AF352671

Teaching Writing in
the Twenty-First Century

Teaching Writing in the Twenty-First Century

Beth L. Hewett, Tiffany Bourelle, and Scott Warnock

Modern Language Association of America
New York   2022

The MLA office is located on the island known as Mannahatta (Manhattan)
in Lenapehoking, the homeland of the Lenape people. The MLA pays respect
to the original stewards of this land and to the diverse and vibrant Native
communities that continue to thrive in New York City.

Figure 2.1 is reprinted with permission of the copyright holder, Michael F.
Giangreco.

Library of Congress Cataloging-in-Publication Data

Names: Hewett, Beth L., author. | Bourelle, Tiffany, 1977– author. | Warnock,
    Scott, 1967- author.
Title: Teaching writing in the twenty-first century / Beth L. Hewett, Tiffany
    Bourelle, and Scott Warnock.
Description: New York : Modern Language Association of America, 2022. |
    Includes bibliographical references. | Summary: "A comprehensive guide
    for students and instructors of composition. Includes an overview of the
    field and discussion of composition purposes and genres, digital education
    modalities, instructional environments, and instructional media. Topics
    include teaching online; composing processes and approaches; designing and
    scaffolding assignments; portfolio assignments; multimodal assignments;
    and response, feedback, and evaluation" — Provided by publisher.
Identifiers: LCCN 2021027820 (print) | LCCN 2021027821 (ebook) |
    ISBN 9781603295451 (hardcover) | ISBN 9781603295468 (paperback) |
    ISBN 9781603295475 (EPUB)
Subjects: LCSH: English language—Rhetoric—Study and teaching (Higher)—
    United States. | Report writing—Study and teaching (Higher)—United
    States. | Academic writing—Study and teaching (Higher)—United States.
Classification: LCC PE1405.U6 H49 2022 (print) | LCC PE1405.U6 (ebook) |
    DDC 808/.0420711—dc23
LC record available at https://lccn.loc.gov/2021027820
LC ebook record available at https://lccn.loc.gov/2021027821

Contents

Dedication and Acknowledgments   ix

Preface   xi

Introduction: A New Rhetoric for Writing Teachers   1

A New Era for Writing Instruction   2

Composition in the Digital Era   8

The Work of the Digital-Era Writing Instructor   15

Composition Learning Outcomes   23

Working Conditions for the Digital-Era Writing Instructor   25

Audience for This Volume   26

Language Choices   27

Human Problems   28

Organization of This Volume   29

Conclusion   31

Part One

**APPROACHING
Composition in the Digital Era**

1. Theorizing Composition and Communication   37

Why Should Literacy Educators Read about Theory?   38

A Thematic Rhetorical History and Theory   40

Conclusion   70

2. Humanizing Composition   72

Diversity and Inclusion   73

Access   76

Cultural Competence   88

Learner Backgrounds for Perceptive Teaching   99

Learning Preferences   104

Conclusion   105

3. Digitalizing Text, Purpose, and Genre   106

Composition Technologies   107

Alphabetic and Multimodal Texts   109

Composition Purposes   111

Exposition   113

Genres   118

Conclusion   135

4. Technologizing Composition Instruction   136

Evolution of Technology in Composition Classrooms   137

Digital Educational Modalities   140

Composition Instructional Environments   143

Composition Instructional Technology   150

Software Applications That Enhance Learning   157

Conclusion   160

5. Teaching Composition in Online Settings   161

Using Technology in Online Settings   162

Preparing to Teach in Online Settings   163

Using Technology in Composition Teaching and Learning Activities   168

Considering the Student   188

Student Access Needs   189

Grading in Online Settings   190

Teaching Multimodality in Online Settings   191

Reflection in Online Settings   192

Conclusion   193

6. Reading Composition — 195

The Need for Critical Media Literacy   196
Learning to Read   199
Reading in the Digital Era   204
Plagiarism: A Reading Problem   209
Teaching Reading Strategically   215
Conclusion   220

Part Two

TEACHING
Composition in the Digital Era

7. Composing Processes and Approaches — 223

Composing Processes for Alphabetic and Multimodal Texts   224
Conclusion   255

8. Designing and Scaffolding Assignments — 256

A Process for Designing Effective Assignments   257
What to Include in a Scaffolded Assignment   267
The Portfolio Assignment   280
Designing Effective Multimodal Assignments   287
Conclusion   295

9. Providing Response, Feedback, and Evaluation — 297

Response and Feedback Guide Students' Composing Processes   297
Elements of Response   302
Peer Review as Evaluation   316
Reflection as Evaluation   317
Instructional Evaluation in Practice   319
Evaluating an ePortfolio   329
Conclusion   333

10. Promoting Effective Communication · 334

Establishing the Classroom Environment   335
Effective Communication in Collaborative Groups   340
Creating Space for Productive Dialogue   345
Establishing a Respectful Learning Environment   347
Recognizing Ineffective Dialogue and Behaviors   349
Building Trust   355
Turning to Administration for Help   360
Conclusion   361

11. Supporting Students · 362

Essential Support in a Contentious Age   363
Literacy Center Support   374
Conclusion   384

12. Imagining the Future of Composition · 385

The Future: Language and Literacy Education   386
Conclusion   395

Notes on the Authors   397
Works Cited   399

Dedication and Acknowledgments

This book is dedicated to all the writing and other literacy instructors who teach because they love students and want to unravel communication with and for them. May they receive the recognition and opportunities they so richly deserve.

To our families, who love us even when we are writing: thank you for your support.

Preface

We ground this book in the principle that rhetoric (and composition as
it engages rhetoric for communication) changes based on the cultural,
social, economic, and political situations of the era. Two months before
Teaching Writing in the Twenty-First Century was to go into production, the
COVID-19 pandemic created seismic changes to literacy education. Because this book already deeply embeds the technologies and communicative changes engendered by the digital era, we have been able to anticipate and account for some of these pandemic-related changes. As we go
to press, the global responses to racism and bigotry—particularly against
people of color and other marginalized individuals and groups—have
shaken society. We are gratified to see that these responses are echoed
in the rhetoric and composition field. For instance, Natasha N. Jones and
Miriam F. Williams recently issued a call for transformation—"The Just
Use of Imagination: A Call to Action"—where they argue for instructors
to use their imagination to replace "oppressive practices with systems
that are founded on equality, access, and opportunity." Our reimagining,
in part, is in this book. Because we live in a time of ever-evolving cultural,
social, economic, and political change, we wrote this book with attention
to diversity, inclusion, access needs, and cultural competence. We hope
the protests currently occurring may bring about genuine change. Protests are rhetorical arguments and have some of the dialogic elements we
examine in this book. But protests alone will not address the problems
the world faces. Another component—among many—must be a reimagining from instructors regarding their teaching practices. We are grateful
to all of the scholars whose transformative approaches have helped shape
this book. As scholars and teachers of rhetoric, we acknowledge that we
are still—in fact, always—learning, and we encourage the same dialogue
among scholars that we also encourage among students. We hope readers

will find the overall approaches, scholarship, and practices we offer in this book useful to teach students to compose and communicate critically, effectively, responsibly, inclusively, and civilly.

Introduction: A New Rhetoric for Writing Teachers

This book was solidly drafted and ready for production before March 2020's COVID-19 outbreak sent the people of the world into a reality of quarantine and physical distancing. In education, digitality is normally the focus of those primarily interested in technology's applications to education, but suddenly it had everyone's attention. As advocates of online writing and literacy instruction, we had spent years making arguments about the value of online environments. Now, this fundamentally life-changing global pandemic underscored these arguments. The pandemic has led 1.5 billion children—or about eighty-five percent of the global youth population—to be often out of school, learning from home and taught by sixty million homebound teachers (Strauss) and underprepared parents. Online educators have used the term "emergency remote teaching" to contrast what is happening at all levels of education with what they know to be "high quality online" instruction (Hodges et al.); in fact, emergency remote *delivery* might be a better term in some situations. Like other countries, the United States was not ready for these circumstances; the so-called digital divide has led "most people in 62% of counties" in the United States to lack "the government's minimum download speed for broadband internet," a significant access problem when education has defaulted to remote settings (Holpuch).

An outlier is an "extremely rare, highly impactful, and only retrospectively predictable" occurrence (Crowe 204), which is what the emergency management field would consider the virus to be. It is a distinct focusing event that directs awareness on facets of life that previously did not have collective attention (C. Rubin): physical closeness and social connections, health care capabilities and inherent inequities, food and lifestyle supplies, and educational delivery, among others. The COVID-19 pandemic is a wake-up call to twenty-first-century global citizens who never thought anything like this could happen to them. As such, it is a blaring message to educators, particularly regarding literacy education. As a focusing event, the pandemic will fade away and other significant occurrences will arise to take its place. Thus, it is important to recognize the lessons it offers for rethinking education's needs and capabilities while acknowledging that there will again be on-site classrooms and physically delivered education. In other words, it is important to make changes while not dismissing what has been good practice. Hence, the exigency for this book is higher than we predicted. Rarely is a kairos, or opportune moment, so clear. *Teaching Writing in the Twenty-First Century* can help readers navigate previously uncharted terrain while mapping the future territory that will encompass both pre- and postpandemic educational needs.

A New Era for Writing Instruction

The world has changed, the prototypical student has changed, and the field's composition education should change, too. Twenty-first-century writing instruction, or composition, is both complicated and enhanced by evolving digital learning technologies; new understandings of access needs and usability design; increasing attention to student diversity; and developing recognition that writing must be taught within the multi-literacies of reading, alphabetic writing (to include nonalphabetic characters), and multimodal composition. Primary among these complications—and a driver of change that cannot be ignored—is the digital era in which composition education occurs and the need to ensure quality education both in person and remotely.

This era is definable by students' discomfort with the uncertainty that is born from the times and culture. Teachers, too, struggle with what and how to teach about communication when digitality has shaken the ground, knocked down beliefs, and torn apart once-cemented relationships. In a time of seismic change, the composition field has both the responsibility and an opportunity to reframe its work. Uncertainty will continue as long as change is afoot, discomfort is a motivator of personal and disciplinary growth, and digitality is the new world of communication.

From the 1980s through the early 2000s, the digital teaching environment affected relatively few teachers—primarily those who elected to teach in networked classrooms, a blended setting where learning occurred partially in the on-site classroom with face-to-face instruction and partially through intranet-based, computer-mediated technology with an asynchronous, reading- and writing-intensive pedagogy. Now, however, millions of students take writing classes in fully online settings, as well as hybrid ones that make use of both synchronous and asynchronous educational, communicative modalities. Of course, traditional, on-site writing classes crucially will continue (outside of pandemic conditions), but many of these are technologically enhanced by digital technologies through such tools as a learning management system (LMS) in which, minimally, students post assignments and receive grades. In many ways, as Beth L. Hewett and Scott Warnock argue in "The Future of OWI," what has become known as *online writing instruction* (OWI) has become "composition writ large because OWI enables teaching students to write with, through, and about the next wave of writing technologies" (547). Hewett and Warnock specifically refer to learning within online classroom environments, yet they argue that all writing instruction is inherently hybrid because of the fluid interconnections among on-site, face-to-face interactions and technologically enhanced ones, including digitally enabled peer response groups. Digital technologies and online teaching principles, theories, and strategies apply even to so-called traditional writing instructional settings of on-site classrooms. Indeed, many students participate in on-site writing classes using mobile technologies, which challenge everyone and merit recognition in any discussion of contemporary writing instruction.

Clearly, the tables have turned, and digitality is more the norm than the traditional settings in which many instructors grew up. In defining the notion of digitality, we rely on the Conference on College Composition and Communication (CCCC) position statement "CCCC Promotion and Tenure Guidelines for Work with Technology":

> *Digital media and work with technology* are defined . . . as any work of teaching, scholarship, or service that is developed and distributed

on computers. . . . Digital media work may be communicated through a number of mediums, including alphabetic text, images, sounds, video, audio, graphics, and animation. Its distribution may be achieved through a variety of methods, including content management systems, personal or professional websites, blogs, social networks, digital archives, and online peer-reviewed publications.

Typically, these digital contexts are addressed in books solely about teaching alphabetic texts in OWI or multimodal texts in multimodal composition (or digital or new media rhetoric or technorhetoric); yet in this book we view multimodal and alphabetic text as inextricable, which "urges us to accept that multimodality isn't something additional to teach, but just another dimension of what we already do," making "the enormity of our instructional edict today feel more possible" (Rule 62) by "pulling multimodality closer to our center" (62–63). Furthermore, it is uncommon to address such contexts with respect to the need all writing teachers have for understanding and functioning in both on-site and online settings. Even though Hewett and Christa Ehmann argue against requiring all instructors to learn to teach in online settings, stating that those with more interest in doing so likely will do a better job (xviiin4), we believe all composition teachers must engage purposefully with the digital era. Therefore, this book weaves attention to digital technology principles and pedagogy into the broader discussion of writing instruction such that teachers may understand that digital instruction is a natural part of their twenty-first-century teaching environment and not a specialty area that they can choose to address or ignore.

Erika Lindemann, in her important *A Rhetoric for Writing Instructors*, defines composition thusly: "Writing is a process of communication that uses a conventional graphic [alphabetic] system to convey a message to a reader" (11). In contrast, we define composition in the digital era as a rhetorical communication process in which both thought and expression are engaged and in which various alphabetic, spoken, and digital modes are used to invent, create, arrange, and deliver a product to readers or viewers in digitally enabled media and in print. Composition instruction should lead students to develop proficiency in communication that expresses a reasoned point of view in various genres and through various media. We consider contemporary composition to encompass writing instruction in all contexts, and we do not separate the traditional idea of composition as writing in print from the nontraditional idea of *digital*, or *multimodal*, *composition*. Rather, composition in the digital era interweaves both of these typically disconnected constructs and includes all sorts of composing genres, processes, technologies, and instructional tools that engage digital technology. This interwoven notion of composition lines up with the threshold concept of writing 2.4, as articulated by Cheryl E. Ball and Colin Charlton in "All Writing is Multimodal": "there is no such thing as a monomodal text" (42–43).

Our definition of composition in the digital era also encompasses OWI. This term was coined as a descriptor for teaching alphabetic writing in online settings; it provides differentiating language from that used in the traditional on-site setting. In 2015, leading OWI scholars realized that, in accordance with what scholars of reading and multimodality had been telling them, a singular focus on alphabetic writing was an insufficient approach to contemporary literacy. These differently focused scholars proposed to work together for *online literacy instruction* (OLI), which acknowledged that reading and multimodal literacies must be joined overtly with alphabetic writing under the online composition instruction umbrella (see GSOLE). However, given the rapid evolution of concepts and the increasing awareness of digital instruction brought about by the pandemic, both OWI and OLI appear to function less than holistically as terms insofar as all composition instruction is now infused with digitality and multiliteracies. Thus, the distinctions made by OWI and OLI are helpful (e.g., for categorizing research and isolating historical practices and theories that remain essential, and for administrative purposes) but no longer strictly necessary. In this volume, therefore, we refer specifically to OWI and OLI only when scholarship and context make it appropriate to do so. And, while we refer to multiliteracies throughout the book, we use the phrase *teaching composition* (or *teaching writing*) in *the digital era* to encompass all these teaching strategies, philosophies, literacies, and environments—because students need educators to focus on all of them. Furthermore, everything we discuss in this book is interconnected and infused with principles and practices of inclusion, access, equity, communication, and dialogue and should be considered in any composition course, no matter the modality (synchronous or asynchronous) or environment (on-site, technologically enhanced, fully online, or hybrid).

Educational change often gets a chilly reception, and historically the inception of what has been called OWI and then OLI has been no different. The fact that we now see OWI and OLI as simply the natural evolutionary consequence of digitality modifies even the most basic language for talking about and doing this instructional work, as chapters 4 and 5 illustrate. Theories, research, and scholarship of OWI and OLI ground much of the most effective practices in any digital teaching environment, so we urge readers to continue to engage with this work while moving forward with a new appreciation for how digitality has changed twenty-first-century composition and its instruction overall. As communication in society evolves, so must OWI and OLI, and we encourage readers to consider how the theories and practices of these subfields are now essential to composition instruction; in other words, these subfields have the capacity to unite writing studies with a common purpose, grounding best practices for all teaching in the digital era. We also encourage readers to consider this argument and expand upon it as social, economic, political, cultural, and technological changes demand (see Berlin, "Writing Instruction"; see also Paine; Kress, *Multimodality*).

To further explain our definition of composition in the digital era, we consider the terms *modes*, *mediums*, and *media*. In *Multimodal Discourse*, Gunther Kress and Theo Van Leeuwen indicate that *mode* and *medium* are hard to separate (7). We agree, noting that even in writing studies, the concepts can be tricky. Using Kress and Van Leeuwen's concepts as a guide, we define *modes* as the semiotic resources students can use to communicate, whether those are words, animation, sound, images, or the like; these resources often are shaped by developments in society (e.g., images that once were hand-drawn now can be digital). While we recognize that *media* is often seen as the plural of *medium*, we use *mediums* to refer to the technologies or tools used to produce a finished product. *Media*, then, becomes the product or deliverable that disseminates a student's message (Kress and Van Leeuwen 6; see also C. Lauer, "Contending"). For example, students may use words, music, and sound (modes) to compose using video software (the medium) in order to disseminate a message through a video (the media). We make this distinction now so that readers are not confused when we suggest that instructors can find media to use in their classrooms to support learning, or when we note that students can compose through various mediums to communicate with outside audiences. Simply put, *media* is associated with the final or deliverable product while *medium*, or *mediums*, engages with the process of using tools and technologies to communicate.

Regarding the digitality of composition, the 2014 "WPA Outcomes Statement for First-Year Composition (3.0)" produced by the Council of Writing Program Administrators (CWPA) affirms that

> "composing" refers broadly to complex writing processes that are increasingly reliant on the use of digital technologies. Writers also attend to elements of design, incorporating images and graphical elements into texts intended for screens as well as printed pages. Writers' composing activities have always been shaped by the technologies available to them, and digital technologies are changing writers' relationships to their texts and audiences in evolving ways.

The outcomes statement for writing program administrators (WPAs) clearly embraces technology and its attendant literacies for students within the definition of composition. What this statement cannot do, however, is explain how writing instructors can address these goals, a challenging task, especially when technology and even the definition of literacy are always in flux. The primary goal of this book, therefore, is to guide instructors in teaching rhetorical strategies for communication, no matter the modality or environment in which they communicate or the mediums through which they communicate; these strategies should offer students flexibility for determining how to communicate in their future lives, regardless of technological changes.

The notion of writing as composition is an old one, as Lindemann's definition illustrates. We use these terms relatively synonymously throughout this book. *Composition* as a noun can be considered both a product (e.g., "The students produced six compositions this term.") and a type of course (e.g., "First-year composition is a general studies course."). Yet composition is not limited to first-year or general studies requirements. Many institutions provide composition courses in upper levels and teach varied genres under the general rubric of composition; such programs as writing across the curriculum (WAC) abound wherein educators understand the core work of composing in disciplinary learning. Composition's scope also is used in verb form in writing studies: educators teach students to compose, or write and create, texts that can be alphabetically based or multimodally constructed with alphabetic text, still images, video, audio, and the like. In this book, we speak both specifically about first-year writing (FYW) and other writing courses as types of composition courses and more generally about composition as what writers do, and how they use a wide variety of rhetorical strategies to compose.

Composition in the Digital Era

The complexity of contemporary composition can be confusing, not only particularly to new instructors but also to instructors accustomed to doing things more traditionally. This book draws on both traditional writing instructional texts and current, relevant OWI, OLI, and digital rhetoric resources but departs from these in significant ways. Instead of addressing composition in one primary environment or genre, this book assumes that writing instruction naturally occurs online as well as on-site and that it is taught in various settings requiring attention to both alphabetic and multimodal composition in print-based and digital contexts. It further assumes that students have differing access needs, reading and writing literacy levels, linguistic backgrounds, and learning preferences. In other words, it presumes there does not exist one single, traditional setting for writing instruction, nor does there exist a prototypical, traditional student of a particular age, race, ethnicity, gender identity, sexual orientation, culture, linguistic background, or technological proficiency.

In the following sections, we briefly address some complexities of composition in the digital era that require new instructional knowledge and decision-making.

Argumentation and Dialogue

People argue about that which has no certain answer, meaning that probable—not certain—and practical reasoning are involved. In "The Good

Writer," John Duffy suggests that people generally consider arguments regarding winning or losing based on authority and control. That is, indeed, one type of argument. Duffy notes this perception of argument opens up communicators to scrutiny, which too often becomes ridicule in contemporary public and private forums, including conversations. Aristotle explains that the counterpart to rhetoric is dialectic, the idea of dialoguing among small groups of speakers, critically examining all sides of a question by testing ideas and opening space for new thinking (3; I.i.1 [1354a]). Whereas dialectic relies mostly on logic, however, rhetoric also addresses the ethos of a speaker and the emotions of the audience. Aristotle believes dialectic and rhetoric go hand in hand—those engaging in argument need to consider the needs and emotions of the audience and treat them in ethical, respectful ways, critically considering and using logical evidence to attempt reasonable solutions to uncertain human problems (17; I.ii.3–7 [1356a]).

It often seems that many citizens in contemporary culture do not engage in productive, or even civil, dialogue. Even so, Duffy suggests current teaching practices of argument do promote dialogue by prompting students to learn to make claims based on evidence, which includes seeking to address all sides of an issue. When people make claims, Duffy writes, they invite others to share in dialogue, which requires mutual trust among participants. He explains that this work invites students "to practice the rhetorical virtues of honesty and mutual respect," as well as accountability, with proofs and counterarguments "considering seriously opinions, facts, or values that contradict their own." This, he asserts, is

> potentially, the most radical and transformative behavior of all: we are asking students to inhabit, at least for a while, the perspective of The Other and to open themselves to the doubts and contradictions that attach to any worthwhile question. In teaching counterarguments, we are teaching the rhetorical virtues of open-mindedness and intellectual generosity. ("Good Writer" 238)

Yet these virtues often are lost in real-life interactive communication, especially when that communication happens in real time through social and other radically evolving media. Trust seems to be broken among those engaging in communicative acts.

Indeed, we believe real dialogue becomes even harder when communicating through mediums, especially when the audience and rhetorical situation and purpose shift constantly. As such, driving questions at the heart of any twenty-first-century writing classroom include asking how educators can

- teach students first to rhetorically listen (and read) and then to critically consider what other participants are saying (Glenn and Ratcliffe);
- help students have productive conversations with others who have very real, quite different lived experiences;
- cultivate a sense of belonging and open space for engaging, productive dialogue that is safe yet responsible;
- add dialogue, or dialectic, to courses as the counterpart of rhetoric; and
- teach students to choose the appropriate genre and medium and to effectively communicate within those spaces.

If readers are looking for straightforward answers to these questions, this book does not provide them. There are no easy answers. Instead, we offer options for instructors to encourage students to read and listen to others' opinions; understand how communication affects audiences by writing and creating documents based on the needs or constraints of various audiences, purposes, and mediums; and consider how the circulation of a document or conversation (e.g., a blog or social media interaction) can have real consequences for real people. Conversations between instructors and students about open-mindedness, intellectual generosity, and inclusivity must occur, especially when a community of inquiry is being established (see Garrison and Akyol), as we advocate. This book touches on these topics and addresses how technology has changed the way people communicate, affecting both how educators teach and students learn. Educators have adopted technology use, whether in on-site classes, hybrid settings, or fully online (sometimes called *remote*) instruction, and most students are now required to create texts using technological tools.

These questions are especially important when considering the needs of the diverse student population that enters twenty-first-century classrooms, whether with brick-and-mortar rooms or virtual spaces. They require instructors to remain open-minded and willing to question their practices critically. These questions are important when considering educational content, teaching processes, and student evaluation. They are important when deciding which readings and conversations to bring into the classroom, what types of writing processes to introduce, and what media to incorporate.

Composition Student Populations in the Digital Era

Another change to contemporary composition is the students themselves. Once upon a time, some will say, most students came from the middle to higher socioeconomic classes and attended college directly from high school. They spoke and wrote a form of so-called standard English and had adequate preparation for postsecondary work. They attended school for philosophical reasons and not merely to get a job. That is a nice fairy tale. On the contrary, students have long come from various socioeconomic classes with different educational backgrounds and financial (dis)advantages. Students have long been of nontraditional ages and attended college for different goals and purposes. They have been English speakers where the home language is a heritage language or a dialect of English, and they have been immigrants who speak English as a second (or third or fourth) language. Moreover, although most students are neurotypical, others have learning challenges (e.g., autism; dyslexia; auditory processing, reading, or writing disorders) not always addressed in teacher preparation. Some students have physical disabilities that require space- and time-based accommodations. Some students struggle with aspects of their identity, including their ethnicity, race, or gender. Therefore, it is critical that educators pay attention to the access needs and inclusion of students, especially in composition classes in the digital era—particularly during and after a pandemic-sized wake-up call.

Nonfiction Composing Genres

When Lindemann's *A Rhetoric for Writing Teachers* was first published, multiple nonfiction written genres—narrations, letters, descriptions, literary arguments, and (vaguely) argumentations—often were assigned in FYW and other composition courses; Lindemann calls these "traditional assignments" (207). Other brief and extended academic essays, consisting of expository and argumentative writing, multiple forms of reports and letters, creative nonfiction, and even fiction genres, were assigned then as they are now. Yet the genres students encounter these days have expanded. Added to the common nonfiction genres are formal and informal emails, which are consequential communications like letters; blog or vlog entries, often understood to be both argumentative and journal- or essay-like; multimodal texts of all sorts; websites and webtexts intended for hypertextual as well as multimodal reading; and social media posts, ranging from informal and personal to formal and academic. Such expanded genres require new approaches to teaching them.

Composing Actions for Alphabetic and Multimodal Texts

The writing studies field has examined, observed, theorized, tested, and suggested various composing actions that work for many writers. These strategies tend to engage a process-based approach that consists of

> finding one's ideas in an invention or brainstorming approach;
>
> developing those ideas through research, which leads to relevant content;
>
> considering one's audience, purpose, and context—as demonstrated through a version of the writer-reader-subject triangle (see fig. 0.1);
>
> seeking and using feedback to revise in a read-write cycle;
>
> editing after revision to prioritize the integrity of the message while addressing stylistic elegance; and
>
> polishing for publication.

These actions work in a twenty-first-century context. The overarching process-based composition strategies are the same, whether for traditional alphabetic or multimodal projects except for the need to select the medium one uses. Yet they take on new dimensions when combined with technologies for broader composition types.

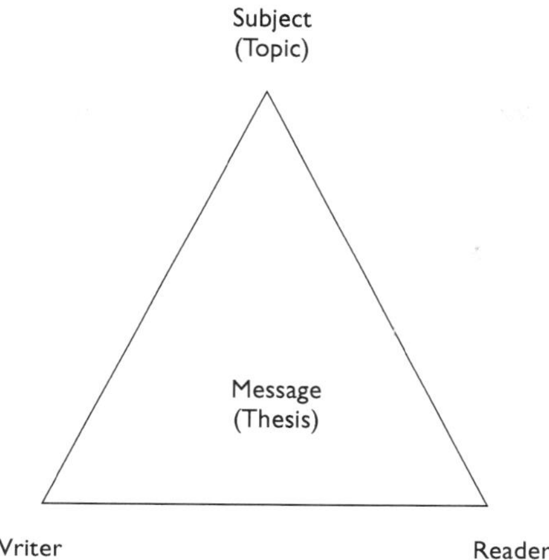

Figure 0.1. Writer-reader-subject triangle, adapted from Lindemann, p. 12.

Composing Technologies for Alphabetic and Multimodal Texts

When Lindemann wrote *A Rhetoric for Writing Teachers* in 1982, writing alphabetic text defined composition. Composing most often occurred first with the technologies of pen or pencil and paper or typewriters; personal microcomputers were rare then. These composing tools work well for those who learned to draft by hand on paper and subsequently type the text. Now, contemporary composing technologies for alphabetic texts include computer-based word processors with keyboarding and voice-to-text applications, introducing their own special challenges to the process and text. Mobile and Internet-based technologies engage other composition tools, such as file transfers, file sharing, and simple copy and pasting. One can collaborate easily with other writers using the Internet, cloud-based apps, and specialized software for shared text development. Despite these digital advances, contemporary students raised to compose on computers may undoubtedly benefit from returning to earlier modalities for brainstorming, drafting, and revising.

All the technologies used for alphabetic texts can be used to compose multimodal texts, another threshold concept. In fact, as we mentioned earlier, Ball and Charlton say in *Naming What We Know* that a "monomodal text" does not exist (43). For instance, graphic novels tell a story with text boxes and images. Yet additional tools for multimodal texts have digital origins beyond the alphabet. Video files emerge from camera features in mobile devices, television, movies, and Internet-based *YouTube* clips. Audio files of all kinds include voice, music, and other natural and synthetic sounds. Still images emerge from hand and computer-aided drawings, photographs, and computer graphics. Tool changes enable genre changes. Marshall McCluhan teaches in *Understanding Media* that the "medium is the message" (7); we believe that in an environment of digital technologies the medium nuances the message by reformulating its presentation for each audience. Multimodal texts invite new, individualized, uniquely independent writing and reading strategies that remain interdependent within the overall text.

Composition Teaching Environment and Tools

Both the genres and technologies for composing create a complex picture for contemporary writing instructors. Adding varied teaching environments or modalities to the mix leads to new challenges. Through the beginning of the twenty-first century, teaching composition—typically alphabetic texts—usually occurred in brick-and-mortar buildings and classrooms where tables and chairs marked student positions and podiums and lecterns marked teacher positions. Even though the theoretical blending of social construction, collaboration, and peer work led to many writing classrooms becoming less proscenium-like and to seating students more equitably in circles or groups, the instruction tended to occur primarily through the teacher's oral lecture, textbook and handout readings, and some in-class writing. In the latter part of the twentieth century, workshops, conferences, and writing tutoring became more popular means of reaching student writers (Bruffee, "Collaborative Learning" and *Collaborative Learning*; J. Harris, "Idea"). Although instructors could use video, audio, and still images through slides and movies, technology-enabled classrooms were rarer. Now most teachers have such technology available. Moreover, most have LMSs that, minimally, enable posting and collecting assignments and recording grades and, maximally, function to connect students to teachers and each other. Understanding the affordances of the synchronous and asynchronous modalities has become more important. Hybrid and fully online classes also are common, changing the environment from one where students and teacher are colocated to one where they may see one another face-to-face some days, as in hybrid or blended courses, or may meet solely through the Internet, as in fully online asynchronous or synchronous courses. Such environmental changes, however, involve more than merely a sense of embodied presence because they require different teaching strategies and reconsidered communicative and instructional skills.

When the range of contemporary students, composing genres, strategies for alphabetic and multimodal texts, available technologies, and new learning environments are considered as a whole, it becomes clear that composition in the digital era requires different approaches that include the technologies of contemporary composing, teaching, and learning. At a minimum, these contexts change the idea of universally defined good writing.

The Work of the Digital-Era Writing Instructor

Defining a multiliteracies pedagogy for writing instruction entails addressing the multiple diversities of students to achieve access for all in the twenty-first-century writing classroom.

Student Diversity

In a post for the CCCC blogspot, Kevin Eric DePew writes that compositionists need to see themselves as Generalists 2.0, particularly regarding student diversity needs:

> All composition instructors are responsible for knowing how to address the challenges and opportunities that their different students bring to the classroom. A movement toward fostering this second generation of generalists will need to build upon the rich corpus of diversity scholarship in our field writ large to bridge the gap between the scholars' advocated practices and the actual classroom practices. ("Moving")

Scholars, Depew says, already have been studying issues like student diversity in what have become their specialty fields, which, we believe, resemble silos of thought that others tend not to read or use if they do not share that specialty area or believe it is their job to do such work. By extension, issues of digitality are part of such diversity concerns if for no other reason than that of access. To address diversity, we include up-to-date research, including webinars, in which authors provide suggestions for recognizing racial bias and microaggressions in online spaces, as well as for designing courses for underserved and marginalized students. We argue for equitable access for all students in all teaching environments, and we encourage readers to engage the resources we provide to educate themselves more on such topics as access, race, inclusion, and equity.

Linguistic Diversity

Students' linguistic abilities long have been recognized as critical to their identities, and questions of how to teach students with different home language experiences were raised in the groundbreaking and contentious 1974 CCCC position statement "Students' Right to Their Own Language." This document addressed key access issues, including the question of whose language is taught in the classroom, and advised all writing teachers to learn about such areas as dialect, idiolect, morphology, language acquisition, grammar, and language diversity, influencing teacher training ever since. Of particular interest, every writing studies educator should understand language change and its effects:

> Diversity of dialects will not degrade language nor hasten deleterious changes. Common sense tells us that if people want to understand one another, they will do so. Experience tells us that we can understand any dialect of English after a reasonably brief exposure to it. And humanity tells us that we should allow [all people] the dignity of [their] own way of talking. (22)

Multilingual students are especially vulnerable. The CCCC indicates, in its "CCCC Statement on Second Language Writing and Multilingual Writers," that any writing or writing-intensive course "that enrolls any second language writers should be taught by an instructor who is able to identify and is prepared to address the linguistic and cultural needs of second language writers." This statement also addresses teacher preparation for multilingual writers, urging student practitioners and scholars to study both native and nonnative English speakers to improve understanding of abilities and differences. Among other documents following from the CCCC's "Students' Right to Their Own Language," the organization's "CCCC Statement on Second Language Writing and Multilingual Writers" also indicates that all students should have linguistic access to education.

In *What Anti-Racist Language Teachers Do* and *Qualities of Anti-Racist ELA Curricula*, the National Council of Teachers of English (NCTE) Committee against Racism and Bias in the Teaching of English suggests that "racism can be enacted through the instructional practices of English language arts teachers," specifically when they promote English-only policies in the classroom. As such, instructors must critically consider their pedagogies to encourage "linguistically, ethnically, and culturally diverse students" and their voices without censorship. Beyond the still-current guidance of the CCCC's "Students' Right to Their Own Language," we have included in chapter 2 strategies supported by scholarship from teachers and scholars of color. These strategies can help instructors work toward anti-racist teaching, using the "CCCC Statement on Second Language Writing and Multilingual Writers" as a guideline, starting with its first principle, which outlines the importance of linguistic diversity in the writing classroom. Additionally, many of the practices we include throughout this book align with anti-racist pedagogy (readers may see overlapping themes with feminist and critical pedagogies as well), including fostering critical analytical skills, guiding students to consider their biases and assumptions, decentering the classroom, and creating a sense of community through collaborative learning (Kishimoto).

Access Needs

The New London Group (NLG), composed of ten international teacher-scholars, suggests in "A Pedagogy of Multiliteracies" that instructors should develop new teaching approaches to provide access to education and classroom opportunities to aid students in becoming successful workforce communicators. The NLG notes that "the changing technological and organizational shape of working life provides some with access to lifestyles unprecedented by affluence, while excluding others in the ways that are increasingly related to the outcomes of education" (61). The necessity for composing and communicating with technology for social and business purposes has prompted changes in educational outcomes, with instructors adopting teaching philosophies that encourage and increase student access to twenty-first-century multiliteracies—reading, alphabetic writing, and multimodal composition—that then may transfer to the workforce. Language, (dis)ability, technology, and rhetorical literacies are part of such access.

Notably, "Students' Right to Their Own Language" addresses key access issues, one of which is the question of whose language gets taught. The authors state that American schools and colleges have been forced "to take a stand on a basic educational question: what should the schools do about the language habits of students who come from a wide variety of social, economic, and cultural backgrounds?" (2). Having asked that question, they clarify "the distinction between speech and writing," noting that educators previously had "taught the language as though the *talk* in any region, even the talk of speakers with prestige and power, were identical to edited *written* English." The "Students' Right to Their Own Language" is a manifesto of access, shouting out that students of all backgrounds have legitimate languages and dialects that are appropriate to various contexts. Instead of uncritically teaching the "English of educated speakers" as the power dialect, educators must question whether they feel "some inherent superiority of the dialect itself or on the social prestige of those who use it," asking "whether our rejection of students who do not adopt the dialect most familiar to us is based on any real merit in our dialect or whether we are actually rejecting the students themselves, rejecting them because of their racial, social, and cultural origins" (3).

Disability studies is another area about which composition instructors must learn. In the CCCC's "Principles for the Postsecondary Teaching of Writing," point nine states that all students require learning support because they arrive in college "with a wide range of writing, reading, and critical analysis experiences." Students also "bring a range of experiences with writing, reading, and analysis from literacy activities outside of school." Also recognizing students' differences and rights to a level educational playing field, the CCCC's "Disability Studies in Composition: Position Statement on Policy and Best Practices" "describes concepts and processes intended to assist members of the field practice active inclusion across the discipline beyond mere compliance measures." The position statement advocates that members of the discipline

> recognize that college campuses include people with a wide range of visible and invisible disabilities;
>
> recognize that people with disabilities bring vital diversity to all of our professional spaces and places;
>
> "acknowledge the contributions disability studies makes" to our disciplines by "advancing theories of difference" and criticizing ideas of normalcy and access;
>
> understand that disabled people are still a marginalized group with a variety of specific needs that "must not be erased in the classroom or in policy"
>
> "strive to create fully inclusive environments"; and
>
> recognize that disability intersects with other identities, so "access work should be approached through an intersectional lens."

Crucial to this position statement is its acknowledgement that meeting the letter of the law, the Americans with Disabilities Act of 1990 (ADA), is insufficient for fair and full inclusion; educators must go beyond what the statement calls "limited legal standards" with flexibility for how to teach literacy with those needing physical access particularly. Those actions should be supported by course content and fully trained teachers who have become sensitized to disability issues.

As digital technologies have become ubiquitous, access and usability have become critically recognized concepts. In 1999 Cynthia L. Selfe famously urged educators to "pay attention" to technologies and their inherent messages about literacy and accessibility ("Technology" and *Technology*). The CCCC Committee for Effective Practices in Online Writing Instruction's *Position Statement of Principles and Example Effective Practices for Online Writing Instruction (OWI)* exemplifies professional groups that have emphasized access and inclusivity. As OWI principle 1 of fifteen, this committee claims that, given its inherent union with technology, OWI fundamentally must reject exclusion by critically reflecting and acting on any technology adoption for writing instruction. Principle 1 therefore addresses "the needs of learners with physical disabilities, learning disabilities, multilingual backgrounds, and learning challenges related to socioeconomic issues" as well as multilingual challenges; furthermore, given OWI's text-intensive nature, in which "reading is a necessary skill, addressing the accessibility needs of the least confident readers increases the potential to reach all types of learners." The Global Society of Online Literacy Educators has taken up the charge, also identifying universal access and inclusion as its first principle in "Online Literacy Instruction Principles and Tenets." Clearly, professional organizations are accepting the high stakes of addressing access, which we support by urging educators to exceed mere ADA compliance to a spirit of generosity that recognizes and actively upholds students' and teachers' rights and needs.

Defining a Multiliteracies Pedagogy

When the NLG first met, its members discussed the broader implications of changes in literacy and education's purposes. They were charged to rethink the "fundamental premises of literacy pedagogy in order to influence practices that will give students the skills and knowledge they need to achieve their aspirations" (63). What students needed to know and learn was shifting, prompting a change in how composition was taught. Until then, literacy pedagogy had meant teaching and learning to read and write in "page-bound, official, standard forms of the national language." Of course, such a need to read and write traditional texts exists; the NLG, however, expanded literacy's scope to account for the digital text forms permeating society. It established two goals of a multiliteracies pedagogy: "to extend the idea and scope of literac[ies] pedagogy to account for the context of our culturally and linguistically diverse and increasingly globalized societies, for the multifarious cultures that interrelate and the plurality of texts that circulate"; and to "account for the burgeoning variety of text forms associated with information and multimedia technologies" (61).

In their introduction to *Multiliteracies*, Bill Cope and Mary Kalantzis suggest social change was the exigence for these two goals, including the "changes in our working lives; our public lives as citizens; and our private lives as members of different community lifeworlds" (7). As American society, and by extension, the college classroom, was becoming more diverse, educators discerned a need to address linguistic diversity because linguistic and cultural diversity impacts professional, civic, and private lives, changing how language is used. Students, therefore, must learn the value of such linguistic diversity while learning to negotiate (and appreciate) difference and while working and living within globally interconnected spaces (6). The changing nature of technological discourse adds to the exigency.

Hence, the multiliteracy needs of composition learners are in the forefront, as the *NCTE Framework for Twenty-First-Century Curriculum and Assessment* affirms:

> Literacy has always been a collection of cultural and communicative practices shared among members of particular groups. As society and technology change, so does literacy. Because technology has increased the intensity and complexity of literate environments, the 21st century demands that a literate person possess a wide range of abilities and competencies, many literacies.
>
> (NCTE, *NCTE Framework*)

The technological concerns of literacy lead NCTE to highlight the following skills for both students and their teachers, who, as "[a]ctive, successful participants in this 21st century global society," must

be fluent with technology;

build cross-cultural relationships, problem-solve collaboratively, "and strengthen independent thought";

design and share information for global audiences;

be able work with and synthesize streams of "simultaneous information";

create and assess multimedia texts; and

consider the ethics of these environments.

Any rhetoric for twenty-first-century writing instructors must address multiliteracy goals by, minimally, considering the principles behind these goals and suggesting strategies for achieving them. Such strategies include selecting the best technology for instruction, thus guiding students to do the same when composing. All parties must learn to question the role of technology, including the affordances and challenges of various software. These skills will remain important as technology evolves; understanding and questioning technology can help students approach new technology in the future, long after a software is defunct. Indeed, learning the rhetorical principles of audience, rhetorical situation and purpose, and medium can guide them in composing, no matter the selected technology.

Finally, GSOLE's "Online Literacy Instruction Principles and Tenets," a statement of online literacy instruction (OLI) principles, includes four principles (quoted below) that require all educators to engage literacy instruction in the context of digitality:

> "Online literacy instruction should be universally accessible and inclusive."

> "All program developers and institutional administrators should commit to supporting and implementing a regular, iterative process of professional development and course/program assessment for online literacy instruction."

> "Instructors and tutors should commit to regular, iterative processes of course and instructional material design, development, assessment, and revision to ensure that online literacy instruction and student support reflect current effective practices."

> "Educators and researchers should initiate, support, and sustain online literacy instruction-related conversations and research efforts within and across institutions and disciplinary boundaries."

These principles foreground literacy in the digital era, and they ask administrators and educators to acknowledge their shared, multidisciplinary work and responsibilities in online literacies to benefit sound instruction.

Summary

Despite repeated urging from writing studies' professional organizations, the high-stakes goals outlined in critical position statements have never been considered fully in one rhetoric of writing instruction. These various issues comprise the twenty-first-century job of all composition instructors who teach contemporary composition students of multiple diversities who need multiliteracies for composing with varied genres, processes, tools, and environments.

Composition Learning Outcomes

To further illustrate the complexity of the twenty-first-century writing instructor's work, we cite the CWPA's "WPA Outcomes Statement," which outlines some skills and knowledge students need, along with advice for instructors on how to help students reach these goals. We highlight the WPA statement, noting that the composition and rhetoric field is at a pivotal moment in overtly questioning foundational ideas about the racial and cultural inclusivity of language, particularly the ways educators teach, represent, and assess writing. We also recommend readers consider Asao Inoue's conference addresses "Friday Plenary Address: Racism in Writing Programs and the CWPA" and "2019 CCCC Chair's Address: How Do We Language So That People Stop Killing Each Other; or, What Do We Do about White Language Supremacy?"[1]

Despite current critique, the CWPA's "WPA Outcomes Statement" can be a place to start when creating outcomes for classrooms or programs. We encourage instructors and administrators to consider the critiques of the outcomes statement, read the scholarship we have provided in this book regarding twenty-first-century teaching practices (including those on anti-racist pedagogy), and revise the outcomes and craft new ones based on their goals and contexts for teaching and administering writing programs. The skill sets put forth by the statement are organized into four knowledge areas and include the following:

Rhetorical Knowledge. Students should gain experience reading, analyzing, and composing diverse texts to understand key rhetorical concepts, genres and their conventions, purposes for writing, and technologies for composing within a variety of environments and for different audiences.

Critical Thinking, Reading, and Composing. Students should use composing and reading for inquiry, learning, and thinking in various rhetorical contexts and should use strategies such as synthesis and critique to compose texts that integrate their ideas and those from other sources.

Processes. Students should develop flexible strategies for reading, writing, drafting, collaborating, revising, and editing, considering and reconsidering ideas while giving productive feedback to peers.

Knowledge of Conventions. Students should develop knowledge of linguistic structures such as grammar and punctuation through practice composing and revising, common formats and design features for different kinds of texts, and intellectual property rights.

These outcomes represent the minimum skill sets students should have when passing FYW and are therefore crucial for writing students to achieve at all levels in all genres, including writing-intensive and WAC courses, upper-level composition, and technical and professional writing courses. In other words, if the skills in these knowledge areas are the ideal outcomes for FYW, they represent the ideal preparatory goals at which teachers should aim in completing secondary writing instruction and the best beginning point for all writing instruction beyond FYW. Minimally, students of postsecondary composition courses should become proficient in the competencies outlined in the statement.

Faculty member goals from the WPA statement are particularly important to consider through the lens of upper-level writing. These goals address the composition ramifications in a wide variety of students' disciplines. No one teacher knows all of these, of course. Therefore, graduate students and new teachers particularly, but all writing instructors generally, require a range of knowledge about how one's disciplinary genres may apply general composition skills. The ability to take the general skill and apply it to the specific field is one that can be developed through asking a series of questions about individual disciplines and teaching students how to do the same. Therefore, educators do not need to be experts in all fields but rather experts in the application of rhetorical principles to any situation, which is an educational approach dating as far back as Aristotle's *The "Art" of Rhetoric* and as recently as the writing-about-writing movement.

Although these outcomes offer clear guidelines for FYW, it is important to remind readers that the WPA statement is an evolving document, indicating the changing nature of composition and the complexities of teaching in the twenty-first century. This iteration, for example, omits "Composing in Electronic Environments" and integrates technology throughout the document (Dryer et al. discuss the revision process). We expect new iterations will address current faults and encourage fresh discussions about students' literacy needs. Throughout this book we focus on the four primary knowledge areas identified above and in the WPA statement. If students have not achieved these skills prior to their upper-level writing and writing-intensive courses, they certainly should achieve them before completing such advanced courses.

Working Conditions for the Digital-Era Writing Instructor

In this book, we acknowledge the real-life needs that twenty-first-century teachers have for excellent training, ongoing professional development, and fair pay. Although these necessary conditions for fairness in teaching are addressed more fully in the companion volume, *Administering Writing Programs in the Twenty-First Century*, by Tiffany Bourelle, Hewett, and Warnock, our commitment to them is built into our approach to teaching writing. All composition educators need theoretical knowledge in rhetorical, linguistic, instructional, ethical, and effective research methods and technical knowledge. As indicated by the CCCC Committee for Effective Practices in Online Writing Instruction's *Position Statement of Principles and Example Effective Practices for Online Writing Instruction (OWI)*, they will need not only to engage and adapt traditional theories and practices but also to develop new theories and practices appropriate to online settings. They will need to assist their WPAs in understanding, working with, and even limiting the number of technologies teachers and students must learn for composing to avoid undue burdens unrelated to curricula. To best assist their WPAs with these important considerations, teachers will need technology-focused teacher preparation and ongoing professional development.

Considering the plethora of skills students need to learn from writing studies scholars and practitioners, DePew's Generalists 2.0 is both apt and, unfortunately, easily misread because the term *generalist* can imply that anyone at all can do the work. Yet the work of the writing instructor in the digital era is anything but general; it requires special training in various areas, including understanding of—and ways to teach—students of all ages and educational, cultural, and linguistic backgrounds. It further requires understanding access and inclusion from a generous spirit that reaches beyond the letter of the ADA law, developing proficiency teaching those with nonneurotypical learning styles, working with the physically and emotionally disabled, and meeting the crucial needs of multilingual and multicultural students—all in the context of alphabetic and multimodal genres, digitalized composing processes and tools, and digital teaching and learning environments. Therefore, we urge instructors to help themselves become and remain employed by embracing the diverse, complex skills they must have and learning how to argue for their own worth, given their education and experiences; they must learn to argue individually and collectively for appropriate-level positions, job security, compensation, and recognition.

Composition instruction in the digital era is not a no-brainer. It requires professional, skilled attention to composing in many genres; for varied purposes; with multiple (digital) tools; in different environments; and with students who each have unique learning background, personal histories, and reasons for composing. The skilled twenty-first-century writing instructor works hard and deserves recognition that includes steady, reliable work (where desired) and fair compensation in various forms, to include monetary remuneration, paid research and study time, access to up-to-date equipment, regular promotions, and professional development opportunities.

Audience for This Volume

The primary audiences for this book are postsecondary and secondary instructors of writing courses. Postsecondary writing instructors who previously have not seen their work as involving digital technologies, attention to access, and a need to address multiliteracies with multilingual and multicultural students must be brought up to speed quickly. Even those who have experienced their teaching with digitality, access, and multiliteracies need additional support (Breuch, "Faculty"; Rice) for their work to remain up-to-date and to develop new strategies and theories. Additionally, we address secondary-level writing and reading instructors because they are key players in preparing students for postsecondary-level writing courses. They also are tasked with teaching multiliterate high school students the multiple and whole literacies of reading, alphabetic writing, and multimodal composition in accessible ways using up-to-date, accessible technologies. Many secondary and postsecondary institutions work together through institutes and partnerships intended to acculturate secondary students into postsecondary writing instructional settings quickly and purposefully. Both postsecondary and secondary teachers will have realized that having succeeded in emergency remote instruction is not enough to provide excellent writing instruction that fully engages digitality. Sticking one's finger in the leaking seawall is not a well-engineered, sustainable solution.

Among the audience are WPAs, master teachers, and writing instructor coaches as teacher-trainers for twenty-first-century writing instruction. Writing program administrators, who are the primary audience for the companion to this book, *Administering Writing Programs in the Twenty-First Century*, by Bourelle, Hewett, and Warnock, offer professional development for both online and on-site faculty; they can incorporate the strategies articulated in this book into their current training practices. These strategies help graduate teaching assistants and secondary-level practice teachers learn to implement access-friendly, multiliteracies-enriched, and multimodal composition instruction, as well as understand the nuances, challenges, and approaches to teaching these important pedagogies. Administrators developing or revising their programs and policies may find some answers in this book. Finally, when training is not available, the book serves as a guide for all writing instructors interested in incorporating accessible approaches to reading, alphabetic writing, and multimodal composition into their classes.

In sum, our readers will reimagine and restructure training practices for global contexts, as well as their own localized ones, ranging from entire writing programs to a single course curriculum.

Language Choices

We use the term *writing studies* to describe our audience's disciplinary affiliation, but we realize this is a contested term. For example, in "Reclaiming Composition," Derek Owens and Tara Roeder argue that this term "privileges traditional alphabetic print at the expense of other strategies and modes of meaning-making," and they prefer the term *composition and design* (290). Although we see their point, we treat multimodal meaning-making approaches as forms of composing. Similarly, we could use *rhetoric and composition*, given rhetoric's tight connections with composition, yet this term risks omitting those who teach technical and business or professional writing, journalism instructors, and teachers in multiple disciplines across the curriculum who engage writing as one of their teaching and learning strategies—any of which easily fall under the label of *writing studies*. To be more precise, we could have called the field *reading and writing studies*. Reading, which has been given short shrift in composition studies, is critical to writing well. (This oversight contributed to the founding of the Global Society of Online Literacy Educators in 2016, which attempted to broaden the *w* of *writing* to the *l* of *literacy*, or, more accurately, *literacies*). Reading is the first literacy skill students learn; writing always comes later. And, like writing, reading is a lifelong skill that needs ongoing attention throughout one's education and beyond. Reading has changed in form and structure in the digital era, and writing studies educators are tasked with reading instruction as the CCCC's "Principles for the Postsecondary Teaching of Writing" and "Disability Studies in Composition" and the CWPA's "WPA Outcomes Statement" indicate. Perhaps the best name for the field simply is *literacy studies*, and we advocate for it. Still, had we designated this book as for literacy instructors, many of our readers would not recognize themselves as the audience. *Reading. Writing. Literacy.* Pick your favorite name for the field. This book is targeted to all educators who must comprehend and teach reading, alphabetic writing, and multimodal composition in the digital era.

Human Problems

We weave throughout this book anecdotes about a particular instructor (Professor Jackson) and administrator (WPA Garcia), who read and follow some of the suggestions provided in this book. We offer these examples to demonstrate how people might understand and negotiate instructional needs and situations. Professor Jackson, while experienced and eager to learn, has mostly taught in on-site environments and could use more training in teaching with technology and in various online settings, and WPA Garcia is a newly minted graduate who is stepping into the role of WPA for the first time. Instead of linking these characters to any one culture or background, we attempt to draw them as broadly representative of educators struggling with common experiences and professional growing pains. To this end, we selected their names from the most common surnames in the United States: *Jackson* ranks eighteenth, and *Garcia* eighth, per the 2000 United States Census (Word 20). Similarly, we have chosen to include example topics that are controversial in current society, attempting to illustrate how students might approach these topics. Although we believe writing can be taught without addressing such topics, they will emerge in many courses, and instructors should be ready for them. Our intention is to show instructors how they might help students manage such challenging human problems responsibly—no matter what they believe personally—through research, appropriate rhetorical strategies, and attention to all sides of an issue. These issues challenged us in writing this book because, given situations we have encountered as teachers, we desired to present them fairly and contextually. Real life is messy, and we want to honor that reality. Thus, these topics are genuine, difficult to address without personal bias, and present challenging opportunities for instruction in the twenty-first century.

Organization of This Volume

This book's two-part organization seeks to explain and support the writing instructor's work. Each part engages core principles from professional organization position statements to help readers use the information in their varied institutional settings and contexts. We attempt to articulate these core principles so instructors in a wide variety of institutional settings might apply them in ways appropriate to those settings and to their students while respecting the principled intention.

Each chapter contextualizes issues of digital-era composition, access, accessibility, usability, and multilingual and multiliteracy concerns. As described earlier, we address writing and writing-intensive courses rather than FYW alone. Therefore, we believe the WPA outcomes offer minimal expectations for any postsecondary writing, and the standards and strategies offer principled starting places for the book and its readers. Due to space limitations, we do not address such important subjects for composition as linguistics, paragraphing, and sentence structure, as Lindemann and others provide adequate coverage of these topics. We acknowledge these sources in the text for additional reading.

In each chapter, the fictitious scenarios involving the fictitious educators WPA Garcia, Professor Jackson, and their students and colleagues demonstrate how people might understand and negotiate instructional needs and situations. We use these common, recognizable, and practical sketches to embody and relate sometimes dense material to everyday instruction. Above all, we hope this book will inspire dialogue about what it means to teach effectively online and on-site in the twenty-first century.

Part 1: Approaching Composition in the Digital Era

Chapter 1, "Theorizing Composition and Communication," addresses four core composition themes rooted in rhetorical history. Knowing these themes grounds instructors who need to teach students strong communication skills in the digital era. Chapter 2, "Humanizing Composition," acknowledges the different needs and goals of contemporary writing students, providing practical strategies for attending to culturally competent and anti-racist approaches for nontraditional, multilingual, and learning and physically challenged learners, such that the needs of all are met.

Chapter 3, "Digitalizing Text, Purpose, and Genre," addresses the inherent digitality of contemporary composition, considering alphabetic and multimodal texts, composition approaches, and writing genres. Chapter 4, "Technologizing Composition Instruction," considers how the digital era affects composition technologies, educational modalities, composition environments, composition and teaching activities, and instructional media.

Chapter 5, "Teaching Composition in Online Settings," addresses instructional strategies and approaches for both fully online and hybrid settings, as well as courses using asynchronous and synchronous modalities. Chapter 6, "Reading Composition," provides theoretical and practical literacy reasons for explicitly teaching reading strategies in print-based, digitally presented, and multimodal readings.

Part 2: Teaching Composition in the Digital Era

Chapter 7, "Composing Processes and Approaches," outlines and addresses a rhetorical approach to alphabetic and multimodal writing with attention to audience, purpose, and social process. Chapter 8, "Designing and Scaffolding Assignments," provides strategies for developing, testing, and presenting well-designed content and assignments based on outcomes.

Chapter 9, "Providing Response, Feedback, and Evaluation," addresses response and feedback strategies for asynchronous (e.g., alphabetic text, video/audio, and screen capture) and synchronous (e.g., teleconference, video conference, and written chat) modalities as means for providing helpful commentary. Chapter 10, "Promoting Effective Communication," addresses a variety of communication strategies, including email; traditional theories of collaboration; online collaborative theories; and concrete strategies for anti-racist collaborative discussion and writing groups in various on-site and online settings.

Chapter 11, "Supporting Students," considers such support structures as time management, writing centers (both traditional on-site and online), embedded instructional assistants, peer mentors, and writing fellows in composition courses. Chapter 12, "Imagining the Future of Composition," considers how the writing studies field may continue to evolve, opening the future to thoughtful research and engaged collaboration among educators while encouraging them to approach the digital era of composition with excitement and readiness for continuing change.

Conclusion

The very ground of education has shifted, and conversations have become actions. Changes in writing instruction related to digitality have challenged us as authors to determine what we must and can include and do justice to in relatively little space. Twenty-first-century writing is part of a whole literacy made up of reading, alphabetic writing, and multimodal composition. Although they have been separated in most discussions of the writing instructor's job, we weave them together, inviting writing instructors to see themselves as literacy teachers who may provide the final, most overt education about core literacies that students ever will experience. The globally connected world into which postsecondary students will graduate requires high levels of these core literacies. *Teaching Writing in the Twenty-First Century* is a rhetoric that fully integrates these literacies and considers twenty-first-century teaching as wholly relying upon ubiquitous digital technologies. Although some teacher-scholars may believe they can teach traditionally in so-called traditional settings, we argue that what once was called *traditional* no longer exists; therefore, writing instructors must rethink the many issues students encounter through the educational filters of pedagogy, settings, and beliefs about writing. Doing so will eliminate some areas of frustration and contention, enlarging the scope of practice and enabling composition educators to reach students more fruitfully. Of special concern is that some teachers believe writing can—or should—be taught outside the considerations of reading and digital literacies and the strategies and tools that enable students to flexibly master and use them. This belief is not well-founded. Therefore, we acknowledge the need for ongoing college-appropriate reading instruction and multimodal composition as a natural part of writing instruction in the digital era.

Although no one book can cover the entirety of contemporary composition—readers will find important areas we have missed or elected not to address—*Teaching Writing in the Twenty-First Century* breaks new ground by accurately addressing the already-expanded educational scope of writing instructors. It embraces twenty-first-century, digital teaching environments with their attendant principles and practices; interpersonally relevant attention to access and usability; and a focus on whole literacy, including multilingual and multicultural concerns, as part of contemporary writing instruction. This rhetoric is supported by position statements that were researched and written by countless advanced scholars in the writing studies field and represented by multiple professional organizations. As such, it addresses how a contemporary writing pedagogy that naturally includes digital elements can be migrated, adapted, theorized, and reconceived for the various teaching and learning environments—including face-to-face, technology-enhanced, hybrid, and fully online courses—to meet students' various literacy needs and learning styles.

NOTE

1. We interweave similar critical considerations throughout the companion to this book, *Administering Writing Programs in the Twenty-First Century*. For additional insight on the conundrum of developing outcomes on a larger scale for writing programs, we recommend readers also review Selfe and Ericsson; Dryer et al.; Yancey, "Standards"; and White, "Origins."

Part One

APPROACHING Composition in the Digital Era

1

Theorizing Composition and Communication

Language is powerful. It is, as Richard Weaver expresses, "sermonic"—it teaches, leads, guides, suggests, frames, argues, encourages, discourages, delights, and expresses the self. Its uses also are contentious.

Professor Jackson jauntily enters the classroom, looking forward to the day's lesson. The students are animated, loudly sharing in agreement and disagreement. They turn to their instructor, who asks, "What's up?"

"We were talking about how wrong people can be. I can't believe what I'm hearing in the world! I read a blog about immigration and the border wall. One of my best friends is undocumented. How dare they talk about her this way?"

"I read another one questioning what to do about immigration during the virus pandemic."

"People are marching and protesting racist actions. I don't know what to say or do. Should I be doing something, too?"

"My father and uncle used to be best friends. Now, they won't talk to each other after my father wrote on *Facebook* about current politics."

"I wrote a *Twitter* post about climate change. People were so ugly in their tweets back. Who do they think they are to talk to me like that?"

"I read a news article about a college student under investigation for hate speech. But what he said wasn't hateful. It was just his opinion! He's allowed to express his opinions. First Amendment rights!"

"I wrote a paper in my history class about gun rights. The professor said I was completely wrong in my opinion and to either rewrite the paper or fail the assignment! It's so unfair!"

"One of my favorite musicians has been accused of horrible things! But it's just accusations right now. Why won't radio stations play her music? You can't just cancel someone for being accused of something, can you?"

Professor Jackson inwardly cringes. It's time for a talk. But how to approach earnest students and such serious issues without losing them in deep disagreement? How to help them negotiate these human issues? This is a writing class, not a sociology course!

Fortunately for Professor Jackson, a writing course is precisely the place to talk about the strategies for developing an informed opinion and communicating the challenges of such human issues—though without addressing the specific issues students raise, since it is not a composition's instructor's job to guide students to one opinion or the other. First, though, Professor Jackson needs a brushup on rhetoric and its connections to the composition and communication issues his course teaches.

Why Should Literacy Educators Read about Theory?

Why should composition instructors read about rhetoric's history and theory? What is the point of delving into ancient matters and those not easily connected to the daily work of reading, writing, and other literacy instruction? Simply put, the composition field is in a critical state of evolution because communication itself is changing in groundbreaking ways: genres, composing tools, delivery media, educational technologies, even words (and especially word meanings). The digital era has led literacy educators to an unknown space and there is no map to show where the field is, or should be, going. Composition's intimate history rooted in rhetoric, however, offers an understanding of the past and its evolution to the present. It offers grounding theories and practices that do not topple with seismic change—although they may quaver. Such grounding means teachers can rely on principles of communication that, although they have been theorized and described differently throughout the ages, will hold, allowing educators to begin their ever-evolving teaching on solid ground no matter what communicative changes arise.

The rules of engagement, so to speak, have changed. Students—people generally—are communicating and arguing more, not less, in the digital era, sometimes compiling hundreds of words daily through social and other digital media, habits that take them beyond the minimal writing that formal education requires and into the real world of consequential communication. Sometimes students imitate the tone and biases of journalistic media; as often, they mimic their favorite celebrities and politicians, who themselves may be unmindful of how their messages are received. Students may not know that communicating well with a reasoned, informed, and civil message is harder than ever because of digitality. Written (and dictated) messages fly out to readers and around the globe as fast as words can be spoken. Mistakes can never be fully erased even when deleted. Even experienced communicators often do not know the impact of what they say and how it will be used. Understanding and implementing the basics of rhetoric allows students to communicate better both privately and publicly.

Teachers need awareness of how thinking and words have been considered historically because some of the tools available to a composer have changed and may be viewed differently now from centuries ago. Regardless, both exposition that explains the why and how of an issue and argumentation that seeks to convince, persuade, or negotiate have important purposes in twenty-first-century life. The goals of such communications include being nonconfrontational but productive and being respectful, responsible, and reasonable beyond mere tolerance of others' positions. Only then can such communication lead to potential understanding at the least and agreement and action at the best.

Just as rhetoric considers "in each case the existing means of persuasion" (Aristotle 15; I.i.2 [1355b]), which have evolved, the available means of composing have changed over the years; therefore, students need guidance using rhetoric in concert with the different means of composing at their disposal. Students already are using many of these tools for a variety of purposes in their extracurricular lives. For instance, in *Writing in the Twenty-First Century*, Kathleen Blake Yancey expresses that people form groups to communicate, such as protesters who connect for a cause or organizations that form and create web media for mass circulation. Given that many students use social media often, composing in spaces that may not seem to count as writing but are composing spaces nonetheless, educators must teach that these spaces have rhetorical context and consequences requiring rhetorical strategies. Thus, instructors like Professor Jackson are charged with teaching students the rhetorical situations for composing, the most effective strategies for researching and constructing the message, and the most efficacious media for communicating it. Instructors also are challenged to connect what students are already doing in the outside world to the classroom, illuminating rhetorical choices and teaching how to hone them for a multiplicity of purposes.

Western rhetoric's history and relation to composition can be traced back approximately 2,500 years to Isocrates, Aristotle, Plato, Cicero, Quintilian, and other classical educators. *Rhetoric* is variously defined as persuasion, the art of seeking all the available means of persuasion in any particular case, a systematic investigative art, or all uses of language or expression (Burroughs 630). Classical oratory—about which rhetorical treatises first were written—often is consciously conceptualized as the knowledge and use of the human faculties of logic, grammar, rhetoric, and poetic. Such conceptualizations involve topoi (topics), formulas, and patterns of discourse taught systematically through influential treatises that not only conveyed rhetoric's theories and uses but influenced the rhetoric of each age.

In this chapter's representation of Western rhetorical history, we hope that readers can see a reconceptualization of traditional rhetoric that supports using it for contemporary communication and composing issues. Reading this chapter provides educators with theoretically powerful strategies to teach students how to communicate proficiently and self-consciously in a contemporary rhetoric that is oratorical, textual, and visual, as well as immediate, enduring, and global. From this brief history, therefore, we hope readers will understand the benefit of learning about and enfolding newer pedagogical practices with such older ones as discussed in this book.

A Thematic Rhetorical History and Theory

This chapter considers rhetoric's history and theory in connection with today's communicative concerns and composition courses, which are highly influenced by digitality. Rather than provide a complete chrono-logical history, however, we take a thematic approach, considering that rhetoric and composition address human problems that have no certain answers, adapt to the age and context, acknowledge audience, and concern both thought and language, allowing for invention. Although other themes can be added, we value these as grounding principles that enable composition instructors to begin teaching while assisting students with the evolutionary changes in contemporary communication, which includes argumentation of all forms.

Theme 1: Rhetoric and composition address human problems that have no certain answers.

It is hard to remember that most of the problems people experience are ones without scientific or absolute answers. For example, concerns about high levels of immigration and emigration abound globally. It is possible to attach definitions to such terms as *citizen, resident, immigrant, emigration, foreigner,* and *border* within the context of any one country (although not everyone will agree with any one definition). It also is possible to scientifically study the number of people any particular city or country can support through adequate resources. Formal definitions and statistics, however, cannot pin down what people believe about immigration and emigration in terms of a person's inherent worth, possible contributions, or positive and negative effects on ecology and economy. Beliefs differ among individuals, and they are connected to personal backgrounds, situational contexts, and actions people want to see occur—all of which stem from their beliefs. Other highly contended legislative issues like gun control, what constitutes an act of treason, and appropriate punishment for sexual abuse are mirrored in such private-life issues as homeowners' association rules about flag and faith symbols, smoking and vaping in public establishments, and neighborhood responses to registered sex offenders.

These concerns about human problems require *probable reasoning* to sort through the issues and find the best possible arguments that might resolve them—not forever but in the context of a time and place. Professor Jackson should teach his students that probable reasoning does not lead to one certain answer—as one might expect of a scientific exploration—but to a potentially usable answer given the situation. Probable reasoning was used in classical civic deliberations of law, legal proceedings, and ceremonial issues of praise and blame. Today, it also is applied to everyday citizens' needs in their homes and neighborhoods. Although rhetors (specially trained orators in ancient Greece and Rome) used to work professionally to offer such assistance by becoming the people's voice, today everyone—citizens and foreigners alike—has the rhetor's responsibility, which is to use probable reasoning to seek answers to everyday problems and then to convey that reasoning thoughtfully and civilly. Today, nearly everybody has a rhetor's duties, but few have the training and self-awareness of what they can do to teach, convince, and persuade people regarding an issue. Hence, too many people think their opinion is the "right" one, which makes everyone else "wrong." With digital communication in use globally, to some people, being "correct" also means being inappropriate, divisive, and even remarkably cruel and hateful. Such thoughtless speech tends to be ineffective at best and interpersonally devastating or violence-inducing at worst.

Gorgias, Isocrates, Plato, and Aristotle, all teachers of ancient Greek rhetoric, grappled with what rhetoric encompasses regarding probable reasoning, which means they contested the nature of truth and Truth.[1] Gorgias, who engaged Athenian civic interests in rhetoric around 427 BCE, believed there is no transcendent knowledge or singular Truth and that humans can only uncover provisional knowledge and express it through ethical, pathetic, and logical appeals (Bizzell and Herzberg 42). That means he believed rhetoric solely considers human affairs for which people have opinions and seek others' belief. Isocrates, the foremost speech teacher of the age, also saw no possibility of transcendent knowledge and, with his focus of serving the state, possibly no use for it anyway (Bizzell and Herzberg 70–71). He espoused sophistry, a belief that knowledge is context-bound and socially constructed. Although the word *sophism* often is used pejoratively today, it was more neutral in Isocrates's time. Arguably, Protagoras introduced sophistry as a formalized way of thinking about human knowledge, which "relies solely on sense perception and therefore is necessarily flawed" (Bizzell and Herzberg 22). His philosophy that one can make contradictory statements about any issue (i.e., *dissoi logoi*) suggests rhetoric assists in negotiating opposing views that might be considered equally reasonable—a concern that should interest Professor Jackson's students in the opening anecdote.

Sophistry's opponents, like Aristotle, believed that, although humans cannot know Truth, they can uncover probable knowledge, deliberate on the best course of action, and use rhetoric to persuade people to the perceived good. Plato also disagreed with teaching sophistically. A friend of Socrates, whose questioning search for metaphysical Truth offers a dialectical model for Plato's dialogues (particularly *Phaedrus*), Plato philosophically considered rhetoric to be a "knack [cleverness] acquired by routine" that "enchant[s] the soul" through words (*Gorgias* 44; sec. 463b; *Phaedrus* 438). He argued strongly against sophistic rhetoric's apparent ability to make the worst case seem to be the better one, which is an approach taken by many tweeters and by defense and prosecution attorneys alike. For him, rhetoric cannot be an art because it does not rest on universal principles; like poetry, rhetoric deals with belief and opinion, which can be false and misleading. Plato's antisophistic theory of rhetoric is that rhetors must know Truth before they speak, which means Truth itself is knowable and not socially constructed. For Plato, at best, Truth might be found through dialectic, a private or academic dialogue process among a few people with different viewpoints who want to establish the truth of a proposition (Moss 183).

Aristotle contributed a full, systematic theory of oratorical invention. He believed that one can learn to be a good rhetor from other's practices and why those practices work (J. Lauer 724). Aristotle refuted Plato by elevating rhetoric, a public practice for defending oneself or another against a proposition, as the counterpart of dialectic. He believed that, although some truth is empirically knowable through scientific demonstration and formal logic (Bizzell and Herzberg 170), there is a gray area of the probable, which is uncertain but open to an educated guess; therefore, the probable is the basis of persuasion, and belief is the highest degree of certainty obtainable in human affairs. In *The "Art" of Rhetoric*, Aristotle responds to Plato's utter disdain for rhetoric, suggesting that even though rhetoric deals with opinion, it is reliable regarding human affairs. Unlike Plato, who believed that dialectic alone can find probable truth, Aristotle believed both dialectic and rhetoric are "not so much to persuade, as to find out in each case the existing means of persuasion" about any topic (13: I.i.141 [355b]). Because rhetoric enables discovering probable truths through *invention* (one of five canons, including *arrangement*, *style*, *memory*, and *delivery*), rhetoric could make truth prevail, as well as instruct, defend, debate issues, and thus inform larger general audiences. Therefore, Aristotle considered *rhetoric* to be the practice of seeking all the available means of persuasion in any particular case. He agreed with Plato's need for truth, believing humans are naturally inclined to prefer the true and the just and that truth is easier to support rhetorically.[2]

These Greek rhetoricians influenced Roman educators Cicero and Quintilian, medieval rhetorician Augustine, and countless other rhetoricians. Cicero educated orators about their civic responsibilities when Roman orators still held political and legal influence (*De inventione* [*The Invention*]). His *De oratore* (*The Orator*) focuses on acquiring necessary wisdom and eloquence for public speaking: To be a strong speaker, the citizen orator should be well educated, understand society and subject matter, be a strong rhetor, and have high moral virtue. During Cicero's time, the moral center of the citizenry resided in the community's best interests, making the state's well-being each citizen's first duty. Quintilian, widely considered the prototypical educator for imperial Rome and author of *Institutio oratoria* (*Institution of Oratory*), held a government-funded chair of rhetoric just when the political atmosphere put rhetoric in the closet and allowed only legal counsel in the courts. For him, the ideal orator is a good person speaking well, strongly suggesting that one's ethics matter (9; I.Pr.9.).

Fast forward to the twentieth century, when Chaim Perelman published *The New Rhetoric* with Lucie Olbrechts-Tyteca, a work that takes a stance similar to Aristotle's regarding rhetoric's province as probable truth argument about human affairs. Perelman and Olbrechts-Tyteca used case study analysis to understand practical argument, mirroring Aristotle's method of observation and analysis of human nature. Perelman came to rhetoric from judicial persuasive concerns of law, like many active classical rhetoricians. The work of Stephen Toulmin, an English philosophical logician and author of *The Uses of Argument*, shares both Aristotle's and Perelman's narrower distinction of rhetoric as belonging to the realm of practical human argument. These different approaches to what rhetoric addresses ground some contemporary composition theories. Expressivism, which prizes writing for personal expression, for example, is Neoplatonic, whereas social construction and social process theories are informed by sophistic rhetoric. Classical rhetoric exists in neoclassical writing programs that consider probable reasoning and persuasive argument as important parts of composition instruction.

Professor Jackson's students would benefit from understanding that, although they have a right to their opinions about human problems, long-held thinking about responsible communication requires they learn about the issues, providing them an informed opinion from which to speak. Students attempt meaningful communication that often is transactional in seeking action: to inform, convince, persuade, negotiate. In ancient Greece, these transactions typically occurred in legislative, judicial, and ceremonial arenas. In the twenty-first century, however, these arenas also include educational settings and the (digital) social realm of the general populace. Classical rhetorical approaches to probable reasoning remind people they have a responsibility to have their facts correct and argue beliefs not only from research but also through proof strategies. Taken largely from Aristotle's astute catalogue of how humans argue, rhetoric can invent proofs, either inartistic (e.g., testimony, law, results of torture or interrogation) or artistic (e.g., ethos, pathos, logos). To seek—or invent—these proofs, Aristotle outlined the topoi, or special and common topics, that make inventing and arranging extemporaneous orations possible; similarly, the topoi support the development of twenty-first-century essays, multimodal texts, social media posts, and other communications (see ch. 4 of this volume).

These tools are helpful for composition students, who need many strategies to manage both postsecondary writing requirements and life-based communications. Professor Jackson's student who questioned canceling a popular singer accused of immoral behavior might consider developing a ceremonial, or epideictic, composition, deciding what to praise or blame about either the singer or her accusers and engaging such topoi as past fact or future fact to compare her to other famous people with failings. Such a composition could exonerate the singer or lead others to want to cancel her memory as one who does not support commonly held values. The student who is interested in what action to take regarding protests might benefit from researching and writing about the nature of protest as a rhetorical act, specifically researching past and current protests against racism. Using the possible-impossible or the more-less as inventive topoi might assist in this process. Such self-education can provide the student with necessary information for determining next steps that match personally held opinions with ethics.

The powerful nature of language means that it can be both harmful and helpful: It can inform and distract; it can imbue hope and instill darkness. In *Gorgias*, Plato (informed by Socrates) famously indicates strong distrust of written text as a substitute for orality, language's most trustworthy and probing mode. He writes that rhetoric itself is merely a knack or cleverness that needs philosophy to create responsible communication (44; sec. 463). Naturally, yet ironically, his views come to educators through text. Plato's concerns emerged when speeches and rhetoric treatises were delivered orally and sometimes written on vellum or parchment. Today, words are spoken and written using digital media. If Plato considered words suspect, what would he think of the rapidly published, globally distributed words of *Twitter, Facebook*, and people's written responses to news, blogs, and other publications? What would Professor Jackson's students say to Plato about their uses of social and other media for communication?

Theme 2: Rhetoric and composition are adaptable to the age and context.

Professor Jackson's students were troubled by language uses and how they were received. In their parents' and grandparents' day, language also could be used poorly, but the way it was delivered and transmitted was different. People did not share their unfiltered thoughts as widely, nor did they necessarily expect everyone to agree with them, as they often do today. Writing instruction is responsive to the culture and always in flux; society has changed how people communicate with different media and modes, making digital composing approaches imperative for students' success both in and outside academia. In *Technology and Literacy in the Twenty-First Century*, Cynthia L. Selfe argues literacy practices have always followed society's demands, as can be seen with the rise of the Industrial Revolution or even literacy crises and the many variations of "why Johnny can't write" that permeate media. One of rhetoric's greatest contributions is how it adapts to time and culture, which is information that Professor Jackson can use to teach his students about the critical language uses that perplex them.

Many of composition's strongest theories are traceable to the education that classical rhetoricians offered, making rhetoric the precursor to composition. Undoubtedly, composition has changed with digitality, yet much remains the same, which is one reason we reframe classical rhetoric for instructor and student accessibility in this book about composition instruction in the digital era. As discussed above, composing typically addresses human concerns, and doing so requires proofs as well as critical thinking. What began as classical discussions of how best to educate an orator, however, quickly encompassed how to represent ideas textually. For example, despite Plato's contempt for prepared texts, Aristotle acknowledges written speeches in *The "Art" of Rhetoric*: "Generally speaking, that which is written should be easy to read or easy to utter, which is the same thing" (373; III.v.6 [1407b]). Three hundred years later, Quintilian offered the first comprehensive Western prescription for childhood to adulthood education in the *Institutio oratoria*. He outlined both written composition and declamation exercises based on paraphrasing stories and fables, translating compositions from other languages, and imitating classic models—all educational methods for developing subject matter common both to oratorical and written composition education.

Rhetoric as both an oratorical and text-based endeavor changed greatly between the classical and Enlightenment periods. It was adapted to different purposes, guided by cultural, social, economic, and political changes. For example, Christian rhetoric began as an apologist approach to persuade nonbelievers of Christianity's legitimacy. Books 1–3 of Augustine's *De doctrina Christiana* (*On Christian Doctrine*), published in 397 CE, adapted Cicero's rhetoric to preaching God's word, and book 4, published in 426, shifted the classical notion of eloquence to Christian eloquence.

The Middle Ages divided education by the trivium (grammar, logic, and rhetoric) and the quadrivium (music, arithmetic, geometry, and astronomy). Cicero's *De inventione* and the pseudo-Ciceronian *Rhetorica ad Herennium* (*Rhetoric for Herrenius*), formerly attributed to Cicero, had the greatest educational influence. Rhetoric's general application to many fields—what made it so vital to the classical orator—splintered it, eventually leading Peter Ramus to reduce rhetoric's province to style and delivery alone. Yet this splintering also led to primarily writing-based interests in poetry (i.e., using literature to demonstrate and analyze tropes and figures), grammar (i.e., assigning figures of thought to rhetoric and figures of speech to grammar), prose (i.e., developing epistolary structure for the art of prose composition and letter writing), and sermons (i.e., emphasizing sin less and rational persuasion more). These communication types also appealed to people without civic responsibilities.

During the Renaissance, a new valuation of human nature gave rise to a secular oratory apart from Christian morals. The Reformation shifted sermons from being about Christian living to being moral teaching tools, and the Counter-Reformation shifted sermons to addressing reason and faith together. The Augustinian purposes of praising God's deeds, truth, and love were revived. Classical oratorical texts were translated and imitated as a paradigm shift toward the practical. For example, neo-Ciceronian influences focused on both Latin and the vernacular, with emphasis on literary and poetic examples. The stylistic school valued the eloquence of tropes and figures, and formularies helped to improve letter-writing skills and engaged models for imitation, giving written media a solid place within rhetoric and enabling more people to make use of the art. For example, people wrote letters prodigiously both to transact business and to maintain connections. People wanted to learn to write letters better, and letters often were saved or collected and sometimes published posthumously—like a diary; yet, unlike online journals and blogs, they were not written for immediate publication. Writers could let their ideas steep, and sometimes they or their families edited out what they did not want published. The Renaissance's wide reach across Europe means that rhetoric developed with geographic differences. European travel inspired crossover learning. At the end of the Renaissance, rhetoric primarily engaged writing over speech and was still adapting to the culture and times. Professor Jackson will recognize this attention to writing over speech as common to both academic and social life, particularly as texting now supersedes phone calling.

Over time, new ways of thinking influenced rhetoric and its uses, leading to various beliefs about its purpose and preferred medium—speech or writing. For example, *empiricism* is the belief that all knowledge is derived from sense experience or experimentation. Such Renaissance empiricist thinkers as Francis Bacon, in his 1605 *The Advancement of Learning*, critiqued rhetoric as the study of ideas and not of real matter. Bacon relegated rhetoric to communication, making elocution, or transmitting ideas, its primary focus. Rationalism, another late-Renaissance movement, replaced dialectics with method. René Descartes's 1637 *Discourse on Method* emphasized science for finding truth, leaving persuasion for when doubt exists. Descartes found truth's kernel within the human thinker through solitary mental analysis, and he believed the scientific method supported this process. Interestingly, about one hundred years later, Giambattista Vico argued with Cartesian science, returning rhetorical attention to Cicero's good person orator. He defended rhetoric as a modern method of study and a superior philosophy of knowledge because knowledge is formed by argument and conviction, indicating that even science deals with probability and not absolute truth (Bizzell and Herzberg 11).

In rhetorical thinking and teaching, the Enlightenment introduced changes responsive to the cultural, social, economic, and political milieu. Innovations included revolutions in philosophy, science, linguistics, and psychology. Neoclassicism in France and Britain represented a turn from the baroque, and the age emphasized classical rhetoric, literature, architecture, sculpture, and painting, leading to a new role for primary rhetoric and preference for Cicero's work. According to Tania Smith, in the early Enlightenment, for example, *The Lady's Rhetorick* epitomized the teachings of classical and French rhetorics for young men and women's everyday communication as conversationalists and letter and journal writers. She explains that leading Blue Stocking salon hostesses were reading English biographies of Cicero and learning the epistolary art in the vernacular.

English translations of classical Latin texts arose in the late seventeenth century, and after the mid-eighteenth century, translations of Greek rhetoric beyond Longinus and Aristotle became more common. Thus, students might see, classical texts were variously ignored, resurrected in the vernacular, and built on during the age of reason. Simultaneously, the Enlightenment's focus on empiricism, rationalism, and psychology led to the psychological-epistemological theory of rhetoric based on scientific empiricism. Belletrism, which focused on polite letters, surfaced in the eighteenth and nineteenth centuries as a reaction against the reemergence of classical rhetoric, whereas an elocutionary movement returned pathos to oratorical rhetoric. As the Enlightenment stretched toward the nineteenth century, rhetoric and oratory were influenced by elocutionism (a focus on the body and voice in oratory) and Romanticism (a focus on the individual). Each major movement influenced the context for rhetorical education (Hewett, *Scholarly Edition* 39–49). By the nineteenth and twentieth centuries, rhetoric had moved into American education as so-called *current-traditional*, Daniel Fogarty's pejorative term for writing instruction that prized product over process; reduced writing to four modes (i.e., narration, description, exposition, and argumentation); and focused on abstractions like unity, coherence, and correctness (see also Berlin, *Writing Instruction*). Professor Jackson's students may have experienced such writing requirements in their earlier English, writing, or language arts courses.

In the 1960s, educators returned to rhetoric, which has always "strived to be useful, to help *reform the way we teach our students*" (Paine 27). In "Who We Were, Who We Should Become," Richard Lloyd-Jones suggests that with the advent of the GI Bill, more nontraditional students entered the classroom, and writing instructors sought ways to respond to the change in student demographics; specifically, teacher-scholars began to question the current-traditional model because it lacked attention to invention and how people actually compose (489). Because rhetoric as composition changes in response to age and context, educators can see rhetorical concepts grounding newer composition pedagogies. In "Contemporary Composition," James Berlin notes these conceptual approaches as the neo-Aristotelians or classicists, the positivists or current-traditionalists, the Neoplatonists or expressionists, and the new rhetoricians (766).

The twentieth century opened rhetoric to a complex series of approaches that connected rhetoric with linguistics (Richards; Bakhtin; Britton et al.; D'Angelo), cognitive development (Flower and Hayes; Berthoff), early childhood development (Moffett, *Teaching*; Britton et al.), collaboration (Bruffee, *Collaborative Learning* and "Collaborative Learning"), classical oratory (Kinneavy; Corbett), and a return to its legal-juridical models of practical argument and probable truth (C. Perelman; Toulmin). The mid-century influx of students prompted increased attention to writing process (Emig), eventually dominating theory because it seems helpful. Linda Flower and John R. Hayes countered this approach, however, citing that a cognitive-process theory necessarily addresses "distinctive thinking processes that writers orchestrate or organize during" composition; "a hierarchical, highly embedded organization in which any given process can be embedded within another"; the "goal-directed thinking process guided by the writer's" own goals; and that "writers create their own goals" by creating them, supporting subgoals, and creating new goals as needed (366). Donald Murray's 1968 *A Writer Teaches Writing* was influential for valuing response and discussion over traditional lectures, and Peter Elbow's 1973 *Writing without Teachers* introduced freewriting for idea generation and late-in-process editing.

In the 1982 essay "Winds of Change," Maxine Hairston argues that the process movement represented the most significant shift, at least until then, in how American postsecondary educators taught writing. This movement from product to process challenged academic writing as everyone knew it by focusing on students' voices (Newkirk). As such, the process movement is often linked to expressivism, characterized by attention to writers, shifting from classical rhetoric's attention to audience.

The process movement has been expanded on and critiqued by post-process scholars, who argue that writing is a public and situated act, never a private one. Process pedagogy remains influential, nevertheless. Susan H. McLeod argues in *Writing Program Administration* that Donald Murray's work, specifically "Teach Writing as a Process Not a Product," became "a rallying cry for WPAs who were involved in staff development and/or TA [teaching assistant] training programs" (68). The paradigm shift from current-traditional rhetoric to process writing also marked the beginning of composition as a discipline in its own right (68), which was aided through the formation of professional organizations dedicated to helping instructors and administrators both teach the new influx of students and manage and direct entire programs. Such professional organizations as the Modern Language Association, National Council of Teachers of English, Conference on College Composition and Communication, Council of Writing Program Administrators, and Global Society of Online Literacy Educators offer Professor Jackson and WPA Garcia association with colleagues and valuable professional development.

In the twenty-first century, a new shift to technology-enhanced teaching (detailed in chs. 3, 4, and 5 and considered throughout the book) paralleled the digital era's addition of new genres and media to composition's work (see chs. 3, 4, and 7). Multimodal composition for digital settings was born, and its effects on people's everyday communications has been massive and, sometimes, interpersonally challenging—as evidenced by Professor Jackson's perplexed students. Variously called *multimedia composition*, *new media*, *digital rhetoric*, and *webtexts*, we use the term *multimodal composition* to represent "texts created primarily in digital environments, composed in multiple media (e.g., film, video, audio, among others), and designed for presentation and exchange in digital venues" (Selfe, "Students" 43). Cheryl Ball defines multimodal texts as having such

> semiotic modes . . . [as] sound, graphics, video, animation, and/or written words. These texts are typically distributed in an online context, and because of their use of modes that readers more typically find in aesthetic texts (i.e., film, audio, animation), their argumentative models are not linear, alphabetic, or reminiscent of traditional print-bound models.   ("Show" 404–05)[3]

Yet such texts almost always use alphabetic text. Until recently, adding imagery to text most often occurred in medieval scriptural texts and children's books, assisting with meaning making (Jewitt 317). Now, however, especially in a digital, screen-based world, the coexistence of other media with text is common and expected. Multimodal composition reading is a literacy required in the "'out-of-school worlds' of most people" (330), which means it must be taught as a core literacy in early school years and supported in college.

Particularly because multimodal texts engage alphabetic text, educators like Professor Jackson should not fear that teaching them functionally, critically, and rhetorically—as Stuart A. Selber's work (*Multiliteracies*, "Reimagining") argues technology itself should be taught—rejects teaching linguistic text. Instead, teaching multimodal texts is the natural outgrowth of contemporary rhetoric and composition (Hawisher and Selfe, "Rhetoric"). It involves considering thought and language, and it robustly reengages the five rhetorical canons. Idea invention, text and media arrangement, conscious uses of style, the audience's memory (distinctly different from the orator's/composer's memory), and especially digital delivery are all crucial to multimodal composition both in and outside of school. According to Andrew Bourelle, Tiffany Bourelle, and Natasha Jones:

> The remix of writing that often occurs in the classroom, and more broadly in the digital workplace, is grounded in rhetorical principles,

with students learning Aristotle's idea of rhetoric, discovering all "available means of persuasion" [13; I.i.14 (1355b)]. The means of persuasion students have available to them may vastly differ from those in Aristotle's day, but the principles are still the same: these new mediums simply give students more available means of persuasion to choose from when communicating.   ("Multimodality" 309)

Arguably—and Professor Jackson's students must consider this point—students engage new media composition every time they text one another, talk using video, mix and mash up music and video, and create or share memes through social media. These genres represent the new secular rhetoric. Some of the cleverest turns of phrase occur through individually created memes and in blogs (i.e., weblog or journal) and vlogs (i.e., video [b]log). Some arguments are pursued through humor, keen insight, and even meanly phrased word-image mixes. Undoubtedly, the selected modes and media influence the rhetorical choices composers make.

Although multimodal pedagogy has gained traction in the last two decades, it has met with resistance. Some instructors and students may not understand the connection between the written word and multimodality. How is a multimodal pedagogy supposed to teach students to write? The bridge between the written word and the image may seem wide; in *Embodied Literacies*, however, Kristie S. Fleckenstein argues that image and text are inextricably tied. She suggests one's waking and sleeping life is "punctuated by the chaotic flow of images, those that we see, smell, hear, feel, and taste. We carry those images with us, consciously and unconsciously seeking their guidance, submitting to their coercion," when completing such everyday tasks as making grocery lists or recalling students' names (12), unavoidably thinking of the product or picturing faces alongside names. Imagery makes creating textual meaning possible. The image and the written or spoken word thus go together, as "thought, meaning, and texts are crafted out of images" (13); hence, alphabetic composing already has a multimodal element.

With its focus on rhetoric and process, multimodal composition has found a natural home in writing studies, and it has gained traction in courses across the disciplines. Geoffrey Sirc's *English Composition as a Happening* indicates instructors often value process over product. Instead, instructors should look at how students move through a text to see fluidity that is hard to define, and they should let this process happen, guiding students as they create. In "Composing Multimodality," Joddy Murray describes this flow as a process of discovery; as students get in the flow of composing multimodally, they should be guided in their choices but allowed to compose freely. Thus, instructors should teach process as variable and creative when adopting a multimodal pedagogy.

Combined with Selfe's and Selber's discussions of critical literacy, composition is much more than students simply creating texts through multiple communicative mediums.[4] Students must understand the rhetorical considerations behind creating text while identifying how their texts may affect their audience and how the piece fits within broader societal communications. Composition draws on the theory of multimodal literacy, which, as Hawisher and Selfe state, "acknowledges that contemporary authors, faced with complex rhetorical situations, need the ability to draw on an increasingly varied set of design resources and representational modalities to make meaning and create texts—among them, still photography, video, audio, alphabetic, animation, graphical drawings, and color" ("Studying" 191; see also B. Horner 24). Thus, it is crucial to help students approach technology with confidence, encouraging them to try new ways of composing with the media and modes that best suit their message. Just because students are living in the digital era does not mean they understand how to use technology in rhetorically effective ways in either academic or real-world situations. Furthermore, students also need to be taught how to critically consider the technology they are using, which means understanding how to operate the software, the rhetorical choices behind technology development, and how certain technologies or media might replicate or change current social structures (Selber, *Multiliteracies* 85).

Professor Jackson's students do not need to know all the people and movements outlined in this section, but even understanding a few of the paths rhetoric has taken over the centuries may help them realize that composing well is a time-honored art worth learning to do skillfully. It also may help them put into perspective the kinds of interactions they experience daily and how—especially with digital devices for technologically rapid delivery—their speaking is a form of oratory and their writing is an argument that affects communications and interpersonal relationships in important ways.

More important, Professor Jackson benefits from learning about rhetoric's historical and contextual changes, in part because when educators do not know their discipline's past, it is harder for them to imagine its potential future. Therefore, newer rhetorical theories and scholarship instructors should review are interwoven throughout this book. Although no list we offer could be complete, we would be remiss if we did not mention emerging rhetoric scholarship that should influence practice, including Native American (Mukavetz), feminist (Royster and Kirsch), cultural (Cui), queer (Bessette), Latinx (Soto Vega and Chávez), and African American (Williams-Farrier) rhetorics, among others. We hope this book helps instructors reconceptualize rhetorical history for the twenty-first century, offering new directions for rhetorical practices, and we include scholarship from a multiplicity of authors our readers can draw from when constructing an inclusive classroom and curriculum, approaching difficult topics, facilitating productive dialogue, incorporating new composing strategies, and communicating with students.

Further, when communicative genres, strategies, and technologies change, approaches to instruction also must change, encouraging educators to relearn teaching from an evolutionary perspective, which opens new philosophical questions of substance and language for the twenty-first century. Through this picture of how rhetoric adapts to one's age and context, Professor Jackson can consider new or different teaching methods. Students and instructors can begin to discuss the critical rhetoricity of the communication problems that Professor Jackson's students expressed in this chapter's opening anecdote.

Theme 3: Rhetoric and composition acknowledge audience.

Who is out there to listen to or read what is composed? Professor Jackson's students certainly know that people are recipients of texts and social media posts and interactions, discipline-specific college essays, and end-of-term portfolios. But they may not be consciously aware of how their words impact real, individual humans in their audience or why, as one student indicated, people can be so mean. The notion of audience is critical to rhetorical theory, and it is crucial to the composing practices and everyday argumentation of Professor Jackson's students and their relatives and friends. Rhetoric as a set of theories and practices has always attended to audience, and students can and should consider audience along with rhetorical situation, purpose, medium, and the rhetorical intention of the documents they read and produce.

Audience has nearly always been considered tripartite: "For every speech is composed of three parts: the speaker, the subject of which he treats, and the person to whom it is addressed. I mean the hearer, to whom the end or object of the speech refers" (Aristotle 33; I.iii.1 [1358a–b]). This notion of speaker, subject, and audience is often presented in a triangular rather than linear or circular configuration because each angle is intimately related to the other two. For example, in *Teaching the Universe of Discourse*, James Moffett used Jean Piaget's developmental language model to explore the intimate relations among writer, reader, and text. Moffett states, "The elements of discourse are a first person, a second person, and a third person; a speaker, listener, and subject; informer, informed, and information; narrator, auditor, and story; transmitter, receiver, and message" (10). Ultimately, these comprise the "super-structure of English," a "set of relations among three persons" (10), often depicted in a communication triangle that relates the first person *I* to the speaker, the second person *you* to the listener, and the third person *it* to the subject. The message—the speech or text—resides in this triangle, connected to all three points. In Moffett's intimate model of communication, children begin with the *I* as their normal point of reference and move in successively more sophisticated ways to the *you* and the *it*. Relations between both the *I* → *you* and the *I* → *it* are necessary to achieve communicative understanding between the *you* → *it*. In transferring the notion of speaker to that of writer, the writer must have intimate understanding of both the reader as audience and the subject to hope that the writing will affect the reader. Figure 1.1 is an illustration of Moffett's theory that writers must learn to span the distances between the *I* (writer), the *you* (reader), and the *it* (subject); this increasingly sophisticated understanding of the reader-as-audience, however, can only come insofar as children are cognitively ready.

Spanning those distances among speaker, listener, and subject is the work of both classical orators and today's speakers and writers. Although all three parts of the triangle must be addressed, rhetorical educators are uniquely concerned with audience. In classical and contemporary deliberative, judicial, and ceremonial oratory, for example, the audience exists

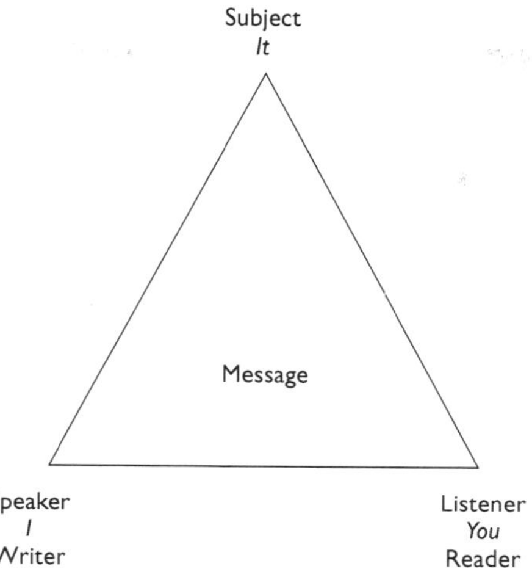

Figure 1.1. Triangle of Moffett's writer-reader-subject model. Moffett, *Teaching*, p. 10.

not only to listen to but participate in the communication by making rational judgments leading to deliberative votes and legal findings or by embracing or decrying the subject of praise or blame. Therefore, educators like Aristotle and Cicero taught people how to influence and affect the audience—how to persuade and move them. Rhetors needed to know not only the facts of the issue and how to portray them—the logos— but also the minds of the listeners, which is ultimately psychological, a view that both Plato and Aristotle held (Freese xxv) as well as modern eighteenth- and nineteenth-century educators like George Campbell, Hugh Blair, and Richard Whately.

Aristotle's rhetoric is a methodical, psychological, and scientific discussion of human nature—how people are persuaded and how speakers may persuade particular audiences. As an educator, he was concerned with the universals of human nature, understanding the speaker's goals, comprehending the audience's needs, and the specific circumstances of speech itself. Among Aristotle's system of persuasive proofs are logos, ethos, and pathos. *Logos* represents the logical parts of an argument, based on dialectic, discussed previously and identified as inartistic and artistic (Freese xxv). *Ethos* addresses speakers' characters, and *pathos* considers the minds and emotions of the audiences who judge the case

(Aristotle 169; II.i.3 [1377b]). In deliberative oratory particularly, the focus is on speakers who need to display good sense, virtue (e.g., justice, courage, temperance, and wisdom), and goodwill toward the audience (171; II.i.6). These personal characteristics help audiences trust speakers and respond positively. In judicial oratory, speakers attempt to appeal to the listener's emotions so that the audience is internally disposed to render a desired judgment (171). Aristotle systematically treated emotions as "affections which cause men to change their opinion in regard to their judgements, and are accompanied by pleasure and pain"; these emotions are "anger, pity, fear, other similar emotions and their contraries" (173; II.i.8). Take anger, for example, which Aristotle defines as "a longing, accompanied by pain, for a real or apparent revenge for a real or apparent slight, affecting a man himself or one of his friends, when such a slight is undeserved" (173; II.ii.2 [1378a]). This emotion is natural, normal, and can be circumstantially raised in people. Any speaker can hook an audience accidentally through its anger, rage, and outrage; a skilled speaker can raise or calm emotions deliberately. Chaim Perelman, among others, might echo Aristotle's concern for seeking adherence to a claim by understanding the psychological (e.g., economic, educational, and age-related) makeup of the audience; yet Perelman believed there is no such thing as a universal audience to which a rhetoric can reliably appeal. One cannot know the audience because it is a construct of the speaker's imagination, which suggests Perelman might reject as futile Aristotle's attempts to define particular audiences. From this position, no audience is reliable; people can make some general and often correct assumptions about others, but (as popularly televised real-time trials of celebrities reveal) what will persuade them often is unpredictable.

According to Kenneth Burke in *A Rhetoric of Motives*, one must address an audience, recognizing the tensions of strife—or division—among them, in order to find potential for cooperation or identification. Division itself introduces the possibility of rhetorical solutions: "But put identification and division ambiguously together, so that you cannot know for certain just where one ends and the other begins, and you have the characteristic invitation to rhetoric" (25). Difference, then, invites speaker-writers to approach listener-readers.

This insight into anger speaks to Professor Jackson's students' need to understand why, in this chapter's opening anecdote, one student's father and uncle no longer speak after a *Facebook* exchange about politics. The father and uncle sound angry—angry enough for best-friend siblings to stop talking about *anything* because of an argument about *one thing*. Underneath their anger, Aristotle suggests, may be pain that they disagree strongly as well as a sense of having been slighted (perhaps way back in childhood). It really does not matter what the topic of the argument was, given the likelihood that they each did not approach that topic displaying their best ethos—their genuine goodwill for each other. Each may have believed he showed good sense, but did each display the virtue of temperance? How about the wisdom to know when to stop talking (writing) and start listening (reading) thoughtfully? The students should recall that this argument was not about certainty or scientific knowledge. It was about probable reasoning: what might happen if different political actions were taken—and, thus, what might be the best action. These human elements can only be guessed at, never fully known. When father and uncle argued over *Facebook*, their differences invited rhetoric, but they may not have known how to approach the argument fruitfully. Additionally, they likely did not consider the result of making each other angry, the development of a "real or apparent slight" that each would experience as "undeserved." They probably did not consider whether *Facebook* was the best venue for this exchange; arguing on social media may lead to public loss of face, which is even more challenging than private disagreements. Audience considerations remain as important today as in classical times—perhaps more so in arguments that, through digitality, can go nuclear, so to speak.

Persuasion is not the only means of approaching audiences to seek change. New thinkers have added to the complex theories of persuasion developed over the centuries. Burke was one such rhetorician; in *A Rhetoric of Motives*, he demonstrates a preference for seeking identification with the audience rather than persuasion over them. His goal was to find common ground in everyday discourse rather than in deliberative, judicial, and ceremonial contexts. Therefore, he looked at how one creates identification with a group. Identification is not agonistic or polemic; instead of having a persuasive goal, it seeks cooperation, looking to humans' common interests and assumptions. When one identifies with another, the person crosses boundaries to consubstantiate with the other, overcoming (however briefly) divisions between them (19–29). This thinking is much like Martin Buber's *I-Thou* (*You*) and *I-It* theory of human connection, a theory to which Moffett also alludes (*Teaching* 11).

Burke's idea was that when person A identifies with person B, person A is "substantially one" with person B, "both joined and separate, at once a distinct substance and consubstantial with another" (*Rhetoric* 21). Each person is autonomous, capable of individuality, but seeking consubstantiality is a way of addressing the tension between them.

Burke's concept of identification with an audience is interesting for Professor Jackson's students because it can reshape the dialogue around the *Twitter* post about climate change or the news article about hate speech on campus. Instead of trying to win such arguments—*to win* being defined as having persuaded other people to one's own side—one would be trying to understand the other's perspective to find commonalities. Drawing on the identification of those commonalities, the students could choose to use their points of agreement to civilize the argument, agree on where to disagree, or even come to agreement. These actions are more difficult to achieve in social media than they may be in other controlled contexts. A type of crowd-sourced emotion—*argumentum ad populum*—may carry the day, a power that can override over those who seek a more consubstantial result.

In the context of audience, we return to Professor Jackson's student struggling with a history professor regarding gun control. The student should determine whether the professor means that the argument is historically inaccurate or otherwise unsupported or that the professor's personal bias means he will not accept another viewpoint; if the professor is expressing a bias that prevents the student from developing a personally held position, the student is in an untenable power position. Although it is inappropriate for the teacher to display personal bias about the student's argumentative position, a focus on audience suggests the student should consider why the instructor may be doing so and seek an opportunity to talk about the problem. But first, to be clear about what he is asking for, he should determine whether his goal is persuasion (e.g., *I want to write my original thesis*) or identification (e.g., *Let's sort out what would be an appropriate thesis given my perspective and your reasons for not letting me write about the original topic*). Because such uneven discourse where power is in one individual's hands is an especially challenging, real situation, it may be useful for Professor Jackson to use similar examples as learning opportunities for the entire class, enabling them to reenvision audience from practical perspectives. For more guidance in encouraging a dialogue surrounding often contentious issues in the classroom, see chapter 10.

Audiences are not always considered from the perspective of the other person, the *you*. The nineteenth century's Romanticism movement constructed audience as the first person *I*, the authors themselves. Romanticism focused on writing creatively and aligned rhetoric with literature, which proponents believed should instruct readers as audience by pleasing them. Yet the Romantic model focused more on the writer and creation of text than the goals of literature to enlighten or please the reader. Moreover, the notion of audience was reduced to writers themselves in that creating literature was considered a solitary discourse like a soliloquy as opposed to an argument for others; the genre was lyric, not oratory or essay. In this sense, the artist's mind—the *I*—became more important than the audience, which is not unlike expressivist composition approaches.

Professor Jackson's students may be self-focused at this juncture. Both Moffett (*Teaching*) and James Britton and colleague's cognitive theories about how children learn to write strongly suggest that young people always begin communication with the personal. Moffett theorizes that discourse begins with (self)-reflection as the first degree of distance between speaker and audience as first and second person. Progressively, discourse increases in distance to take in conversation, correspondence, and publication (*Teaching* 33). Britton and colleagues, on the other hand, engage both Piaget's cognitive language developmental theory and Edward Sapir's language model to arrive at their own model for written communication: Transactional → Expressive → Poetic. Children begin learning language as expressive and they work outward to poetic or transactional uses. Britton and colleagues stress that, whereas young children learn to adjust spoken language to the "sense of the person" they address, "when children begin to write, this process of adjusting to their audience presents them with new problems even though they may fail to recognize them" (58). With this sense of audience in mind for less experienced writers, it seems likely that—even more so than in the 1970s, when Britton and colleagues were writing—students weaned on social media may not yet realize the complexity of audience conditions related to their self-expression on social media and their need to express themselves differently in transactional situations.

By extension, the notion of audience considers not only the *other* and the *I*, the ones outside writers or writers themselves; it also considers the *we* or *us*, writers plus their peers or colleagues who function transactionally as assistance givers. In other words, sometimes writers and their intended audience, or even those outside their intended audience, function as a substitute audience for a composition, which occurs whenever one person reads a draft to help the writer (thus, the instructor also can function as part of a *we*). But such readers cannot be fully objective, considering a composition outside themselves as if they have no thoughts about or stake in the reading. In fact, when they function as the *we* in peer association to provide feedback for further drafting and revision, they have a stake as audience. Theories regarding collaboration and connectivism offer a sense of how the third person plural works as audience.

In his 1984 "Collaborative Learning and the 'Conversation of Mankind,'" Kenneth A. Bruffee notes the rise of collaboration as an important pedagogical tool within 1980s composition. Underprepared students often did not ask instructors for assistance, so institutions started offering tutoring opportunities that, unfortunately, were underutilized. Bruffee suggests that undergraduate students did not use these resources because they saw tutoring as an extension of the traditional classroom, where tutoring mimicked the social structure of the classroom—the same aspect they struggled with adapting to when entering academia. Thus, peer collaboration, or educationally induced collaborative learning, emerged wherein instructors would pair students to cosolve a problem or work out an idea together (see Moffett, *Teaching* 12). From such peer interactions, the idea of peer paper reviews arose, and students shared their writing, critiquing and offering suggestions. In some processes, the instructor reviewed both the initial writing and the peer review critique, providing feedback to both writers and peers on how to improve the writing as well as the critique (Bruffee, "Collaborative Learning" 638). Because peer review can work well to encourage students to understand various perspectives (Grant and Thornton) and to encourage deeper learning (Bruffee, *Collaborative Learning*), this form of collaboration has become a composition course mainstay.

Meaningful collaboration corresponds to the situated practices a multiliteracies pedagogy demands. The *we* involved in such interaction sometimes is visible as two students talk, overtly guided by the student author's questions; they may interact freely and come to agreement about a composition's meaning, intention, and strategy. Other times, the *we* is less visible, as they may interact guided by predesigned rubrics to prompt responses to the text. In either case, the interaction may be oral or textual, face-to-face or computer-mediated, and in both cases—particularly when they engage in reflection regarding how the peer review may influence revisions—peers influence one another's views of the composition. Even choosing not to revise can be done in connection with the other, joining the authors in a *we* interaction.

The technological advances of web 2.0 technologies, such as wikis and shared document software, promote collaborative, *we*-audience learning since student authors can contribute to the document simultaneously. Collaboration also can be implemented during the multimodal composing process. An instructor can partner students or create peer groups according to students' technological skills; one student may know how to create a video using particular software and can teach others in the group. Thus, students are one another's audiences and absorb information from one another through situated learning, specifically through peripheral participation, wherein students are immersed in a community of practice (i.e., the peer group) and learn from one another through watching others perform a task (Lave and Wenger).

A *we* audience widens with connectivism in that students learn from each other, with an often messy interaction stemming from the inclusion of various voices or opinions. For example, users or readers of a hyperlinked text can often interact with the author in some form and, depending on format, change the text or leave comments. Such changes and interactions affect both readers and writers, joining them in a *we* association. Students learn from not only peer review or collaborative projects but also a multiplicity of voices. Carmen Luke, in "Cyber-Schooling and Technological Change," notes the millions of Internet users who collaborate through chat groups, message boards, email, and so on, and these users communicate and write by negotiating meaning with each other. In such online spaces, the learning process is often cyclical in that learners connect to a network to share and find information. During that process, they may change or modify their beliefs and their comprehension of ideas may increase; in turn, they are likely to share this new information and their own inferences within other spaces and with other groups.

This *we*-audience process undoubtedly multiplies as more users enter online conversations throughout even one day, let alone the lifespan of the communication.

Connectivism is a term often used regarding digitality, as people create chat and blog posts digitally and others post comments in response—the original author and users interact and cannot help but influence each other; in *The Shifting Sands of Authority in the Age of Digital Convergence*, Leah Frieda Cassorla calls this process *interblogging* (73–99). This kind of *we* interaction clearly confuses Professor Jackson's students; they may know instinctively they influence one another, yet they resist the impact when disagreement with others creates a soured message. They need to learn that when the audience becomes *we*, they cannot choose or control the response, nor can they stop that response from interacting with their own minds. They can, however, choose how they respond to a response, using probable reasoning to help persuade or create identification. Finally, Professor Jackson also can help these students recognize that such digital communications as videos, podcasts, and even course ePortfolios are open for Internet circulation and can prompt the formation of a broader community beyond the classroom, leading to still more *we*-based interactions for which they should prepare carefully.

Theme 4: Rhetoric and composition concern both thought and language, allowing for invention.

As Professor Jackson's students should see by now, learning to compose well and responsibly entails finding not only what words to say—the subject, knowledge, ideas—but also how to express them. In ancient Greek rhetorical history, these two parts of rhetoric were called *res* (variably translated as "thought," "things," "knowledge," or "subject matter") and *verba* (variably translated as "words," "form," "eloquence," or "style")—but their connections within rhetoric's province were far from uncontested (Howell 131). The story of invention, one of the five canons of rhetoric, is intimately connected to whether thought inhabits rhetoric with language. For Professor Jackson's students who need tools for managing the challenges of daily and academic composition, how to find subject matter is particularly important. When rhetoric cannot invent or find subject matter, thought cannot reside within its purview. Style or language with no thought cannot invent. Undoubtedly, students must learn how to access both thoughts and style.

The question of whether both thought and language reside in rhetoric regards "a fundamental division between *what* is communicated through language and *how* this is communicated" (Burton). According to A. C. Howell, the terms *thought* and *language* have become commonplace, yet they have been confused in rhetorical literature, depending on translation (131) and, likely, the prevailing questions of the times. *Thought* is not the same as *subject matter* for composition and *words* are not the same as *style* or *eloquence*, yet all these meanings have importance and sometimes are elided in the literature. These terms underpin some of the most controversial concerns about what rhetoric—and composition—encompass. One of the primary characteristics of humans is their ability to communicate using words and symbols. But from where do thoughts or ideas originate? Under what discipline does rhetoric fall? Science? Ethics? Writing studies? All studies? And how does one take thought and put it into words that create stylistically elegant—or merely comprehensible— representations of thoughts? Philosophers, linguists, psychologists, and rhetoricians have long asked these and other questions, and just as they have translated *res* and *verba* differently, they have answered the questions differently. Some have offered highly philosophical and ideological responses; yet these responses nearly always are grounded in practicality.

Professor Jackson should consider how educators have represented and taught the connections between thought and language over the centuries because these connections and disconnections offer guidance for teaching invention as heuristics and research. Although the challenges of teaching twenty-first-century students to compose may seem unique to this age, countless earlier educators struggled with similar concerns and provided different—yet intimately connected—answers. Philosophically, the issue of what one can say within the auspices of rhetoric or composition often turns on whether there is an apprehensible Truth. Practically, the issue often turns on whether and how one can discover or invent ideas. Does rhetoric provide people with the means to find the subject matter or does it only provide guidance about words and how to use them well or correctly? If the former, then composition, as an academic discipline into which rhetoric has morphed, provides writers with ways to discover, or invent, and discern ideas, distilling them into aptly communicative word sets in both alphabetic essays and multimodal texts. In this case, composition becomes a full art, providing numerous ways into composing. If rhetoric as composition has no connection to thoughts and subject matter except to convey them through words, then it is concerned primarily with expression or style, leaving the finding of ideas outside composition instruction and—for many learners—outside their ken. One's definition affects not only instructional thinking about composition but also the ability to provide composition strategies regarding content development.

How are Professor Jackson's students affected practically? Take, for example, the student who was shocked at the flashpoint emotional responses to posts about climate change. By now, this student knows that positions people take on the topic stem from probable reasoning—not opinion or fact (despite scientific evidence) alone. This student is aware that rhetoric has shifted to accommodate social media and digital delivery of thoughts and ideas. Finally, this student understands how to analyze and appeal to an audience persuasively or through identification. What this student now needs to know is how to find subject matter for communicating successfully about climate change. If invention, or uncovering the ideas, is not part of the composition course, then how will this student find content for any communication about climate change? What Professor Jackson teaches reveals the writing program's philosophy about whether composition courses should assist in finding subject matter.

History continually reveals disagreement about the epistemologies, or theories of knowledge, that rhetoric instruction entails. For example, any review of rhetorical history clearly shows that thought (and invention) eventually were relegated to outside rhetoric's purview. In the fourteenth century, Ramus particularly advocated for separating invention, arrangement, and memory from rhetoric—giving these to the study of logic and leaving only style and delivery to rhetoric (Herzberg 587). This approach became entrenched in the seventeenth through the nineteenth centuries. As we mention earlier, American education in the nineteenth century was especially heavily enveloped in current-traditional rhetoric, teaching composition practices grounded in the belief that all knowledge is founded on a simple correspondence between sense impressions and the faculties of the mind, a denial of deductive (syllogistic) reasoning as valuable to rhetoric, and a belief that truth is discovered in induction alone—therefore, locating thought outside rhetoric. Strongly connected to John Locke's and Bacon's scientific logic, fact and truth were believed to stem from observation and experiment. Because thought was considered outside rhetoric, language as arrangement and expression became rhetoric's main concerns. The distinction between dialectic as learned discourse and rhetoric as a discipline of popular discourse was destroyed (Hewett, *Scholarly Edition* 40–43, 47–49). Rhetoric thereby became the study of all forms of communication, following Edward T. Channing's approach as Harvard's third Boylston Professor of Rhetoric and Oratory. Because of Harvard's vast influence on other American colleges, he almost single-handedly derailed rhetoric from postsecondary writing programs, leaving it to communication studies, and he began the first English department of literature (Reid).

Professor Jackson should know that for many years after Channing, composition was taught reductively without access to invention, emphasizing product over process, concreteness over abstraction, four-mode writing, and rigid five-paragraph essays. Some of Professor Jackson's colleagues may teach that way today, using textbooks still designed for such instruction. It is highly likely that Professor Jackson's students have learned writing—at least partially and especially for standardized exam purposes—in the current-traditional approach, which means there is some unlearning to do and some introduction to rhetorical invention to offer.

What kinds of invention strategies might help students in Professor Jackson's class? One is Burke's concept of the *pentad*, outlined in *A Grammar of Motives* (xv). Burke invented five "dramatistic" terms as a method of analyzing the form of thought at work in attributing motives to other people (21, xv–xx). The pentad offers complex layering and interweaving of people's motivations, which may lead to identification of people with one another and a useful way into composing. The definitions of Burke's five original terms and a sixth, added years later, are followed by prompts for student responses:

Act. What took place. Narrate the actions.

Scene. The "background of the act." Explain the situation and context.

Agent. What person(s) or kind of person(s) performed the act. Provide details about agents to illustrate who they are.

Agency. What "means or instruments" were used. Discuss how the act occurred and through what means.

Purpose. Motive or reason for the act. Consider the reasons the agents might have had or the general *why* of the occurrence (xv).

Attitude. The agents' state of mind. Examine possible beliefs, biases, and intentionality of the agents (Anderson and Althouse).

As a simple invention schema, the pentad can encourage greater complexity of thought. Taken together, these six elements can enlighten writers by enabling them to systematically think about a problem. For example, both the student struggling with wanting to write about gun control in history class and the student puzzling out the issues surrounding immigration might contextualize their respective topics from these questioning perspectives. Writers bring with them, of course, their own biases and beliefs, but they can work to mitigate those in purposeful ways (we address implicit bias in chs. 2 and 10). When students critically engage Burke's questions, the complications of what, once again, are human problems with no certain answers, become obvious. The pentad requires students to do more background research than merely taking on one or two news sites' initial case presentations. The pentad and other invention strategies (see ch. 7) can assist writers in developing material and learning what needs to be researched, helping them to construct stronger communications about things that matter to them.

Lacking heuristics like Burke's pentad and with insufficient rhetorical training from their own professors, nineteenth-century teachers likely knew little about invention and how to help students find the ideas words are meant to express. The powerful tug of current-traditional rhetoric was infused into North American composition instruction by the mid-nineteenth century and remained there well into the mid-twentieth century. Yet even in the 1920s, rhetoric and composition scholars started to rethink what they had been teaching and theorized new ways of approaching writing. In a sort of rhetorical renaissance, writing studies educators drew from such fields as psychology, logic, linguistics, and philosophy and reached back to classical rhetoric, finding new inspiration for research and speculation about how students write, leading to novel instructional approaches that relocated invention within composition's responsibility and reinfused thought with language. Eclectic approaches reinvigorated what had become a stale, formulaic subject and generically rigid skill set.

As described earlier in this chapter, the 1940s and 1950s brought new focus to composition, and through the process movement in part, rhetorical invention and other, newer heuristics were adopted into composition. Process pedagogy, although much more fleshed out in early scholarship, eventually was whittled down to what are known (and still valued) as stages of writing, which include (but are not limited to) prewriting or freewriting, drafting, writing, and then revising (Tobin 11), yet in a generative, recursive, and nonsequential manner. Process theory began to provide students with invention tools, among other strategies—again reuniting thought and language.

Process theory is not without its challenges, one of which is that it has been wrangled into sometimes simplistic explanations that suggest all one has to do to succeed is plug into a brainstorm → write → revise → repeat cycle. Flower and Hayes' cognitive theory of writing was developed in part to counter focus on "the growth of the written product," placing it instead on "the inner process of the person producing it" (367). Post-process theory emerged to reposition process, suggesting writing processes vary by students' culture, educational background, and linguistic history. In *Post-Process Theory*, Thomas Kent states that "no codifiable or generalizable writing process exists or could exist" (1), a striking blow against process pedagogy. In a somewhat gentler approach, Chris M. Anson expresses in "Process Pedagogy and Its Legacy" that scholars have suggested "post-process was not really another paradigm shift but a loose, undifferentiated set of assumptions and theories that pushed back, sometimes gently, sometimes more strongly, against the process movement— suggesting not so much a rift in the field as a period of major development" (224). As a result, more attention began to be paid to "cultural, social, ideological, public, situated, and interactive dimensions of writing" (224–25; see also Breuch, "Post-Process 'Pedagogy'"). In the wake of such attention, writers sometimes lost the focus of how one might compose in favor of the topic or subject matter, a sort of inversion of thought over language, which is starkly contrary to rhetoric and composition's history. As a corrective, intentional or not, the writing-about-writing movement returned the focus to both the subject (i.e., writing, rhetoric, language, and literature) and its expression (i.e., how learning about writing can shift students' approaches to the actual process) (Anson, "Process" 225). Because it always has a subject (i.e., writing) for the composition, the writing-about-writing approach may help mitigate some of the challenges Professor Jackson's students face regarding contemporary communication (see Downs and Wardle).

However one thinks about the linkage of thought and language, it is clear that twenty-first-century composition theory continues to grapple with questions related to *res*, *verba*, invention, and how human problems can be conceived, discerned, and conveyed. Some of the newer rhetoric approaches to which we connect in this book (e.g., feminist and African American or, more commonly, Black rhetoric) allow for helping students identify their own writing processes while focusing attention to the situatedness of rhetoric within cultures and societies that are ever-changing.

Conclusion

Contemporary writing studies is a discipline that encourages looking inside and outside itself for explanations and ideas about uniquely human language literacies: reading, alphabetic writing, new media composition, digital technologies, and the unending possibilities for genuine communication between one human and another. Professor Jackson's mind may be reeling after this brief introduction to only some of the historically held rhetoric and composition theories and how they have affected composing. It is useful to remember that this chapter, like every chapter in this book, is developed to connect directly to the practical work of composition instruction in the digital era. We hope that Professor Jackson's questions—and those of the students—will be answered throughout the book.

NOTES

1. In this chapter, *Truth* with a capital *T* symbolizes belief in a foundational, metaphysically ascertainable knowledge of nature in contrast to a relativistic *truth* that is created sophistically by reducing knowledge to contextuality and the social construction of agreement.

2. Of truth, Aristotle says: "For, in fact, the true and that which resembles it come under the purview of the same faculty, and at the same time men have a sufficient natural capacity for the truth and indeed in most cases attain to it . . ." (11; I.i.11 [1355a]).

3. Video, according to Ball, can be used as a mode in online contexts, not just as a medium for composing or communicating. See the introduction for our definitions of *mode* and *medium*.

4. Selfe, "Movement," *Multimodal Composition*, "Students," "Technology," and *Technology*; Selber, *Multiliteracies* and "Reimagining."

2

Humanizing Composition

The student population at Professor Jackson's institution has shifted in the past few years. The college has admitted international students for decades, but it recently started promoting its services more vigorously to disabled students and local urban students. Additionally, its growing online education programs encourage students from distant rural areas and military bases to enroll. Professor Jackson is an uneasy Generalist 3.0 because he's unfamiliar with working with students from this wide range of demographics, and he's concerned about his ability to be appropriately supportive. WPA Garcia, also noticing this shift, has arranged a midday faculty seminar series to explore students' backgrounds and needs.

Just as writers have an audience for their compositions, writing instructors have an audience for teaching: students. Teaching about communication skills itself requires strong communication and interpersonal skills, which means carefully considering those with whom one interacts. As we explain about audiences in chapters 1 and 7, it is critical to analyze, understand, and speak to the audience as human beings with genuine contexts, needs, fears, and concerns. Student diversity challenges educators to set aside stereotypical thinking about students and see them both as individual persons and unique learner groups. Using the primary lens of diversity and access competence, this chapter assists writing studies' educators in inclusively welcoming and working with diverse students. Finally, throughout this chapter and others, specifically chapter 10, the strategies we discuss offer actionable practices that align with the National Council of Teachers of English (NCTE) Committee against Racism and Bias in the Teaching of English publications *What Anti-Racist Language Teachers Do* and *Qualities of Anti-Racist ELA Curricula*. We encourage readers to read and incorporate these documents, as well as such supporting scholarship as *Performing Antiracist Pedagogy in Rhetoric, Writing, and Communication* by Frankie Condon and Vershawn Ashanti Young, into their teaching practices.

Diversity and Inclusion

Educators like John Dewey (*Democracy and Education*), Paolo Freire (*Pedagogy of the Oppressed*), and James Moffett ("Coming") considered equity and multicultural concerns. For Moffett, a student-centered curriculum and diversity approach were natural—if not easy—and he instilled in mid-twentieth-century educators that even if they had not been taught explicitly to work with heterogenous classes, they could do it by assuming "the power to do what you know" ("Coming" 533). Twenty-first-century students are diverse, as Professor Jackson has learned, but he knows his job is to treat all students with dignity and respect. *Difference* is a tricky notion, and one that is particularly sensitive. Although it is possible to approach students from points of similarity, in some cases seeing only where people are alike can invalidate them because differences matter (Sue et al.); difference helps define people's self-perceptions and how they want others to view them. Pedagogically, acknowledging and straightforwardly embracing students' rich diversity may enable writing instructors to encourage stronger, deeper compositions.

People see difference more often than they realize, yet the culture of the United States sometimes encourages denying its existence (Sue et al. 271). In *Cultural Competence in Process and Practice*, sociologist Juliet Rothman notes that human differences include gender, race, ethnic group, nationality, skin color and shades of color, language, religion, ability/disability, sexual orientation, age, social class, immigration status, region of country, size and appearance, economic class, financial resources, level of education, and marital status (8). Even fashion can divide people because humans make judgments about almost everything others do, are, or seem to be. Such judgment often comes from stereotyping, which Rothman defines as an act that "destroys uniqueness, self-esteem, and creativity in all of us. Bias, discrimination, and oppression based on our group affiliations, and the effects of internalized oppression, do affect us all—but not all in the same way" (7). Stereotyping oppresses people and denies them access to precious resources, including education. To be clear, oppression consists of "racist remarks, exclusion, stereotyping, and other behaviors. Institutional oppression limits accessibility by not providing materials and services in appropriate languages, physical conditions, or locations. *Structural oppression* includes the norms, habits, and world views of society as a whole, which create and support a system that privileges some groups and stigmatizes others" (Rothman 25; emphasis ours). Oppression leads to a sense of powerlessness that can be made worse in certain settings, including ones where educators are perceived as having the power to dismiss students' needs and concerns. Because teaching is a transactional—often gatekeeping—interaction with learners, the educational setting rarely is level. Yet opposing oppression in class settings is imperative to offering an inclusive and critical education.

The United States was once touted as a melting pot comprising different ethnic and racial groups, where people with no economic resources and humble beginnings could—with hard work—improve their economic circumstances and elevate their social status. These generalizations were true for some, but they remained inaccessible goals for many. The grand goals of assimilation and acculturation often fail and are, indeed, problematic because they require a two-step dance: those in the majority must wholeheartedly fling open closed doors and those in the minority must give up identifying features of their heritage language and familial customs (Rothman 19). There must be ways for individuals to maintain cultural customs, including the use of their various languages, dialects, and registers; as such, educators must value these differences and help their students value them too.

In figure 2.1, a man chooses to clear snow from a school's steps before clearing a ramp because the majority of the children are able to use the steps; however, clearing the ramp first would enable everyone, including a child in a wheelchair, to get inside. This cartoon expresses the essence of an inclusive approach to diversity. Including everyone means clearing

Figure 2.1. A cartoon about inclusion. Michael F. Giangreco, *Absurdities and Realities of Special Education: The Best of Ants . . . , Flying . . . , and Logs . . . ,* full color edition, Corwin, 2002.

the access route such that everyone can enter the building at the same time; it is not about providing two routes if one will do. If two routes are necessary, though, they must be accessible in equal ways. An inclusive education, like societal aspects of inclusion, is ethically right, practically appropriate, and legally necessary. Such need for access was made more obvious by the experience of COVID-19 home sheltering, where it quickly became apparent which students already had at-home computer and Internet access and which ones required these tools.

Access

Access is about being inclusive, whether students need accommodations for diverse learning needs, additional skills training, access to technology, or other adjustments to provide opportunities to learn.

Principles of Access

The 2020 document "Disability Studies in Composition," by the Conference on College Composition and Communication (CCCC), calls attention to student and faculty diversity. This document is both an ethical position and a mandate to meet and exceed the letter of the law, describing "concepts and processes intended to assist members of the field practice active inclusion across the discipline beyond mere compliance measures." In 2013, the CCCC Committee for Effective Practices in Online Writing Instruction took up that call, addressing access and inclusion as the first of fifteen principles published in an NCTE position statement. Its online writing instruction (OWI) principle 1 states, "Online writing instruction should be universally inclusive and accessible." In 2020, the Global Society for Online Literacy Educators published its principles for online literacy instruction; the first principle similarly asserts, "Online literacy instruction should be universally accessible and inclusive." What do these principled statements mean? In essence, as the rationale for OWI principle 1 states, they indicate that

> the needs of learners with physical disabilities, learning disabilities, multilingual backgrounds, and learning challenges related to socioeconomic issues (i.e., often called the *digital divide*, where access is the primary issue) must be addressed in an OWI environment to the maximum degree possible for the given institutional setting. Furthermore, given that OWI typically is a text-intensive medium [environment] where reading is a necessary skill, addressing the accessibility needs of the least confident readers increases the potential to reach all types of learners. (CCCC, Committee)

Given composition's inherent twenty-first-century digitality, this principled position of putting access and inclusion first should guide all composition instruction: educators should provide access and inclusion at every point of their work, humanizing composition at every level. As Beth L. Hewett writes, this welcoming and proactive mindset requires "a *spirit of generosity* toward all of our students" by rejecting the retrofit model of fixing problems after students point out their lack of access ("Grounding Principles" 42). As becomes obvious regarding access and inclusion laws, seeking to "accommodate more students with more varied challenges than we might imagine—without them even having to self-disclose their issues" benefits everyone, including those who recognize they have specific learning needs that "may be difficult for them to name let alone disclose" (42).

Technology and Access

The New London Group, too, indicates that effective multiliteracies teaching requires "include[ing] a vision of meaningful success for all; a vision of success that is not defined exclusively in economic terms and that has embedded within it a critique of hierarchy and economic justice" (13). Narrowly construed, access means providing students with opportunities to develop skills for entrance into a new workforce where language use is changing with the rise of technologically and linguistically diverse constituents. More broadly, the New London Group suggests that educators should harness diversity as a resource in a digital global market. In her classic *Technology and Literacy in the Twenty-First Century*, however, Cynthia L. Selfe notes that the shift toward technological literacy, a literacy at the forefront of the digital revolution, inevitably leaves out entire groups and cultures (see also Hawisher and Selfe, "Rhetoric"). Selfe argues that in America, technology primarily supports divisions among class, race, and gender; she warns about the myth that technological instruction can close the gap between the literate and illiterate, clearing the snowy ramp for all.

Research suggests that even when students have access to digital technologies at home, they may not know how to use them for composition unless they have been exposed to or socialized into these types of practices (see, for example, Buckingham; see also Gos). Multiliteracies access means students must be able to critically examine digital media and reproduce the media for various contexts. Merely bringing technology to the classroom does not create access, however; as Selfe posits in *Technology and Literacy in the Twenty-First Century*, instructors must first consider how, when, why, and to what ends they are using technology, which involves critically questioning the role of technology and who might get left behind when assigning technology-intense projects. Critical technological literacy must be a design-stage component of any composition curriculum, and instructors should teach students to think critically about technology and the social implications for its use. Selfe suggests guiding students to research who has access to the Internet and digital technologies and then to analyze the global digital divide's impact. Such critical examination, she believes, engages access issues by encouraging students to make critically informed decisions about technology instead of being passive consumers (155).

In *Literacy Theories for the Digital Age*, Kathy Mills examines the link between access and oppression, noting that although increased opportunities into literacy practices open economic avenues, these literacy skills do not necessarily equate to employment, and patterns of inequities will continue even as literacy skills increase. Like Selfe, Mills indicates the need to teach students to be agents in their learning, be critical consumers and producers of media, and question who decides what literacy really means. Although these conversations may not clear the snowy ramp for socioeconomically challenged students regarding their physical access to technology, they may lead to broader social change, a key concept of multiliteracies pedagogy.

Laws Supporting Access

Educators should know about several laws that support placing access before other educational concerns, including Section 504 of the Rehabilitation Act of 1973, the 1974 Family Educational Rights and Privacy Act (FERPA), and the 1990 Americans with Disabilities Act (ADA).

SECTION 504

Section 504 protects "qualified students with disabilities who attend schools receiving Federal financial assistance" and mandates that postsecondary institutions with federal funding must provide students with appropriate academic adjustments and auxiliary aids and services that are necessary to afford an individual with a disability an equal opportunity to participate in a school's program. Recipients [institutions] are not required to make adjustments or provide aids or services that would result in a fundamental alteration of a recipient's program or impose an undue burden. (Office)

Coverage includes students that "(1) have a physical or mental impairment that substantially limits one or more major life activities; or (2) have a record of such an impairment; or (3) be regarded as having such an impairment." Additionally, in postsecondary education, "a qualified student with a disability is a student with a disability who meets the academic and technical standards requisite for admission or participation in the institution's educational program or activity" (Office). In other words, given appropriate accommodations, such students should be capable of meeting the institution's academic standards.

From a postsecondary perspective, Section 504 often is interpreted to mean that students must have a documented physical or cognitive impairment that they willingly disclose (see discussion of FERPA below) to receive educational accommodations in a federally funded school. First, however, not every student can afford the testing or doctors' diagnoses that prove an impairment, which means some students are denied formal access to accommodations. Providing accommodations to students without proper documentation may be perceived as favoritism or may not be allowed by the institution. Second, reading Section 504 in connection to FERPA presupposes students must willingly disclose their disabilities, meaning teachers may not ask whether the student has specific problems and may not seek out parents or previous records. Third, this law does not apply outside federally funded institutions, which leaves out students in nonfederally funded institutions.

FAMILY EDUCATIONAL RIGHTS AND PRIVACY ACT

The Family Educational Rights and Privacy Act protects student education, personally identifiable, and directory information. It applies to any educational institution that receives federal funding from the

United States Department of Education. An example FERPA requirement is that federally funded postsecondary educators are prohibited from discussing with parents the grades and progress of students eighteen and older without explicit student permission because, at eighteen years of age, students receive all rights formerly given to parents ("Family Educational Rights and Privacy Act"; see also "FERPA"). The requirements FERPA outlines are important for composition instructors because they limit educators' discussions of students' disability or learning needs with the students themselves, meaning if students elect not to disclose their learning needs, there is no parental avenue to that information.

AMERICANS WITH DISABILITIES ACT

The Americans with Disabilities Act is far-reaching civil rights legislation that prohibits discrimination on the same basis as such legislation regarding "race, color, sex, national origin, age, and religion." Its mandate is to eliminate discrimination against people with disabilities in "public accommodations, employment, transportation, state and local government services, and telecommunications" ("What Is"). Most important for our purposes, the ADA applies to all postsecondary institutions regardless of federal funding status, which means that what Section 504 does not cover, the ADA does.

The ADA mandates that "both public and private colleges and universities must provide equal access to postsecondary education for students with disabilities" through its Title 2, which "covers publicly-funded universities, community colleges and vocational schools," and Title 3, which deals with schools with private funding ("What Are"). The ADA addresses all postsecondary programs, including extracurricular activities, through such actions as

> providing architectural access to buildings, including residential facilities; by providing aids and services necessary for effective communication, like sign language interpreters, Braille or electronic formats and assistive listening devices; and by modifying policies, practices and procedures, such as testing accommodations and access to school facilities for service animals.　　　　("What Are")

The unique accommodations and program modification requirements for any disabled student should be designed individually. Notably, "[a]ccommodations and modifications of policies and practices are not required when it would fundamentally alter the nature of the service, program, or activity or give rise to an undue financial or administrative burden" ("What Are").

Educators may not understand the notion of "reasonable accommodations," thinking that such accommodations give disabled students advantages over others without disabilities. This reasoning is incorrect. Reasonable accommodations are academic adjustments, modifications, and auxiliary aids and services. Their goal is to clear the snowy ramp for those with applicable impairments, which makes postsecondary education possible for them. It is important to note that students whose educational backgrounds have not included due attention to their potential disabilities, who have physical or cognitive challenges that yet fall within the range of normal, or who cannot afford testing do not receive such accommodations, thereby situationally shoveling only the stairs and ignoring the snowy ramp. Furthermore, accommodations do not fix but merely help mitigate issues on a day-by-day, case-by-case basis. Disabilities cannot be taught away; students wake up with them daily, making developing workable strategies necessary.

Victoria Scanlan Stefanakos of *Understood for All* describes common accommodations one might find at the postsecondary level, including longer testing times and laptop or calculator use during exams; classroom accommodations such as access to audiobooks, notes, or recordings of class materials; curricular adjustments like smaller course loads and priority course registration; and aids like voice recognition software. Stefanakos identifies "[e]xtended time on papers and projects," "[c]ourse waivers and substitutions," and "[a]lternative exam formats" as accommodations that may be harder to get. Other useful services include access to technology training; assistance with study skills and time management; and help from "[l]earning specialists, support groups, and mentoring." We strongly advocate that instructors build access-focused strategies into all teaching and learning activities so students who would benefit from accommodations—whether or not they self-disclose or have received formal testing—receive assistance that might help.

Our stance of providing access to all students does not mean attempting to diagnose a student with a disability; it means being flexible in teaching and testing strategies and presenting curricula in various formats. When curricula are presented in varied formats from the onset, the burden may be off students to request accommodations. Examples include teaching using a variety of modes and media, including in person (when not in fully online settings), asynchronous reading and video (with transcripts or closed captioning), and synchronous talk opportunities, as well as teacher skills modeling, hands-on practice, and choices among assignments. We address access throughout this book and outline access-focused assignments and feedback strategies in chapters 8 and 9.

Physical Disabilities and Learning Challenges

A traumatic brain injury, sudden illness, or accident can change anyone's life forever. This knowledge—if nothing else—should raise educators' awareness of the difficulties people with physical disabilities and learning challenges face daily. Just like educators, students with physical disabilities and learning challenges typically are bright, inquisitive, teachable people, and they rightly expect to be treated as such. Physical, embodied disabilities include, but are not limited to, vision and hearing impairments, paraplegia or other limiting movement disorders like cerebral palsy, and loss of limbs. Cognitive disorders that create learning challenges include dyslexia, dysgraphia, aphasia, autism and other non-neurotypical brain patterns, auditory-processing disorders, and attention-hyperactivity disorders, among others. Acute or chronic mental health issues like depression, bipolar disorder, high anxiety, and schizophrenia may impact students with or without such other challenges. Grief, while not a mental health disorder, can cause cognitive and energy challenges.

Section 504, FERPA, and ADA in Play

Students with these ranges of challenges require access by virtue of Section 504 and the ADA, as we discussed earlier. Typically, a college has an office of special or disabilities services that will work with WPAs and instructors to teach them accommodation skills and that meet with students who self-disclose their needs. With such disabilities and challenges, it is important to recognize how Section 504 and FERPA work and how accommodations are made, or not, in postsecondary settings compared to those in K–12, as detailed in the following list adapted from the *Understood for All* website (Understood Team):

> Colleges do not have the same legal responsibilities as high schools. Although they fall under the ADA, they do not have to provide Individualized Educational Programs (IEPs) or the same level of support services.

> Students—not their parents—must register with the disability services office to receive accommodations.

> Requirements for documentation of residency and eligibility may not be the same across all postsecondary settings.

> Students do not get case managers in postsecondary institutions, although someone will work with them to determine reasonable accommodations. Students must self-disclose and self-assert, which are *learned behaviors some do not yet know.*

> All colleges receiving federal funding must provide reasonable accommodations, and some offer higher levels of support.

> Because of FERPA, parents are no longer automatically in the loop, meaning both the school and the student must provide permission to parents for them to participate in discussions.

> Colleges may require but do not provide evaluations for learning and attention issues or other abilities.

Access Actions

We already have listed common postsecondary accommodations and cannot cover all the individualized academic adjustments for students. Each institution's disability services office will have that information and can provide materials explaining how various conditions may affect student learning. Although no two students have identical needs or respond the same way to interventions, the following access actions can help with inclusion for a variety of student needs. Here we align with Sushil K. Oswal's approach in "Physical and Learning Disabilities in OWI" to building in rather than retrofitting access and refusing to see students as "stock audiences who were assumed to be able-bodied and enjoying all the access to technology that an institution of higher education offers" (259–60).

Thus, we indicate here which educational settings and modalities might best suit students with particular abilities (see also chs. 4 and 5).

Students' reading skills may be compromised, leading to slow reading rate or inability to read at sufficiently high levels, uneven comprehension and retention, difficulty finding important points or themes, poor mastery of phonics, word confusion, and inability to read for lengthy periods. Students may need to pay special attention to acquiring such skills as text-annotating, note-taking, outlining, summarizing, and paraphrasing (see ch. 6). Books on tape and video presentations may help. These students may be served best in technology-enhanced, hybrid, or synchronous online classes in which teachers offer more oral instruction, as well as classes with podcast and video instruction.

Students' writing skills may be compromised, leading to illegible handwriting; an inability to move ideas from thought to writing; difficulties planning and organizing; a tendency toward simple sentence patterns and lack of complex vocabulary; incorrect copying from a source to one's notes; transpositions of letters, words, or both; and insufficient details or content. Students may benefit from composing with voice-to-text translation software, presenting compositions orally or in podcast or video media, having a tutor or editor's assistance at appropriate times, reading and discussing peer writing for implicit comparison, and participating in such activities as in-class workshops and class-based brainstorming and organization. These students may be less well-served in asynchronous online reading- and writing-intensive courses, benefiting instead from less text-intensive and more oral instruction (Hewett, "Characteristics" 273n7).

Students with oral language and auditory-processing difficulties may have trouble attending to and comprehending oral lectures, may not be able to orally express difficult concepts, may speak ungrammatical English, may tell stories nonsequentially or have other organizational problems, and may not follow oral or written directions well. They may benefit from text-based transcripts or teachers' notes to accompany oral lectures, opportunities to write their ideas (as with journaling or brainstorming) before being asked to talk about them, permission to read their notes aloud when asked to talk in class, individualized help in outlining chronologically organized material, and a safe environment for speaking ungrammatical English as well as dialect infusion. These students may benefit from hybrid and asynchronous online courses because of the higher propensity for text-based lesson design (Hewett, "Characteristics" 270n5).

Students with aural disabilities have linguistic differences from hearing students, and they may be multilingual with American Sign Language (ASL) as their first language. They may have had insufficient oral/aural language acquisition opportunities regarding access to spoken or written English (or both), interaction with other speakers, modifications suited to their needs, and expansion opportunities. They may demonstrate overgeneralized inflectional errors from an intuited language structure they use ungrammatically. As with most students, they benefit from imitation; modeling (not just parroting); text bolding; outlining; questioning; cloze exercises; and survey, question, read, recite, and review (SQ3R, a reading comprehension strategy). Additionally, they may need a language interpreter in the classroom, requiring instructors to learn how to interact both with the student and interpreter (e.g., everything spoken is signed and interpreted; those in the class should talk directly to the student and not include the interpreter in the class activities). In online settings, we believe these students may be well served in asynchronous online courses where they can listen as fully as hearing students through reading text; videos must be closed-captioned.

Students with vision impairment typically read text with assistive magnification, Braille, voice-based recordings, or screen readers. Most cannot see sufficiently well to read without adaptive technologies that clear the snowy ramp. Peer response workshops in all types of settings may be inaccessible unless reading such texts is aided by students reading aloud or screen readers that can interact with the learning management system (LMS), websites, and text. Because note-taking can be hampered by lack of sight, these students may benefit from audio recordings of class lectures and oral discussions as well as video transcripts and accessible PDFs. In online settings, they are at a disadvantage unless the LMS and other interactive software are facilitated by accessible technology. According to Oswal, most LMS "interactivity tools—the chat programs and discussion boards—have serious accessibility flaws because they have been designed only for ocular efficiency and ease requiring significantly greater effort and time investment on part of the keyboard users" (267). Students with visual impairments may be less hampered in technologically enhanced and hybrid courses than in fully online courses, even though any of these might use insufficiently accessible LMSs.

Students with various physical disabilities have limited motor capabilities. A student without legs who uses a wheelchair is differently affected in a writing course from one who has lost arms or who is a quadriplegic. As with students who are visually impaired, adaptive technologies are key to providing adequate access, and instructors should learn about them: adaptive mouse pointers and trackballs, head pointers, voice-to-text translation software, multiple interfaces, and other adaptive devices that enable students to compose in multiple media for multiple audiences and rhetorical situations. Again, LMSs fail to meet basic needs because "a software package that can function perfectly only with a mouse might be a useless string of code to a high percentage of users who have not been considered by its designer" (Oswal 263). Instructors and the school's disability services office should help students select a composition learning environment by examining overall campus accessibility to traditional classrooms and technologies against potential LMS assistance or interference in technologically enhanced, hybrid, and fully online settings.

Students with attention, concentration, and organizational skill needs may exhibit time management challenges, overall slowness in beginning and completing writing tasks, recall problems, unorganized note-taking, inability to read and interpret graphic images (e.g., tables and charts), difficulty focusing on academic tasks, short attention spans, distractibility, and especially poor multitasking (see ch. 6), among other characteristics. These types of educational management problems are especially challenging in the digital era because computers and portable devices are among the most helpful and distracting technologies available. Furthermore, these management issues are crucial to the hard work of self-teaching inherent in most online settings. Instructors can help these students through strategies outlined in chapters 7 and 8: scaffolding assignments, teaching invention, reinforcing reading and research, and the like. Time management stands out as a critical concern for composition courses in any learning setting and modality; it helps to scaffold the learning by requiring frequent posting of drafts and self-reflection that receive feedback.

To our general suggestions, we recommend "invest[ing] resources in accessible content development from the start" (Oswal 269). As such, we offer Oswal's heuristic designed to help Professor Jackson and his colleagues as they prepare to integrate "accessibility at every level of the course design," particularly for digital settings. Questions include the following:

"Do course goals address students with disabilities?" Has the curriculum been developed to serve all students' needs?

Has course content been selected "with prior consideration of disabled students" (272)? Could more accessible content serve this group better?

Have disabled students been part of the testing of technology choices, especially the LMS?

Are pedagogical methods and techniques differentiated through "multiple means of representation," "expression and action," and "engagement" as described by Universal Design for Learning? Do these techniques match and support the learning goals of a range of abilities and skills (273)?

LEARNING MANAGEMENT SYSTEM ACCESS PROBLEMS

Because they tend not to be designed with access or even writing instruction in mind, LMSs are particularly fraught. Even software (and curricula) that have attempted to meet the checklist guidance of the Quality Matters (QM) Rubric, Universal Design for Learning (UDL), and the Web Content Accessibility Guidelines (WCAG) still may present interference to students with various disabilities and learning challenges ("Higher Ed Course Design Rubric Standards"; "UDL Guidelines"; "Web Content Accessibility Guidelines"). These checklists, often produced outside educational institutions, attempt to "facilitate inclusive and accessible classrooms (both online and face-to-face) by providing faculty [members] a starting place on issues where they may not have a lot of experience," but they sometimes become the beginning and end of access attempts (Oswal and Melonçon 63). In "Saying No to the Checklist," Oswal and Lisa Melonçon critique these bandage checklist approaches to access that imply a "machine-centric *ethos*" over a "living experience architecture" (66). Such checklist attempts at access imply a formulaic focus on policy and not on "individuals and learners" (67). A participatory design phase in LMS and course development with any digital or online features is best, and it begins with "giv[ing] students a voice in curriculum design" (69), which can help eliminate "after-the-fact fixes or retrofits" (71). Nonetheless, these ideals have not yet come to fruition.

The reality of teaching in the digital era is that not every environment works well for every student, disabled or not, and current LMSs are woefully inadequate both for access generally and often for composition instruction specifically. We assert that all students have different abilities requiring different learning approaches, whether oral, aural, text-based, multimodal, or other. Consciously engaging such learning approaches clears the snowy ramps and helps all students. One important way to accomplish such engagement is to have a reciprocal relationship with the institution's disability services office. Faculty members should learn from disability services professionals; they also should teach disability services professionals and other support personnel about how digitality infuses contemporary composition instruction and how and why some students may not succeed in particular learning settings. Ideals aside, educators should inform students and student support services of which writing instructional environments might make their learning journey less steep. Thriving supersedes merely surviving the course.

Cultural Competence

Teaching diverse students calls for cultural competence. According to Rothman, who cites the "NASW (National Association of Social Workers) Standards for Cultural Competence in Social Work Practice, Definitions," "Cultural competence involves responding 'respectfully and effectively' to 'people of all cultures, languages, classes, races, ethnic backgrounds, religions, and other diversity factors in a manner that recognizes, affirms, and values the worth of individuals, families, and communities and protects and preserves the dignity of each'" (10; see also Bennett). Simply put, composition educators should be respectful in all encounters with students regardless of individual difference or similarity.

Composition instructors often teach immigrants with multiethnic backgrounds and various levels of multilingual skills, possibly not realizing the sheer intellectual and linguistic scope of bilingual, trilingual, or other multilingual students because of English-language interference. To be culturally competent, educators first need "to recognize the strengths that have made survival possible for the [student], to build on these, and to expand choices and opportunities" (Rothman 26). To do so, it is important to recognize that diversity, as "variations between and among social groups based on" differences (9), exists both *between groups* and *within groups* (10). In other words, it is possible to become sensitive about group diversity while failing to recognize that students within ethnic and other groups differ among themselves. Stereotyping never works. Therefore, educators need to develop sensitivity, which "involves an awareness of the feelings and reactions of others to events, crises, stress, and special conditions in the context of their unique set of life experiences and situations" (10). Such sensitivity enables a better understanding of the challenges facing vulnerable populations that hold minority status, ascribed to "nondominant groups in our society" like Latinx, African Americans, Asian Americans, Middle Eastern and Arab Americans, and Native Americans, who may have "experienced generations of oppression, discrimination, and prejudice" (11). Vulnerable populations include LGBTQ+ people and individuals with AIDS, mental illness, and physical and cognitive disabilities.

Cultural competence enables educators to provide vulnerable students with "responsible, caring, culturally congruent service . . ." (13). To this end, composition instructors—who work with writing that may connect students with core personal events, issues, and needs—must commit themselves to being personally aware, to growing, and to "unlearning (as possible) any biases, stereotypes, or prejudices that may interfere with [their] ability to assist the [students and colleagues] toward culturally appropriate personal goals" (15). This approach aligns with the NCTE Committee against Racism and Bias in the Teaching of English resource, *What Anti-Racist Language Teachers Do*, which suggests instructors should work against implicit bias. Simply being aware of implicit bias is not enough, and educators should seek out resources and training on their campus that encourage more action than acknowledgement. Chapter 4 in *Administering Writing Programs in the Twenty-First Century*, by Tiffany Bourelle, Hewett, and Scott Warnock, offers concrete exercises to raise awareness of implicit bias and its potential for harm in the classroom.

Furthermore, instructors must not assume that their experiences with one student can be extrapolated to a whole group. Culturally competent writing teachers explore—through reading, research, and respectful observation—the experiences of other members of that group (39). In *Multiliteracies, Emerging Media, and College Writing Instruction*,

Santosh Khadka argues for "intercultural communication competence" as a rhetorical skill that "asks for respect for multicultural identities and differences" (215). Instructors owe it to their students to learn this rhetorical skill and help their students learn it, too. Chapter 10 provides more specifics on this topic.

Language Diversity

Language, a performative act, comes in "varieties of Englishes, [non-Englishes], discourses, media, or modalities" (Lu and Horner 208), and recognizing and accepting language's different uses is a core aspect of humanizing composition. The CCCC, in its "CCCC Statement on Second Language Writing and Multilingual Writers," argues that multilingual students "may demonstrate different expectations for and understandings of discourse" and that "[t]he process of acquiring academic literacies—including syntactic and lexical competence—in an additional language is a complex, recursive, lifelong process." Significantly, regardless of English experience, all students are engaged in the same rhetorical learning processes as native speakers of English, and they do so with varied literacy backgrounds in diverse languages and dialects.

Here we describe a range of linguistic roots students may bring to composition courses.

English Only. Monolingual English-speaking students will have had primary exposure only to English (possibly not in the United States), may not have had foreign language classes in primary or secondary school, and may know words from other languages only through exposure to other-language speakers or media.

Multilingual (English First). Multilingual English-first students are native-English speakers, readers, and writers. They may have learned second or third languages from their family setting, schools, or time in other countries. Depending on whether most of their education occurred in English-language schools, their writing education needs may be similar to monolingual peers; their additional language knowledge may offer better or different grammatical understanding, however, and may inflect their speech and writing.

Heritage Language. Children of immigrants may have difficulty learning to write even if they were born in the United States because they may have entered school speaking only their family's language; they may not have learned to read or write in the heritage language. Their spoken English may be nonstandard or mixed dialect with translingual (see below) characteristics. Although they may have had some English as a second language (ESL) classes in school, most instruction likely would have been geared to native-English-speaking peers. These students may have good vocabulary but may not have native-speaker intuition about using prepositions, articles, infinitives, and gerunds, and they may drop noun and verb word endings.

Immigrant. Immigrant students generally are fluent and literate in a home language and maybe in other languages. Their English fluency depends on when, how, and where they immigrated. They may have learned English through oral/aural immersion and may lack reading and writing literacies, meaning they lack formal standardized English grammar study.

Multilingual or International (English Not First). International students may be fluent and literate in their first language and possibly other languages. They likely have studied English deeply and know a set of grammar and mechanics rules (e.g., those found in British English) that may differ from those common in American English. Yet their grammar knowledge may not transfer to writing because they may have done little writing in English prior to postsecondary education. International students' cultural approaches to writing also vary among languages, and they may not be comfortable with typical American English logic, organization, development, and style.

Translingual. More an approach to language writing and writing instruction than a language background, translingual writers *code switch*, or alternate among languages, in an utterance, writing, or conversation—usually by choice and sometimes to fit in or communicate in a situationally appropriate register. More likely, they may *code mesh*, or "blend dialects, international languages, local idioms, chat-room lingo, and the rhetorical styles of various ethnic and cultural groups in both formal *and* informal speech acts" (V. Young 114; see also V. Young et al.; Lu and Horner).

We see at least two important issues for educators considering such linguistic differences. First, there is no such thing as "linguistic homogeneity," a misperception leading "teachers (both online and in the classroom) to outsource language-specific help that students need in writing classes to other places such as Intensive English Programs, remedial courses, and writing centers" (Miller-Cochran 292; see also Matsuda). Composition literacy educators should receive teacher preparation, "sustained" professional development, and resources to address these concerns in the common course setting, as the CCCC describes in its "CCCC Statement on Second Language Writing and Multilingual Writers." All writing educators should be aware of how to include these students' linguistic and cultural needs, and these should be addressed at the theory and course development phases as well as in courses.

Second, we agree with the CCCC's position in the "CCCC Statement on Globalization" that WPAs "should push institutions to provide all students (including and especially English monolinguals) with support structures to expand their language repertoires" in not just introductory classes but also writing across the curriculum courses. It is especially vital to support multilingual writers because most will continue to inflect their written English with their native language while they learn more common American English rhetorical structures. This inflection is as it should be; the composition instructor's job is not to eradicate a first or other language. As the NCTE Committee against Racism and Bias in the Teaching of English's *Qualities of Anti-Racist ELA Curricula* suggests, instructors working toward an anti-racist pedagogy must lead students to become critical users of language while honoring their home and cultural codes. We also agree with the CCCC's position in the "CCCC Statement on Globalization" that "WPAs should devise local assessment tools to evaluate multilingual students' writing performance that reflect the values of both the institution and individual students and teachers." To judge multilingual students solely on the basis of native-language speakers or monolingual English speakers' abilities or desirable features is a harsh, unfair, and unrealistic system. For guidance, we adapt Susan Miller-Cochran's support structures for multilingual students, described in "Multilingual Writers and OWI" (295–96), which also benefit native-English-speaking students and encourage recognition of language diversity:

> Design the course by accommodating linguistic variation to avoid the need to retrofit.
>
> Offer additional resources (online or hard copy) for multilingual success, use multiple instructional modalities, and be sensitive when designing assignments requiring cultural knowledge.
>
> Be aware of cultural differences in interpersonal communications and writing styles; offer appropriate technological and pedagogical support.
>
> All WPAs, instructors, tutoring administrators, and tutors need to be trained to work with multilingual writers in both online and on-site environments.
>
> Set maximum course caps of fifteen students for online writing courses composed only of multilingual writers.
>
> Set up question and answer forums where students can ask questions or converse freely (but respectfully of one another) in any language and any dialect.

Other approaches include bell hooks's suggestion in *Teaching to Transgress* that students be encouraged to use their various languages in the classroom, not only so students do not feel that "seeking higher education will estrange them from that language and culture they know most intimately" (172) but also so that all students recognize and honor linguistic diversity and push beyond the homogenized idea of standardized English. Similarly, Staci M. Perryman-Clark's "African American Language, Rhetoric, and Students' Writing" discusses ways instructors can guide students to understand the "purposeful and strategic choices about language choices in the composition classroom," illustrating students' essays that explore this idea across various genres and rhetorical situations (470). Further, hooks calls for an "acknowledgement and celebration of diverse voices, and consequently of diverse language and speech," which includes bringing texts into the classroom that enable continued diversity exploration (173). Even further, as Bonnie J. Williams-Farrier argues in "'Talkin' bout Good and Bad' Pedagogies," students from "racial/ethnic backgrounds can benefit from learning AVT [African American Verbal Tradition] strategies, because AVT is a major component of the writing process" (231). She indicates all students can benefit from understanding rhetorical strategies evident in AVT such as anecdotal leads and repetition. The practices offered here also align with the NCTE Committee against Racism and Bias in the Teaching of English's *What Anti-Racist Language Teachers Do* and *Qualities of Anti-Racist ELA Curricula*, which stress the importance of including culturally and ethnically relevant and sustaining texts that reflect students' backgrounds and linguistic varieties. These texts and activities should be thoughtfully woven into the entire curriculum, not with just one unit or assignment on cultural diversity or multiculturalism; otherwise, instructors risk further marginalizing students, doing more harm than good (Pimentel et al.). Williams-Farrier's essay illustrates how to integrate diverse readings and approach them meaningfully while establishing AVT as a language with rhetorical power (231).

Inclusion and Error

Instructors can be inclusive of language differences and teach all levels of composition accessibly by attending to individual students' language usage. In the following example strategies, as in any examples in this book, remember that students are never a checklist of errors or a series of categories; they are people who use language in often categorizable, patterned ways, some of which veer from standardized English. Indeed, using the word *errors* implies working from a deficit model in which what is wrong counts more than what is right, strong, or effective. One way to combat the deficit model is to not grade errors—as many do not interfere with comprehensibility—but to note them for students who wish to improve their English language use. Many semantic and syntactic patterns are differences rather than problems to be corrected, as the CCCC's "Students' Right to Their Own Language" indicates. In language learning, however, the word *errors* does usefully indicate a mistake or linguistic choice that teachers can address thoughtfully and kindly with students. We recommend the following strategies:

> Give students choices among writing prompts or assignments, particularly in high-stakes assessments. Avoid topics requiring cul-

tural, historical, or political knowledge inaccessible to students from other countries, cultures, or linguistic backgrounds.

Assess composition learning through more than one piece, using end-of-term portfolios (see chs. 8 and 9), which allow students to showcase their best work.

Use self-reflection and other reflective activities to enable students to comment on their rhetorical and linguistic choices in relation to course outcomes and assignment goals.

Conference with all writers, knowing that instructors may need more time to understand what second language writers are communicating in their writing and to attend first to global and second to local issues.

Dispel the myth that most multilingual writers will want feedback on the lower-order concerns only; they often want and need both lower- and higher-order work (Thonus 209; Raimes 59).

Be aware of cultural differences in eye contact, hand gestures, touching, and talking back to persons in authority, which could be deemed offensive in students' home cultures. Instructors and students should work together to find their comfort levels in one-to-one, in-person, or online conferencing.

Ask students questions gently and respectfully. "You seem to be saying XYZ. Is that what you mean?" Multilingual students' language skills may not keep up with their complex thoughts (often formed in the first language), so they may need more time to express their ideas in English. New content creates dysfluency of ideas for all students; it is doubly so if students are translating from another language.

Emphasize that recursive writing processes might be viewed as possible phases to undertake consciously. We note that this recommendation differs from that found in chapter 7, which suggests a less linear, more recursive approach to process; students' linguistic contexts warrant flexibility in suggesting and describing approaches to them. For multilingual writers particularly, students may need help analyzing and understanding the assignment as well as the organizational structures of an essay or multimodal project before editing and revising. Therefore, whereas outlining may be too rigid a requirement for many native speakers, it may help some multilingual writers.

Look for *performance* versus *competence* errors, which often emerge in the oral reading of their writing. When reading their writing aloud, students sometimes read an incorrect word or sentence correctly or as they intended, despite what is written, revealing a writing performance error that students may not recognize. Note these with students to illustrate their competence. A competence error often is a personal trouble spot, as with skipping articles or error clusters. Such competence errors usually will be systematic and thereby a lower-order concern worth addressing together or with a handbook.

Be judicious about assigning lower marks to multilingual students with competence errors, as these may be glaring while not affecting the piece's comprehensibility. For all students, multilingual or otherwise, teachers should attend more to the higher-order concerns of content and form.

Assign priorities to error clusters and give them due focus only. Multilingual speakers will make numerous, various errors. Address the most important and leave the rest for later. Sentence structure, verbs (forms, tense, agreement), and nouns (forms and articles) should be ranked higher than prepositions and phrasal verbs, punctuation (other than main clauses), and mechanics (spelling, capitalization).

Encourage multistep editing: (1) Read aloud, (2) reread looking for personal trouble spots (especially content detail and organization), and (3) read again sentence-by-sentence from the end of the paper to the beginning to isolate sentence and word errors, especially spelling.

Be specific (and correct) when teaching grammar because multilingual students who may have learned many rules likely will apply what is taught. Handbooks can be friends!

Try to understand what causes an error. Such issues can stem from language interference, interlanguage application of rules, vocabulary or spelling interference, use of the thesaurus or dictionary, misunderstood oral forms, avoidance of uncomfortable issues for which they may lack appropriate vocabulary or cultural experience, and misused patterns.

Even though errors can seem glaring, it is crucial to note multilingual students' strengths because strengths can be developed most readily. Look for the main point, organizational strategy, parallelism, and imagery; consider the student's apparent composing process; then analyze what is going wrong and why.

Multicultural Writing

Undoubtedly cultural differences may also occur in student writing. The following list of such differences is adapted from Paul V. Anderson's "Professional and Technical Writing/Ethics/Cultures":

Amount of Detail Expected. Writers may provide less detail in higher-context cultures, where more is known and assumed (e.g., China, Japan, France). High-context cultures are "based on fewer, deeper relations with people" and "expect readers to have enough knowledge about the communication before they begin reading." Writers provide more detail in lower-context cultures, where people have more surface-level relationships (e.g., the United States, Great Britain, Germany). Readers "expect detailed writing that explains" everything.

Distance between the Top and Bottom of Organizational Hierarchies. Formal writing is heightened where hierarchical relations are greatly distant, as in many companies in the United States and Europe. Writing that is less formal occurs in organizations with flattened hierarchies. Writers may engage formality implicitly in relation to their home cultures.

Individual versus Group Organizations. Writers may write implicitly to audiences of their home culture, and those cultures can have widely different orientations, from collectivist, *we*-oriented cultures (e.g., those of Asia and South America) to individualist, *me*-oriented cultures (e.g., those of the United States and Northern Europe).

In-Person Learning Communications. Writers' peer and student-to-teacher communications may reflect their home culture in personal distance, eye contact, and decisions to ask questions of or disagree with others.

Preference for Direct or Indirect Statements. Writers from Western cultures (e.g., cultures of the United States and Northern Europe) may be more linguistically—and pedagogically—direct compared with those from Eastern cultures (e.g., cultures of Japan and Korea).

Basis of Writing Decisions. Objective, goal-oriented cultures (e.g., those of the United States and Europe) and subjective, interpersonal cultures (e.g., Arab cultures) have different preferences for written products, and students may reveal such preferences in email or other interpersonal communications.

Interpretation of Images, Gestures, and Words. Writers of all cultures should learn to avoid religious and political language in interpersonal communications and their writing generally—depending on rhetorical situation, of course. Any graphics showing hand gestures of any sort should be avoided as they are interpreted differently among cultures.

Instructors can address these differences in a variety of ways, but mainly by having direct, explicit conversations about areas of concern. Audience analysis and communication modeling can help. As needed, instructors should connect individually with students to create a safe learning environment. Also, the instruction cycle should include multiple safe opportunities for ungraded risk-taking.

According to the CCCC's "Students' Right to Their Own Language," students have an inherent right "to play roles in dialects other than their own, they should be encouraged to experiment, but they can acquire the fundamental skills of writing in their own dialect. Their experiments are ways of becoming more versatile" (12). "Students' Right to Their Own Language" speaks not only to language diversity but also to cultural difference and students' rights—and needs—to explore their cultures and those of others. Culturally competent instructors will provide assignments allowing for this experimentation.

Learner Backgrounds for Perceptive Teaching

Paul Kei Matsuda argues in "The Myth of Linguistic Homogeneity in U.S. College Composition" that composition instructors have widely (and wrongly) accepted a dominant image of composition students "as native speakers of a privileged variety of English" (638); he suggests that nontraditional writers' needs often are overlooked in research or programmatic design. Despite Matsuda's message, there remains a dearth of research regarding multilingual writers' needs with technology in composition classrooms. Here, we draw on Miller-Cochran's suggestion that all nontraditional students may have different needs and goals within a technologically driven composition class, but that instructors have a moral imperative to address their needs in the context of the course and in alignment with accessibility requirements. Therefore, instructors must acknowledge these differences and create their courses for what Jennifer L. Bowie in "Beyond the Universal" calls a "universe of users" rather than base them on a "universal design" that fails to consider the needs of diverse learners. We provide practical strategies for attending to these learners such that nonmultilingual learners' needs are also met.

Socioeconomic Background

Socioeconomic background affects students' college experiences as well as their potential success. Money is a strong motivator for entering and completing college, but its lack can hinder students. According to Michael Gos in "Nontraditional Student Access to OWI," particularly underserved populations—especially in online settings—include working-class, older adult, remotely rural, urban, veteran and active duty, and incarcerated students. Access issues related to finances, technology, and geography block education among these populations. Unemployed students may attend full-time with their education paid by parents, savings, scholarships, or loans. Students of low- to middle-income backgrounds also face such situations. Many students are employed part-time to full-time, working as many as thirty-five or more hours weekly while carrying heavy course loads. Such situations impede study and academic opportunities and make experiencing an active extracurricular college life impossible.

Such work-life contexts make online asynchronous courses attractive yet reduce study time, challenging adequate composing and drafting. Students may return to college from a previous attempt—or begin from scratch—because they are underemployed and want to boost a current career or change careers altogether. Additionally, some people enter or reenter college when retired from a first or second career. Generally, the more students must work for money outside college, the more challenged they may be in completing their studies, exploring new options, and making practical connections among their courses.

Educational Backgrounds

Students enter postsecondary education from various educational contexts that may affect how they approach composition in the digital era. For example, some secondary school districts have partnered with colleges to admit secondary students for postsecondary credit. This concurrent teaching scenario allows students to earn both high school diplomas and postsecondary credit. Certain secondary honors and advanced placement courses can lead to postsecondary credits in composition, mathematics, and other common core subjects. Other students enter college directly after high school, a phenomenon that leads to calling them traditional (eighteen-year-olds who might complete college in four to five years). Some students take a break between secondary and postsecondary school, working while exploring options and saving tuition money.

Age-Appropriate Learning Needs

Many students enter college after age twenty-four, so-called nontraditional students. Still others begin college after high school and then interrupt their education with work and other life experiences before returning to college. Of course, some students never complete college. In *Reading to Learn and Writing to Teach*, Hewett highlights how all contemporary students are influenced by the digital era, making them "nontraditional to traditional college expectations" (11). Thus, she considers the "new" nontraditional student with mixed youth-adult traits (i.e., adolegogy) and digital experiences previously unknown to educators. According to the current *U.S. News and World Report* "Best College" rankings, between thirty percent and eighty-three percent of students were over age twenty-five in 2019–20 ("Most Students"). With so many adult students in college, the terms *adolegogy* and *andragogy* help to understand the twenty-first century's new nontraditional digital students.

Young students have just come from lower-school settings in which they were treated educationally as children—being led by their teachers, a pedagogical stance (Knowles et al.). But they are entering adulthood and transitioning into adult learner, or andragogical, traits. This transitional stage, which Robert Marshak calls adolegogy and Hewett illustrates regarding literacy and OWI in *Reading to Learn*, engages mixed learning traits from both child and adult learners. For example, an adolescent-like learning stance that both younger and older learners might take involves the learner's self-concept. Whereas child learners' self-concepts are shaped by both teachers and themselves as "dependent personalit[ies] with slow independency growth rate," and an adult learner's self-concept is shaped by taking "responsibility for [one's] own decisions and life, and the learner needs to be seen by others as responsible [and] self-directing," an adolegogical learner may see the "self as sometimes dependent (and rebels against this) and sometimes independent (and feels uncomfortable with this, too)"; simultaneously such learners may be "okay with the label of irresponsible if it means not moving out of [their] comfort zone" (22–23). These adolegogical learning traits may reveal themselves particularly in the context of digitality.

Hewett explains that from a digital perspective, younger undergraduates between the ages of seventeen and twenty-four have nontraditional aspects. Access to devices, software, and technological interactivity permitting, many of this student generation have had some relation with digital technology most of their lives. Yet they likely have more experience with computer gaming and social media than with digital education. They may have a higher acceptance-level of multicultural peers and may be accustomed to global connections, but their interpersonal and one-on-one communicative skills may be low (*Reading* 26). Their world is and has been changing rapidly, and they expect rapid-fire communications, which typically do not occur in writing courses. These students may be digital-era natives (Levine and Dean xii) but not necessarily digital natives (Prensky). Hence, their relation to composition education using digital tools or in a hybrid or fully online setting often differs from what instructors expect, causing frustrations and requiring adjustments.

Interestingly, these younger nontraditional students have potentially shallow relations with textual literacy (Hewett, *Reading* 28). They may have read few lengthy books, a literacy need addressed in chapter 6. Likely, they are more comfortable with instructional images, videos, and podcasts than with text-based information. These students may or may not learn best from these media, but they have deep familiarity with them. If they need a new skill, many will turn to *YouTube* videos; they learn from *Google* searches and *Wikipedia* briefs rather than print-bound books. Furthermore, they are frequent multitaskers with digital tools and other activities, leading to "mere surface-level interactions both with learning material and people" (32). Of course, although older adults have had other learning experiences, they also have learned some of this behavior, since having social-to-national news perpetually available is habit-forming; nonetheless, younger students have known little else.

Many adult students also have developed a "working relationship with digital technology in their home and work lives" (33). They necessarily must grapple with the educational aspects of technology, as do their younger counterparts, but potentially from a more fraught and less experienced digital relation. Although the idea of online learning may appeal for logistical reasons, adult students may express anxiety about managing these digital courses. Given lifelong understanding that books, not images or video, constitute the literacy work of school, they may wonder, too, about the validity of multimodal projects as part of their literacy education. Additionally, adult students come to composition education from involved work, family, and social relationships and responsibilities, meaning they shoehorn school into already tight spaces.

Their differing experiences and backgrounds mean adult students may bring the following observed traits to composition instruction:

> *Adult learners are purpose-driven.* They often can identify what they need to learn and how they best receive such learning. They want just-in-time learning, getting needs met in the moment. They may want to try out new skills right away.

> *Adult learners may need help becoming aware of what they do not know.* They benefit from opportunities to explore alternative belief

and action systems and may need assistance in working through sometimes painful transitions from one system to another (Apps 97–98).

Adult learners need to connect their learning directly with their goals. They may rebel at disconnected school activities, seeing them as busywork. Direct connection with outcomes and scaffolded learning help connect the learning to the goals (see ch. 8).

Adult learners have life experience to direct, connect with, and expand their learning. They have transfer skills beyond those of younger learners and may value their education differently.

Adult learners often want clear-cut rules and orientation to the course and its expectations. They need to know when and where to accomplish work, particularly in online settings where learning may be new. Assignments and due date changes must be necessary and in their favor as adults often organize school around family and employment.

Adult learners bring a wide variety of past experiences to their education, including negative self-images from prior schooling. As with all learners, they may battle diversity issues, linguistic differences, learning and physical disabilities, as well as worries about their qualifications to continue their education. Anecdotally, many confess (with embarrassment) they do not know how to write.

With these learning traits, adult learners benefit from hands-on opportunities, time to integrate learning into thinking and practice, explicitly stated outcomes expectations, reflection opportunities for applying past experiences to new skills and future needs, few scheduling changes, and interpersonal opportunities to talk with instructors who also see themselves as lifelong learners.

Given their life phases, adult learners may hold the composition instructor and course to a higher level of accountability. Some concerns adult students may have include the course's value for its cost, whether students have a voice in the content, the quality of the teacher's knowledge and skill set, the teacher's concern for students and their needs, and the course's convenience and accessibility (Apps 121–23). Certainly, some of these adult learner traits also fit younger new nontraditional students, but acknowledging students' ages as a humanizing factor involves understanding and caring about them as a group and individually, clearing the snowy ramp before the stairs and embracing inclusivity.

Learning Preferences

People naturally differ in how they prefer to take in and integrate information. That preference is not always conscious or changeable. Learning preferences may be aural, visual, kinesthetic (learning by doing), text-based (reading and writing), and multimodal. Some people have strong preferences for a single way, whereas others may have multiple ways to interact with new information and skills. In a handout called "Imitation Copying for Students," Gerald Nelms indicates that students learn by (1) *precept*, "from others through reading, listening, and viewing"; (2) *practice*, by "doing something"; and (3) *imitation*, through "copying what others do" (1). Imitation of experienced writers is a powerful learning process, as Quintilian and others understood and taught as the ancient progymnasmata (rhetorical exercises for beginning students; *Institutio* 225–47; II.iv.1–42). Put another way, some people prefer listening to teachers or audiobooks. Others prefer watching demonstrations or video lessons and trying the skill later. Some need to manipulate the information or try the skill as they are learning it. Still others prefer to read and write about the subject.

People often know how they learn best and can articulate that; targeting learning to this revelation is easy, and changing teaching styles frequently keeps students attentive. For example, students who learn aurally and by precept may understand composition feedback best multimodally through video or screen-capture software. Instructors can plan to provide feedback this way at least once to meet such students' needs. Or, they can survey students and learn their preferences, providing text-based feedback to those who prefer reading and imitation and multimodal feedback to others. Chapter 9 outlines how the feedback itself remains similar, and only the medium changes to meet individual preferences.

Visual learners may need diagrams and charts, written material, colors or highlighting to differentiate material, gestures and animated body language, and concrete visual representations of writing plans. Auditory learners may need oral reading of material, oral discussions, audio recording of classes or podcasts for replay, and voice-to-text dictation for initial composing. Kinesthetic learners may want to do their own writing and underlining, manipulate sentences by copying and pasting or using index cards, act out their thoughts, copy out or imitate other authors, and use physical gestures to connect composing to thinking. Finally, multisensory learners may want to present their ideas orally, through images, and in writing—in other words, multimodally; their creativity may be deeply connected to their ability to think with combined techniques (adapted from Konstant 110–11). In sum, when all else fails, first ask students what they need and then change the approach to match.

Conclusion

All students are entitled to full access and inclusion. Although diversity may make providing such access challenging, it remains the educator's job to do so. Access and inclusion are not one-way streets, however. Faculty members also are diverse and entitled to accessible, inclusive workplaces, as we discuss in chapter 2 of *Administering Writing Programs in the Twenty-First Century*. The more educators learn to develop safe, respectful academic spaces for students, the more they can create safe, respectful academic workplaces for one another—humanizing composition in all ways.

3

Digitalizing Text, Purpose, and Genre

WPA Garcia has asked Professor Jackson to develop a new composition course that will be taught in a technologically enhanced classroom; at least one student project must engage multimodality. Professor Jackson's job is to consider the purposes for writing, as well as the various genres he can teach students to write in, including multimodal genres. He needs to understand some common purposes for writing and to recognize genres are flexible regarding conventions, purposes, and audiences, often changing the very definition of the genres themselves.

All composition courses—whether technologically enhanced on-site, fully online, or hybrid (see chs. 4 and 5)—now have digital features, and teaching has changed significantly. Instructors must help students learn to compose all types of texts using various technologies; they also must teach students to read those texts rhetorically and thoughtfully, and this reading should occur in both traditional print and digital formats. Undeniably, alphabetic text-based composition has morphed into an inherently digital enterprise involving screen reading and multimodal projects, which means it needs different attention from practitioners and scholars. Instructors like Professor Jackson must understand how to address these differences and why; students also need such knowledge to make more conscious, rhetorically effective uses of their composition education both in and outside the academy.

This chapter highlights recent changes in composing technologies and defines multimodal texts alongside alphabetic texts to demonstrate their inherent relation. Then, it outlines exposition and argumentation as common approaches to postsecondary composition. Finally, it addresses some basic considerations of teaching genres in digital settings. Because digitalizing text, purpose, and genre are deeply linked to the technologizing of teaching and learning environments and instructional processes, as well as to the different needs of OWI, this chapter is best read alongside chapters 4 and 5.

Composition Technologies

With what technologies, or tools, do writers compose? The inherent digitality of contemporary composition is revealed strongly in the wide variety of composing technologies available for educators and students. With these technologies, many of them newly digital, comes a period of rapid change to which writers must adjust. Of course, composing technologies have undergone change before. Pencils, first invented in the sixteenth century, became plentiful when machining made them easier to make and use. In time, the ubiquity of inexpensive pencils replaced quill and ink writing instruments; mass production of paper and later the typewriter encouraged more people to engage in writing for various purposes. According to Dennis Baron, with increased use over time, technology becomes "automatic and invisible" to users (82). Nonetheless, the rapidity of technological changes—from the onset of personal microcomputers in the 1980s to smaller, portable devices such as laptop and notebook computers in the 1990s to tablets and smartphones in the 2000s to smart notebooks in the 2010s—has drastically altered when and how people compose.

Not everyone adapts well to rapid change. Many experienced composition instructors in postsecondary education learned to compose or teach writing differently from today's practices. Many adult students, too, developed their early composition skills writing in cursive or lettering with hand-operated pen or pencil and paper and pecking on manual typewriters. Such composing engaged rhythm, balance, and hand-eye coordination, as well as thinking skill sets that people needed to adjust for digital composing tools. Although most people appear to make these kinesthetic and brain-based changes smoothly, not everyone does, and many adults' preferred composing technologies may remain those learned years earlier.

Additionally, as chapter 2 describes, access to new technologies often is unequal (Gos; Oswal). Access issues span age, socioeconomic, racial, geographic, cultural, and other divides; they affect writers with physical, learning, and emotional challenges as well. For example, left-handed people are most affected when handwriting in notebooks and on desks assembled for right-handed people, which is the default construction; left-handed people's arms awkwardly cover the page as they write, smearing ink. They also suffer when digital tools like document cameras are not designed to accommodate left-hand dominance. Similarly, people with certain physical disabilities cannot type by hand whereas others require a screen reader.

In the digital era, pen or pencil and paper remain composing tools, but even in elementary school, keyboarding is a curricular requirement. Word processing machines became popular in the early 1980s and personal microcomputers followed shortly thereafter—for those who could afford them. In the 1990s and early 2000s, many colleges created dedicated computer labs to enable students—particularly those without home access—to complete their work using computers and school printers. Writing programs also devoted significant money to dedicated computer labs for networked and hybrid courses. Now, however, as students of all ages take notes using personal notebook computers, tablets, and mobile devices, such dedicated labs may be considered passé—to the detriment of those without such access. Where laptops once were banned in postsecondary courses as a distraction, now they are a natural part of learning and classroom environments.

As machines have become prevalent technology for alphabetic writing, teaching handwriting has declined. Printing or lettering still is taught in early education, although in 2013 cursive, or script, handwriting was dropped in the United States from schools' Common Core standards, guidance shared among all fifty states (Chemin). Interestingly, script and lettering may enhance learning, improving the "memory of factual detail, conceptual understanding of the material, and ability to synthesize and generalize information" (Jessie S.), which suggests the value of smart notebooks or tablets on which handwriting is translated to the computer as typeface. Some neuroscience studies reveal cognitive advantages to handwriting versus keyboarding. Because writing by hand requires a series of highly coordinated touch and hand-eye movement-focused skills, whereas using the keyboard merely requires spatial memory and pressure for each key, there is a difference in their motor movement and body-to-brain skills (Chemin), and handwriting may have its benefits in engaging listening, comprehension, and summarization skills, as Cessie S. indicates in "Note-Taking."

Increasing numbers of students are learning through mobile devices, particularly phones (see Magda and Aslanian 6). Many make it work fine; mobile technologies certainly have potential for learning generally and composition courses specifically. It is unknown how many students are using mobile devices to compose and complete alphabetic-text-based assignments (Martinez et al.; Rodrigo). Writers may have difficulty gaining a sense of the entire composition without seeing it on a larger screen or in hard copy. Writers relying on grammar and spell check apps may not engage these processes when producing a composition on a mobile device. In sum, even though handwriting remains a viable (and, we think, exceptionally helpful) strategy for note-taking and composing, we realize that digital keyboarding and dictation applications are overtaking them, changing the nature of composing and composition instruction.

Alphabetic and Multimodal Texts

Alphabetic, or linguistic, writing might sound like an odd way of describing the kinds of texts students and educators have composed all their lives. Yet if there were only one composing modality, there would be no need for the qualifier *alphabetic* or *linguistic* to differentiate such text because there would be no distinction to make; at the same time, this distinction suggests a binary of competition instead of a synergistic blending (Reichert Powell, "Writing" 1). Recent decades have brought new attention to multimodal texts, made both available and necessary through digitality. Increased attention to multimodality has erased alphabetic text's exclusivity, but not its need, ubiquity, or usefulness. Most books about writing instruction address alphabetic text specifically as writing, which has been most compositionists' primary purview. Frankly, our decision in this book to purposefully address the interconnectedness of multimodal and alphabetic texts has made writing it far more difficult, continually challenging our thinking about writing instruction in the digital era. Because alphabetic text reflects the symbol system representing how English-speaking people learn to speak and read, it certainly is not going extinct, and it will not soon (if ever) be overshadowed by the need to teach multimodality. The role of multimodal texts in the world outside education—both the work and social worlds—is becoming more crucial to communication, however, making composing multimodal texts also the natural work of composition (see also Horner). Hence, understanding how multimodal texts function in contemporary writing instruction is the work of composition instructors like Professor Jackson.

Multimodal texts (also known as *multimedia, digital rhetoric, new media*, and *webtexts*) use more than one communicative mode, or semiotic resource, to communicate (Kress, *Multimodality* 5). To compose and present a message rhetorically for digital distribution, multimodal texts could consist of a mix of alphabetic text and such media as still, moving, and animated images; music, voice, and other sound; and video. Whether required to use or volunteering to try multimodality, instructors may forget that alphabetic text also is used for producing multimodal texts. In fact, speech and writing should be viewed as significant in multimodal texts and seen as parts of a multimodal ensemble (Jewitt 250). Simply, instructors need to teach alphabetic writing as an inextricable part of multimodality.

Multimodality, as described in chapter 1, is an especially common term, yet it does not solely convey digital composition or delivery because multimodal projects can involve such modes as tactile paper, paint, or sculpture, and they can be delivered by hand in a traditional classroom setting (see Shipka, *Toward*). Digital multimodal texts may engage these same modes but are composed on a computer or mobile device screen and delivered digitally. As Carey Jewitt notes in "Multimodality and Literacy in School Classrooms," "[D]igital technologies are of particular importance to multimodality because they make a wide range of modes available" for communication (250). Digital technologies create opportunities for wider meaning making and offer students chances to transform or remake existing genres; they also enable wider distribution to various audiences. Although we acknowledge multimodal texts do not have to be created for the screen or through technology, throughout this book we rely on a digital definition of multimodality, and this definition is especially significant as we consider the digital environments in which students compose and the various digital technologies they use, and the digital tools instructors employ in the twenty-first century.

Heavily influenced by digitality, such multimodal compositions are too rarely taught in educational settings, despite writing studies professional position statements recommending otherwise. We believe students should learn to compose multimodal texts (see also Bowen and Whithaus; Hull and Nelson; Khadka and Lee; Takayoshi and Selfe). For example, learning to create a webtext that rhetorically appeals to readers enables students to develop an impressive portfolio, create unique advertisements for an employer, represent ideas in accessible ways, or generate thought-provoking materials for other endeavors. Furthermore, technology influences how people think about the modes they use, and the presentation medium affects how they deliver the message. As another example, mobile devices are used to video-connect family visits; create insightful memes; message with text, video, and images; and generally communicate, with users often rejecting the voice features of the phone itself in lieu of other semiotic resources. The available medium deeply affects rhetorical choices. No one can deny that technology has changed how people think about these things, and digital literacy means confronting these changes by learning about them.

Not everyone has equal access to or knowledge about these technologies; yet equitable literacy education compels educators to consider access issues and to teach students about them. With multimodal texts, alphabetic text may (or may not) be the primary communicative means because art images, audio, video, and so on can enhance the message and engage both writers and readers with different learning preferences. Multimodal texts attract people who consume information through reading but expand the audience to those who prefer to listen and view. Students need to learn to base their choices of specific modes and mediums on not only their own communicative preferences but also audience needs and preferences. Multimodal texts can increase access to information production and consumption for people with such different sensory preferences as visual or aural learning, potentially enhancing comprehension.

Composition Purposes

"Language is sermonic," says Richard Weaver. "Everything's an argument," state Andrea Lunsford, John J. Ruszkiewicz, and Keith Walters. These ideas about language and argumentation, although debated among rhetoricians, have merit for writing instruction because students need to know that from topic selection to genre, word choice, and design, every decision is inflected by writers' purposes for influencing audiences.

Recall that rhetoricians through the centuries have named and re-named the aims of rhetoric, which variously have been to teach, to move, and to delight. Particularly in current-traditional rhetoric (see ch. 1), these aims were reduced to four rhetorical modes: narration, description, exposition, and argumentation. To avoid confusing our discussion here with the difficulties of current-traditional rhetoric, in this chapter we address exposition and argumentation as overarching purposes for writing (not as modes); to these two purposes, we add dialogue. In chapter 7, we consider narration, description, and other writing patterns as topoi, or common topics (again, not as modes), that aid invention and arrangement of ideas. Because of their digital features, also to avoid confusion, we use *mode* to refer to media choices and *modality* to denote temporal and interpersonal communicative choices (see chs. 1 and 4).

Exposition and *argumentation* may have other names among compositionists with different backgrounds, but their features tend to be similar. As overarching purposes for composition, exposition and argumentation address the aims of informing or educating and of arguing a claim or persuading about an action, respectively. Exposition and argumentation provide the backbone of most nonfiction composing genres used in academic writing in that students typically are asked to explain a phenomenon or to argue for or against something. Both aims might be used in any genre discussed in this chapter. Finally, both tend to be researched writing in that research is necessary to enable writers to express informed ideas and opinions and support them with reasons, examples, and justifications (see ch. 7).

It is worth reminding readers that these primary purposes run through so-called traditional composition instruction to digitally inflected twenty-first-century composition instruction. The nature of exposition and argument remain the same. How writers attend to the composing process regarding technologies and audience are what have changed. Therefore, throughout the book, we trace the evolution of instruction, illustrating composition instruction's features in the digital era.

Exposition

Exposition is a core composing skill that all writers need. It typically asks writers to analyze (i.e., break into constituent parts) and explain either what something is and is not or why or how something happens.

The first type of exposition has an element of argumentation in that explicating a point of view about the topic and its thesis, or major claim, often is stated as a simple matter of fact: for example, *Animal husbandry remains an important field of study.* Yet bias is enfolded in that statement, suggesting an opposite perspective exists (i.e., animal husbandry no longer is relevant); therefore, exposition has an evaluative nature. A thesis may inform about qualities, for example, leading to answering questions of *what* (e.g., *What functional vocabulary do toddlers gain before learning to speak?*). When a thesis asks *why* (e.g., *Why are colleges moving away from requiring standardized tests for admission?*), the natural response is *because,* guiding the research by seeking good reasons that convey cause. Exposition typically requires a series of reasons and supportive detail such as statistics and other facts as well as examples. It often engages the topoi of definition, description, narration, comparison/contrast, and cause and effect analysis as patterns for writing because the topoi enable reader comprehension of sophisticated topics (Fleming 254; see ch. 7).

Exposition that answers how-to questions typically conveys a process and often the reasons grounding it. Using descriptive details and concrete language, process writing can address anything from how to make a peanut butter and jelly sandwich to how (and why) Mount Kilauea's current eruption cycle began in 1983 and continues to emit lava into the 2020s. Writers use a thesis that enables the essay to foreground a series of steps, which means they must understand the process and be clear about it upfront. These steps provide a natural organizational structure assisted by transition words like *afterwards, next, during, finally, later, first/second/third, previously, eventually,* and *simultaneously.* Of course, the ability not only to write about a process but to demonstrate it for readers to see has changed considerably because of digital composition tools and multimodal presentation that allow capturing and visualizing it.

Position versus Thesis

A *position* is a stance or informed opinion that presents an overall summarizing attitude or judgment about an issue. Examples of positions include *Recycling is an important environmental strategy* and *Universities often exploit student athletes.*

To be a *thesis*, typically the position should be focused, qualified, and narrow enough for the assignment's depth and breadth. Although an expository thesis uses a focused position to explain why or how, it does not need to be pointedly argumentative. An argumentative thesis (i.e., assertion or claim) is more specific, precise, strategic, and arguable, as in *College students, as the new generation of adults, should recycle avidly* and *Student athletes in revenue-generative sports ought to be paid for their services.*

Argumentative claims often express duty, obligation, and probability through the use of modals like *should, ought*, and *must.*

Argumentation

Argumentation is well studied by compositionists. Lunsford, Ruszkiewicz, and Walters's *Everything's an Argument* and Annette Rottenberg and Donna Winchell's *Elements of Argument* provide two popular approaches. We especially like Timothy W. Crusius and Carolyn E. Channell's *The Aims of Argument* for their categorization of argumentation's purposes, which include arguing to inquire, convince, persuade, and resolve conflict. Their two-part structure of first stating an informed opinion and then providing one or more reasons for holding that opinion helps students understand that opinions alone are insufficient to move a problem to satisfactory conclusion. That each reason then requires inquiry into the problem takes students deeper—from raw thinking into thoughtful thesis support (3). In these argumentative approaches, all language may be considered persuasive.

Arguing to inquire, also called *writing to discover,* enables one to develop informed opinions and to self-question already owned opinions. Donald Murray indicates in "Teaching the Other Self" that writing is not thinking reported; "writing *is* thinking" (143, emphasis ours). Students may believe that writers first think and then jot down ideas. But writing is itself an act of inquiring into a topic to discover what it reveals, as Heidi Estrem writes straightforwardly in "Writing Is a Knowledge-Making Activity" (threshold concept 1.1): "We write *to* think" (19). Writers often do not know where their writing will take them or how the project will end, but the very act of writing takes them on a journey to that ultimate point. Using writing to inquire or discover can occur with any genre and with exposition, argumentation, or dialogue; discovery comprises anything the writer has not known, considered, or consciously thought before composing. Sometimes discovery happens explicitly, as with research, freewriting, journaling, or pre- and post-reflections; other times it happens implicitly through talking with others, drafting, and revising. Written inquiry, which also might be expressed as exposition, may never end or resolve (e.g., blog posts where reader comments are welcome), yet sometimes it has a decisive conclusion (Crusius and Channell 5).

Arguing to convince conveys one's conviction, which is an "earned opinion, achieved through careful thought, research, and discussion" (Crusius and Channell 5–6). In other words, when one's inquiry has reached resolution, one wants to convey it to others and induce their agreement, which is typical of academic arguments. Logical appeals that speak to readers are appropriate to the aims of arguing to convince. We like to tell students that, although it would be terrific for readers to agree, another good result is for readers merely to think differently about the subject, figuratively scratching their heads and saying, "Hmmm. I hadn't thought about it like that." This kind of argument requires knowing one's audience, rhetorical situation, and purpose; developing a thesis (claim, assertion); having good reasons and logical evidence; and providing counterarguments, which consider (and typically reject) alternative arguments.

Arguing to persuade is "convincing *plus*" because it appeals to the whole person (Crusius and Channell 6). Persuasion asks for change and for readers to do or act somehow differently. As such, it requires logos, but it also needs writers' ethos to convince readers of their goodwill and earned opinion (as shown through expressed knowledge) as well as appeals to readers' pathos, or emotions, to move readers to action. Humans can agree based on logos while doing nothing about a situation if the writer has little or no ethos or fails to appeal to emotions successfully. This kind of argument also requires knowing one's audience and purpose, but it relies on a doable proposal for realistic action. With persuasion, readers need something specific to do, so a proposal offers possible action steps relevant to the argument's claim. Such action need not be major. For example, *Readers should quit their jobs and join Habitat for Humanity to build houses for the impoverished* is unrealistic. Proposed action is more doable in small bites: *Readers should take one week of annual vacation to help the impoverished through Habitat for Humanity and other action-oriented charitable organizations.* Counterproposals also are important as they consider (and typically reject) alternatives to the proposed action. Thoughtful uses of rhetorical devices and style enable successful persuasion, as detailed in chapter 7.

Arguing to negotiate, a form of *dialogue*, is undertaught, which is why Crusius and Channell address it as an argumentative form. Negotiation acknowledges that audience members may have completely different beliefs from writers and have real, lived experiences different from their own. Those who stand on the other side of the issue also will have arguments intended to convince and persuade. When an argument comes to a standstill, it is tempting to call names and throw metaphorical stones (if the argument did not already begin there), as too often is seen in contemporary mass and social media. Negotiation, instead, may be something that—given the resources—interlocutors can handle alone, or it may require mediation. Although negotiation necessitates logic, clear reasons, and powerful presentation, it challenges interpersonal skills when "[e]xchanging viewpoints and information and building empathy" that "enables all parties to make concessions, to loosen their hold on their original positions, and finally to reach consensus—or at least a resolution that all participants find satisfactory" (8). Rogerian argument (R. Young et al.), taken from psychologist Carl Rogers' threat-reducing approaches to interpersonal communication, provides specific strategies for listening empathetically while being heard. Listening to others and restating their positions enables finding commonalities from which to move forward. Such an approach also engages Kenneth Burke's notion of *identification* with the audience (*Rhetoric*), critical for creating connections rather than merely winning points.

These negotiation approaches entail dialogue as a social act and type of dialectic. In traditional dialectic, a small group of people engage in conversation aimed at finding the truth among differing opinions through reasoned argument. As chapter 1 explains, Plato preferred the logos of dialectic for getting at the truth, whereas Aristotle positioned rhetoric as the counterpart—the equal—of dialectic. Plato made the Socratic dialogue famous through *Phaedrus* and *Gorgias*, in which individual speakers represent different points of view. Dialectic remains a type of argument, however, and when one wants to move away from traditional argumentation into negotiation, dialogue provides a less contentious, oppositional approach.

Theories from James Britton and colleagues and from Martin Buber inform dialogue as an act of cooperative listening, reasoned talking, and responsiveness to others. The audience categories developed by Britton and colleagues highlight different levels of relationships writers can have with their readers, beginning with the self (often expressed as prewriting) and moving outward to wider audiences (→ a teacher-student relationship → the peer-to-peer relationship(s) → the unknown public audience; 65–73). Such relationships can range from transactional ("some kind of participation in the world's affairs"; 83) to expressive ("utterance at its most relaxed and intimate"; 82) to poetic ("verbal object as work of art"; 83). Whereas dialectic might be considered more transactional in that the aim is to reason through informed opinions, dialogue relies less on oppositionality and more on relationality. A dialogic conversation, therefore, prizes the connection being made over winning a point. Buber, whose interpersonal *I-thou* philosophy, which emerged post–World War II, touches on rhetorical theory, examines and identifies levels through which people talk with one another, ranging from a primarily dialogic relationship—in which individuals see, experience, and value their interlocutors (i.e., *I* → *thou*)—to a monologic relationship—in which they turn inward and talk at, rather than to, their listeners (i.e., *I* → *it*). Buber found genuine dialogue to be rare, yet his continuum among the *I, thou,* and *it* describes the social nature of the writer-reader relationship and remains pertinent. The ideas of Britton and colleagues and of Buber were not the only ones that addressed crucial needs for cooperative dialogue among members of an audience. In *The New Rhetoric*, Chaim Perelman and Lucie Olbrechts-Tyteca define the nature of particular and universal audiences, which is important for understanding how to reach agreement with any audience (26–40). Similarly, Burke in *A Rhetoric of Motives* considers how identification with an audience could be reached (19–29); particularly important is the notion of identification and consubstantiality:

"For substance, in the old philosophies, was an *act*; and a way of life is an *acting together*; and in acting together, men have common sensations, concepts, images, ideas, attitudes that make them *consubstantial*" (21). These notions form a theory of how people interactively and connectively communicate, particularly with the use of probable reasoning.

Educators should help students understand the differences among the foundational composition approaches of exposition, argumentation and its types, and dialogue. Certainly, as Professor Jackson observes with his students, people may be confused about their communicative aims, mixing and blending goals within media that may be inappropriate to the aim (see ch. 4). Most media can be used for both transactional and interpersonal purposes, but just because the writer intends the message one way does not guarantee it will be received as such; this idea forms threshold concept 1.3, Charles Bazerman's "Writing Expresses and Shares Meaning to Be Reconstructed by the Reader." A friendly attempt at an objective statement of what the writer believes to be factual can be read as uninformed opinion, posturing, picking a fight, or unkindness. Genuinely civil dialogue challenges writers (and readers) in such forums. Similarly, an attempt to be interpersonally connected through a public forum that is widely distributed—like messaging through *Facebook*, *Instagram*, or *Twitter*—can be misread and cause discomfort or worse for writers and intended recipients.

Genres

Perhaps the most common writing genres learned in secondary school are English course literary analyses. Often rigidified into five-paragraph essays, such current-traditional writing types are inflexible "rhetorical acts" framed by "recurrent situations" where writers need to make similar strategic choices, or "rhetorical actions," that "readers come to expect" (Devitt 146). They often focus more on essay shape, arrangement (e.g., five paragraphs, each with its own job), and correctness than on content. Literary analysis papers usually dissect prose or poetry to discuss themes, plots, and characters. Other commonly taught genres include research papers and science lab reports. Course and standardized exams require brief essays, for which the five-paragraph strategy can be useful. These genres remain staples in many secondary writing curricula although learning them alone falls significantly short of the depth and breadth needed for college or—more important—for life, with or without college. Even though the five-paragraph essay form and the notions taught about what a thesis sentence is, what it must contain, and where it belongs were debunked years ago (Nunes), these current-traditional strategies still are taught at all school levels.

A standard five-paragraph essay literally consists of five paragraphs with rigid rules: an introduction paragraph that always contains a one-sentence thesis as the last sentence of the paragraph; three body paragraphs, each discussing one of three main points supporting that thesis, typically requiring overt topic sentences beginning each paragraph; and a conclusion paragraph repeating the essay's main points and thesis. It is a useful formula for beginning writers who need to practice writing and supporting a thesis. As a formula, it provides boundaries for what may and may not go into an essay, giving instructors a briefer essay to read and assess. The genre is so rigidly defined, however, that if the essay does not meet the guidelines, it may fail regardless of content. Furthermore, it constrains thinking and eliminates exploring supportive points thoroughly, thus leading to minimalistic analysis with little to no opportunity for synthesis.

Instructors can use the following approaches to unteach the five-paragraph essay:

Require essays with no fewer than six to eight paragraphs.

Teach students to deepen essays and vary structure by examining how logical and descriptive content is missing or overly condensed in a five-paragraph essay.

Talk about genre as responsive to audience and purpose, placing five-paragraph essays in context (e.g., spontaneous exam questions) as insufficient for most school and life writing.

Work with students to synthesize ideas developed through analysis. What new or different conclusions emerge? How can they be expressed?

In postsecondary school, students have more opportunities to write, but in many cases, the genres may remain few: short (e.g., five to seven pages for first-year writing) to lengthier (e.g., fifteen to twenty pages for advanced courses) expositions explaining a process or expressing the results of an analysis; some argumentation of a claim; an occasional lab report for science; and many five-paragraph essay exams to demonstrate mastery of knowledge. In some ways, college and high school composing genres differ little, although college composition typically requires more substantive thinking and increasingly more mature stylistic turns.

Yet genres are not narrowly defined by thesis style and placement, paragraphing requirements, and the texts about which one writes. In the Conference on College Composition and Communication's position statement "Principles for the Postsecondary Teaching of Writing," the authors note: "Sound writing instruction enables students to analyze and practice with a variety of genres." They define genres as "distinctive types of texts [that] emerge from particular social, disciplinary, and cultural contexts. Genres are distinguished by writing, design conventions, and functions within specific contexts. Over time, genres typically evolve to meet the changing demands of those contexts," which indicates genres "change over time." Writing is communication about something to someone, and its various genres provide "containers" to help the writer consider the content, purpose, and audience.

Genre, a term Anis S. Bawarshi and Mary Jo Reiff acknowledge in *Genre: An Introduction to History, Theory, Research, and Pedagogy* is "fraught with confusion, competing with popular theories of genre as text type and as an artificial system of classification" (3), move beyond formal features to include "knowledge of what and whose purpose genres serve; how to negotiate one's intentions in relation to genres' social expectations and motives; when and why and where to use genres; what reader/writer relationships genres maintain; and how genres relate to other genres in the coordination of social life" (4). Writers need to learn about audience and purpose for genres, how formal and informal genre conventions relate to communication, and—significantly—that such knowledge and writing flexibility enables writers to engage with standard genres and to create new ones. One's intention affects both content and its reception by the audience. Therefore, instructors need to teach about genres using example documents and attending "to textual conventions such as organization, register, style, and the use of evidence. It also includes attention to visual design principles and visual rhetorics" (CCCC, "Principles for the Postsecondary Teaching of Writing"). Especially in the twenty-first century, analyzing genre conventions—their what, why, and how—should be combined with composing genres and should test rhetorical principles and students' skills through that process.

The twenty-first-century genre possibilities for composition instruction, however defined, have changed substantially; many now are connected to digitality, as expressed by scholars who study how multimodal composition fuels rhetorical invention (e.g., Ball and Charlton; Miller and Kelly; Sheridan et al.). Here, we outline common nonfiction composing genres that students may need to learn or that writing programs may require. Although they may be covered in particular writing programs, we do not discuss fiction genres because these typically are not addressed in general and advanced composition courses, but they too are changed in the digital era, and students may blend them with nonfiction genres, particularly in multimodal compositions. We define and review these genres as types of texts with various design conventions and functions, primarily considering them for both their traditionally understood stable features and those changed by digitality while glossing audience expectations and social, disciplinary, and cultural contexts. As such, our discussion moves from those genres that traditionally are heavily text-based, to genres that use more blended modes (including alphabetic text), to more multimodal genres like podcasts that only use voice and sound, as figure 3.1 shows. Although all genres, including academic essays, can have multimodal elements, we suggest viewing these genres as a continuum, fluidly engaging various modes to communicate. From our discussion below, readers also may note that genre and medium overlap or blend; this overlapping or blending often occurs because genre conventions in the digital age are flexible depending on context, audience, and purpose.

As we indicate in chapter 1, American society used aurality as the primary communicative mode until the Industrial Revolution. Arguably,

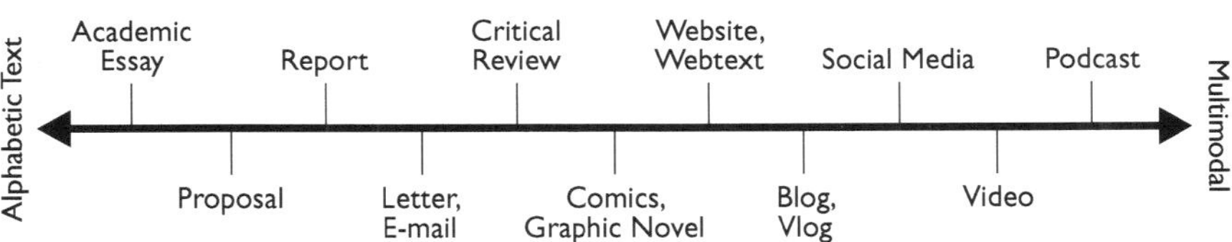

Figure 3.1. Continuum of genres in the digital age.

contemporary culture has returned to the primacy of aurality with the podcast genre; to illustrate this cultural turn, we start this continuum with the traditional academic essay and end with the podcast. Although nowhere near exhaustive, this list offers a general sense of genres that can be introduced into such composition courses as those Professor Jackson teaches.

Academic Essay

Academic essays, typically alphabetically written, can be constructed in both brief and long forms. Brief forms help students learn to address complex issues succinctly and provide instructors with shorter projects to assess. Learning succinctness may seem a more valid reason for short projects than giving instructors shorter essays to evaluate, but assessing writing is complicated by the unfortunate administrative problem of overcrowding a course and giving instructors—especially part-time faculty members who work at more than one institution—too many writing courses and students to manage well. Another concern with briefer essays relates directly to addressing complex issues succinctly: Students may never address a subject's complexity in brief essays, instead considering the subject shallowly just to complete the assignment. We have experienced this tendency with many students despite attempts to provide them with adequate materials and time to read, think, and write about the topic. As mature writers may know, sometimes it is more difficult to write a good succinct piece, hence the value of lengthier essays or of writing longer drafts that later can be purposefully edited (e.g., from two thousand words to one thousand to five hundred), which teaches final-draft concision. In an era of brief Internet articles composed for easy screen reading and short site visits, people may be less inclined to read (see ch. 6) and write lengthy pieces. Therefore, writing longer academic essays provides important occasions to analyze and consider complex issues deeply, which may help students develop meaningful briefer essays. These kinds of thinking and writing opportunities have a generative and recursive nature.

Academic essays need not be scholarly, although students may benefit from learning this important approach to explaining and arguing in academic settings. Essays written in academic settings can have a wide range of purposes, some drawn from ancient rhetorical goals and some much newer. For example, because rhetoric engages probable reasoning about human affairs, Aristotle indicates rhetoric is useful to make truth prevail, instruct in popular rather than scientific language, defend, and debate issues (3; I.i.1 [1354a]). Similarly, Cicero's aims of rhetoric are to teach or to prove the case, to move or persuade, and to delight the audience or arouse its emotions (*Ideal Orator* 357; I.3). Most argumentative essays and multimodal projects do ask writers to explain a point, prove a case, or persuade an audience to some action, which is why exposition and argumentation are most frequently used in academic writing, but these strategies also are useful for composing projects outside school settings. The ancient form of epideictic, or ceremonial, writing offers interesting projects, for instance. Whereas eulogies praise the deceased and encomiums praise the living, such tasks offer students opportunity to delve into someone's life (one they know personally or admire from afar) to find character strengths, virtues, and positive actions—the ethos— of the subject. Writing to blame or expose the negative characteristics and behaviors of others is undertaken frequently in contemporary news and social media; doing it well—with researched opinions and reasonable evidence presented without hyperbole (unless engaging in satire) is challenging even for mature writers. Writing that entertains—like fiction, parables, and poetry—also can teach, defend, and debate human issues. Creative nonfiction, in which literary techniques like narrative are combined with expository and argumentative writing, can achieve all three aims of teaching, moving, and delighting in one powerful piece. When researched writing is involved and the principles of exposition and argumentation are observed, all these writing genres provide variety and challenge while provoking student interest.

In "The Essay as Form in a Digital Age," Joseph Harris argues that essays "can center on almost any subject so long as a teacher gets students invested in working on it" (127). Hence, educators can individualize approaching the "affordances of the Web to reinvigorate how we teach a form of writing, the critical essay, that has long been part of a dissenting tradition of work in the academy" (131). Harris reminds readers that a so-called academic essay need not be dull or lack dimension and intellectual spark; it is neither a long gone genre nor a staid requirement of education—although we believe students benefit from writing essays.

When designed in traditional ways, academic essays tend to have common parts that students need to learn so they can make choices for particular pieces:

introduction and background

thesis (claim, assertion)

body (supported by research), containing main points, a series of reasons, and examples and details

proposals (for persuasive arguments)

counterarguments or counterproposals

conclusions with summations and recommendations

Introductions typically include

the issue;

its background or history;

its importance; and

the writer's position (thesis).

Conclusions typically include

a summary of the project and its main points;

further consideration of the problem or needed research; and

sometimes, questions for which the writer has no answers, leaving readers thinking.

Once students learn such parts, they have tools for consciously varying their writing to create their ideal pieces.

To this point, digitality has not affected routine, alphabetic academic essays as much as it has some other genres; yet when such essays are genuinely published, as to the web, they become differently and newly alive (see J. Harris, "Essay"). Although they now typically are keyboarded into word processing programs (or dictated with voice-to-text apps), these essays often have the same generic requirements as they have had for more than a century when handwriting and typewriting were necessary: such structural and formatting conventions as an alphabetic text-based title or title page; double-spaced lines; one-inch margins; text comprising an introduction, body, and conclusion; and references. Aside from composing processes, which we discuss in chapter 7, few essay features have changed due to digitality. Academic essays remain an important staple of both secondary and postsecondary composition education; and writing them teaches core composing skills applicable to other genres—or, minimally, these essays carry potential to accomplish this challenging transfer task.

New media can be engaged for academic essays. Instructors may encourage students to use a variety of modes to create a text, where text is broadly defined. Students who create multimodal essays in a digital space (e.g., a website) may use a combination of images, video, animation, sound, or alphabetic text based on the rhetorical context and purpose for communicating. The intended distribution also affects rhetorical decisions for composing. For instance, in a blog distributed widely on the Internet, students may find they are limited to using their own pictures instead of images that require copyright permission.

Like traditional academic essays, multimodal texts also may have an introduction, body, and conclusion, although these elements may be more fluid in nature and arrangement. Any multimodal text can be expository or argumentative, with a thesis to drive the communication and suggest a logical progression. Students may think supportive research is necessary only with traditional academic essays, but multimodal essays require both sufficient research and choices of appropriate, effective media, as well as self-reflection about why such choices were made. Syntax and word choice still matter since writers typically use words in multimodal texts either through traditional alphabetic text that supplements other modes (e.g., text overlaying a video) or through oral narration (e.g., voice-over in a video or sound project). Essentially, elements that students learn through traditional academic essay writing also can be learned through multimodal text composing. Teaching multimodal academic texts, however, requires instructors to rethink the process and provide pedagogical reasons for using various media to expand—not replace—the written word.

Proposal

As described in this chapter and illustrated in chapter 8, proposals are persuasive, requiring writers to attempt moving the audience to action through a recommended solution. When students write a topic pitch to argue for and flesh out their subjects, the pitch is a proposal that provides a solution to an assignment. These types of proposals, which can be composed in various forms such as alphabetic outlines and videos, help students receive instructional feedback before developing the project. A brief version of a proposal is an *elevator pitch*, which helps students plan a project, determine its audience and purpose, and draft a proposal or outline concisely, making them hone the project's most important aspects.

Proposals also are common workplace projects often taught in writing classes. Although somewhat different from more academic persuasive arguments, proposals offer solutions to problems and arguments for considering them, which may include decreased budget costs, for example, and comparisons of other possible solutions to argue for the best one. In the workplace, proposals typically are written for either internal or external purposes. Internal proposals address a problem within the company. For instance, if an organization's restrooms need upgrading, the proposal might outline the problem and pitch the most cost-effective solution. External proposals, on the other hand, often are written to sell a company's products or services. In an engineering firm, a proposal might suggest the company for a specific job, outline why they are the best choice, and provide a budget projecting costs. As with persuasive argumentation generally, the proposal genre outlines a problem, describes a solution, and offers logical and other appeals to persuade readers to accept the proposal. Whether for academic or workplace purposes, proposals can be multimodally composed with graphics and pictures to supplement the text and illustrate the problem or solution (e.g., with the case of needing upgraded restrooms, a photograph of a broken sink is invaluable).

Report

Reports have many uses in both academic and workplace settings, and they can be delivered both alphabetically and multimodally. For example, reports convey expository information in science laboratory settings and have generic disciplinary qualities. Reports also are used in workplace settings with specific structure and feature requirements. Similarly, technical reports provide information about such issues as product requirements and consumer information and safety. Primarily expository in nature, reports may have argumentative functions when authors seek funding (e.g., grant requests) or changes to processes and procedures. Students typically learn report writing after first-year writing, in advanced and specialized courses, particularly professional and technical writing for business settings. Lab report writing may be taught—or expected without overt instruction—in science courses at any level.

Report writing typically engages alphabetic text. The ability to include other media (e.g., video, voice, music, still images, charts, and tables), however, potentially improves their readability and interest levels. Reports often are delivered both digitally and through interpersonal meetings in person and online using slideware. Authors benefit from learning the rhetorical nature of multiple mediums, allowing them to create reports that thoughtfully appeal to audiences' technical needs and reading strengths.

Letter and Email

Letters may seem passé, but they, along with emails, remain important formal and informal interpersonal alphabetic-text communications that often convey requests; they straddle the digital line for production and delivery. Both letters and emails may engage persuasive argumentation. Letters of application, for example, request employers to consider one's job or funding application thoughtfully and positively. Letters of request use persuasive strategies to ask for contract concessions, request refunds, or invite recipients to meet other needs. Letters of refusal may not engage argument, but they typically require exposition to explain how and why the refusal has come about. If the letter writer also wants to retain a relationship with the recipient, there may be elements of persuasion because the writer's ethos and skilled use of pathos may help reject the request while limiting the recipient's disappointment. Personal letters, many of which are still handwritten for interpersonal connection and etiquette purposes, may engage any of these written genres. Regarding digitality, the heart of letter writing is not especially changed by technology, yet new media can be used to great effect. Emailed and mailed letters use similar generic writing conventions.

Like traditional letters, email is an asynchronous communication genre, but it more efficiently targets many individuals, which changes its rhetorical features. Email is developed completely around digitality; as a genre, it has developed different shapes and formality levels depending on purpose. Email's digital immediacy means people can send and receive it within seconds, speeding up the communication and increasing the potential for interpersonal or technical error. Emails can be dashed off and sent so quickly that they may reveal unformed thinking, harsh language or tone, and embarrassing errors. Email is worthy of study because thoughtfully writing and responding to email not only is respectful communication but also may mean the difference between success and failure. The rhetorical requirements of audience, context, and purpose; the need for appropriate tone; and the mechanics of more formal texts remain important to teach students, who may not recognize there are rhetorical conventions in this seemingly no-rules genre. Although an email can be deleted, it often can be retrieved, making it an especially sensitive communication. Furthermore, email can tempt people to remain connected to their Internet devices when, years ago, they would have considered themselves out of network and unavailable. Email access at home has thus changed the concept of a workday and workspace, suggesting students should learn about developing appropriate communication boundaries (see ch. 10), as well as time and project management (see ch. 11).

Critical Review

The critical review genre allows students to be commentators, whether they review a restaurant, movie, or favorite place like a park or library. It engages evaluative criteria, as students argue for or against something being critiqued, and involves common, context-specific expectations readers have for such evaluations. For example, a movie review should not reveal too much plot, particularly regarding the climax, although it should address actors and their performance quality, creative elements (e.g., costumes, scenery, or animation), and thoughts about the director's work in comparison to other works. Alternatively, a restaurant review should consider food costs and quality, atmosphere, decor, and service, typically summarizing both site and experience.

Critical reviews themselves illustrate differences among mediums because they may appear as text-based news reviews, brief video reviews on the web, and smaller app reviews like those found on *Yelp*. The review genre easily shifts from text with or without images and from publication in print to a multimodal project published digitally.

Comic and Graphic Novel

When instructors think of multimodal project genres, they might not consider comic books and graphic novels (despite Scott McCloud's *Understanding Comics*), yet comics require both words and images for harmoniously creating meaning. Unlike an illustrated novel, where alphabetic text can stand alone and images merely enhance the imagination, comics require both image and text. To interpret comics, readers must read text, view images, and cognitively connect them. Although comics are sometimes dismissed as an inferior, children's genre, this reductive perspective fails to consider that comic books require an entirely different literacy skill set. Readers who have never read comics may have trouble reading a graphic novel for the first time because, as with other forms of multimodal literacy, comics require practice to learn and understand. Moreover, whereas comics were once left to magazine racks or specialty shops, comics and graphic novels are now found in bookstores, libraries, and respected literary and scholarly journals. Increasingly, comics are being used in postsecondary classrooms, including composition and cross-curricular courses.

Comics and graphic novels can be used to teach multimodal literacy because they can be created with a wide range of technologies. For example, comics can be created with nothing more than a pen or pencil and paper—less technology than a typed report. Therefore, where technology is limited or students lack access to home computers, comic creation can teach the rhetorical aspects of a project without overreliance on digitality. Yet comics and graphic novels can be created or enhanced using a variety of specialized computer programs. Published examples from both ends of the spectrum abound, showing students not only a range of possibilities within the genre, but also that professional writers do not need to use highly sophisticated computer technology to communicate.

Website and Webtext

Websites are another digital composing genre (as well as a site) entirely enabled by technology. The first page of a website is the home or landing page, which typically contains a site menu that leads readers to a series of embedded pages; the deeper the embedding, the narrower, potentially more specific, the topic found on that page. Although the landing page uses generic components like a site navigation map, the goal of the website itself can be expressed uniquely.

Websites engage alphabetic text in nonfiction expository and argumentative genres as well as fictional genres depending on the intended purpose. They are designed for hyperlinking, a quality of webtexts described above, and engaging multimodal applications. Composing for a website typically differs from writing a traditional academic essay because it calls for shorter, chunkier paragraphs that briefly cover an idea; deeper coverage may be accessed through hyperlinked pages or essays. These writing changes assist people in reading from the screen, but they also may have helped to decrease people's ability or desire to read lengthy paragraphs and texts, as we discuss in chapter 6.

Some postsecondary settings require students to have a website on which to post an academic portfolio, or compilation of their best work (see ch. 8). Presumably, in those institutions, students learn both the technical and rhetorical nature of website creation to best showcase themselves; however, there exist both commercial and free website software, including what-you-see-is-what-you-get (WYSIWYG) formats, that enable students to build their sites without having HTML, programming, or other technical knowledge. Because websites have a high Internet profile, students should be taught how to read and analyze them, design their own sites to meet a purpose and audience, and seek feedback regarding readability and access needs. Students must be taught how to address access issues (e.g., having audible and readable closed captioning, written transcripts, and textual descriptions for audio and visual material). Free website access checkers help writers make conscious accessibility choices.

Webtexts are another example of websites through which authors can make a scholarly argument within webtext space. *Kairos* is an example of a digital journal that publishes webtexts, differing from typical scholarly publications. They include internal hyperlinking, which takes readers to different nodes and provides different reading strategies and the ability for readers in effect to rewrite the text by reading it in individualized ways and with unique meanings. As Cheryl E. Ball indicates in "Show, Not Tell," when texts are designed using "multimodal elements and navigational strategies" (421), they become interactive and provide open access, giving authors opportunities to compose for various audiences and interact with those audiences differently. These webtexts, like websites, allow for interaction and varied navigational and reading strategies.

Blog and Vlog

Blogs are a particularly Internet-based, hence digitally developed, genre. The name *blog* has its origin in *weblog* or web-based journaling. A blog is a website—often premade in WYSIWYG software—in which writers create entries. These entries can be informal or formal and audience-focused or self-focused with no expectation of outside readers. Either way, blogs—typically in alphabetic text but often accompanied by images and music—are published pieces made available through the Internet, and writers should anticipate that someone else will read them. Vlogs are blogs in which the primary medium is video, posted as a stand-alone communication but sometimes shared through embedded links within text-based or image-rich blogs.

Blogs and vlogs are interesting composing genres because digitality enables people to publish who otherwise might never have their words read or images viewed by others, making them exceptionally important means of contemporary communication. Blogs and vlogs are taught as genres in some educational settings, and their rhetorical potential as nonfiction expository and argumentative essays is powerful. They have an equally powerful draw as a forum for short fiction, poetry, and particularly for personal narrative and memoir. Although the principles of genre that would guide such composition are not unlike those of other essays, many blogs and vlogs allow commenting, which means that prior to publishing, writers should compose rhetorically and polish carefully. The public nature of blogs and vlogs suggests that students should learn to write mature, thoughtful responses to both positive and negative feedback.

Social Media

Social media are Internet-based technologies that connect users in a virtual community, typically chosen based on one's personally constructed profile. These media use both alphabetic text (often in abbreviated forms) and multimedia. Increased access to smartphones means that many social media users include audio, video, photographs, and other still images when posting. That social media is based on the very act of being social, however, means that the definition, audience, and purpose change based on those who use it to communicate. Human interaction can be easy to see on networked pages such as *Facebook*, but what about podcasts? Although podcasts, which are audio-based and reminiscent of radio, are not traditionally considered social media, authors can post their podcasts online and ask for audience interaction, sometimes changing their topics or adding to their list of topics based on audience participation and input. Social media encourage comments and dialogue within web-based spaces that allow them to alter the texts they create. Does that mean an interactive podcast allowing such participation from the audience is considered social media? There is no easy answer, but even offering these variations for students will help them consider the ever-changing nature of genres and the rhetoricity of digitality (see DePew, "Preparing").

Typical social media venues include alphabetic texting through cell phone or app. Texting apps enable sharing of Internet links, links to files, emoji, and other visual and audio media. Popular apps share information, photos, and videos. All these social media forms engage informal, global communications and connect people interpersonally in ways not available prior to the end of the twentieth century. Although images often represent the sender's message, compact alphabetic text typically accompanies it. This informal, often terse writing style may engender misunderstanding due to rapid-fire communication, garnering agreement and approbation from like-thinking recipients, anger and vilification from those who disagree, and even professional repercussions.

More formal, professional networking apps include commercial, educational, and professional organization apps. People use such networking sites to increase their employment and service-providing reach, often asking relative strangers to link them into their circles. News and social networking services enable people to follow others with brief posts, so effective messages must be tightly composed; ineffective messages include poorly worded or insufficiently stated thoughts and ill-considered messages trolling others.

People also invite others to become respondents to their blogs, news articles, advice columns, and such, which means some people are writing and posting many words in public spaces daily, suggesting high literacy in these genres. Often, they can do so anonymously even if they must provide an email address. Although some of these response venues are moderated, as are many email lists, anonymous (and even fully identified) respondents can be cruel, snarky, and harsh in postings. The anonymity inherent in many posts seems to encourage people to express themselves in ways they might not in face-to-face settings. Students must learn rhetorically appropriate strategies for approaching these crucial register, tone, and audience issues because they can affect both personal and working relationships.

The vast importance of social media in current society strongly indicates students should learn more of the rhetoricity of these digital genres, their virtual permanence, and the importance of developing the Internet persona they want to represent themselves. Even though individual social media formats are ephemeral and apt to be supplanted by newer social media inventions, postings may be accessible for years to come. Exposition, argumentation, and—let us hope—dialogue tend to ground social media communications, yet many people would not consider themselves as explaining, arguing, or discussing a point. Social media use should be a composition subject in some form, and instructors should address the rhetorical nature and ethics of using social media, the development of an online persona, and the consequences of posting inflammatory language.

Video

Video is a challenging genre to define because there are many genres nested within it. Videos are often created based on the rhetorical situation in which they will be viewed. For instance, videos found on certain websites might illustrate how viewers can make a face mask, whereas the TED Talk–like genre might inform or persuade, normally with a one-person narrator talking to a live audience. Video has a long, evolutionary history from film, to music videos, to *YouTube*. In "What's Going On? Challenges and Opportunities for Social Media Use in the Writing Classroom," Stephanie Vie argues that *YouTube* is a social media space because participants can comment and interact with one another, often changing what they post or posting new videos in response to viewers' questions or prompting. Perhaps because there are genres within this genre, the video has become popular for classroom instruction, with creators using voice, sound, images, text, and even animation to communicate. Clearly there are subgenres within the genre, as well as different digital platforms for viewing, and all elements influence creators' rhetorical decisions.

Podcast

Podcasts, as mentioned above, reflect aural genres; speakers typically use voice as the primary communication mode although other sound elements, such as music, echoes, reverberations, and jingles, may indicate the narrator or interviewer's change of topics, guests, or interviews. Gunther Kress and Theo Van Leeuwen argue in *Multimodal Discourse* that inflection and tone can be considered variations in mode, even when authors just use voice to convey messages (66–85). Thus, podcasts are truly multimodal as narrators make use of both speech and other sound. In content, podcasts are much like traditional radio programs, hosting interviews about books, opinions, activities, and events. From an academic perspective, podcasts can include interviews with scholars or others with varying opinions, carrying a thesis and offering alternative viewpoints, stories, and interpretations. Podcasts have evolved past the radio interview, however, to a genre with nested genres—like video—making it tricky to define genre conventions. For instance, podcasts may be made by authors simply talking about their work without interaction from a host or alternative narrator, or they can be created to tell an entertaining or educational story that audiences consume while commuting. These variations make podcasts an excellent illustration of genre malleability and fluidity.

Video Game and Virtual Reality

Video games are inherently multimodal, as they use different modes to communicate with the audience, including sound and animation; arguably, within multiplayer games, the human characters in dialogue with one another can be interpreted as modes, as players can talk and interact with each other and make decisions based on this interaction. Students can observe the input of their peers, reflecting on the choices made by others in multiplayer games and considering how these actions influenced their own choices during the game. Video games also offer a chance to see multiple literacies at play at once (Alexander and Rhodes 129), and many classes have started incorporating them into the curriculum through learning exercises. Video games might not seem like an obvious choice for composing, yet as James Paul Gee and Elisabeth F. Hayes suggest in *Language and Learning in the Digital Age*, many of the games today come with software that allows the user to modify the game in some way. Such modifications include changing environments, achieving new levels, and creating entirely new games (86). Students also may have composition learning opportunities through game-making software. In addition, virtual reality games allow players to create their own lifelike environments, including the characters within their family, houses, and entire environments. Teachers may use virtual reality games to teach students about geography, immersing them in other parts of the world without leaving their couches; students also can use these tools to design their own tours of art museums and other interactive spaces. The choices and representations behind video games and virtual reality are rhetorical, and ignoring these as genres omits a world of possibilities for expanding students' literacies.

Conclusion

Alphabetic writing in academic settings is enhanced, not replaced, by multimodal composition. To teach them well, instructors like Professor Jackson need experience composing with both digital and traditional alphabetic features in all or most of these genres, which professional development can address. We argue that ignoring the digital educational revolution and its effect on students' composing education has serious implications for students' developing literacy skills. We also think preparing students for communicating digitally in the world outside academe will benefit both them and their educators.

4

Technologizing Composition Instruction

Professor Jackson has been talking with other writing faculty members. Their institution now requires all teachers to use newer teaching technologies, including the institution's learning management system, in all their courses. WPA Garcia is leading the writing program's charge, and she wants everyone to understand that the elements of good writing instruction remain the same regardless of modality and environment. Professor Jackson and his colleagues are a little concerned because they know writing courses use the learning management system and other technologies differently from other disciplinary courses. In part to address these concerns, WPA Garcia has scheduled a required professional development workshop to review newer composition technologies and their placement in various educational settings. The faculty members are skeptical but interested in these new developments.

As composing has changed in the digital era, by necessity, teaching has adapted, augmenting long-standing practices with new techniques and tools and adding new technologies. We stress, however, that teaching writing in any modality and environment is first about teaching writing well, which always requires engaging students with writing. This entire volume is developed to emphasize the basic elements of strong composition instruction. We add to these the necessary information to function competently in both on-site and online settings. The hallmarks of good writing instruction in the digital era are (1) teaching writing well, (2) teaching using digital affordances, and (3) teaching in any modality and environment—always with the aim of developing students' skills (see Hewett, "Grounding Principles" 66).

In this chapter, we briefly trace the evolution of technology use in the composition classroom to offer a foundation for understanding online education. We then describe contemporary teaching and learning settings as educational modalities and instructional environments; we also describe instructional tools instructors can use in these settings. Because instructional processes are intimately linked to the ways text, purpose, and genre have been digitalized, as well as to the specialized needs of online writing instruction (OWI) and online literacy instruction—and what we now see more holistically as writing in the digital era—this chapter is best read alongside chapters 3 and 5.

Evolution of Technology in Composition Classrooms

Although computers and digital media have offered various ways to provide instruction, technology has revolutionized the composition classroom as a learning environment, not only offering new ways for instructors to connect with students (and help them connect with each other) but also helping connect what students do outside the classroom with the classroom space.

The 1970s saw composition subspecialties emerging as educators sought to link the classroom with students' extracurricular lives and the technologies available to them. For example, some instructors were interested in how films might pair educationally with students' written work (Adams and Kline). Similarly, in the 1980s, the field of writing studies turned to computers as a new means of connecting with students, and an influx of articles and books discussed how to use this new technology educationally. John Bean's "Computerized Word-Processing as an Aid to Revision" highlights the value of computers for helping beginning writers learn to write and revise first drafts globally rather than locally through grammatical correctness. In "The Computer as Stylus and Audience," Colette Daiute expresses an early view about how computers could aid students in the writing process by allowing them to write without the lag time of handwriting and thus easing the revision process. The desire to integrate new technologies into the classroom enabled scholars and instructors to branch into subspecialties like computers and composition, OWI, and multimodal composing.

The evolution of personal computers led to a teaching revolution. In *Computers and the Teaching of Writing in American Higher Education*, Gail E. Hawisher, Paul LeBlanc, Charles Moran, and Cynthia L. Selfe discuss how the computer's promise for teaching led to the development of computer classrooms at postsecondary institutions that could afford such technologies. Given that digital networks can link students in working groups using text as their primary communication mode, the writing classroom took a new shape around the workshop model. Students began sitting at desktop computer stations, working with peers (one-to-many) and with their instructors (one-to-one) to craft and share writing (29). During this time, Hawisher, LeBlanc, Moran, and Selfe argue, the threat of current-traditional theory's focus on sentence-level correctness rather than overall cohesiveness was never far away, and scholars warned about the dangers of software such as spellcheckers and other aids helping students produce more polished, finished-looking products. In the ongoing effort to avoid returning to the current-traditional paradigm, Hawisher notes, multiple studies were conducted to see how much computers affected students' writing and whether the technology could make students better writers ("Research Update"). The late 1990s saw a growth in the scholarship of using computers in composition instruction, and the subspecialty of computers and composition developed. As often happens with composition subspecialties, however, the topics were not considered mainstream, evidenced in Selfe's "Technology and Literacy," in which Selfe states that instructors interested in using technology had been relegated to a siloed subgroup at conferences: "We assign them to a peculiar kind of professional isolation 'in their own separate world' of computer sessions and computer workshops and computers and writing conferences" (412). Meanwhile, other instructors simply ignored technology in the classroom. A glance at conference proposal submission forms and scheduled meetings reveals that professional groups still segment composition instructors overall from instructors who use computers to teach writing and from those who teach digital, or multimodal, composition. Selfe challenges educators to understand how technology is "inextricably linked to literacy and literacy education in this country" and urges them to question how computers are used in writing classrooms, which is crucial to enabling students to critically consider their own uses of composing technologies (414).

In *Multiliteracies for a Digital Age*, Stuart A. Selber expands on the need for computer literacy, urging instructors to help students learn to think "critically, contextually, and historically about the ways computer technologies are developed and used within our culture and how such use, in turn, intersects with writing and communication practices in the classroom" (9). Selber argues that students need to acquire three different kinds of computer literacies:

Functional literacy asks students to understand how computers operate as tools to aid learning (e.g., how to use software, how computers can help writing and research processes).

Critical literacy asks students to recognize and question the politics of computers (e.g., critically considering Internet content, examining how these artifacts contribute to or challenge societal structures, and considering what they can do to change the status quo).

Rhetorical literacy asks students to become producers of technology, considering the rhetorical context and medium for composing or communicating (e.g., effectively using computers, being informed questioners, and functioning as reflective agents of change).

Figure 4.1 depicts these literacies alongside the multiliteracies we outline in chapters 2 and 3, illustrating the breadth of the instructors' teaching and students' learning tasks.

Selber's argument reveals that technology itself must be taught in composition, engaging the functional, critical, and rhetorical natures of the means with which one composes. Hawisher and Selfe indicate in "Studying Literacy in Digital Contexts" that failing to acknowledge the

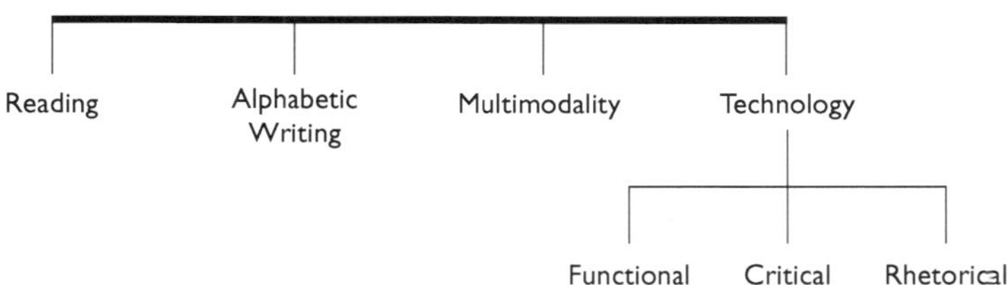

Figure 4.1. Twenty-first-century literacies.

roles that digital environments play "as people make meaning in their homes, in schools, and communities is, in sum, to be blind to the realities of contemporary communication" (188). Like Hawisher and Selfe, we argue that writing instructors can no longer ignore the digital nature of all contemporary composition, because digital communication technologies and new media texts permeate society. Over time, scholarship on using computers in writing classrooms became more sophisticated, and computers and composition emerged as a verifiable subdiscipline of composition and a permanent fixture in writing instruction, although often divided into the separate specialty areas of OWI and multimodal composition, which seldom interact. The concept of online literacy instruction was developed to help mitigate the silo effect of this common separation (rightly adding reading back to the mix), yet even that broader understanding separates online from on-site education and therefore does not fully recognize that all composition instruction is digital in one form or another.

To establish that recognition, what follows in the remainder of this chapter is an in-depth look at how technology is used as modalities for various teaching environments. Readers should learn the intricacies of these modalities before reading chapter 5, which outlines pedagogical strategies for digital composition that are important for teaching writing in all environments.

Digital Educational Modalities

One of Professor Jackson's first lessons about teaching writing in online settings is that when one learns to compose is connected to the time orientation of the learning environment. There are two primary educational modalities falling under time orientation: *synchronous* and *asynchronous*. These modalities are interpersonally communicative because they are the only two modalities through which people can interact. They encompass notions of presence and embodiment as well as time orientation. The term *modality* used here is not to be confused with the modes through which students can communicate when composing multimodally; instead, used here, *modality* represents when and how students and instructors can communicate across technology.

Synchronicity provides an immediate (*real-time*) or nearly immediate (*near-real-time*) time frame during which the participants communicate.

Interactions in on-site course settings are almost always synchronous, with the major exception of the feedback teachers provide to students' compositions. Teacher-student and student-student interactions are immediate, now-based, and real-time. One person talks, one listens, and—typically oral—conversation ensues. When composing activities occur in on-site classrooms, students work synchronously and simultaneously; when these activities occur outside the on-site classroom, they are asynchronous. Interactions in both the online portion of a hybrid course and a fully online course, as discussed below, may be synchronous or asynchronous.

Asynchronicity engages a time lag (*nonreal time*) between and among interactions, making it likely student interactions may occur at different times during a week, for example. Again, even on-site composition courses have asynchronous qualities: student writing typically is written, read, evaluated, and graded asynchronously with the instructor in one place and students in another. Writing studies educators, however, may think of asynchronous settings as Internet-based interactions where activities take place during different time frames. Students enroll in asynchronous courses for their promised (often overpromised) time flexibility. They want the freedom to sign in and work when they like, which may translate to some students (and instructors) believing the course requires less work. Fortunately, this freedom means asynchronous courses play brilliantly into the hands of writing instructors in online settings because such courses become highly focused on writing and reading—the very literacy goals educators seek.

Professor Jackson's entrée into new teaching technologies occurred just one term before the pandemic. So, when his school and others moved wholesale into what people were calling *remote education*, he knew there was a difference between emergency remote assignment and lesson delivery and the carefully considered use of synchronous and asynchronous digital classroom modalities. Educators and the public unfamiliar with online education may imagine that a wholesale migration of lessons and instruction—particularly through video—replicates the face-to-face classroom. They do not realize that online education has developed and argued for its own theories and best practices over the past thirty years. Therefore, they are unaware of the known benefits and strategies for using proven asynchronous strategies alongside synchronous video conferencing for excellent distance education. Regardless of the recent pandemic-prompted movement to online instruction, the terms people use to delineate distance-based instruction and even the definitions themselves are less important than what instructors consider the best ways to deliver their courses. Mistaken beliefs that video interactions replicate traditional classrooms and misunderstandings about asynchronous instruction hurt students and cause instructors to work overtime for little gain. We urge readers to continue to learn how to use a full range of digital technology for instruction and, most crucially, to consider access and who may be left behind if online courses are offered only synchronously with set, required meeting times. Although such synchronous "remote" courses may have seemed necessary during the COVID-19 pandemic, it is critical not to forget the benefits of asynchronicity for student access and learning.

Educational modality changes the instructional dynamic and affects both how a course is taught and the media used in it. Typically, a synchronous course is embodied through real-time voice and video if not in physical, colocated presence. An asynchronous course is differently embodied, typically occurring through text, which becomes the voice and presence of instructors and students. Prerecorded video content is asynchronous and viewable at any time; its nature can lend a stronger sense of embodiment and presence to asynchronous lessons. Access is an issue regarding synchronous and asynchronous courses, however. When students enroll in an asynchronous course, they do not expect to need to reshape their personal time schedules for synchronous meetings. Changing those expectations midstream can eliminate access for students who have set work schedules or live in geographically remote areas.

Although the value and usefulness of synchronous and asynchronous settings are debated, neither has been proved to be superior, and each has benefits for writing students and instructors. For example, students and instructors with writing disabilities may be served best in synchronous settings that require less interactive discussion writing, while students and instructors with auditory processing disorders may fare better in asynchronous settings that limit the need to process interactive vocalized speech (Hewett, "Characteristics" 270n5 and 273n7; see ch. 2). Since instructors often have little choice about the required modality of given courses and because each modality has its strengths, they should learn about both. Technologies evolve quickly, and there are both theoretical and practical guides based around how to create stimulating and engaging learning through both modalities. Additionally, many campus-based and Internet support resources exist to help instructors learn software that enable synchronicity and asynchronicity. Effective teaching through technology-enhanced educational modalities requires more than a functional understanding of the technology, however; it also requires targeted composition-based strategies. Unlike teaching in other disciplines, good writing instruction always means that rather than instructors merely providing information through text or lecture, they ask students to read and write alphabetic and multimodal texts and they read and offer ongoing instruction through those texts.

Composition Instructional Environments

The environments, or place settings, in which composition is taught also have changed dramatically with the digital technological revolution, as Professor Jackson is learning. Certainly, contemporary composition instruction relies a great deal on the setting in which teaching and learning occurs. Where students compose or learn to compose is about space orientation, and this orientation often is determined by administrative priorities regarding how many students can be seated in on-site classrooms at any one time; instructors may have different priorities in how they use these settings, as this chapter and chapter 5 illustrate. Here, we review five settings, most of which can make use of both synchronous and asynchronous modalities to some degree. In each setting, students may use different tools to complete meetings and writing work (e.g., computers, tablets, and other mobile devices), which often change the writing process and overall dynamic of the teaching model (see Hewett, "Fully Online").

On-Site Classroom with No Digital Technology Features

The traditional educational setting involves students attending class synchronously in on-site, colocated physical spaces. In the nineteenth century, composition classrooms often featured a proscenium theater arrangement with the instructor in front; students were staggered in rows to watch and hear the "sage on the stage," who dictated to diligent student notetakers. In 1970, Paolo Freire's *Pedagogy of the Oppressed* urged educators to change what he called the *banking model* of depositing information into students' minds without instructor or peer interaction (72). Freire's work instead encouraged educators to develop more inclusive, student-centered, problem-posing frameworks in which students seek knowledge outside the instructor. In the second half of the twentieth century, instructors began to prompt students to learn more actively by sharing ideas and cocreating knowledge. Such a social constructivist approach led to physically redesigning classrooms: moving desks for circle discussions, small-group meetings, and other more interpersonally friendly learning arrangements.

On-Site Classroom with Digital Technology–Enhanced Features

Traditional settings unaided by digital technology are becoming rarer, and on-site classrooms with technology-enhanced features increasingly are used. Such classrooms may have desks with receptacles for laptop or tablet access, computers for student use, projection technology, Wi-Fi, and instructor laptop stations. The physical space of the technology-enhanced, on-site classroom may pose challenges to instructors seeking collaborative learning spaces. When instructors in the latter part of the twentieth century began to adopt a critical, student-centered pedagogy, classroom seating was restyled into small circles or U shapes to enhance discussion, facilitated by easily movable chair desks. Instructors may have little control over classroom design, however, especially in proscenium auditoriums and predesigned computer labs. In fact, technology-enriched classrooms may hinder oral discussion, as computer stations with permanently placed screens may be configured in face-blocking rows, inadvertently recreating the banking model. Therefore, collaborative communication among students may occur digitally through an LMS, audio, video, or email. Given that most classrooms involve some type of facilitative technology, the primary differences in these environments seem to reside in how students write, communicate, and interact with technology and for what purposes.

Fully Online Classroom

Fully online settings evolved before and then again in response to the COVID-19 pandemic. Here, we describe the nature of such settings and then their two core categories: synchronous and asynchronous fully online classrooms.

Prior to fully online courses, correspondence courses existed for nearly two hundred years, with mail, film, cassettes, radio programs, and educational television connecting instructors and students. The Internet shifted the correspondence to email, and educators began using digital technology to extend education to computer-enhanced, Internet-based settings. Fully online classes were developed to address geographically distributed students' needs while helping institutional budgets use fewer resources to teach more courses, ostensibly leading to savings. The digital revolution has caused a massive growth of distance education students, with the National Center for Education Statistics indicating that in fall 2018, there were "6,932,074 students enrolled in any distance education courses at degree-granting postsecondary institutions" ("Fast Facts"). As this book goes to press, it is likely that most college students have taken at least one course using online technology, at least tripling the numbers cited in these data. These numbers undoubtedly will continue to increase even without such distinct focusing events as COVID-19. Fully online education is a popular alternative to traditional education settings among geographically distributed students who cannot access campus classes because of physical distancing restrictions, family responsibilities, work hours, disabilities, and location. Some campus-based students who could attend their writing courses on-site prefer online education. Alongside setting, the concept of what constitutes computer technology for education also has changed, with many students taking online courses through cell phones, requiring instructors to redesign courses to accommodate student demographics, learning styles, and technologies, all critical access issues.

Fully online courses are pedagogically—as well as administratively—defined by the lack of on-site meetings; this definition varies, however. For instance, an institution may require students to attend an on-site orientation before the course begins to familiarize themselves with course layout and content, preparing them for what to expect during the term;

or, it may require on-campus final exams. Principle 1's effective practice 1.2 in the Conference on College Composition and Communication's OWI position statement contextualizes this need: "students should receive mandatory technology orientation sessions in advance of the teaching term, which will assist with providing adequately accessible online writing courses" (CCCC, Committee 9). Nonetheless, such orientation need not occur on campus, and requiring students to visit campus to take exams or write timed essays obviates the value of fully online courses for geographically distributed students—and their instructors—and such courses cannot be considered fully online.

The two categories of fully online classrooms are synchronous (also called *remote*, a term that gained traction with the pandemic) and asynchronous. Which one is used depends on the institution's available software and philosophical approach to online work. Whether the fully online setting is synchronous or asynchronous, instructors meet students solely through computer mediation.

The recent pandemic has sent many courses to fully online settings, and in an apparent effort to replicate the real-time nature of on-site teaching and to make a more seamless transition, many of those courses have been synchronous. Synchronous courses use video technology to meet at a set time and allow for real-time interaction, but even in such courses, asynchronicity could be used for document distribution, writing assignment posting, grading, and extending discussions beyond synchronous formats. While synchronous courses can create a comfortable sense of familiarity for lecture and discussion, we worry that they may not be used as well for in-class writing and written chat. Additionally, access is a critical equity concern in that students may not be able to move work or other scheduled activities to attend classes at offered times, or they may lack Internet access and cameras for video meetings.

By definition, asynchronous courses do not have required real-time meetings. Instead, they tend to use LMSs to contain and distribute assignments, email, written discussions, and video lectures and for posting writing and grades. Nothing is done in real time, which means that instructors need to find ways to meet with students through chat or email, by phone, or through other options and that time-based issues need to be addressed overtly. While somewhat more challenging to develop, as we describe in chapter 5, asynchronous courses offer benefits in access for high-level literacy instruction given their intensive use of written text for communication.

Hybrid Classroom

Hybrid settings, like fully online settings, evolved before and in response to the pandemic. Here, we describe the nature of hybridity and then the two core categories of hybrid classrooms, which we identify as traditional *spatio-hybrid* and evolved *chrono-hybrid* classrooms (Warnock, "New Teaching Modality" and "'Spatio-hybrid'").

Hybrids involve using more than one environment or modality to teach writing. They can ease the transition between on-site and fully online courses, helping instructors learn to teach and explain writing constructs more clearly and succinctly—typically through writing. With the embodied, voice-based synchronous qualities of an on-site environment, instructors may have an easier experience navigating and teaching students to navigate the online elements of courses. Additionally, hybrids have advantages in enabling interpersonal connections in different ways and in using technologies to enhance face-to-face connection and learning. Without appropriate training and opportunities to practice developing a scaffolded course, however, instructors may misuse hybrid settings by, for example, using the online segments to require extra work not asked of students in on-site courses or failing to explain the reasoning for online work, leading students to sense they are doing busywork rather than essential composition practice. Hybrids, like fully online courses, require students to have time-management skills and a desire to connect to the course and to peers when outside the classroom (Snart, *Hybrid Learning*). Hybrids also require an institutional framework that supports ongoing curricular and professional development as well as evaluation to learn what is, indeed, successful and sustainable for that institution (Paull and Snart). Effective hybrid learning requires careful scaffolding and building on known effective approaches.

Before the pandemic, the most popular hybrid options were developed in spatio-hybrid settings (Warnock, "New Teaching Modality"). By nature, spatio-hybrid settings have both on-site and fully online features; instructors meet students some days on-site and other days through (usually) asynchronous digital tools, often through an LMS. Spatio-hybrid classes usually have required time for physical, colocated attendance, often one or two days a week, with other work completed outside class, often with digital technology. According to Jason Snart in "Hybrid and Fully Online OWI," although the definition of spatio-hybrid classes varies, "there will always be both a physical classroom component and an online component"; how the two settings are combined depends on instructor choices and institutional requirements (100). Low-residency (often graduate) courses may meet on-site only once or twice a term or in a summer institute, whereas the rest of the time the course meets fully online. Snart asserts that clear, consistent course meeting articulation is crucial to student and instructor satisfaction. Instructors may require students to participate in written discussion boards before attending class to talk through ideas or—to their disadvantage, we think—could require such asynchronous discussion while physically meeting in the computer-equipped classroom. Spatio-hybrid courses have become popular among students and administrators. Students say they like the personalized learning both in and outside the classroom (Martinez et al.). Teachers and students like the inherent flexibility of such courses, according to Joanna N. Paull and Snart in *Making Hybrids Work* (16). Administrators appreciate that hybrid courses spread out seat time, enabling them to meet budget demands while accommodating more students on-site.

The rush to emergency remote instruction in spring 2020 highlighted the blending of fully online synchronous and asynchronous modalities in a way that could be confusing. In his 2021 Global Society for Online Literacy Educators plenary talk "'Spatio-hybrid,' 'Chrono-hybrid,' 'Classroom,' 'Homework,' and Other Puzzling OLI Terms," Scott Warnock calls these courses chrono-hybrid courses, or "a different conception of hybrid course" (slide 15). While a traditional, spatio-hybrid course involves a difference of space, with students spending part of the course in an on-site classroom and part online, *chrono-hybrid* is a way of describing a course that "has scheduled synchronous videoconferencing some days and asynchronous activities other days" (Warnock, "New Teaching Modality Terms"). Time is the differentiator instead of place; one advantage to such a designation is that it becomes clear that students (and instructors) must work outside the synchronous session using the LMS or other technologies to interact, read, and write. This chrono-hybrid identifier clearly signals the work that occurs in these classes, enabling instructors, students, and administrators to make informed choices. Nonetheless, access remains a major issue for students who cannot meet synchronously at specific days and times as well as for those who have limited access to Internet and cameras for synchronous work.

The Flipped Approach to Digitalizing Courses

Flipped classrooms are not so much a teaching modality as an approach that engages modality and environment to pedagogical purpose, offering students a different type of interaction in both traditional and technology-enhanced settings. Flipped teaching approaches provide students with materials (e.g., readings) and instructors' lecture notes (often through the LMS) to preview prior to the class meeting. Students then can use course meetings to work individually and with peers; the instructor serves as guide, a just-in-time learning concept touted by adult learning theory (e.g., Andriotis; Knowles et al.) and redeveloped by numerous educators. This process differs from the traditional model of providing reading to be completed prior to an instructor-focused lecture in that the learning is more student-centered; students use class time to explore concepts more deeply and may develop their own learning activities to enhance their understanding. Flipped learning uses concepts of active learning, offering students more opportunities to teach themselves and each other through their interactions. When lectures and course material are moved online and viewed before class, classroom time can be rededicated to student-focused learning activities. For instance, instructors like Professor Jackson may create video lectures or short screencast videos of difficult concepts, requiring students to view them before class. One digital difference is that LMSs enable predeveloped materials to be presented online rather than through textbooks and instructor-provided handouts. They may not realize it, but composition instructors have been flipping classrooms for years, providing students with materials essential to developing early writing and asking them to write during in-class workshops.

Flipped classrooms have advantages and disadvantages, but advantages particularly abound for on-site classrooms. Instructors can save precious meeting time by explaining key concepts before an on-site or fully online synchronous discussion. They can do this similarly in asynchronous courses. For hybrid settings, instructors can continue a discussion after the in-class discussion occurs by using asynchronous discussion boards in the LMS, adding to students' learning before class so everyone can focus more on collaborative inquiry and learning during class. As Richard Mayer and Roxana Moreno conclude in "Nine Ways to Reduce Cognitive Load in Multimedia Learning," student learning is deepened through using such multimodal instructional tools as screencast videos to explain key concepts (43); therefore, building a website where instructors and students can find or make, post, and view educational videos is one flipping strategy to enhance learning. Of course, the opposite truth is that learning can be hindered if videos are poor in quality or if students do not understand the concepts explained in the video and remain unprepared to contribute to the discussion or other activity. In "Multimodal Instruction," Sherry Rankins-Robertson, Tiffany Bourelle, Andrew Bourelle, and David Fisher express that instructors need to create or use instructional tools that model multimodality, rhetorically considering how they use technology to facilitate learning, just as they ask students to consider how technology can be used to create multimodal texts. Whereas an on-site classroom does not require instructors to instruct through technology, the flipped model has become popular as one way to advance students' learning and to have students engage with digital tools in meaningful composition-focused ways.

Composition Instructional Technology

Finally, Professor Jackson needs to know the digital learning environment has made significant changes to the instructional technology, including software, available to composition teachers. In many cases, the same technologies through which faculty members teach are the ones through which students compose. We discuss composing tools in chapter 3, but overlaps exist between composing and instructional technologies. In this section, we move beyond traditional oral instruction in the on-site classroom and address types of software and apps often used as tools for contemporary writing instruction in both on-site and online settings. In doing so, we offer two specific cautions. First, it is important to be flexible. Students may have trouble with the learning modality, environment, or expectations for using the technologies. We recommend meeting them in the middle whenever possible. Second, we suggest doing a usability test of technologies after the first week and again at the end of the course. Consider what is and is not working for the students and what can be tweaked for the next course.

Mobile Technologies

The broad category of mobile technologies has implications for instructors and learners. As Jessica Schreyer writes about teaching with these technologies, "I wondered if meeting students where they were might encourage more engagement and interactivity in the writing and research process," especially since "more of them had access to a phone than a pencil at any given class session" (99). Yet many students' composing lives take place on these types of devices (see ch. 3). As such, OWI instructors must consider what their course content looks like on a phone. In an online writing course, not only must links and documents operate properly, as they must in all classes, but if the course is grounded in asynchronous discussions, instructors must consider what those conversations look like from the phone interface. Will it be like moving an on-site classroom into a very narrow hallway and hoping for a good conversation? Usability or user-centered testing is important in twenty-first-century composition classes, and it is even more important considering that many students will access online writing courses on their mobile devices. To get a more complete understanding, as part of early-term icebreakers and opening conversations, OWI instructors could inquire how their students are participating in the course; the answers will likely be of interest to everyone. Many students will be using mobile devices, mainly phones. Considerations range from pedagogy (e.g., how does one compose on a phone?) to platform. In considering the latter, in "OWI on the Go," Rochelle Rodrigo writes that as the use of such devices increases, "instructors—ideally through their institutions—will need to make students aware of whether or not their institution's LMS has a mobile application as well as on which mobile operating systems that application runs" (505). Most likely, instructors are undertrained in this area, and studies suggest that changing technologies or introducing new technologies may not present a smooth process for instructors. Based on a device-specific study on her campus, in "An Introduction to Multimodal Composition Theory and Practice," Claire Lutkewitte finds that "faculty [members] face many challenges trying to incorporate iPads [only one of many device types] into their pedagogy" (xi), including not having a mobile-friendly LMS.

Mobile devices have considerable potential both for composing and subject matter for compositions, and even if they did not, students would use them anyway. Assignments specifically designed for mobile devices can enhance their use (see Schreyer). Similarly, Lutkewitte suggests instructors can design activities "*about* mobile devices rather than those with them" ("Introduction" xii), which is a way to help students learn the rhetoric of technology. Such metawork asks students to think deeply about ways they interact, not just with the class but also with the world.

One temporal concern is worth mentioning. People who teach composition often have a love for the profession and teaching that can be consuming. Most LMSs have phone apps that instructors can use to establish a kind of perpetual connectivity to not only email but also texts, discussion board conversations, and other course dialogue. Instructors need to establish smart boundaries to avoid being a 24-7 connection, especially if they are teaching fully online, which we discuss in chapter 5.

Learning Management Systems

Educational institutions often provide an LMS (also known as a course management system, or CMS) platform that, having made the investment, its administrators expect all disciplines to use. Professor Jackson and his colleagues realize that LMSs typically have not been developed with writing instruction in mind and that these systems tend to have a top-down structure connecting teachers to students (DePew and Lettner-Rust); instructors must consciously and purposefully engage peer-to-peer and student-to-teacher interactions. Despite its problems, it is unhelpful to dismiss the LMS for writing-focused uses; it is an essential part of contemporary pedagogy (Salisbury), and even poorly designed LMSs are adaptable. Following Selber's concept of rhetorical literacy (*Multiliteracies*), instructors should consider the functional affordances of an LMS carefully, learning what works for aiding student retention and what tools might be limited, supplementing with context-appropriate instructional tools; we further discuss using these multimodal tools in the sections below. Overall, instructors need to build a robust course within the LMS that supports students' learning—one that can be utilized in any teaching environment.

Most LMS platforms tend to have similar functionality connected to often comparable features, despite a variety of options that vary in cost, and it behooves instructors to become familiar with their institution's LMS and its features and functions. Among common LMS elements are grade books, calendars, instruction delivery spaces, discussion boards, virtual workrooms, chat spaces, internal email, and document posting and retrieval spaces. Given that such features are available to all disciplines in just about any LMS, it is helpful to understand how their functions can be applied to writing instruction differently and advantageously. In other words, LMSs should not be used in writing courses as a dumping ground for materials when their affordances enable robust teaching opportunities.

Grade books and calendars have general applications across disciplines for keeping educational records of student progress and for keeping track of time and assignments. Instruction delivery spaces also have generalized uses for class messages (particularly on the course landing page) and for housing, organizing, and retrieving the course syllabus, readings, and assignments. These systems will accept video files and links, so creating educational videos and podcasts are becoming more popular among teachers who meet students' needs by varying learning media.

Discussion boards (also called *message boards* or *forums*) have the general function of enabling students to post and share answers, opinions, or discussions. In some content courses, students may be asked to respond to factual questions about readings or think about issues using discussion boards, but in composition courses, they may be asked to conduct interactive conversations about both content and writing process and product. Some students who have used an LMS prior to a writing course may never have used discussion forums at all. In writing courses, particularly hybrid and fully online ones, written discussion boards may substitute for the oral discussions that writing teachers otherwise would use to share ideas, respond to readings, and talk about writing processes and other issues connected to necessary critical thinking and composing skills. Because they are asynchronous, discussion board conversations are organized or threaded by subject, person, or date and time, making them potentially challenging to read and consistently interactive dialogue even harder to achieve; both usefully and unfortunately, people respond in their own time, a feature of asynchronicity that interferes with conversational immediacy. In a recent survey of student writers in online courses, discussion boards were noted as a particularly unpopular tool (Martinez et al.). In *Teaching Writing Online*, however, Warnock explains that discussion boards are a foundational part of a successful asynchronous course; with clear rules, teacher modeling, and innovative interpersonal approaches, the talk morphs into increased writing practice and meaningful dialogue (see ch. 5; also see Warnock, "Teaching").

Anecdotally, instructors as trainees in professional development settings have indicated they struggle sometimes to be genuine and pertinent when conversing through discussion boards; being in the student seat as trainees helpfully mirrors student experiences (Hewett and Ehmann, 10–14). These specialty uses of discussion boards are important, however, to working out ideas necessary for learners to compose as classmates instead of experiencing the writing course as solitary writers. Therefore, such uses also are important for students' getting to know one another and creating an association as a class, particularly in fully online courses (17–20). Strong uses of discussion boards are an art, as Warnock's work shows (*Teaching*; "Teaching"; Warnock and Gasiewski), and training should center on how to conduct satisfying dialogue in this forum, enabling teachers to analyze their successes and determine guiding principles that may work for students of various learning backgrounds and styles. Chapter 5 more fully engages how to create effective discussion boards when such training is not available.

Similarly, group work virtual rooms may be used differently in writing courses. Writing course group work may be centered around small-group idea sharing and, particularly, peer workshops, where individual student writing is shared, commented on, and discussed more broadly; team writing is also possible. Such work differs from other disciplinary group projects because, again, students need vocabulary to talk—asynchronously, in writing—about the writing; providing that vocabulary is another advantage of the writing-about-writing approach. Students also need an understanding of how to be helpful peer readers; the empowerment to provide genuine, yet kind, constructive feedback; and the confidence to do these in a semipublic forum in which the teacher can view and examine their progress at any time. Composition peer-group work in on-site groups is challenging and worthy of learning to do well.[1] Using an LMS makes the peer-group work more challenging because not only do students need to learn the necessary peer-group skills, as with discussion forums, but they also need to learn to write through alphabetic text as well as other modes and mediums, which means teachers need to be exceptionally good at their own instructional writing (Hewett, *Reading* part 3). Challenged student readers or students who elect not to read instructions or even their peers' work will not fare well in such forums.

Most LMSs have chat space available where students can talk individually to one another and teachers can chat with students. Such one-to-one talk usually is text-based, but oral and video options sometimes are available. Even when these options are not available in the LMS itself, free apps make such synchronous, face-based chat easily accessible. Chat can encompass all kinds of communication and business related to the class, but these spaces are especially nice for getting to know peers individually. For instructors, they are ideal spaces for reaching out to students one-on-one and for seeing them as individuals.

Rapport-building strategies using an LMS also include connecting with students through personal email, video updates, and personalized comments on assignments—all of which have the potential to lower attrition and improve grades (Glazier 13–14). Many LMSs have internal email, which also can provide the interpersonal touch needed to communicate outside of classes, although it likely is used more often for course business rather than interpersonal connection. LMS email can keep personal email accounts from being clogged with course concerns. That said, using such email usually requires logging in to the LMS, a feature that makes mobile devices attractive for addressing student concerns on the fly but that requires instructors to log in regularly. Since many students use mobile devices—possibly with the unreliable voice-to-text feature that scrambles words and drops punctuation—for such interactions, it is helpful for instructors and students to negotiate, and instructors to model, appropriate communication etiquette.

Finally, an LMS by its nature has document posting and retrieval spaces that enable delivery of papers and assignments and retrieval of read papers with feedback and grades. These features are particularly important for delivering materials for prestudy in flipped classrooms. Students whose teachers do not use the LMS for any other function besides grade posting likely will use this feature, so nearly everyone will be familiar with where and how to post and retrieve work. That said, such spaces can be used in composition courses for unique projects like student-to-teacher journal entries, where students respond to a journal prompt and teachers respond to the student's thoughts. It offers opportunities for ungraded writing to be reviewed and for one-on-one interactions to occur.

Multimodal Instructional Tools

Instructors should recognize the potential of the LMS and use the digital space to its fullest capacity, designing their courses with multimodality in mind, using sound bites or podcasts integrated into lessons or as readings, and asking students to consider message and medium at the same time. It is good practice to include projects from former students (with permission); these example assignments can be in an online gallery, but they should be used in specific lessons. If instructors do not have access to former students' projects, they should create the projects themselves. We discuss this idea in more detail in chapter 8 because creating projects from the student's perspective reveals the project's problem areas (which is especially important for online course settings, where instructors cannot field all questions at one time). Regardless of what tools are used in an online writing course, it is important to vary the technology (e.g., podcasts, sound bites, video, text) to model and teach multimodality and to attend to different learning styles by providing transcripts, captioning, image tagging, and privacy and accessibility statements for all software used.

To aid in the retention of key assignment concepts, instructors should use multimodal instructional tools that model multimodality for students. For example, creating videos to supplement each assignment helps when reviewing important aspects or tasks of the assignment while also explaining the different mediums available and why students might choose one over another. One easy method is to design a slideshow and then narrate a video of the slides. Using a script ensures minimal errors and provides a transcript for accessibility. Essentially, the instructor also should model how students might choose a topic, conduct a review, and then choose a medium. Since the instructional tools model multimodality concepts, instructors can creatively use pictures, music, animation, voice-over, and other modes. While instructors may not be exceptionally technologically savvy, students should experience well-composed multimodality models, even if that means finding predesigned, open-source videos from the Internet. Self-made multimodal instructional tools can be imperfect; in fact, instructors can integrate them into course discussions to ask students what could be done differently if they had more time or technological knowledge, also conveying their rhetorical choices.

This way, students recognize that their projects do not have to be perfect, keeping the focus on rhetorical and compositional considerations.

As we have illustrated, technology is an important aspect to consider when designing a course; instructors must consider how they will communicate with students and how students will communicate with one another. It takes time to build a truly multimodal course, so instructors must be aware of the preterm design time necessary to populate the LMS with complete course materials and media integrated throughout. Instructors should also leave enough time for students to learn to use technology to communicate. In online classrooms specifically, it is a good idea to interweave time for students to play with and become comfortable using technology to create projects. We suggest giving students low-stakes opportunities to use technology about halfway through a unit or project, enabling them to learn how software tools work and potentially to change tools if the learning curve is too steep. Media labs provide low-stakes ways for students to play with technology and are discussed in more detail in chapter 8.

Software Applications That Enhance Learning

Instructors can consider using various software applications to develop a robust, multimodal LMS and to enhance students' learning of course concepts.

Reading and Annotating Tools and Applications

Because so much reading takes place on screens, companies have developed ways to help people engage in literacy activities in such environments more effectively. A variety of reading and annotating applications can help students take notes on websites or (preferably accessible) PDFs, organizing and even sharing such notes. Students may use e-reader technologies, some of which offer similar capabilities.

Response Tools Software

Although some instructors may prefer offering feedback on hard copies, exchanging texts in digital environments means they can respond electronically, which can alter this significant component of a writing instructor's professional life considerably. Easy-to-use response tools and applications exist inside word processing programs, even cloud-based versions. They allow instructors to comment within texts and provide side annotations; teachers who have software-inking capabilities can use those tools to sustain that pen-on-paper feeling. There also are dozens of applications that can assist teachers in commenting and responding, including providing ways of storing libraries of comments. Some are built directly into LMSs.

Writing instructors have been using audio capabilities to provide feedback for decades, and such technologies are relatively accessible. Screen-capture applications allow teachers to display a student paper on-screen and annotate it while commenting with voice to provide a different response experience for both teachers and students. For some students, such audio- and video-based media may shift how well they understand instructional responses to their drafts (Mrkich and Sommers 4).

Rubric Software

Rubric software applications are not new, and teachers at all levels likely have worked with such programs for some time. Many LMSs have rubrics built into their assignment applications, and some rubric applications offer back-end capabilities that provide ways for instructors to chart performance across a whole class or cohort.

Bookmarking Applications

Students are not alone, of course, in being deluged with websites, links, and social media. Bookmarking applications are digital tools that help students (and instructors) keep track of the virtual pile, and some have capabilities that enable students to create digital spaces where they can share such materials easily and quickly with classmates.

Slideware Applications

Slideware applications offer composition instructors workspaces to develop instructional presentations. Slideware provides more than just a place for bulleted lists of sentences, perhaps its worst use, but is rather an adaptable space for images, figures, charts, and even embedded movies. Typically, a slide project will be accompanied by voice, which is one way to blend slides with video software. Access principles recommend "ALT tags, pre-recorded description of visual elements," and transcripts to accompany project delivery (Oswal and Hewett 142).

Video Composition Software

The use of video composition software, available in both free and low-cost options, enables instructors to develop their own television broadcasts, *YouTube* videos, and other video and movie clips for teaching students. These typically are easy to use and allow even technologically inexperienced people to edit and provide transcripts for access purposes. By combining video compositions with slideware, instructors can develop interesting lectures regarding course readings, assignments, and composing processes. They can demonstrate writing, a visual access approach we highly recommend, given that many students need help with the cognitive leap from the instruction they receive to their own writing (Hewett, *Reading* 60). Similarly, audio software for voice, music, and other sounds can be used to overlay text and slides, potentially increasing interest levels.

Website Development Software

Composition teachers may want to experiment with WYSIWYG website development software for showcasing and publishing teacher and student writing, particularly ePortfolios (see chs. 8, 9, and 12). Basic websites engage multimodal text, as well as alphabetic text-based, text-only, and hyperlinked text that enable audiences to make their own reading choices. Because multimodal text is important in a digital world, students should be able to create and post it for review and sharing, and WYSIWYG software offers a reasonable option. Instructors should be available as guides, but students often can figure out how to develop websites and blogs with such software on their own; they even can teach such skills to each other.

Digital Image and Graphics Software

The incorporation of software for digital images and graphic design may push the boundaries of what some time-challenged teachers can handle, but it can be ideal for those who thrill at working with visuals and thinking outside the box using rhetorical principles. Such software can be used for developing hand-drawn art, enhancing photographs, and creating basic computer graphics. If these are within the scope of the composition genres in the writing program's courses, they can be engaged for teaching students to create and analyze ideograms and ideographs, which are words, phrases, and symbols used rhetorically to represent ambiguous ideas. Another creative visual space, 3D software enables students to focus and dimensionalize their writing differently; for example, it teaches them attention to detail in instructions and how materiality can emphasize or demonstrate an argument or other composition aim.

Conclusion

Instructors need experience with the digital features of twenty-first-century composition technologies. Particularly, they benefit from teaching (and, preferably, learning) through a variety of activities and using and evaluating different composing technologies, modalities, environments, and media. Above all, they need a willingness to approach new technologies and learn to use them successfully in the classroom. Ultimately, these are the literacies—traditional and digital—through which contemporary writing teachers do their work. Instructors like Professor Jackson no longer have the luxury of determining whether they plan to teach with or through technology; ignoring the digitality of contemporary composition education hobbles students and may have serious implications for teachers' careers.

NOTE

1. For more on how to facilitate effective composition peer groups, see Gere; Spear; Hunzer.

5

Teaching Composition in Online Settings

Because of the COVID-19 pandemic, Professor Jackson, a veteran of on-site instruction, is being asked by WPA Garcia to teach through different modalities and environments, which might be synchronous, asynchronous, or even chrono-hybrid. Although Jackson knows effective practices for teaching writing in technologically enhanced on-site classrooms, he also knows that migrating his pedagogy wholesale online won't work. He's beginning to understand the nature of teaching with technology generally, but he's nervous about this change. How can he build and facilitate courses that encourage students' success in any modality and environment?

A fully online writing course or the online portion of a hybrid course offers some different instructional challenges and opportunities than those found in traditional on-site or technologically enhanced settings. Instructors need to pay special attention to modality (i.e., whether a course is synchronous or asynchronous) within these online environments to make the best uses of their affordances. While this chapter should be read in the context that all twenty-first-century writing instruction is digital, it focuses on the challenges and opportunities involved in teaching composition in online settings, which includes using the various modalities, environments, and technologies that we discuss in chapter 4. Because teaching and learning composition online are inextricably linked with how text, purpose, and genre have been digitalized as well as the technologizing of instructional processes, this chapter is best read alongside chapters 3 and 4. This chapter discusses how instructors like Professor Jackson can use teaching strategies and technological tools to enhance student success in online settings. Further, this chapter illustrates that the very environments in which *studenting* (Warnock and

Gasiewski) happens have changed in the digital era and offers ways to approach those changes to support student success.

Using Technology in Online Settings

In the introduction to this volume, we mention that educational changes like those encompassed in digitality often are coldly received. For example, some writing instructors have expressed concern about online education's potential to commercialize teaching and depersonalize writing instruction (Kanuka 92). More generally, some educators have worried that fully online writing courses (more so than hybrids) might hinder deep learning and might not have the general effectiveness and rigor of their on-site counterparts. Nonetheless, hundreds of studies have illustrated "no significant difference"—a term that emerged from Thomas L. Russell's book *The No Significant Difference Phenomenon*—in learning that takes place online instead of on-site (Arbaugh; Neuhauser; Sapp and Simon; Warnock, "Studies"). In fact, research suggests that the outcomes of fully online courses are highly dependent on instructor motivation, student participation, variances in learning styles, and instructor-student rapport (Glazier 13–14). For instance, Andrew Bourelle, Tiffany Bourelle, Anna Knutson, and Stephanie Spong's research on composition students' acquisition of multimodal literacies indicates such acquisition was higher in fully online courses than in on-site classes, and they speculate this result might be related to student interaction with highly trained instructors and tutors who worked in the online courses ("Sites" 64). Unfortunately, many WPAs and instructors do not have access to such training or the ability to provide adequate training for online settings, leading first-time (and even experienced) teachers of online writing instruction (OWI) to feel unprepared.

Although many aspects of interacting with student compositions and texts are similar regardless of modality and environment, a big question persists for some instructors, including Professor Jackson, who might ask, "Yes, but how do I *teach* in these environments?" As Scott Warnock states in his and Diana Gasiewski's *Writing Together*, "Even after an extensive, multiday workshop, some faculty still voice uncertainty about what the actual experience of an online writing course will be like" (x). Although we can claim with some assurance that immersion into the environment from both the teacher's and students' perspectives will help, instructors who have considerable expertise in on-site teaching may find themselves adrift when reconceiving their fundamental teaching activities for online settings and uncertain about how to create the kind of classroom culture and sense of community key to contemporary teaching (see ch. 10). To address this problem, we also recommend specific training in practices developed for OWI that make sense for any composition instruction in the digital era; reading chapter 4 of *Administering Writing Programs in the Twenty-First Century*, by Tiffany Bourelle, Beth L. Hewett, and Scott Warnock, our companion volume to this book, can guide WPAs in this effort.

Preparing to Teach in Online Settings

Instructors' experiences with preparing to teach writing courses online differ considerably depending on many factors, including the institution. Warnock and Adrienne Cassel indicate in "Teaching Writing Online" that instructors should ask certain questions to help better understand their teaching context: Who is responsible for setting up a course? Do course curricula, outcomes, or syllabi need to be approved, particularly for first-year writing courses that are part of a large program? Who coordinates course development, delivery, and support? What experiential training opportunities are available? (104–05). Instructors should consult their WPAs about these questions and other local resources including, perhaps, a campus teaching and learning support center. Instructors also should investigate their institutions' student demographics and learn about institutional supports for students. As Warnock and Cassel write, "In an ideal situation, the students will receive institution-level as well as instructor support, as recommended by OWI principle 10: 'Students should be prepared by the institution and their instructors for the unique technological and pedagogical components of OWI'" (104). These supports might include a virtual help desk focused on distance learners' technological needs.

We recognize some readers may have a core worry: Is teaching writing in online settings more difficult? Those moving rapidly from face-to-face settings into remote emergency instruction may have found themselves floundering, and they would benefit from supportive training and professional development to imagine how their online instruction can foster stronger student learning. Certainly with experience, flexibility, and a good nature about engaging the Internet and digital resources for learning, instructors need not find teaching writing online to be more difficult, although at first it might seem more time consuming. Nonetheless, we ask readers to keep this essential difference in mind: teaching literacy skills online—reading, alphabetic writing, and multimodal composing—requires an attention to language and linguistics beyond what is required for on-site instruction. Clarity of spoken and written instruction is critical, as is knowing when to use linguistically direct over indirect speech acts (Hewett, *Online Writing Conference* 116–21, 183–91). Such teaching is an educational adventure that hones one's instructional and communicative skills not only online but for on-site settings, too.

Unique Course Materials Development and Migration for Online Settings

Despite the sizable number of online composition courses taught at all levels and the surge of remote instruction in spring 2020, many instructors like Professor Jackson come to the teaching of writing through on-site instruction. Even veteran writing instructors in online settings may use an on-site paradigm in creating, conceptualizing, and teaching online. There is nothing wrong with this approach as a foundation for such courses. In fact, thinking about the process of teaching as a blend that includes migration (Warnock, *Teaching*) and a specifically online praxis (Hewett, *Online Writing Conference*) may help instructors put their best teaching face forward.

Writing instructors in online settings should allow the membrane between teaching modalities to be permeable, enabling movement in both directions. This concept was reflected well in the yin and yang principles articulated in the OWI position statement issued by the Conference on College Composition and Communication (CCCC):

> "OWI Principle 3: Appropriate composition teaching/learning strategies should be developed for the unique features of the online instructional environment" (CCCC, Committee 12).

> "OWI Principle 4: Appropriate onsite composition theories, pedagogies, and strategies should be migrated and adapted to the online instructional environment" (14).

These principles were reinforced by principle 3, tenets 4 and 5, in a document issued by the Global Society of Online Literacy Educators (GSOLE). The document says that teachers should migrate "appropriate" practices online while also seeking to apply "appropriate . . . theories to their [online literacy instruction] environment(s)." Essentially, the yin and yang principles of OWI and all the literacies involved concern learning when to apply on-site composing theories and strategies and when to engage theories and strategies developed specifically for online settings and for digital genres, composing and delivery technologies, and rhetorical processes that shift in digital settings.

To this end, OWI principle 4 indicates that while migration is a good foundation for many aspects of an online writing course, instructors should approach information, instructional materials, and other communications somewhat differently. For instance, information may be more readable when "chunked" in shorter paragraphs, as Robin Smith points out in *Conquering the Content*, and becomes more memorable yet through strategic use of repetition (64; see also Hewett, *Reading* 173, 217; Warnock, *Teaching* 56). Repetition helps build awareness of important ideas when reading on the screen, because screen reading often lacks spatial identifiers that enable memory. Additionally, key information should be provided in various media and places in the learning management system (LMS). For example, instructors might provide weekly notices on the course landing page as well as through specific announcements; they might offer a brief overview of assignments in the syllabus, extensive assignment details in an assignments folder, and reminders about assignments in weekly home page notices. We describe challenges of reading in online settings in chapter 6.

In fully online courses and the online portion of hybrid courses, as well as in any digital communications through the LMS, instructors should organize materials especially thoughtfully, down to such specifics as smart file-naming conventions that enable them to easily store, find, and retrieve course texts and digital student projects. This detail may sound trivial but instructors moving from paper-and-folder teaching to online teaching can find the shift abrupt; when materials are filed appropriately, digital searching on computer hard drives or in a cloud-based folder enables instructors to spend more time teaching. Therefore, to avoid receiving multiple essay files named "essay 1" with no student identifiers, it is wise to require students to name files using a simple, uniform file-naming convention, such as last name, first initial, essay number, and (if appropriate) draft number.

In approaching any course with online features—whether technologically enhanced, hybrid, or fully online courses—instructors should keep the technology simple. There are many different opinions about the effectiveness of popular LMSs for online composition, but those systems do most of the things that writing courses need: provide syllabi, notices, and assignments; share files between teacher and students; enable large- and small-group discussion and other interactions; and post comments, writing feedback, and grades. Simplicity is an accessibility issue, as more technologically challenging software may be too much for students whose main purpose is to improve their writing skills.

Content-Based versus Skill-Based Teaching

As we reiterate throughout this book, teaching is a complex activity, skill, art, and profession constituted by many possibilities, variables, and opportunities. Instructors certainly vary in their approaches, and part of the appeal of teaching is that it allows for individuality and creativity. Here, we attempt to reduce at least some of the complexity of teaching the online portion of any writing course by separating teaching into two broad areas: content-based courses and skill-based courses. Acknowledging these broad categorizations can help educators think about what they do and how they do it in online environments.

Content-based courses help students learn course material and are driven by the need for students to master a knowledge set, often with the goal of upwardly moving to the next knowledge level (e.g., Algebra I leads to Algebra II). These courses, which encourage objective test evaluation, constitute the bulk of higher education instruction through content-focused courses in both STEM and humanities fields. Skill-based courses, however, focus on developing abilities and competencies, including reading, alphabetic writing, multimodal composition, and speech literacies. Although such courses still may include content (e.g., courses using the writing-about-writing approach to composition and theme- and literature-based writing courses), skill-based courses often focus on developing a practice-driven skill or technique. Evaluation is subjective for such skills as rhetorical effectiveness, audience and purpose analysis, stylistic strategies, and reflective acuity. A general pedagogical goal is to help students individually develop their own effective composing process or method.

Because the majority of courses in higher education are content-based, much of the technological support for teaching naturally has focused on these types of courses. As online learning emerged to supplement on-site learning, that emphasis carried over into training and development materials and resources, creating a content-delivery focus for online learning environments and popular LMSs. This reality indicates one reason that the CCCC principles, the GSOLE tenets, and the resources like the books we cite are so necessary. The literacies we engage in this book are not content per se but a mindset, skill set, and operational philosophy of communication; they require overt attention for how to teach them effectively and how to encourage students to find their best learning stance for receiving and practicing them.

This content versus skills dichotomy is helpful to remember as instructors prepare online courses, since, at a minimum, most asynchronous online courses that will reside on an LMS must be completely outlined, fully fleshed out, and accessibly designed before the term begins; a clearly written syllabus and concurrent assignments require some depth that will remain relatively firm. Preparing a content course is different from preparing a writing course of any type. As the emergency remote teaching environment of the pandemic quickly revealed, even when the affordances of online learning are not fully understood, content courses can be moved to an LMS almost wholesale and rapidly (although not always aptly) from teaching and learning perspectives. Lectures delivered synchronously by recorded or live video will not look or feel much different from those delivered on-site without engaging such affordances as breakout rooms or written chat. Assignments, readings, discussions (when they actually occur online), and exams can be uploaded to an LMS—and many of those materials were already on LMSs whether the course was on-site or online. When teaching writing and other skill-based literacies, however, instructors cannot merely move oral, on-site lectures to the text-based presentation or the video of the online course, partly because lectures are not the pedagogy of choice. The content of a writing course tends to be students' actual drafted writing, their oral and written discussions about that writing, the instructor's responses to the writing, revisions, reflections, and portfolios for public (inside and outside the class) review. Course mastery is not dependent on moving through a sequence of material and passing a test, which is why many preprogrammed, commercial writing courses do not work. Instead, writing instruction largely is about developing ways "for students to interact with their writing, themselves, and each other" (Warnock and Cassel 104). Thus, teaching writing online is a process rather than a product of syllabus and assignments, and each writing course section differs from another.

Connectedness

Literacy courses like composition need a connectedness some might call "community" or "association." Helping students move beyond their comfort zones in both process and peer review requires an interpersonal connection between writer and audience, and writing instructors in online settings must find ways to safely generate this connectivity, not just among students but between themselves and students. This connectivity is a key challenge in teaching writing online, and it can be accomplished in many ways through the assignments and overall course experience. For example, instructors should make clear that they want to know each student individually, which might be accomplished through brief individual text or video chats and interactive student→instructor→student journal entries. Instructors can create early connection among students with well-structured small group activities that have clear instructions for interacting. When connection is done well, students will feel safer and be more trusting of one another and the instructor. We elaborate in chapter 10 on how to form a classroom community.

Using Technology in Composition Teaching and Learning Activities

Below we focus on how composition teaching and learning activities function and sometimes shift when technologies are used and when activities occur in online settings.

Reading

Because reading is a critical literacy for any composition course, we address it in most chapters of this book while also providing a full chapter about it (see ch. 6). Undoubtedly, reading activities present ongoing opportunities for functional literacy instruction in and beyond school. In contemporary composition classes, readings are provided both in print-based and digitally distributed alphabetic and multimodal texts. The media through which readings are offered may change how students approach them. Reading from a screen is done ubiquitously, but it may not be done well. Lacking tactile opportunities for touching (and dog-earing) a page, writing on it, and having other spatial, visual cues to where something appeared (e.g., right or left side of the page, mid-page), students may quickly read what can look and feel like endless words on the screen. Handy "find" or search features for digital alphabetic text both support readers in finding what they recall having read and encourage an approach less focused on what one reads on screen.

Unfortunately, reading often is given short shrift in composition courses of all types, with teachers assuming students will do it, leading to thin discussions, or that they will not do it, leading to excessive quizzing (although we think thoughtfully developed reading-based quizzing can support learning). Readings range from instructional material about composing to topical materials that provide information and content for writing assignments. Readings can enrich writing by providing contextual materials that deepen students' topical knowledge and understanding and offering details that help them reach informed opinions. Instructors may not want to hear this, but they need to teach and reinforce reading skills at all levels and in all courses, including how students should read what they are provided, why readings are assigned, how readings fit into the scaffolded course, and when and how to use readings as part of their (researched) writing.

Reading about writing (as well as about how to read better) may be challenging for some students to move from their cognition to writing action—what Hewett calls a cognitive leap (*Reading* 60)—suggesting that brief video lectures with demonstrations of reading strategies as well as brief reading assignments that overtly engage these reading strategies may work. One helpful approach is the writing-about-writing approach described by Doug Downs and Elizabeth Wardle, which takes what students read about writing (and reading) and makes it primary and secondary source materials as students "explore their own writing practices" (560). This approach enforces reading as a critical literacy worth attention. Chapter 6 outlines approaches to thinking about and teaching reading in the digital era, including useful reading assignments that support writing development.

Lectures

Lectures are a time-honored (and equally dishonored) teaching approach; although they are contested, in this section we offer technological strategies to incorporate lectures in more active-learning ways regardless of teaching environment. As we discuss, the traditional lecture format is the sage-on-the-stage teaching approach that Paolo Freire decried. Lectures traditionally have enabled teachers to share information to everyone and, for the teacher, to do it once. It is efficient (for the teacher), inexpensive (for the institution), and requires focused attention (from the student). Those who have auditory processing disorders, however, may have difficulty cognitively leaping from hearing to comprehension for note-taking. Additionally, lectures are a passive learning activity that do not work well for composition instruction because they engender little student participation or writing practice. The process movement taught educators that lecture is less helpful than actual writing practice, thus opening the door for teacher demonstration or modeling, peer response groups, and writing workshops. Nonetheless, lectures remain popular among writing teachers, as a walk down many college hallways verifies and the massive open online course (MOOC) movement in the 2010s shows. Large-class online lectures, MOOCs have thousands of enrolled students who receive little to no teacher or peer feedback. Their form might be attractive when education is forced into online settings without preparation for individualized courses (see Monske and Blair's *Writing and Composing*), although we think these are not writing instruction friendly.[1] Lectures arguably retain value (educators also encounter them in professional development and meetings), but they are not the most effective writing instruction option.

In on-site and fully online, synchronous video-enhanced teaching settings, lectures are delivered orally, requiring students to listen and take notes. In computing terms, students in a synchronous classroom may get a verbal download from the teacher as hard drive, what Freire describes as "banking" (72). Video-based lectures may be made with visual enhancement from slideware and images that connect the words symbolically and may include accompanying notes. We suggest a more active learning approach to lecturing, where fully online instructors with synchronous capabilities engage students by sharing their screens, asking questions, and describing their understanding. Screen sharing easily enables writing in real time for students, which Robert Zoellner recommends in "Talk-Write" as a way to teach students about how experienced writers begin, stop, think, and revise. Other effective practices include the following:

Use web conferencing software that offers transcription as text for students with accessibility challenges.

Ask students to comment and ask questions using the chat features enabled in most video meeting software.

Have a student moderate the chat, and rotate this responsibility. Provide the chat transcript to students who miss class that day.

Provide the chat (and the option of not using video) for students who do not want to or cannot participate in video conferencing.

In lieu of lecturing, have students lead presentations or discussions, but first model them. Ask students to prepare a summary of readings and questions to lead the class on a specific day.

In a fully online asynchronous setting, where lectures might seem necessary, students either download the information as a reading or view it from video. These lectures can be more active when combined with immediate writing exercises (or mini-lessons) posted to the teacher after reading or viewing or linked to class-wide small peer group or student-to-teacher discussions. It is helpful to ask them to have at least one question prepared based on the asynchronous work they did before class. Students also can be asked to create short video lectures that reveal understanding and assist peers. It is helpful to encourage student connections whether through a writers' lounge space in the LMS or through social media spaces that are private to the class.

Discussion

In process-based instruction, strategies for doing writing typically supersede talking about it, whereas in writing about writing, talking, reading, and writing about writing as a subject and a process become central. Regardless of epistemology, both oral and text-based discussions, or conversations, have a place, and they can be a powerful means to enable students to think critically about writing content and process. Discussions can prime the pump for writing, enable students to practice making a case, and reveal students' knowledge for further research and reflection. Additionally, discussions offer students opportunities to talk and express their thinking about what they have read, heard, or done—essentially enabling them to prewrite aloud. Well-executed discussions are democratic in allowing all students a chance for self-expression, and they level the ground between teacher and students. Writing instructors often share that they do not get the results they want, however. Some students will not participate, and a few others may say too much. Instructors may do nearly all the talking, both asking and answering the questions themselves. Therefore, we consider discussions especially deeply.

When discussions fail, the problem often is a lack of conversation structure. Structure is a key point for both oral (i.e., on-site or online synchronous) and text-based (i.e., online, asynchronous discussion board) settings. When instructors supply processes and goals (including stating that silences while students think are natural), stay quiet, and teach students how to discuss successfully, students can contribute more fully and confidently to the conversation. In on-site settings, teacher silence can encourage students to talk; in online—especially asynchronous—settings, however, teacher silence can seem like abandonment of presence. Teaching students how to have powerful conversations online often means more teacher participation, guidance, and even prodding (Warnock, *Teaching* 75 and "Teaching" 163–64)—at least in the beginning. Students can learn to lead their own discussions by talking and actively listening. Discussions always should have an overtly stated value to the development of writing skills and acquisition of course outcomes in a composition course, however, and students need to be told what that value is (Martinez et al.). Students should know how important it is to participate in the discussion, whether and how it will be graded, and—especially for asynchronous discussions—the amount of expected participation and when it is to be completed. Students also should know how the discussion relates to their current writing assignments and processes. In any setting, strong discussion prompts make or break the discussion, which means they should include variations of open-ended questions and issues directly relevant to composition course content and related reading, thinking, or composing skills. Practice makes the process more intuitive. Additionally, depending on how the students are doing, teachers can remain silent or enter whole-class or small-group conversations to participate fully or just to help spur the talk. Overall, a metadiscussion with students about how to discuss and participate in the course environment helps to set the tone.

A wealth of discussion structures can be found in educational materials geared to K–12, postsecondary, and professional workshop audiences. In many cases, these discussion structures work at all ages; even simple structures apply well to increasingly more complex questions. Examples include teacher- or student-developed questions using stasis theory or Rogerian (e.g., *I heard you say . . .*) approaches, three-to-five-minute writing in response to a question prior to talking, think-write-pair-share exercises, Socratic seminars, and snowball structures. Example 5.1 presents sample directions for a think-write-pair-share exercise.

Example 5.1. Sample Directions for a Think-Write-Pair-Share Exercise

This brief exercise provides students with an opportunity to write and then to talk with each other, helping them think through a specific problem, challenge, or issue. The instructor can start class with this exercise or introduce it when students seem stuck:

- Ask a question or pose a problem stemming from a pertinent reading or writing assignment.

- Give students no more than one to two minutes to think about it.

- Ask them to write out their ideas, giving them only one to two minutes to write. Writing extends the typical think-pair-share strategy to solidify thinking through the sensory process of handwriting (in an on-site course) or keyboarding (in a fully online course or an online segment of a hybrid course).

- Instruct on-site students to pair up and talk about what they thought and wrote, limiting time to three to four minutes. Likewise, online students can pair up in asynchronous groups of two using the LMS or meeting through text-based chat or a video conference in a small-group setting.

- Ask the pair to report to the class. Ask someone to be a scribe on a whiteboard or other recording device. On-site, these steps can be accomplished seamlessly; online, they may require opening a new class discussion space for pairs to report.

These opportunities for thinking, writing, and pairing should be brief to encourage students to remain actively engaged and to respond quickly. Reporting to the class through a sharing opportunity helps students learn collaboratively. The activity can be repeated with the same pairing, a new pairing, or the addition of a third person. Likewise, the activity can lead to a broader conversation or turned into a writing opportunity.

In synchronous online classes, instructors still may draw on their talents and skills as moderators, but they must accommodate the layer of complexity introduced in the digital meeting space. As Kimberly Fahle writes in *Collaboration and Community in Undergraduate Writing Synchronous Video Courses (SVCs)*, "SVCs, while sharing features of both f2f [face-to-face] and asynchronous instruction, are a unique learning and teaching modality which require specific training for both faculty and students" (223). Fahle offers a simple but powerful example of the uniqueness of synchronous courses; in the online meeting software she studied, the last person to speak remains on screen in a large frame, which made students uncomfortable and became a disincentive for them to speak (191). Video does introduce some embodiedness and connectivity, yet it also forces participants to hear and see themselves, which can make close communication awkward for some students. It can be mitigated somewhat when instructors acknowledge this awkwardness and normalize the experience. Some students might not want others to see their home surroundings or their personal appearance, however, leading them to request to use only the audio feature; such an accommodation may require measures to ensure students actually are attending classes (e.g., calling on them occasionally or asking them a private question in the chat box), but it is reasonable and does not require an explanation to the class. To enhance community building, instructors can ask students who do not feel comfortable being on camera to add a picture of themselves; this replacement of a blank screen with a picture allows students to get a sense of who else is in the class and who is speaking at any given time.

Setting up discussion activities in synchronous settings is somewhat straightforward, as these discussions would seem to imitate in-person conversations. In fact, video meeting software often enables small-group discussions through breakout rooms. Some effective practices include the following:

Choose several comments students have posted in the LMS discussion boards to highlight during the synchronous discussion and to get students talking (but never make someone talk if they don't want to). This strategy works especially well in chrono-hybrid settings.

Use smaller breakout groups to facilitate discussion, providing structured questions for students; alternatively, have students think of questions for the day. Breakout rooms will always take a little longer to get rolling, so plan accordingly.

Assign roles in the breakout rooms. Someone should be a scribe taking notes, and someone else should be the reporter who will report on the breakout group to the main class. Although all students should be encouraged to talk, these roles will ensure discussion starts rolling again as an entire class. This strategy also works well in writing workshops, which we discuss below.

Save time after the breakouts to come together as an entire class to review what was said in the rooms.

Using discussion boards for asynchronous discussions can present some challenges, as students must learn how to use discussion forums to meet expected outcomes and instructional needs for writing courses since these expectations and needs differ from those of other content or disciplinary courses. For example, one simply cannot assume students will be familiar with the vocabulary necessary for writing (or talking) about a reading, essay, or webtext, nor can one assume students will know how and when to respond—on their own time, asynchronously—to sustain meaningful discussion. The result can be a disconnected discussion, where some students try to talk, some never really engage, and others don't participate until an hour before the discussion is closed for grading purposes. However, when guided by appropriate pedagogy, these asynchronous, conversational writing environments can present strong learning opportunities for students (see Seward; Warnock and Gasiewski). Without such guidance, discussions may not be extended and students will seldom return to them for any sort of continued dialogue. Instructors should provide examples of strong and weak discussions with some commentary to show what is expected and why. Some of these issues can be overcome by teaching and repeating only two or three discussion structures throughout the term instead of changing them for every discussion.

In asynchronous classes, building conversation is not about orality, faces, and immediate discomfort. Students can use asynchronous apps or tools, including common technologies like discussion or message boards, to have conversations that have distinct differences from on-site conversations: everything occurs through writing, is time-delayed, and is posted individually per students' choice or availability. On the plus side, students talk by writing, and they can think about what they have written before posting. They write more when they discuss textually, which is one reason June Griffin and Deborah Minter express that the literacy load is heavier in such courses. They can respond to peers and instructors, even if they are shy speakers. They may learn, as Leslie Blair says in "Teaching Composition Online," about "the biases, opinions, and preconceived notions of their audience, which allows them to practice writing for the addressee" (sec. 2, par. 5). On the minus side, students may not respond to peers or may do so insufficiently. They may choose to enter the conversation at the last minute, making themselves onlookers at best or unheard at worst. Their writing skills may cause a sort of talker's block that minimizes their presence. Moderating and developing text-based, asynchronous conversations can feel alien to instructors like Professor Jackson who are used to teaching on-site. Typically, however, LMSs have a discussion tool, making setting up a message board easy; again, campus IT or instructional support can help.

Like all teaching, moderating fruitful online discussions is a kind of art. Warnock and Gasiewski's *Writing Together* describes a variety of different prompts, adapted here, to help students talk asynchronously online (52):

> Have a conversation about assigned texts or media.
>
> Write to learn about specific content (in writing about writing, that content is often writing itself).
>
> Work on or explore a specific aspect of writing.
>
> Generate ideas.
>
> Metawrite about your own texts and writing, about texts composed by other students, and about the course itself.
>
> Argue or debate.

Reflect.

Develop course community with other students or meet one another individually.

Work through course logistics.

Example 5.2 illustrates a discussion board prompt that encourages productive interaction between students and promotes effective practices for composing. The prompt asks students to generate ideas about their writing process and can be implemented at any point during a project.

Example 5.2. Sample Prompt for a Discussion Board

Now that you have turned in a rough draft of your project, walk us through your writing process so that the class can see the differences in how we all work. Consider the following questions as you write a solid paragraph (around 250 to three hundred words) that shares your process from brainstorming through the publishing phase. Your response does not have to be written; instead, you can use the tools we have been playing with during this project to convey your process multimodally. Either way, share your posts within this discussion board space. If you choose a multimodal option, keep your video or audio clip under five minutes in length (also post the transcription or use captioning so all of us can follow along). Below these questions, I have posted more guidance for your responses to peers.

- How do you start a project? For example, do you take time to think first before you put ideas to the page? Do you listen to music while you consider ideas or while you draft?

- What does the brainstorming process look like for you? For example, do you create a mind map? Do you use dictation to take notes? Do you freewrite?

- How do you organize your project? For example, do you write an outline? Do you create a rough draft with notes to return to later? Do you write your introduction last?

- How do you decide what medium to compose in? At what point in the composing process do you reach this decision? How much time do you devote to learning the technology?

- What do you do when you receive peer, tutor, or instructor feedback? How do you incorporate revisions?

- Once you're finished with drafting, what are your next steps before you turn in the project to your instructor?

After you have posted a response to the prompt, respond to two of your peers. How is your writing process similar and how does it differ from theirs? When composing future projects, what will you try that your peers do? What processes of yours might your peers benefit from trying? Feel free to include links to different resources that might help during any of the phases (mind-map generators, storyboard templates, etc.). Make sure your two responses are around 250 to three hundred words each.

After posting the prompt, the instructor also should consider writing the first post to model the exercise and must check in frequently during the student-response cycle to keep the conversation moving. Moderating asynchronous conversations requires practice, but George Collison, Bonnie Elbaum, Sarah Haavind, and Robert Tinker's *Facilitating Online Learning* provides great models. To support their goal of helping to "clarify and extend the thinking of other people" (72), they offer six personas, summarized here, that instructors can inhabit as moderators (106–17):

> The *generative guide* provides a range of positions indicating different questioning avenues students might pursue in a conversation.
>
> The *conceptual facilitator* resembles a lecturer but addresses elements of student posts and course readings beyond content delivery.
>
> The *reflective guide* restates elements of posts.
>
> The *personal muse* offers an individual perspective about issues in the conversation.
>
> The *mediator* attempts to determine participants' sometimes unstated reasons for posts and reactions, while not avoiding the productive argument tension that can sometimes occur on discussions.
>
> The *role player* assumes the persona or voice of different characters.

These personas provide ways for instructors to act in different roles as discussion moderators and can inspire new thinking (and playfulness) in students. Although moderating can be key to the success of online discussions, instructors should find a good balance; students will feel their absence, but they also will notice overzealous instructors who cut into every student conversation.

Discussion environments will be different for students as well. Many, of course, will be well accustomed to communicating through text in asynchronous situations, but far fewer will have done so for professional or academic reasons. Instructors should provide clear guidelines about these conversations in early-term materials; Warnock and Gasiewski provide an example of such guidelines in the prechapter of *Writing Together*

(1–13). Students need support to help them through the conversations in their composition courses, and guidelines should include straightforward rules about discussion board etiquette along with instructive modeling. Whereas some instructors may use the discussion board only as a kind of open drop box, others will require highly interactive written conversations, making rules for communication critical.

Conference

Individual conferences are a common teaching strategy in which instructors meet writers one-on-one, traditionally in person. This individual time provides teachers precious opportunities for listening respectfully to how students are faring in the course. Moreover, it offers students a rare opportunity for immediate, in-process instructor feedback, which is ideal for encouraging students to take drafts to the next stage of competence or completion, shaping them through questions and fostering student ownership of the text. In "The Listening Eye," Donald Murray refers to this crucial work as a "strange, exposed kind of teaching, one to one" in which he operates from the desire "to stay out of their way and to not interfere with their learning" (14). No doubt, individual writing conferences retain such power for instructors who do, indeed, allow students room to grow but who also guide them in discovering fruitful directions. Although appropriation of student text for the purposes of moving a draft in a new direction that the teacher wants generally is rejected (Brannon and Knoblauch 157), instructor modeling through writing for and with students is a useful conferencing process, enabling students to imitate instructional feedback in ways that Lev S. Vygotsky might approve of (see also Spear). Teachers are the ideal mentors to demonstrate in-the-moment strategies for achieving one's composing goals. Showing students how two or three different revision choices can redirect the message is one way to avoid appropriating student text (Hewett, *Online Writing Conference* 83–84 and *Reading* 95–96).

Murray expresses that he successfully uses conferences to inspire the kind of revision he had hoped for when he had diligently corrected and remarked on student writing textually ("Listening Eye"). Yet few teachers will have administrative leeway to substitute individualized conferences as their sole teaching method. In compressed six- or eight-week classes, time to teach one-on-one becomes still more precious. A common practice in on-site, hybrid, and fully online asynchronous writing courses is to cancel one or two class meetings to conference with students. In fully online asynchronous courses, however, canceling classes for one-on-one meetings is functionally impossible because there are no group meeting sessions to cancel. Spontaneous and planned voice or chat conferences remain helpful, however. Instructors can use polls or assessment surveys in the beginning of the semester to learn when students are doing schoolwork and can then plan to be online during those times to provide individualized help. The assessment survey should ask what challenges students have (e.g., time, access to technology or the Internet). Appointments should be made using a time structure that also suits the instructor's needs. Conferencing also can be implemented through student-to-instructor journaling and as emailed outreach to individual students to check in or connect with things they said in class. Finally, instructors should understand that conferences per se occur every time teachers respond to student writing (Hewett, *Online Writing Conference*). Particularly in asynchronous settings, audio, audio-video, and text-based feedback and mini-lessons shape instructional response and should provide students with explicit, limited global and local feedback that can help them move their drafts forward.

Writing Workshop

Writing workshops allow students to do learning-centered work (typically writing-focused) in the classroom during dedicated class time, with the instructor available for conversation, demonstration, and modeling. Whether students work as individuals or in groups, the processes of reading, writing, and talking about writing engage three of their five senses (i.e., sight, touch, and hearing with reading aloud), which engages cognition differently from writing quietly and solitarily. Student-led workshops use various formats, including round robin, partners, small groups, and five-minute "dating." They enable students to work on their writing individually or collectively by, for example, brainstorming, analyzing audiences, and testing reasons that support a claim. Sometimes students complain they find workshops unhelpful or boring. *Boring* may mean "I don't know what to do or how to do it" or "I didn't understand the assignment, so I didn't do anything." Workshops give teachers important one-on-one time for connecting with and supporting such students, and they do not require canceling class meetings, as conferences often do. When students are free to talk with peers in their groups, they can help each other with writer's block or in learning to translate their thinking to text. When students take control under the instructor's supervision, they gain skills and confidence that can enable them to work better in groups outside the classroom. Allowing students to determine the point of the workshop and to set the ground rules encourages them to take responsibility for their learning and provides instructors time to visit with individuals or groups to observe, ask questions, and offer guidance and deserved praise.

In-person workshops can occur in various settings. On-site, the ability to move desks or chairs creates privacy and, when needed, interpersonal connection among students in pairs or groups. In fully online synchronous settings, small-group video workshops enable instructors to participate and observe (or not), staying out of the way as students write, talk, and share. Students can record their meetings if they need to demonstrate that they met or show what they did. Text-based workshops in asynchronous settings are somewhat more complicated. When students are in asynchronous workshops to write, discuss readings, or help each other brainstorm, they must write to talk; therefore, they need writing-based vocabulary that helps them make meaningful statements and ask useful questions. Such language can come from assignment prompts or worksheets that provide the steps they must follow, possibly preceded by a brief teaching video that models what is needed. Additionally, asynchronous workshops are challenging because some students assigned to the group may never log in to participate, and the work doesn't occur in real time, so students may never get in sync, such that the first participants to do the work may not get their own writing addressed in time for the next writing steps. We talk about how to mitigate some of these challenges in chapter 9. Finally, asking students— particularly any fully online ones—to provide a brief written or video-based after-action report can meet the same goal with the advantage of their not feeling watched over by the instructor and the bonus of their practicing expository composition that explains how the group managed the workshop.

Peer Review

As we describe in chapter 4, there are many ways to conduct peer reviews online. Some of these approaches may work better within technologically enhanced on-site, fully online, and hybrid settings because these writing-intensive environments engage thinking and reviewing processes that are connected closely to student writing. Peer review may happen in structured asynchronous discussion boards or in synchronous environments where students are assigned partners and placed in small groups that work in real time. Peer review does not mean, however, that a teacher simply pairs students up and asks them to read each other's papers, nor does its use imply teachers have no responsibility for in-process review and feedback. Instructors must create clear guidelines, letting students know what is expected of them and modeling those expectations. Therefore, focusing students on the task and offering ways to connect to peers as readers and writers include writing specific prompts for the review, providing well-defined directions about how to engage the review and provide responses, and requesting reviewer reflections on the review processes. Good peer review requires structure, prompts, hands-on participation, and instructor involvement.

In our experiences, some across-the-disciplines faculty members resist student peer review activities because they believe it just does not work. Certainly, unless they are taught differently, peers may be too focused on low-end concerns, such as grammar and punctuation, which are problematic if they are suggesting the wrong fixes. In addition, they may not have developed the skills to know what needs revising in their own papers and may therefore have difficulty seeing it in others' writing. Successful peer review depends on how instructors set up the activity, as we detail in chapter 9.

Group Work

Social process theory encourages group work as a way to enable collaborative learning, yet engaging students well in distributed group work is challenging on-site and in synchronous settings. Does group work suffer still more in asynchronous online courses? The definitive answer is sometimes it does. The lack of face-to-face interaction can enable students to abdicate responsibility in group projects. Still, good assignment and course design coupled with smart technology use can facilitate smooth, effective group and collaborative work in asynchronous courses. As research has reinforced (Handayani), the instructor's role should be more prominent in online course group projects than it is in similar on-site projects. Instructors cannot simply set up online meeting spaces and let students go; they must provide clear benchmarks in the design of collaborative assignments and teach students how to conduct productive meetings that include clear, goal-driven responsibilities and deliverables. Despite obstacles, online collaborative projects certainly prepare students for working environments outside school.

Peer collaboration is a learning-and-doing strategy that is becoming more important as digitality connects people globally. Planning, writing, and revising in group or team settings are important academic skills, but they are even more vital workplace skills. Peer collaboration is a cooperative venture that in composition courses consists of such tasks as brainstorming; discussion planning; peer review workshops for feedback; and collaborative research, writing, revision, and editing. Traditional and technologically enhanced on-site classrooms and hybrid and fully online settings are all useful sites for collaborative work that includes both feedback about others' compositions and direct revision into the documents. Even though both experienced and novice writers naturally may be reticent about changing others' texts to demonstrate revision ideas (Robidoux and Hewett 409–10), learning to do so respectfully is a dynamic cooperative skill important to both work and school settings. To co-opt, in this sense, is a positive notion of working together toward a common goal. Writing teams can learn to manage both the composing and interactive skills necessary for success. Digital, cloud-based document sharing software particularly support these skills because students can write together at a distance while conversing by phone or video.

Anecdotally, one problem instructors express about peer collaboration regards a complete lack of collaboration. When students do not know how to work together toward an assignment goal, such as a discussion or a writing workshop, they may default to individual work. For peer collaboration to work, students need to be empowered in what they compose and in their group roles (e.g., feedback providers or direct revision editors). Empowerment stems from having choices, genuine goals, and clear processes. For example, in *Team Writing*, Joanna Wolfe outlines three processes for writing together: *face-to-face*, meaning talking and writing together simultaneously, which can be done on-site or at a distance through collaborative software; *divided*, where each team member has a different writing task and the pieces are combined to form a whole; and *layered*, which invites one peer to write first, another to continue and refine the writing, a third to build on what had been written and revised earlier, and so on (6–9). Students need to learn about such processes and find the right one for different tasks and settings because they likely will be using such writing strategies in upper-level group assignments and workplace writing projects. They also need to learn how to accomplish such goals in online settings.

Wolfe offers reasons for assigning peer collaboration and for its challenges. Project management, for example, requires a project manager, division of tasks, task schedules, meeting agendas and minutes, reminder strategies like email and text, and after-action reporting (13–24). Writing together requires students to learn approaches for constructive conflict (51–55), revising with and for others—complete with overtly stated ground rules and an understanding of the software or other technologies to be used (59–78)—and how to listen to one another (80–100). Most writers benefit from learning to listen to one another without too much ego tied to the composition; certainly, listening with a physical ear is different from listening through reading someone else's written feedback or examining direct revisions and understanding what compelled those revision choices (see ch. 9 regarding reflection and reading and using feedback). Ultimately, peer collaboration is as much about communication as it is about composing skills, processes, and tools. As such, although how it looks varies depending on how much technology is engaged, peer collaboration has similar qualities in on-site and online settings.

Presentations

In many courses, students must present to their classmates, and this need remains important online. Students benefit not only from presentation opportunities but also from learning to be active, engaged audience members. Many online meeting apps provide platforms for gathering virtually, and they include ways to facilitate presentations along with question and answer sessions. In synchronous online courses, presentations are a natural extension of the online class meeting experience and provide opportunities to flip the classroom. In asynchronous courses, presentations offer similar benefits, but they must engage video technology differently, using narration software or screen-capturing the content to record and present the material to classmates and the instructor asynchronously.

Instructors offer presentations whenever they lecture orally or through slideshow or video. Such presentations typically are designed to teach something about writing, a theme, or other course-based knowledge or skill. Asking students to create presentations that teach their peers what they know engages them in deeper attention to the work at hand. Public presentations can be challenging, however, for shy students and those with certain learning and physical challenges. Presentations need not be out of reach, however, as they do not always require all composers to be in front of classmates; sometimes presentations can be given for the instructor alone. Group presentations can enable some to take a less public role by writing some of the material, constructing multimodal parts of the project, or even organizing and directing the process for the group.

Teacher Modeling

Most skills that people learn involve some kind of modeling—from how to start and stop (e.g., skiing, skateboarding) to efficient uses of tools (e.g., photography, bicycle repair) to techniques (e.g., piano playing, computer programming). Modeling skills is an effective means for teaching new abilities and strategies; Quintilian popularized the use of modeling and imitation for teaching writing and oratory (*Institutio* 225–47; II. iv.1–42). Writing is a skill as well as an art, and students benefit from watching teachers demonstrate how to do it (Zoellner). Students need not only to see examples of strong and weak compositions to comprehend the features of a desirable product but also to observe writers as they handwrite (or keyboard), hesitate over words, delete, begin again, become confident, get lost in thought, change tracks, and revise, revise, revise. One of the best ways to communicate such writing behaviors is to show students how instructors themselves compose. Instructor modeling can be as non-technical as writing a paragraph spontaneously on a whiteboard, or it can be as technologically complex as using a projector to demonstrate early brainstorming in a zero draft; show an in-progress preliminary draft;

and, later, present a revised draft with word-processed tracked changes and embedded personal comments to share one's reasoning with students. When digitality is fully integrated into the course, instructors can use multimodal demonstrations through software to produce a simple project, which helps students gain the confidence to try new technology themselves.

Tutoring

Tutoring is a well-established learning method through which either peer or professional coaches (e.g., consultants, mentors, and tutors) provide feedback and writing guidance. Students benefit from tutoring when they have questions or want feedback about their compositions outside of what they may get from teachers (which, as we have said, can be all too minimal) and peers, whether trained or not. Educational institutions and composition programs often offer tutoring using in-class peer mentors, instructional assistants, and writing fellows; out-of-class assistance usually comes from writing or other literacy learning centers. Typically, the goal is to guide student writing rather than fix it and to support developing writers rather than the writing itself (North, "Idea" 435).

Ideally, tutors should be able to help students with reading skills and strategies; brainstorming through revision, researching, summarizing, paraphrasing, and quoting; and understanding and making choices about how to use feedback in revision. In this digital era, we argue, tutors should be able to help students with technology-based decisions, such as what mediums to use for composing. Online tutoring is gaining popularity among students and tutors for its ability to reach those who cannot or will not attend on-site tutoring sessions. Online writing tutors are available at many institutions, providing students with support in the same learning environment and modality as their instruction.[2] Digitality enables tutors to work with writers textually and asynchronously, by voice over the phone synchronously, and by voice and video both asynchronously and synchronously. Text-based tutoring feedback benefits from being structured as both global and local, with a personalized mini-lesson relative to the student's own writing (Hewett, *Online Writing Conference* 107–11); such structuring can help students in understanding and making use of any feedback. Chapter 11 considers writing center and other support integration into composition programs.

Self-Teaching

Self-teaching occurs anytime students write outside classroom settings, read and follow explicit instructions, and experiment with words and ideas. Through practice and trial and error, students learn by doing, which is always connected to self-taught skills and processes. Students teach themselves by checking out topics in *Wikipedia* before doing deeper research, sifting through general information on the Internet, learning to use software through a video, and making choices among the learning strategies and topics teachers offer. Because the web itself is grounded in self-teaching concepts, moving online may provide instructors opportunities to encourage such behaviors. It can still be a jarring experience on-site when an instructor asks a question and students offer answers from quick search engine hunts, but online, students are connected directly to their computers during the course. This continual Internet connection alleviates the longtime teaching challenge of comprehensiveness: teachers do not need to know it all. Students who seek information can reasonably be expected to find it. Information differs from knowledge. To look up reliable information by means of text or video, therefore, is an appropriate digital-era learning approach, one we use frequently. Reading and composing alphabetically and multimodally then enable students to assimilate mere information into owned knowledge. We consider self-teaching as a teaching and learning strategy precisely because instructors may forget how much work students must do on their own when figuring out how to apply what they are taught to composing processes or products. Unfairly, we think, many students have to do a great deal more self-teaching in asynchronous online settings because too many teachers think their own work is merely to set up and deliver the course through an LMS and grade papers, abandoning additional educational or interpersonal connections and opportunities for individualized instruction (Glazier 5–6, 13–14; Martinez et al.; see also ch. 4). Whether the actions occur on-site or online and with or without digital technology, students must teach themselves how to make cognitive leaps from instruction to action and from thinking to composing (Hewett, *Reading* 60). As such, instructors can help students with self-teaching by overtly acknowledging it. They can explain when students should try out several strategies, make choices about which to use, and adapt them to their own learning and composing processes; such explanation is a way of addressing students' possible misconception that education is about having their heads filled with information to regurgitate, undigested.

Considering the Student

The above strategies are intended to aid student success, but it also is imperative that instructors consider how the content and design of a course will be received and what challenge students might face. Warnock and Gasiewski say that "students need a more prominent place in our conversations" (239). They cite Mary Louise Pratt, who in "Arts of the Contact Zone" states, "Teacher-pupil language, for example, tends to be described almost entirely from the point of view of the instructor and teaching, not from the point of view of pupils and pupiling (the word doesn't even exist, though the thing certainly does)" (Pratt 38; Warnock and Gasiewski xiii). From *pupiling*, they developed the word *studenting* to prompt change in the dialogue driving much of education, which tends to exclude or overlook most of the people involved in it: students! By providing a close-up view of the student-author, Gasiewski's experience through an entire term in an online writing course, the authors aim to help instructors see what an online course looks like from the student side. Many LMSs provide instructors with options for viewing and experiencing the course interface from a student's perspective, and instructors should make use of them if for no other reason than to check accessibility. Instructors also should peer review each other's courses to see what they look like—placing themselves in both the teacher and student seats—primarily because what instructors and students see are often quite different, particularly in terms of access. Whenever possible, instructors should talk to students about their studenting experience. This process includes asking students to evaluate the course mid-stream and at the end of the term to find out what they learned that they did not expect to learn, what they wanted to learn that they did not learn, how they helped themselves as learners, and how instructors helped (or failed to help) them learn. Students may reveal important information, such as time and project management inefficiencies, that instructors can then teach about to generate better outcomes (see ch. 10).

Student Access Needs

As with all the pedagogical advice, guidance, and discussion in this book, our overarching concept of access means instructors should design their courses with all their students in mind. This means that students' physical, learning, and emotional challenges and differences as well as their cultural and linguistic backgrounds require attention. Although a functional online class should help students succeed in ways suggested in this chapter, instructors also should consider students' access needs and offer helpful accommodations. Technological equality and high-speed wireless Internet access are considered standards for education, for example, but these are not universal to all students or even all instructors. Although it might seem antiquated, a hardwired Internet connection can be a good workaround for consistent video access. Some students cannot take online courses from their homes because they do not have computers, let alone Internet access, leading them to use public libraries for school; if libraries are closed—because of pandemic quarantine requirements, for example—these students may need to drop out. Instructors therefore need to know something about their students' technology access and their subsequent educational experiences with technology. Similarly, instructors should be aware of the institution's outreach to students of various cultural, economic, age, and other backgrounds in order to be inclusive in their online instruction, as we discuss throughout this book. Physical challenges and learning differences also should be considered from an access standpoint because they may require varied due dates, additional tutoring or personal assistants, or such assistive devices as screen readers and text-to-speech readers of which instructors should be aware. Online instructors also should be aware of and able to address the reading and writing instructional concerns of students with varied home languages and dialects. Multilingual learners, for another example, may experience different challenges in fully online courses—both synchronous and asynchronous—in which writing is the dominant, if not sole, means of interaction. Writing-centered courses can help multilingual students because they will have many opportunities to hone their literacy practices, but, as Susan Miller-Cochran states, "In an online writing course with multilingual writers, language is an additional element that can create distance in the course because instructors often use language to build bridges intended to span the other gaps in transactional distance" (305). The instructor's use of course language and writing will need to be careful, specific, and thoughtfully planned with this in mind.

Certainly, some multilingual students will be glad to write instead of speaking to represent themselves in class, but others may resent how their identities are elided online or may be even more self-conscious about their writing. Discussing online writing center tutoring, Sarah Rilling describes two "areas of concern" in meeting multilingual students' needs online: error correction and increased interactivity, or "meeting second language writer expectations and creating autonomous learners" (359). Error may arise as a distinct problem when the course is solely text-based, as Paul Matsuda and Michelle Cox express in "Reading an ESL Writer's Text": "Readers with little or no experience in working with ESL writers may be drawn to surface-level errors and differences that they see as problematic" (3–4). Hypercorrecting for small errors shuts down the open dialogue that can make an online writing course so rich. Rilling discusses issues of plagiarism, which can be quite different for multilingual students, who may have different educational and cultural experiences with citing and referencing texts. Again, in the broader spirit of access, composition instructors need to examine how elements of their courses ranging from syllabi to assignments to conversation platforms operate for multilingual students.

Grading in Online Settings

Students will need regular and timely feedback throughout the course and during different stages of drafting their final projects. Some instructors are surprised at how similar grading in an online writing course is to grading in an on-site course. Major projects and papers can be evaluated and graded using the same criteria, facilitated by text-based or video-based feedback; these criteria provide consistency and redundancy that students need to succeed. In other words, when the same rubric is throughout a course, students will know what to expect regarding goals or outcomes for all of the course projects. Online students, especially with asynchronous, text-based courses, will be doing more composing and writing work because all their interactions are written, and instructors will have to decide whether and how that work should be evaluated. Although instructors need not grade every informal assignment and discussion, evaluations may include weekly writing grades or portfolios that encompass—and engage reflections on—students' written work in the course. Students may need feedback on informal assignments, and we encourage instructors to check in with students to let them express these needs (a usability or midsemester survey may help achieve these insights). Evaluation also may encourage participation because students who otherwise might think they can hide by not "talking" by means of their writing will be attuned to grades as a reward.

Teaching Multimodality in Online Settings

In this book, we define composition as including both alphabetic-text-based writing and multimodal compositions. Students in any environment may feel trepidation when creating multimodal projects, and this fear may be heightened in online environments. Although many aspects of interacting with student compositions and texts in online settings are similar regardless of modality, for many instructors, like Professor Jackson, a question persists: How do I teach assignments in these environments so that students can acquire multimodal literacies? Even instructors who are supremely comfortable and demonstrate considerable expertise in online instruction may find themselves adrift when reconceiving fundamental activities for teaching multimodal composition online (see K. Blair 478). In our experiences, instructors with no background in teaching multimodality may feel especially intimidated by teaching multimodality online; instructors who are new to online teaching but not to multimodality may feel the same trepidation. There are fundamental differences in teaching a multimodal pedagogy online rather than on-site, and here we outline effective practices in designing and teaching an online multimodal composition class. Although these practices can be used in on-site classes, especially hybrid and technologically enhanced classes incorporating a supplemental LMS, the recommendations we provide are aimed at designing a fully online class emphasizing multimodal composition.

As we describe in chapter 8, instructors should design assignments that give students choices within parameters. This means that instead of a "you choose the medium" assignment with no guidance, instructors should give online students at least two choices of mediums, carefully describing the parameters of each. In online settings particularly, giving students too many choices is unnecessarily daunting, as is giving them a free-for-all assignment without any guidance about appropriate composing mediums. Remember that everything instructors teach in online settings will be through text, voice, and video. Such instruction should be particularly clear because often students cannot or will not ask questions at the time of need.

For instance, for an assignment in which students review their favorite place, an assignment we describe in more detail in chapter 8, students could choose between two mediums, perhaps composing a blog or a travel agency newsletter. The parameters of each also must be established: Length in word count, pages, or time? Number of images or other media? Although these parameters should be discussed on discussion boards or in other course communications, they also should be repeated in the assignment sheet. Another effective practice is to create emphasis through font changes like bolding or highlighting, signaling words to which students should pay close attention, especially regarding the fact that they are working on a multimodal project; otherwise, students may miss that fact and submit a text-only document.

Reflection in Online Settings

Finally, reflection is crucial to understanding what students are learning and the challenges they may be facing, no matter the environment; interestingly, the online classroom can encourage more robust reflection. A powerful aspect of online writing courses is that every discussion board, journal, or communication with peers and instructors can be used as an archive of student learning. Instructors should ask students to reflect throughout the term about their learning of course concepts or outcomes for each project, looking back at earlier learning and quoting themselves, their peers, or the instructor as evidence to support their argument for learning. These reflections can be posted in discussion boards, allowing students to see and comment on each other's reflections, and instructors can use this space to guide students to review the archive for more material. Students (and instructors) should be able to clearly see where they need more guidance toward learning specific outcomes. This learning evidence is clearly demonstrated and readily available through archived material, so much so that we recommend incorporating a robust LMS in both traditional and technologically enhanced on-site classes, especially when teaching multimodality and using portfolios as the culminating multimodal course project.

Conclusion

Teaching composition online can offer new challenges, but such teaching also creates opportunities for instructors, as Professor Jackson is learning—and for students. Teachers should remember that regardless of modality, they are still instructors with valuable knowledge and skills. The CCCC's OWI yin and yang principles 3 and 4—reinforced by GSOLE's principle 3, tenets 4 and 5—demonstrate well that, whereas "[a]ppropriate . . . strategies should be developed for the unique features of the online instructional environment," instructors should be mindful of ways their teaching practices should be "migrated and adapted to the online instructional environment" (CCCC, Committee 12, 14). Technology should not—and need not—upend or supplant literacy instructors' professional approaches, but it will require some adaptation and critical thinking. Indeed, because *all* instructional writing and literacy practices are digital in some way, technologies and online settings offer instructors tremendous opportunities to rethink and revolutionize how they teach, including expanding the composing repertoire to multimodal projects.

NOTES

1. Massive open online educational experiences (MOOEEs) as reconceived through the OWI principles may offer better access and less confusion about

huge, nonintimate writing courses for instructors and students (Hewett and Warnock "Writing MOOEEs?").

2. The CCCC's principle 13 states that "OWI students should be provided support components through online/digital media as a primary resource; they should have access to onsite support components as a secondary set of resources" (CCCC, Committee 3).

6

Reading Composition

Professor Jackson sees his students struggle with—or fail to do—the reading he requires for writing courses. But they're constantly reading something online: texts, *Twitter* feeds, blog posts, and Internet newsfeeds. Is it that they just don't want to read his assignments, or can't they? He knows reading is part of the programmatic outcomes, but wasn't all that work done in elementary school? Why should he take precious time away from writing instruction to focus on reading? Like many of his colleagues, Professor Jackson doesn't realize that reading is a more essential literacy than ever in the digital era. He needs to teach reading to teach writing well.

Reading has never been more important than now, in the digital era. Without reading there is no composition; computing has not lessened the literacy load but rather increased it (Griffin and Minter). Yet, despite the explicit endorsement of such documents as the Council of Writing Program Administrators' "WPA Outcomes Statement"; *Standards for the English Language Arts*, by the International Reading Association and the National Council of Teachers of English (*Standards*); and the Conference on College Composition and Communication's "Students' Right to Their Own Language," reading praxis continues to get short shrift in writing program curricula. We think this problem emerges not from educators' ignorance of reading's importance or disdain for reading as an "elementary" skill; instead, we think most educators do not know how to encourage deepened reading skills appropriate to digital needs. This chapter addresses theoretical concerns about reading in the digital era and provides practical strategies for helping students consciously connect reading to writing in various educational settings and genres.

The Need for Critical Media Literacy

Undoubtedly, reading in the digital era requires media literacy, which is the critical consumption of texts, alphabetic and multimodal, necessitating deeply analytical skills. Critical media literacy asks students to question the validity of what they read and to research topics extensively and fairly before they add to the conversation. Henry Jenkins, Joshua Green, and Sam Ford in *Spreadable Media* name *spreadable media* as media that "refers to the potential—both technical and cultural—for audiences to share content for their own purposes, sometimes with the permission of rights holders, sometimes against their wishes" (3). In such an era, students need to consider what they read and what they create in terms of who might see and share the media. With media being produced—sometimes poorly—for quick consumption and circulation, students need to question what they consume and analyze it logically in terms of the author's argument; in turn, they need to consider their own ethos and how it is established and represented in the media they create and share.

Hypertext exemplifies that digital media reading has changed how people read and comprehend information. Where reading was once a linear, left-to-right, and whole-page and next-page process, hypertextuality enables users to read in various sequences: from left to right, top to bottom, in Z or F configurations, or by clicking to various pages, or nodes, and reading information more uniquely. There is no single process or right way to read webtexts, which are ubiquitous. Even in academic publications, the linear, text-based scholarly article is no longer the predetermined standard. Journals like *Kairos* require authors to develop web pages within webtexts that are nonlinear and multimodal; each page stands alone and enables users to read the material at any entry point and through any sequence. Just like a traditional website, the webtext itself must have a thesis or overarching theme; readers can freely click to different pages, however, and have a one-off experience. Much of the reading outside school that students encounter daily is hypertextual and multimodal. Yet, webtext reading processes can be so unique to individual readers that they can link to various pages, never to return to the landing or home page again. Whereas such mobility may not seem like a problem, as students click from page to page, they may lose the initial idea or thesis, and they may not make clear connections to what they are reading. The amount of information to which readers may link can be overwhelming, which suggests instructors need to help students learn to read hypertext and make relevant connections.

Reading is an essential part of literacy education, not distant in any way from composition. Among many literacy scholars, in his *Chasing Literacy*, Daniel Keller recognizes reading and writing as "literacy counterparts" reliant on each other and only comprehensible in the context of the other (36). James Paul Gee considers such literacy connections when he expresses in *Teaching, Learning, Literacy in Our High-Risk High-Tech World* that education, as our adapted list indicates, should prepare people to be the following (17):

Resilient: flexible and able to incorporate change into one's life, as well as to be persistent in the face of difficulties and past failure.

Proactive Agents: able to participate in life and to be producers—not merely consumers—of ideas, texts, and media.

Deliberate Learners: able to be self-directed, purposeful learners who seek challenges and new experiences and insights.

Insightful: able to engage with knowledge over information, analyze and understand how things work, and involve themselves and others in dialogue and reflection.

Good Choosers: able to use knowledge to make thoughtful decisions and to thrive—more than just survive—after making bad ones; able to seek good mentors, guides, teachers, and help.

These goals for education are impossible without reading literacy practice in both traditional print and digital media. As Bruce Horner indicates in "Modality as Social Practice in Written Language," both reading practices need "to be explored in terms, too, of the conditions of such practices, as part of those practices. That is to say, practices themselves must be understood as contingent and (therefore) material and social rather than individual choices or habits or universals." Thus, not only should students be asked to metacognitively explore their marking, note-taking, and experiences of alphabetic text, and how these affect "meaning, learning, and pleasure" but they should experiment with "alternative practices in such reading" (33) to include formatting, "line spacing, margin size, not to mention paper versus digital 'files' and use of images, graphs, sound clips (and not), and the conditions of such practices (time, labor, equipment, training, as well as intent and submission requirements)" (33–34).

Ellen Carillo argues in *Securing a Place for Reading in Composition* that reading education must lead to mindful reading, which has the deliberate goal of making connections and transferring knowledge from one subject, discipline, or plane to another. Metacognitive readers are students who "become *knowledgeable, deliberate,* and *reflective* about *how* they read and the demands that contexts place on their reading" (117). Carillo suggests instructors should move from seeking one primary reading model and, instead, engage a "framework within which teaching and learning occur that largely determines if and how that learning translates into other and future contexts," which is knowledge transfer (128; see also DePalma). Writing courses provide a natural fit for reading often and learning to read better (Bartholomae and Petrosky). We agree all writing courses should address reading instruction. Liberal arts education, to which many students are not exposed, demonstrates connections among all courses and a natural redundancy signaling an interconnectedness of human life as demonstrated about known history, science, and other intellectual endeavors and lived experiences. Students whose literacy skills are weak or whose course curricula are narrowly configured may need help making those connections—transferring knowledge gained in reading—but that is the work of reading instruction, too.

Certainly, professional organizations have called for attention to reading in college. We summarize here eight outcomes related to reading in the International Reading Association and the National Council of Teachers of English's jointly written *Standards for the English Language Arts*:

> Students read a wide range of literature from various periods and genres in both print and nonprint texts to build an understanding not only of the texts but also of the human experience, of themselves, and of various cultures. Such reading allows them to acquire new information; create, criticize, and discuss such texts; and meet the demands of their future workplaces and of society.

> Students draw on their prior experience and learn to "comprehend, interpret, evaluate, and appreciate texts." In addition, "[s]tudents whose first language is not English make use of their

first language to develop competency in English language arts and to develop understanding of content across the curriculum" (*Standards* 3).

Students conduct research (using a variety of resources like libraries, databases, and videos), synthesize data from different sources, generate ideas and questions, and pose problems to successfully communicate through spoken, written, and visual language to accomplish their purpose based on the needs.

Similarly, the *NCTE Framework for Twenty-First-Century Curriculum and Assessment* asks that students be able to "[m]anage, analyze, and synthesize multiple streams of simultaneously presented information." Doing so requires them "to take information from multiple places and in a variety of different formats, determine its reliability, and create new knowledge from that information." As the following list of questions about student performance reveals, this work certainly is the task of reading:

Do students create new ideas using knowledge gained?

Do students locate information from a variety of sources?

Do students analyze the credibility of information and its appropriateness in meeting their needs?

Do students synthesize information from a variety of sources?

Do students manage new information to help them solve problems?

Do students use information to make decisions as informed citizens?

Do students strive to see limitations and overlaps between multiple streams of information? (NCTE, *NCTE Framework*)

Each of these performance questions signals complex goals for students as they blend reading, writing, speaking, and listening to become more literate twenty-first-century lifelong learners. How can Professor Jackson attend to them? First, he should understand the building blocks of reading and how the act affects the human brain.

Learning to Read

Reading is a stunning use of the brain's inherent plasticity. Although people may take it for granted that everyone can read, it is not an automatic skill and many fail to achieve fluency. Learning to read, which differs from reading to learn, has several requisites.

First, there must be a writing system, a technology for symbolizing "linguistic representations to linguistics and conceptual information" (Wolf, *Proust* 30). Writing has been invented many times in various cultures. Among the first such systems were tokens, Sumerian cuneiform, and Egyptian hieroglyphics, each of which had pictographic characters encompassing a visual system matching an object name with the spoken language (33). In time, Sumerian cuneiform crossed particularly well into logographic representations that "convey the concepts in the oral language rather than the sounds in the words" (34) and eventually moved into representing oral Sumerian syllables. Such sophisticated writing engages many areas of the brain and creates new neural pathways, including "visual areas in the occipital lobes, to language areas in the temporal lobes, and to the frontal lobes" involving executive functioning (34). In sum, the human brain adapts—individually, person by person—for learning to read in any writing system. One such system is the Latin alphabet used by speakers of English and some other contemporary languages. Different alphabets wire, or organize, brains differently, but that does not make one alphabet superior to another (61–62). With the advent of any writing system comes the opportunity to learn to read and write in that system, which generatively and recursively leads to increased opportunities for reading and writing across time. Today, given that the Latin alphabet is stable, people first learn to read and then to write, making reading skills essential to composition.

In the Latin alphabetic system, the second reading requisite is a linguistic structure. In English, these systems are phonology, morphology, syntax, semantics, pragmatics, and orthography. Writing instructors minimally should know the following about these linguistic systems (as adapted from Wolf, *Tales* 14–34; see also Lindemann 63–67):

> *Phonology* is sound: melody, rhythm, sonority, tone, stress, and pauses that together comprise units of speech of syllables and phonemes.
>
> *Morphology* is a system of rules for forming words—using stems, prefixes, suffixes, and infixes—which are internalized in the native speaker and crucial to fluent reading.

Syntax is the grammar of a language and its sentence-formation rules: generative capacity, combinatorial property, and recursive property. Multilingual students must learn these rules functionally for each language, typically consciously and purposefully.

Semantics is "capacity to convey meaning not simply through the single word itself, but also through its function within particular syntactic contexts," which is what makes Lewis Carroll's "Jabberwocky" so brilliantly comprehensible (Wolf, *Tales* 24; Carroll, *Jabberwocky*).

Pragmatics is the cultural and contextual usage rule system setting the stage for a speaker's intention: addressing what is and is not said, what can and cannot be uttered, and how and why.

Orthography is "both the type of writing system of a particular language and also the rules each language has for representing and/ or spelling its words with its characters or letters": how the language "represent[s] the word, morpheme, syllable, or phoneme, or some combination of these levels, and according to their properties" (Wolf, *Tales* 29). Orthography differs for different alphabets, which many international multilingual students must master.

A third requisite for reading is cultural adhesion. Arguably, according to cognitive neuroscientist Maryanne Wolf in *Tales of Literacy for the Twenty-First Century*, reading begins at birth with language acquisition and a home culture in which parents talk to, listen to, and read to children daily (39, 135). Literacy has a more difficult time entering a home in which it is not prized as necessary in daily life. Orality, Walter Ong teaches in *Orality and Literacy*, is primary and innate to humans; reading and writing literacies, therefore, are secondary and must be modeled and taught explicitly. In *Thought and Language*, Vygotsky suggests it is in response to the presence and absence of social relationships that people develop and use language to express their thoughts (56). Social experience is most critical in externalizing thought to language, which is how babies begin to talk. Without hearing varied words frequently, concepts may go unlearned (Wolf, *Proust* 102). Vygotsky distinguishes among inner speech, verbal (social) speech, and written speech, finding inner speech to be an internalization of, and a developmentally higher step than, egocentric speech, the verbal speech from which all children begin (35) and to which adults richly return when puzzled or otherwise thinking aloud (32). Vygotsky further observes that written language, which always comes well after both spoken language and inner thought, "is the most elaborate form of speech." Because writing takes place outside "situational and expressive supports" like an immediate context, tone, and body language, it must take on "complicated forms—hence the use of first drafts" (242). Wolf follows Vygotsky and indicates that written language promotes human intellectual thought development—particularly abstraction (*Proust* 65). To reach such levels of abstraction, one must learn to read and write, which are deliberate, developmentally challenging acts that must be accomplished consciously because their connection to thinking is more closely related to inner speech than to orally verbalized speech. Therefore, oratorical rhetoric, which millennia ago morphed into written (and read) composition and now is shifting back to a combined focus on orality, alphabetic text, and multimodal productions, is intimately connected to learning to read and write. Reading—and, by extension, writing—is a secondary faculty, one that Wolf asserts is not genetically innate to humans. Although most humans have the mental capacity to learn to read and write, every human must learn these skills individually. Unlike speech, the neurological wiring for reading and writing is not passed down genetically or generationally. Every human's brain must undergo the process of neurological rewiring that occurs when one learns to read and write—on one's own and without the neural capacities gained by one's parents or more distant ancestors. The gap between speech and text is both wider (through human genetics) and narrower (through digitality) than one might think.

A fourth requisite for reading that composition instructors should know regards basic skills that people use when, after learning to read, they begin reading to learn. The brain typically is ready for learning to read at about ages four and five whereas reading to learn starts in about fourth grade, when students without fluency fall behind (Wolf, *Proust* 135). Fluency occurs when readers gain both efficiency and automaticity. For example, fluent readers have a strong working vocabulary, their vocabulary grows with increasingly more and higher-level reading, and they can decode words with different meanings, using the apt meaning most often (123–24). Fluency occurs over time, as the brain forms efficient neural pathways, leading to automaticity (125), and it most often develops for students within a literacy-valuing home (81–107; see also Wolf, *Tales* 47–48). Without these developed skills, students are disadvantaged, may be poor or slow readers, and may be left behind These problems are different from those that occur because of multilingual reading needs and reading disabilities like dyslexia, and they are different from natural orthographic considerations like learning that capital and lowercase letters are still the same letters and that different fonts do not change the letter's basic nature (120), although they may change how certain texts are read and perceived (Horner 30).

In *Reading to Learn and Writing to Teach*, Beth L. Hewett outlines eight commonly taught comprehension themes for overt instruction to students who are reading to learn:

Metacognition is thinking about thinking and an awareness of thoughts as they happen; it helps readers anchor information and transform it to knowledge (106).

Schema represents the constructs of people's individual, unique existence in "memories, opinions, and background, as well as the extant conceptual knowledge" they engage in learning and general life; it is a worldview through which people filter what they read (116).

Inference is a skillful use of guesswork, often called an educated guess or detective work; inference enables readers to predict what might happen and why, leading to active, interested, and apt reading (123).

Questioning shows curiosity about the world; it can be cultivated as a deliberate, strategic way to interrogate text, as with Burke's pentad or classical stasis (130; see chs. 1 and 7 of this book).

Relevance considers and categorizes the important from the unimportant in text; it enables readers to dismiss distracting ideas and connect with core meaning (136).

Visualizing uses readers' visual and sensory capacities to imagine and bring to the mind what is being read; it enables readers to live in the moment of the reading and actively enter the text (146).

Analyzing is taking apart, breaking down, or categorizing what is read to form a conceptual model of its meaning; it is a high-level literacy skill essential to understanding whether and how texts support claims and theories (154).

Synthesizing is combining a series of ideas from different reading sources or other data to create something new, a unique perspective or approach to a problem; it is a high-level literacy skill that needs conscious attention and ongoing instruction (161).

These eight comprehension themes are developed in elementary school, as are others like sound awareness (e.g., alliteration and assonance), analogy, and discerning underlying meaning in figurative language. As skills, they have a shared need to be retaught and reinforced consistently at each learning level—including postsecondary and graduate studies— to help students engage them consciously and actively at increasingly higher critical thinking levels. No one is ever finished learning to use these comprehension themes, either in reading or in writing, which is why Professor Jackson and his colleagues should address them as part of composition instruction.

Reading in the Digital Era

As chapter 1 indicates, the ancient Greeks highly valued orality and the capacity to memorize stories and speeches. Plato, caught in a technological transition of massive proportions, carefully inscribed his teacher Socrates' beliefs that the written word would be disastrous to orality. Just as twenty-first-century instructors exist in digital transition, Socrates lived during a marked transition from orality for rhetorical oratory and dialectic to writing as a technology. Like most adults, Socrates worried about the changes literacy would bring in communication for youths. He wanted his students to question deeply and think about words, concepts, and beliefs conveyed through spoken language (Wolf, *Proust* 70–71); written words, after all, cannot talk back or engage in dialogue that peels back meaning and evaluates thinking (73). His focus on examining knowledge differed somewhat from previous Greek teachings using oral stories to learn the collective wisdom. Socrates taught that "the greatest good of man is to converse about virtue, and all that concerning which you hear me examining myself and others, and that the life which is unexamined is not worth living" (Plato, *Apology* 128–29). Literacy challenged the intellectual life once developed by orality; it changed the requirement to use one's memory in pursuit of knowledge, "creat[ing] forgetfulness in the learners' souls"; and it negatively affected one's pursuit of justice and morality as a citizen (Plato, *Phaedrus* 442). In other words, citizenship responsibilities required people to make their way in the world successfully and as moral and ethical people. Literacy jarred that process for Socrates, who paid for his teaching with his life. Plato dutifully recorded Socrates' lectures, demonstrating that he was ambiguous about orality and literacy. Aristotle, Plato's student, was himself entrenched in literacy—merely one generation later.

Just as Socrates struggled with writing as technology, contemporary educators have struggled with digitality for teaching students to read and write. Students read prodigiously through digital devices—perhaps more than they do with hard copy print—and educators worry about what is lost and ponder what may be gained with this technological shift. Reading on screen certainly differs from reading print. Minimally, there is the brevity of screen text, which writers are cautioned to provide in short, chunky paragraphs that facilitate screen reading—as we caution in this book. In *Tales of Literacy for the Twenty-First Century*, Wolf worries "about the formation of deep reading capacities in the young" (since these are developed by reading longer texts as part of knowledge formation), "the deterioration of these capacities in expert readers[,] and the indifference and/or lack of knowledge about the consequences of both" (142). Neurologically speaking, the digital reading brain differs from that of the print-based reading brain. She asks:

> From a developmental perspective, several intimately connected questions press upon us: first, what is the reality of our *digital habits* from the earliest years on? Second, what are the consequences of these digital habits for the *nature of attention*? Specifically, what are the relationships between *how we attend* and *how and what we read* (e.g., decisions about text length and complexity for both reader *and* writer)? And third, given the immediacy and overwhelming volume of easily accessed information, what are our relationships to this *information overload* and its effects? (143)

In exploring these questions, Wolf considers the nature of attention, distraction, and multitasking, particularly in that "human attentional systems are evolutionarily predisposed to move immediately to any new or novel stimulus" (147); such movement indeed is what the Internet and other hyperlinked materials encourage in today's readers. Worries of shallow and distracted reading are not new, as Rebecca Moore Howard, Tricia Serviss, and Tanya K. Rodrigue report in "Writing from Sources, Writing from Sentences," regarding how inattention to what a text means can lead to patchwriting and plagiarism (178). These are real educational concerns at all levels.

Maintaining reading attention was problematic prior to digital reading tools; it may be harder work with those tools. For example, people may fake read when they look at words, moving their eyes across a page without considering or digesting the text as having meaning (Hewett, *Reading* 107). In the digital era of increased distractibility, how do readers' comprehension abilities change with digitality? How do they develop and attend consciously to thinking sequentially when hypertext changes reading strategies? How is deep reading affected as an expected ability in education and for lifelong family, work, and civic purposes? Wolf posits that humans are developing a *biliterate brain* (*Tales* 158), wired for two different types of reading from early youth, requiring a *biliteracy agenda* for education to "incorporate what we view as the best characteristics of each medium for different cognitive capacities and different types of text [including, we think, multimodal text] at specific developmental epochs in the child's life" (159). Figure 6.1 illustrates the biliteracy theory, which, when connected with the breadth of literacies shown in figure 4.1, suggests the brain's plasticity may support making new neural pathways for all these literacies. Such biliteracy differs, of course, for multilingual readers, who must read and write in multiple languages, sometimes with different alphabets, and across print-based and digital media.

Keller tackles some of Wolf's questions from a writing educator's perspective. He uses Deborah Brandt's notion of literacy accumulation, which involves a horizontal "'spreading out' of literacy's influence on more parts of our lives" and a "'piling up' of old and new literacy materials and expectations" (4). These horizontal and vertical influences on literacy mean that readers' (and writers') jobs are bigger than in the early twentieth century and growing still larger now. Simultaneous to accumulation is "a culture of acceleration," or speed, in that, narrowly, "literacy technologies and practices . . . aim to achieve some end faster" and, broadly, "litera-

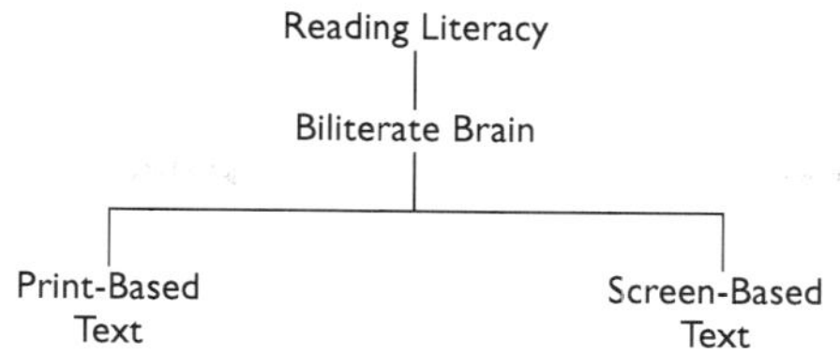

Figure 6.1. Biliterate brain.

cies can accelerate: appearing, changing, merging with other literacies, or fading at a faster rate" (7). Accumulation and acceleration lead to the competing options for readers' attention, as Wolf claims when talking about a lessening of deep reading and an increase in multitasking and less attentive reading (*Tales* 146–48). The answer, Keller believes, is not to try to stop acceleration and accumulation (because how would that even be possible?) but to retheorize reading in the light of them. Reading pedagogy should engage "readers, texts, and contexts: What does it mean to be a reader today? What should count as text? What is the reader's relationship to text and context? How is a reader constructed by the situation and previous reading experiences?" (31).

Ultimately, Keller argues, educators must rethink the nature of reading in the digital era, which asks so much of readers. One solution is to move beyond assigning material about how to read, such as that which appears in the beginning of anthologies, to teaching that material (25) to help students understand reading as actively constructing meaning. That kind of teaching requires the eight reading comprehension themes detailed above and Keller's insight into acceleration and accumulation, which together lead to competing options for students' attention (89). Although educators can worry that students may be reading everything too fast instead of engaging the slower, deeper, close reading that writing instruction has called for in the past, Keller asks, "How might we view fast and slow rhetorics [reading] more productively?" (96). His answer, not unlike Wolf's concept of biliteracy (*Tales*), is to move pedagogically from the binary of fast and slow to a continuum that considers purposefully incorporating the "slow, sustained reading" (100) that instructors value and know how to teach with other types of reading, directing students' attention to them overtly.

These strategies require educators' validation that different speeds and depths of reading are necessary and that "hybrid forms of literacy" exist (Keller 108). They include the following:

Teaching purposeful multitasking that acknowledges not every task is of equal cognitive difficulty or purpose. Multitasking is inherent in multimodal composition and reading, given hyperlinking, different media (e.g., text, image, sound) to which attention must be given, pop-ups, menus, and clickable buttons and links (101–04).

Teaching students why they easily navigate certain reading types delivered in particular forms (e.g., print book, journal article, website, blog); they do so not only because of well-planned design but also because of remediation (per Bolter and Grusin)—a familiarity with blurred older and newer forms of media that they recognize and to which they adapt quickly (Keller 108).

Teaching how and why certain websites and other reading formats work as they do through their purpose and audience as well as the technology's functions and limits, which is a type of functional literacy (110; see also Selber, *Multiliteracies*).

Teaching students the technique of *oscillation*, which, according to Keller, involves adjusting the speed and depth of reading: *depth* refers here to the degree of attention paid in reading and varies between the extremes of skimming and deep reading (116–20). Keller argues for "teach[ing] a range of reading speeds for a variety of purposes" (121). Controlled reading oscillation techniques include skimming (116), foraging (109–10), filtering (113–14), deep-reading bursts and sustained deep reading (110–18), scanning, and reflecting.

Teaching *patchwriting* (see Howard; Howard et al.) as an appropriation that is plagiarism but that society has accepted as occasionally appropriate. Instead of merely condemning patchwriting for its insufficient reading, faulty use of paraphrase, and plagiarism qualities, discuss it overtly as an oft used strategy that is more ethical in some settings than in others (e.g., business memos, reports, and interpersonal communications) and explain why it does not work in traditional academic writing, and compare it with remixing, sampling, and meme digital composing.

Teaching imitation (per Quintilian's rhetorical exercises in *Institutio oratoria* II.iv) in writing (thus, reading) as both inappropriate appropriation for traditional academic writing and appropriate practice for reading and writing. Use stem sentences and resources such as Gerald Graff and Cathy Birkenstein's *They Say, I Say* as examples of how to imitate appropriately.

We recommend extending Keller's pedagogical theory of reading oscillation to encompass a more complex series of choices and reading activities. A reader might, for any given text, vary the speed and depth of reading, which might lead to missing a main point or having to reread it. Competing activities, the reader's literacy level and comfort with reading in English, and the text's purported reading level also affect reading speed. Furthermore, reading environments can vary in any given activity, further affecting a reader's decisions about speed and depth of reading: to fulfill an assignment, a student might choose between printing out an article, reading it on screen, or reading articles both in print and on screen, and the student might also watch a video. Oscillation, therefore, can be understood to fluctuate in waves within the multiple activities (and their conditions) of reading that include not only speed and depth but also reading environment and the literacies employed by the reader, which range from alphabetic to multimodal texts (see fig. 6.2). In the context of the digital era, Keller's theory suggests that the biliteracy Wolf proposes (*Tales*) is possible to achieve deliberately. We believe decisions about reading speed and depth, the reading environment, and the type of text to be read often are made unconsciously but can and should be brought to the conscious attention of students. Educators can teach students to harness reading oscillation to their advantage when reading both print- and screen-based texts.

Plagiarism: A Reading Problem

The *NCTE Framework for Twenty-First-Century Curriculum and Assessment* calls for students to learn how to "[a]ttend to the ethical responsibilities required by complex environments," which includes "legal and ethical practices as they use resources and create information." The framework asks, "Do students share information in ways that consider all sources? Do students practice the safe and legal use of technology? Do students

Reading Activity Boundaries: Alphabetic Text, Fast Reading, Skim Reading, Print-Based Text

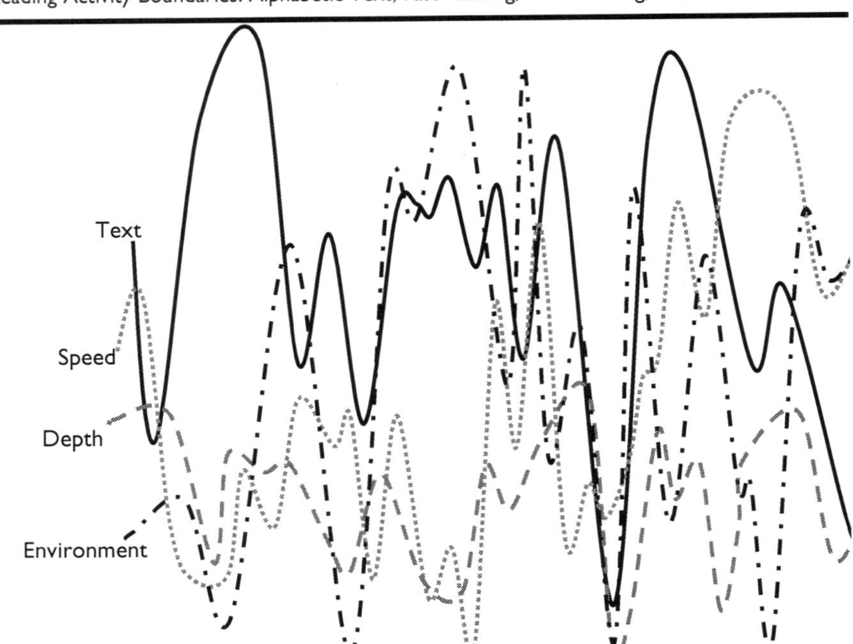

Reading Activity Boundaries: Multimodal Text, Slow Reading, Deep Reading, Screen-Based Text

Figure 6.2. Reading oscillation. Type of text, reading speed and depth, and reading environment oscillate between conventionally understood extremes, or boundaries.

create products that are both informative and ethical?" (NCTE, *NCTE Framework*). The result of not doing these things is plagiarism.

Plagiarism is one of the most significant results of insufficient reading in composition instruction, which is why we address it in this chapter as a reading, not writing, problem. Alice Horning in "Writing and Reading Across the Curriculum" expresses that "underlying true plagiarism (i.e., not simple theft or fraud) is an inability to read well enough to understand, analyze, synthesize, and evaluate sources and then use those sources in support of an argument. The problem appears not only in writing courses, but in courses in every discipline" (9). By *plagiarism*, Horning refers not to cheating by using a term-paper mill that sells es-

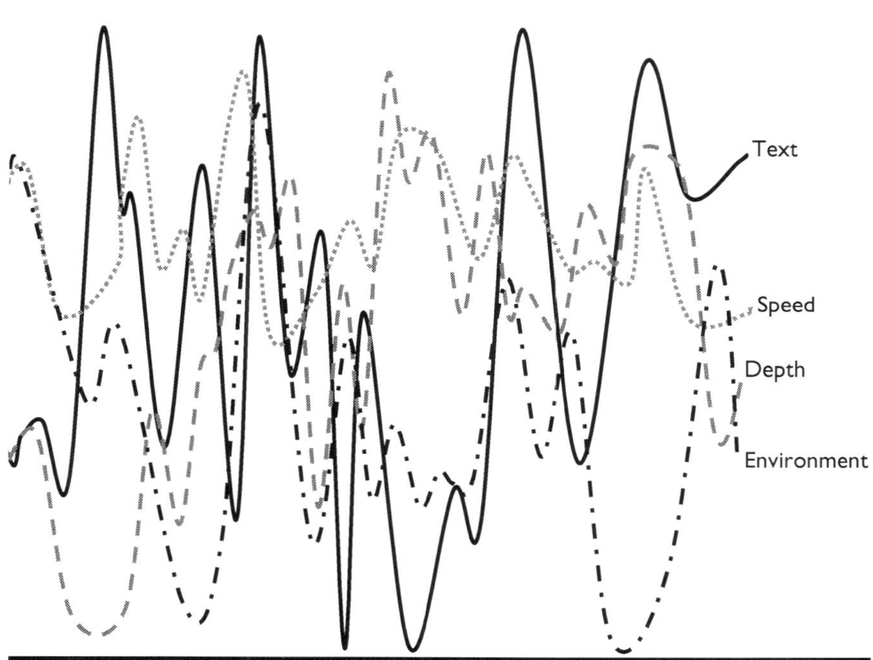

says nor to taking an essay from a previous class and using it in a current one. She speaks, instead, of what often is called *patchwriting* (Howard and Jamieson 233–34), when students copy word-for-word without quotation marks or attribution or when they paraphrase, producing something like the original, and fail to provide attribution (Horning 9). Such reading and writing behavior often happens, as Effie Maclellan indicates in "Reading to Learn": "Students who conceive of learning only as 'more things to know or remember' are going to treat the text as though it were a repository of facts to be raided. On the other hand, students who recognize that a text might radically affect the way they think about aspects of reality are going to engage with the line of reasoning expounded and evaluated in terms of a range of criteria" (285). Lack of engagement with the text is the common thread between raiding a text and patchwriting.

Plagiarism is unfortunately common because students may fake read or skim, failing to read far enough to come to their own ideas; word-spot without reading surrounding text; or be uncertain of when and how to cite outside sources. Some students find the vagaries of citation overwhelming and inaccessible. Others are convinced that a copious use of outside sources sprinkled with their own sentences is what makes writing good regardless of context. Some few students prefer not to do their own writing and look to other essays or written sources for their papers. There are two types of plagiarism that writing instructors tend to see: primary and secondary.

Primary plagiarism is considered intentional theft of another's words either by wholesale copying of an entire piece or by copying substantial parts of that piece without using quotation marks or attribution. It usually entails no evidence of an attempt to blend the material with the writer's own words or to offer credit through internal citation or a bibliographic citation at the end of the piece. Often, primary plagiarism is obvious, and instructors may find the original works through a Google search or may be signaled to talk to the student through information provided by plagiarism software. Students may resort to primary plagiarism for reasons ranging from poor time management to lack of understanding of the assignment to laziness to learning disabilities. Additionally, multilingual students may bring to their reading different cultural rules for full-on appropriation of others' texts.

Secondary plagiarism is considered unintentional theft of another's words, and it is common among first-year-writing and even more experienced students. The copied material—which may constitute a significant part of the writing—usually is stylistically, tonally, and substantially different in content or approach from the student's own writing. There may be an attempt at citing the source in text or a reference to the material through a bibliographic citation, however. Often, secondary plagiarism occurs through insufficient reading and insubstantial understanding of research's purpose and academic style. It may be, in other words, an unintentional combination of poor reading and imitation.

Secondary plagiarism tends to be a problem among students who have not learned how to summarize or paraphrase using their own words, how to quote accurately, or how to write in-text citations that accurately represent the use of another's words. When asked, many students express confusion about these requirements: when to use their own words, when to use quotation marks, and how to use in-text citations. Therefore, it is composition instructors' work to teach these skills—repeatedly, if necessary, as each higher level of sophistication may reveal students' lack of confidence in their skills.

The CWPA's "WPA Outcomes Statement" offers the following advice, adapted here, for helping students avoid plagiarism by attending to the sources they use and their reading of them:

Ask students to draw on and document a variety of sources. Instructors should build such opportunities into their assignments, asking students to gather, assess, and read sources, as well as use a variety of research methods, including observations, interviews, and simple surveys.

Consider conventions. Instructors should design low-stakes assignments and activities that guide students in becoming familiar with conventions appropriate to different genres.

Show students how to evaluate their sources. Through discussions or reflective assignments, instructors should offer opportunities for students to discuss with their peers their research, including how the sources support their argument.

Focus on reading. Instructors should create reading-related heuristics and exercises to help students critically consider what they read and how such information will be useful to their research projects.

Along with this advice, we suggest giving students strategies for copying and pasting text from digital sources, summarizing, and paraphrasing, such as the following:

Learn to identify borrowed material. To avoid plagiarism while copying and pasting from a digital source, develop a method to distinguish your words from the ones you are borrowing. For example, open a new document and name it "Notes from Sources," or use an app that encourages responsible copying and pasting. Use quotation marks around the copied text as a reminder that these are not your own words. Paste the URL into the text along with the author and title. Provide the page numbers or the paragraph number. Make notes about why you copied it, what portions may be helpful to your thesis, and what it means to you. Use brackets [ ] around your notes or a different color font to distinguish your words from the author's.

Learn to summarize well. Summary is a master writing skill that objectively explains what you have read. Summarizing requires not only condensing the text but also judging for importance and organizing for comprehension of the importance. It should provide the author's name, title, thesis, and some examples or supporting points using your own words. A summary of a five-page text will be a paragraph of about five to seven sentences.

Learn to paraphrase well. Paraphrase is a master writing skill that requires completely understanding what you have read. To paraphrase is to restate someone else's idea in your own words with the goal of tightening, shortening, or providing additional clarity. A paraphrased idea may come from a single sentence, or it may come from a lengthy section (e.g., a paragraph or section of an essay); it may be as brief as one to five sentences or as long as the source text. Paraphrased material also must have proper attribution, minimally the author's name and information origin.

Finally, we recommend providing straightforward text that clearly explains the parameters under which students are reading and writing, as example 6.1 shows.

Example 6.1. Clear Directions about Plagiarism

Many students mistake using quotations from sources for the skill of analysis or synthesis. They take whole chunks of text (sometimes several paragraphs!) from a source, put it into their own essays or projects, and decide they have finished writing. That's neither analyzing from a source nor synthesizing from several sources. It's called "patchwriting" (like quilting together pieces of unmatched cloth), and it is a form of plagiarism. Although you might not mean to be doing anything wrong, using other people's texts like this is stealing. I will help you learn how to fix the problem through summary writing and paraphrase. Remember, though, plagiarism (even unintentional) is a serious disciplinary offense at this institution.

To avoid plagiarism:

- Use the reading strategies I have taught you.
- Write either a summary or paraphrase of the text.
- Only use direct quotes when they provide especially important or unique material.
- Only use a few of the author's words or sentences at most.
- Always put quotation marks around words you've taken from another source.
- Always cite the source and page or paragraph number.

Teaching Reading Strategically

Reading in the digital era is dependent on various abilities: to use recall, memory, conscious thinking, and flexibility, among others. Flexibility particularly is developed through numerous cognitive abilities as described throughout this chapter. In *Reading, Writing, and Digitizing*, Horning outlines five appeals that engage these mental capacities and stimulate brain work in novice readers and writers.

> *Reading enables one to learn voice implicitly* (204). In other words, by reading various genres often and well, students can infer what makes writing strong and interesting. Adding explicit analysis and reflection about the reading helps students name and use these qualities overtly.

> *Students can gain pleasure from reading* by learning complex skills from it and learning how others live; both fiction and nonfiction serve these purposes (205–06).

> *Reading can develop students' empathic abilities and connections to others*, which can help to lower violence and potentially increase humanitarian relationships (206).

> *Students gain efficiency from reading more text, more diversely, and more often*, desirable when multitasking and distractions abound and time for schoolwork may be limited by other life objectives (207).

> *Reading is inherently connected to career development*, which students likely think about a lot (207). We think all workplaces somehow require or prize reading and writing literacy at some point. Strong readers and writers tend to be valued in the world, particularly in a globally connected world where communication often happens through text.

When writing instructors approach reading from such real-life perspectives, they may draw out students who otherwise might wonder why they are being asked to read in a writing class or how that practice might help them. Practice, which students sorely lack (Horning, "Reading" 5), means to enforce skills, but such enforcement need not happen only with grades at stake (e.g., quizzes). Other overt, interesting approaches exist. As we describe in chapter 2, student diversity means they differ in age, economic backgrounds, cultural approaches to literacy, physical and learning disabilities, as well as home and past school access to books and digital technologies. It is helpful, therefore, to remember that part of education is to learn what has not been fully achieved in the past; to be reminded of what one may have forgotten; and to be encouraged to use skills and knowledge in myriad ways to anchor, enforce, and extend them. Therefore, unquestionably, students benefit "from direct instruction in the use of personal and rhetorical reading strategies, especially when they are expected to read on unfamiliar topics" (5). Additionally, they may need to learn that reading is more important than ever given the influx of technology; massive interpersonal and international misunderstandings occur when people do not read messages by appropriately and insightfully interpreting meaning. Moreover, as Horning notes, critical reading might be thought to be unnecessary because anything can be looked up on the Internet (6); although that may be true, the distinction between information and knowledge is important. People do not need to remember all the information in the world; that is, indeed, why information pools like libraries and the Internet exist. Yet people do need to acquire knowledge and critical decision making around that knowledge, just as Socrates knew millennia ago. For him, the written word did not substitute for knowledge earned dialogically and through memory; for us, digital technology also does not meet the criteria for such substitution.

Reading Strategies

In both "Reading across the Curriculum" and "Writing and Reading across the Curriculum," Horning offers a series of strategies that we adapt and represent here as one set. After each strategy, we suggest exercises that Professor Jackson and other instructors can adapt to any course setting and at various writing course levels.

> **Strategy 1: Understanding Reading.** Readers need to comprehend reading as an activity that has similarities and differences in both print and digital forms. They need to understand that fluent and effective reading is not necessarily fast; it is reading through depth and speed per its particular purpose.
>
> *Exercise:* Teach students when to skim and when to read carefully for comprehension or memory. Teach them to word-spot or graze as needed (Wolf, *Tales* 148) but help them understand when these skills work best (e.g., seeking keywords) and when they do not work as well (e.g., seeking a word match for quoting without reading what comes before and after it).

Strategy 2: Overt Teaching of Critical Reading Skills. Critical reading skills are part of the reading to learn that began in fourth grade. They engage the eight comprehension themes of metacognition, schema, inference, questioning, visualizing, relevance, analysis, and synthesis. Analysis particularly involves summarizing key points and main ideas. Synthesis requires pulling together ideas from various sources to create new ideas or thinking. Evaluation is another critical reading skill that involves "judging authority, accuracy, relevance, timeliness, and bias" (Horning, "Reading" 11).

Exercise: Ask students to read and analyze several *Wikipedia* entries. Based on reading and analyzing a subject, prompt them to write an entry that looks beyond mere information about something and develops and shares knowledge about it. Require them to explain their process.

Strategy 3: Providing Opportunities for Practice. Reading is a learned skill, individually gained through practice. Practice does not have to be tedious because each reading opportunity can open new windows of the mind, entertaining, informing, and challenging thinking. Each composition course should provide reading practice, but all reading should have clear connections to the course as instructional material, examples, illustrations, or content for writing projects; teachers should inform students how the readings connect to assignments and outcomes.

Exercise: Assign a reading about reading project, much like engaging writing about writing, to consider such issues as distraction, partial attention, deep reading, and the like. After reading, conduct an oral or asynchronous discussion, ask students to write a journal entry about what they learned, or both.

Strategy 4: Learning to Read in Specific Disciplines. Each discipline has its own reading needs because it has its own writing genres. Whether to read a science report deeply or to skim for the main points depends on one's purpose and whether the reader needs the data for another research project. Literary reading of longer and shorter fiction and poetry typically is taught as slow, close reading, whereas textbook reading sometimes may be glossed.

Exercise: Offer at least one reading and writing assignment that crosses course boundaries. For example, ask students to choose several alphabetic and multimodal texts that provide background to writing something in their major discipline. Ask them to reflect on how the reading connects to their writing.

Strategy 5: Modeling by Reading Aloud. Reading aloud does not have to be public, as it may have been in elementary school, potentially causing less confident readers embarrassment. Privately reading aloud is excellent practice for avoiding fake reading. Significantly, it forces focus on the text and, by engaging one's speech, hearing, and sight senses, may improve comprehension.

Exercise: Ask students to read their drafted writing from hard copy print as well as from the screen. Encourage them to read aloud to engage carefully (like their own drafts and those of peers) or to remember (again connecting Socrates' orality with memory). Have them read aloud and video or audio record themselves for their own review or for posting to the instructor alone.

Strategy 6: Intensive Reading through Using Reading Guides. Reading guides offer prompts, typically formed as questions about the reading. Teachers often create prompts to help students focus attention on main ideas and relevant smaller details. With popular fiction, reading guides help book readers to focus their discussion about what happened, what they predicted (expected), and why.

Exercise: Create a reading guide to help students read about so-called fake news. Ask them to highlight and annotate where the story went wrong. Prompt them to find stories that have borrowed from and repeat the misinformation and to find stories that report accurately. Discuss how one can know what is accurate and what is not.

Strategy 7: Discourse Synthesis through Exercises Geared to Audience and Purpose. When students write academic assignments, they usually must synthesize various texts as support for their own theses and scaffold ideas that are new for them. Focusing such synthesis more tightly to the texts' audience and purpose helps to sort through various opinions and positions about a single topic.

Exercise: Explain that analysis is a process of taking apart, while synthesis is about putting things together, typically in a new way. Discuss with students the concept from chapter 7 that all writing is researched writing. If this statement is true, how does it change the concept of reading in college? Of reading for your course?

Strategy 8: Scaffolding with Text Apparatus. Scaffolding engages Vygotsky's "zone of proximal development," which is the difference between what students can do on their own at their developmental level and what they can do with a teacher or peer's assistance, indicating a potentially higher developmental level (Chaiklin). Textbook writers often include assistance, such as textboxes to call out main ideas or illustrative examples, prereading chapter maps, postreading summaries, and keyword definitions.

Exercise: Review a core textbook with students. Find the text apparatuses and teach students what each does and how to read them. Particular chapters might have especially useful materials to review with students.

Strategy 9: Scaffolding with Graphic Organizers. Students often benefit from making their own charts, tables, and illustrative maps of texts they read. They can employ exclamation points or vertical arrows (↑↓) to indicate importance, horizontal arrows for directionality (←→), highlighted colors for calling out particular language or facts, and the like. Such graphic organizers are ways to annotate and personalize reading, which students should be encouraged to do (although those who rent books or want to sell them might be reluctant).

Exercise: Ask students to create an outline or conceptual map of how they have read a webtext and reflect on why they did it that way. What might another path have yielded? Use oral or text-based, asynchronous discussions and/or journals to anchor the learning.

Strategy 10: Learning to Read Critically on Screens. Screen reading can prove challenging for those who do not see the organizational structures (particularly those who use screen readers to facilitate poor sight). Columns, text chunks, hyperlink buttons, colored background or font, font type and size, and pop-up boxes all challenge screen reading. Website or content maps, typically laid out vertically down the left side or horizontally across the top, help with organizing reading. Inability to annotate such sites requires overt discussion about note-taking strategies.

Exercise: Ask students to write about the differences between print and screen text. Consider multimodality in both media. For starters, describe possible challenges with the lack of spatial identifiers (e.g., top/middle/bottom of page, page numbers) that help readers remember and return to particular words, necessitating other technologies such as (digital and hand-drawn) highlighting or notating.

Additional Reading Exercises

Here we provide additional reading exercises that Professor Jackson and other instructors can engage outside of and within writing assignments.

Review metacognition, schema, inference, questioning, relevance, visualizing, analyzing, and synthesizing. Discuss why and how analysis and synthesis are high-level cognitive tools. Use a few of these comprehension theme terms in every assignment to remind students overtly of their value to reading and writing and the need to engage them consciously.

Consider reading as human adaptable and not limited to one way, purpose, need, or style. Determine how this perspective shifts your instructional thinking about reading in the digital era. Ask students about how it shifts their own thinking about reading in the digital era.

Discuss the concepts of information (overload) versus knowledge with students. Together, consider how acceleration and accumulation have affected both.

Introduce the notion of *cognitive patience* (Wolf, *Tales* 152) and discuss how it might be developed in a world of hurry, distractions, and multitasking.

Metacognitively practice with polysemy (i.e., a word or phrase having more than one meaning) to remind students about wordplay. Create or analyze memes or other wordplay like puns, poetry, and jokes.

Explain how texting using shortcut words makes an equivalency of letter (*u*) to word (*you*), a reversal of early reading instruction, which conceptually taught that the sound (*ruh*) a letter (*r*) makes does not correspond to the letter itself or to a word (*are*) (Wolf, *Proust* 97). Ask students to find other texting or digital shortcuts that reverse such early learning yet remain comprehensible in informal language use.

Define and discuss the concept of *fake reading*. Ask students to journal about one time they remember doing fake reading or when they recognized someone else doing it. Ask them to describe how they knew it was fake reading (even without a term for the action).

Conclusion

In her epilogue to *Securing a Place for Reading in Composition*, Carillo charges composition instructors, WPAs, and professional organizations to change their approaches to reading:

> "We must commit ourselves to studying reading in ways that are recognizable and valued outside of our discipline so that we have more opportunities to fund these studies [of reading that are absent from the published literature]" (144).

> "In order to prepare graduate students and new instructors to study reading, we must rethink graduate education in rhetoric and composition, as well as the professional development opportunities offered to instructors" (146).

> "Composition needs to continue encouraging studies on the transfer of learning and specifically those that consider the transfer of reading knowledge from first-year composition courses to future courses" (147).

> "We must adjust our mindset so that text selection does not overshadow attention to reading as a practice" (148).

> "Composition's professional organizations should revise the outcomes statements and other documents to first-year writing instruction to better reflect reading's role in the teaching of writing" (149).

We end this chapter with Carillo's charges because they reflect our understanding of the importance of reading for composition in the digital era. Reading is an astonishing accomplishment of the brain, as Professor Jackson now understands, and it deserves concerted attention in all writing courses at every level. If educators teach postsecondary students to use their biliterate brains overtly through the concept of oscillation and through reading that connects clearly to writing, students will benefit with lifelong skills and the ability to make conscious choices about what and how they read.

Part Two

TEACHING Composition in the Digital Era

7

Composing Processes and Approaches

Professor Jackson has been teaching composition at different levels for a few years, but now he is teaching more advanced courses and multimodal approaches to composing. Addressing two new focal points simultaneously is stressful. What if he doesn't know how to teach the courses well and responsibly? What if he just confuses students who already question their ability to compose? Fortunately, WPA Garcia has provided some professional development opportunities and recommended reading in just these areas.

As chapter 1 demonstrates, rhetoric grounds composition whether the text is purely alphabetic or has multimodal elements. Engaging rhetorical skills can enable one to get a point across civilly and effectively while seeking to engage in constructive dialogue or argue a point. Doing so often requires supporting the process of composing, which includes making rhetorically situated choices and strategies—all skills students need practice developing (C. Lauer, "Contending" 237). Composers must consider their audience and the rhetorical situation and purpose; additionally, they need to address how these factors influence medium choices, how the selected medium might affect the audience, and how different mediums have different effects and may change the meaning or enhance the communication. Otherwise, the problems students cited in chapter 1's opening anecdote may go unresolved.

Cynthia L. Selfe affirms in "The Movement of Air, the Breath of Meaning" that the major responsibility of twenty-first-century composition, alphabetic and multimodal, is to teach "rhetorically-based strategies for taking advantage of all available means of communicating effectively and productively as literate citizens" (260), a direct connection to Aristotle's rhetoric. When possible, instead of choosing tools for students, Selfe says, an instructor should leave these choices to students, encouraging rhetorical agency. For instructors who worry they may flounder in new technological territory, Anne Frances Wysocki suggests in *Writing New Media* that they already are skilled in teaching how writing for alphabetic, aural, and visual texts is "embedded among the relations of agency and extensive material practices and structures that are our lives" ("Opening" 7). She argues that educators should use their skills to help students attend to the "materiality, production, and consumption" of such texts, a conversation missing within most composition classes. Educators should guide students to consider the following questions: What medium best suits the rhetorical situation and purpose for communicating? What modes work best within that medium and for the message? Who is or will be the audience or consumer for this product? How do the needs of that audience dictate or guide the choice of medium?

This chapter describes composing processes from classical rhetoric and contemporary social-process composition and applies them to alphabetic and multimodal texts, enabling instructors to teach them contextually for different delivery options. The processes we discuss can guide students to use multiple composing strategies, responding to these questions in relation to their compositions.

Composing Processes for Alphabetic and Multimodal Texts

A variety of theories ground composition instruction, as chapter 1 discusses (and Professor Jackson is learning!). Because many composition educators commonly engage these theories, we primarily use the languages of classical rhetorical and contemporary social-process theory to describe the varied composing actions, or processes, students might encounter in any composition course. A classical rhetorical approach to text development uses the canons of invention, arrangement, style, memory, and delivery, and it engages logos, ethos, and pathos as appeals. A contemporary process-based approach to composing includes several recursive, generative phases. These phases are *recursive* in that one might engage and reengage various phases repeatedly and in a different order. For example, writers may begin drafting with an idea; support and reinforce it; and then end with the same, a new, or a more developed idea. These phases also are *generative* in that each can spawn new thinking, ideas for research, and enlightened revision; the composing act itself generates new or different ideas. Each writer has a unique writing process, yet the notion of phases offers identifiable, teachable strategies writers can adapt.

Process theory recognizes that a composition is never genuinely finished in that it can be developed, changed, edited, and revised endlessly—particularly when it receives thoughtful peer or other reader response. Nonetheless, the school-based need for assessment requires that at some point the writer must offer the piece to an audience for review, which creates an artificial, if necessary, completion. In workplace and publication settings, however, the same issue occurs; at some point, the work must be considered done.

The composing processes outlined in this chapter are flexible enough that individual writers can engage one process and discard another. Therefore, although we suggest that instructors be familiar with all these processes and be able to demonstrate them to students—particularly in online settings using various technologies—we do not recommend a dogmatic approach or requirement. Finally, these composing processes are mostly similar for both alphabetic and multimodal texts, and instructors should be able to help students engage them flexibly for all kinds of texts in various teaching environments.

Genre Conventions

As chapter 3 describes, genre conventions may comprise formal characteristics of what the audience expects when reading, seeing, or hearing a text. Genre conventions might be considered the framework for writing, as they can be benchmarks one must address when composing within that genre. For example, if consumers visit a popular website to determine whether they should buy a product, they will find consumer reviews that address the product's cost and quality in relation to cost. Consumers will find information about the unique features of the product and any challenges of putting it together or using it. These expectations constitute genre conventions, which also may dictate the general structure of a document. For example, when readers review a workplace proposal, they expect to read first about the problem, and then about potential solutions; they expect a detailed description of the best solution, budget, timeline, and possibly a comparison of vendors. In any case, students may experience genres as both constraining and freeing. Moreover, for any genre, expectations are bounded by social, disciplinary, and cultural contexts. Even with expected conventions, however, genres can be malleable; students should learn that rules are best broken only after they are understood in context. Instructors can teach that play within genre is possible if writers meet readers' needs.

Rhetorical Invention and Brainstorming

Composition instruction often begins with rhetorical invention, from the classical rhetoric canon. According to Richard Young, *invention* involves "an explicit and organized way of discovering the content of a discourse, especially persuasive discourse" (350). Rhetorical invention has been defined differently over the past 2,500 years, each definition valid and none completely satisfactory because each is "embedded in history, in the theoretical, psychological, political, ethical, and educational beliefs prevalent at a particular time" (350). Young defines the art of rhetorical invention as "a method or suggestions for proceeding effectively in complex, nonroutine situations, the general purpose being the use of what is known to go beyond it to what is not known" (351). Invention often occurs before writers start composing, as with Kenneth Burke's pentad described in chapter 1; however, invention can, and arguably should, happen at any phase of the composing process. For instance, invention strategies like freewriting can aid writer's block, simply allowing writers to crank out words without judging them.

One method is *stasis* (or *status*), which provides a series of questions for determining the main issue to be argued through questions about the issue or occurrence (i.e., the *it*):

> **Fact.** "[D]oes it exist? did it happen as claimed?"
>
> **Definition.** "[I]f it happened, what kind of thing is it that happened?"
>
> **Quality.** "[I]s it desirable?"

Procedure. "[I]n law, does the court have jurisdiction? is the charge proper?" (Young 351).

Applying the *wh*-questions (i.e., what, when, why, where, who, and how) to these four issues deepens understanding of the problem. Achieving stasis means reaching consensus with oneself or others about the issue, though not necessarily its solution.

The appeals to logos, ethos, and pathos also develop content, especially for argumentation. Logos engages facts and numbers to reason out a problem; examples and statistics are especially helpful. Logos works with what is considered true, particularly science or other seemingly proven issues. Ethos engages the writer or speaker's own (presumably good) character and knowledge, indicating that the composer has the audience's best interests in mind. Particularly in today's *Twitter* world, a powerful or famous person's position may begin as an ethos marker of authority or reputation, prompting others to believe in the message; these markers are tricky, however, and audiences can flip quickly to nonbelief—and even scorn—with miscommunication or ill-advised behaviors. Pathos appeals to emotions, seeking to create an impassioned audience response that can move people from mere belief to action. For example, animal rights groups pursuing funding may use emotionally charged images and videos of mistreated animals, publishing them strategically for certain demographic groups to consume.

Other heuristics involve the deliberative, forensic, and epideictic types of classical speeches, addressing, respectively, "the ethical considerations of advantage, justice, and honor" (351). Heuristics also include the Greek *idioi topoi*, or special topics, that assist with idea discovery in particular subjects (352). Special topics prompt writers to find information in known things. For example, deliberative topics involve legislative issues (e.g., ways and means, peace and war, national defense), forensic topics involve judicial concerns (e.g., motives, states of mind, just and unjust actions), and epideictic topics involve ceremonial considerations (e.g., virtues such as justice, courage, temperance, and wisdom). These topics respectively address the future, past, and present. In other words, if students want to write about whether *WikiLeaks* whistleblowers had acted against the law, the special topics of what people can or should do in the interests of national defense would help to find or invent arguments.

The *koinoi topoi*, or common topics, can be applied broadly as talking points. These are stock formulas (e.g., more/less, possible/impossible, and past fact / future fact) that can be used with various subjects (Aristotle 37; I.iii.6–9 [1359a]); they include puns, proverbs, causes and effects, comparison and contrast, opposites, analogies, description, definition, consistency of action or being, hypocrisy, testimony, and circumstance. For students seeking to discuss *WikiLeaks*, for example, after establishing points of law regarding national defense, engaging historical facts about how whistleblowers have been treated with respect to national defense could ground an argument about what should happen in this case. Using the topos of definition would establish *national defense* and *whistleblowers* in the context of the nation.

Professor Jackson can teach the topoi for both invention (see ex. 7.1) and organization (see ex. 7.2); we discuss arrangement later in this chapter. *Topoi* consist of thinking patterns such as narration, description, definition, comparison, contrast, analogy, and the like. Unfortunately, having begun in the classical era as common topics for rhetorical invention and oratorical arrangement, they were rigidified into writing "modes" and paragraphing strategies in the nineteenth and early twentieth centuries (see ch. 1). Popular rhetorics and textbooks—particularly those written for developmental and some multilingual student courses—still employ such rigid single-mode structures without considering that most complex subjects composed in any genre become more comprehensible when organized using patterned approaches and that those patterns can vary within any one composition. We recommend teaching the topoi as invention and arrangement devices, not as modes. Unaffected by digitality, they can be used both alphabetically and multimodally. Example 7.1's topoi exemplify invention patterns.

Example 7.1. Topical Invention Patterns

Cause and Effect Analysis

What it is: An examination of why something happened and what its consequences are or will be.

How to use it: Illuminate what writers know and do not know; reasoning from cause to effect or effect to cause, move from what writers know to what they want to learn. The analysis

- considers whether a cause is necessary (i.e., must be present for the effect to occur), sufficient (i.e., can produce an effect unaided), or contributory (i.e., helps to produce an effect but cannot do so alone)
- reflects a best guess from available facts: a case study investigates a single occurrence or situation, leading to a big-picture discussion; a global analysis investigates the big picture in more general terms, drawing on a range of cases and sources
- requires abundant, reasonable evidence that is reliable, relevant, and sufficient: writers must search diligently for as many likely causes as possible to trace the chain of cause and effect to the root and demonstrate a relationship

Classification and Division

What it is: A pattern that enables analyzing a plural, multipart, or complex subject and breaking it into named groups and subgroups.

How to use it: Achieve understanding by examining the smaller parts of the main subject; division does so by dividing a singular subject into its constituent parts, using categories of equal abstraction that, ideally, do not overlap too much.

- Method 1: Analyze the subject and divide it into logical and complete categories.
- Method 2: Organize a body of material using a particular purpose.

Comparison and/or Contrast

What it is: A means for finding likenesses and/or differences within and among topics.

How to use it: Examine how two items, things, people, or processes share qualities and/or how they differ. Comparison and/or contrast

- works best when the two elements are similar or different in an obvious but perhaps unexpected or unusual way or area
- can lead to new perspectives if developed using other composition patterns to expose details, processes, and reasons for the similarities or differences
- uses a divided or block pattern to help find the unique quality that both subjects share or in which they differ

Definition

What it is: A process of explaining what something is and is not, what it includes and excludes, and what its purposes are.

How to use it: Determine the boundaries around a term, idea, topic, or thing, usually in more than a simple sentence.

- Simple definition provides an in-context word, phrase, or sentence.
- Stipulative definition addresses the specific meaning the writer wants for a particular purpose, either operational (i.e., what a term does rather than what it is) or lexical (i.e., the word's meaning, history, etymology, and evolution).

- Extended definition may be an entire essay with length and complexity centering on the writer's aims and the audience's needs. Other idea development patterns (e.g., description, process, comparison and/or contrast, and classification) may play a role in an extended definition.

Description

What it is: An illustration of how something looks, feels, tastes, smells, sounds, or simply is in its inherent state of being; static or dynamic (process).

How to use it: Provide the reader with a connection to or mental picture of what is being read.

- Description may use narrative strategies to help complete a picture it draws.
- Writers filter the subject matter either subjectively through their own biases and emotions or objectively as an attempt to eliminate the self as filter.
- A controlling filter or metaphor aids choosing words that bring the image to mind and eliminates distracting details.

Narration

What it is: A story related to an event—fictitious or true—such as anecdote, life episode, observation, memoir, autobiography, or biography, among other genres.

How to use it: Help the reader make connections to a point or theme. Storytelling may

- engage a logical approach that brings past events to mind.
- use chronology or time-based occurrences that assist recall (for self-focused stories), investigate someone else's experiences (for nonfiction), and/or create a plausible series of events (for fiction).

Process

What it is: A dynamic description of how to do something or a narrative of how a problem originated, why it is a problem, and what steps might fix or address it.

How to use it: Guide the reader to better understanding of a problem and its solutions.

- Consider the process as events occurring in a straight-line, cyclically, simply, complexly, once, repeatedly, logically, or in no particular order.
- Engage other topoi patterns such as detailed description, definition, and narrative.

Testimony

What it is: An appeal to reliable authority, usually a public figure or an expert's research, including what others interested in the subject believe to be true.

How to use it: Requires understanding current common thinking about an issue.

- Use maxims, quotations, proverbs, and laws and their precedents and implications for the present and future.

- Use with cautious selectivity (e.g., consider that public figures or celebrities may be famous for inconsequential reasons rather than for public service).

These invention patterns typically overlap within any one composition, blending to enrich the writing and benefit the audience.

Topoi also offer strategic advantages for students struggling with limiting or narrowing a topic to something they can explore thoroughly in a short time and in a relatively brief composition. Like stasis, such topoi as definition, cause and effect analysis, comparison and contrast, and classification prove helpful. For example, stem questions engaging definition include the following:

How do I define _______?

How do various dictionaries define _______?

In the sense that I am using _______, are there other people in the field or news that define _______ differently? If so, how?

How do people tend to confuse _______ with _______?

What are synonyms (or antonyms) for _______?

Whereas rhetorical invention can be considered a formalized or plan-based way of finding one's ideas, *brainstorming*, a term often used synonymously, may involve as simple a process as freewriting every thought until ideas have emerged that warrant more formal exploration. Generally, heuristics may or may not have set forms. Some techniques include

listing ideas and concepts

team idea mapping

clustering, mapping, webbing, and storyboarding

Venn, cluster, and other diagramming

Burke's pentad (see ch. 1)

Richard Young, Alton Becker, and Kenneth Pike's tagmemics[1]

Toulmin's model of claim, evidence, warrants, backing, counterargument, and qualifier

questioning or starbursting

word and visual image association

mind mapping

finding pros and cons

SWOT analysis (strengths, weaknesses, opportunities, threats)

charting, smart art, tables, and shapes

considering audience, purpose, and occasion

Brainstorming techniques, which can be used by teams or individuals, enable critical and creative thinking about a project or problem without immediately judging any single thought's merit. Although they are practical for students learning to compose more sophisticated projects or struggling to engage one another in team-based writing projects, these techniques are cognitively useful for problem solving. Team brainstorming (or brain-netting), processes include talking in on-site and live video settings, working by phone or text, and using synchronously or asynchronously shared documents.

Rhetorical invention and brainstorming can lead to making claims or developing tentative thesis statements that can be tested through research, discussion, and drafting. A claim is the view, thesis, or conclusion the writer states about the subject. Typical advice is that a claim must be explainable or arguable, clear, and qualified such that the writer can argue it completely. Categories for claims include the following:

Judgment. What is your position on the issue?

Policy. What should be done to solve the problem?

Value. What is something worth (to someone)?

Cause. Why is something the way it is?

Interpretation. What does something mean?

Claims always need to be supported by sufficient reasons and strong evidence, which is why good research (discussed below) is critical.

Both rhetorical invention and brainstorming can be accomplished with teachers' direct support in face-to-face or synchronous video settings. Instructors can use pencil or pen and paper, chalkboards and whiteboards, as well as cloud-shared typed and handwritten documents. In asynchronous settings, as we discuss below, teaching rhetorical invention and brainstorming may require prerecorded videos that demonstrate different strategies; rather than being generic, such direct instruction should be tuned to the students' assignments, which helps them transfer the processes to their own writing. Most heuristics work equally well using alphabetic text and multiple media and in both on-site and online settings.

Audience Analysis

Professor Jackson knows that a composition without an intended audience is flat and may lack focus. Writing with readers in mind is an invention tool that sharpens writers' plans. Therefore, students benefit from learning how to determine and analyze readers for compositions. If they select an inappropriate audience, they may go down the wrong path toward composing and production. Instructors act as coaches in such instances, guiding students to choose and understand the audience that might be the most receptive of their developed project. Choosing an appropriate audience enables writers to engage their composition's purpose and determine the best medium for the project. This process works best when instructors buy in to the students' selected audiences and read the composition from the intended readers' perspective as well as their own as teachers.

The notion of audience is connected to more than two millennia of rhetorical education for orators, who had real-time listeners to consider as they spoke, often extemporaneously. In *The "Art" of Rhetoric*, Aristotle lists some of an audience's qualities that rhetors should consider when composing, including what causes the audience to experience anger, shame, pity, envy, fear, and desire (247–63; I.xii–xvii [1388b–1391b]). Such emotions influence reception to and potential agreement with an argument. Millennia later, George Campbell articulates connections between what an audience might think and look like and how to use that sense of audience in invention, data choices, and composing strategies like arrangement (Porter, "Audience" 44). Teaching about and developing an audience analysis are strategies that have not been overtly affected by digitality, except that any investigation into a potential readership can be conducted through the Internet and social media. Professor Jackson's students might profile audiences by interviewing them orally (through phone, audio recording, or video), returning to the interview to listen and think, and then analyzing audience preferences. They even can repurpose the clips to splice into the project itself.

Questions like the following are helpful in conducting an audience analysis regarding who might be influenced by the piece:

Who is this audience? Is it an imaginative construct of who may read compositions or an actual reader or readers, like the teacher, one's classmates, or the local city council?

What does this audience look like in terms of demographics, age, sex, faith base, economic background, education, work experience, and geographic location?

What primary beliefs, values, thoughts, needs, or emotions might the audience experience regarding the topic under discussion or how it is presented?

How might this topic and the claim being made affect their lives?

Is it realistic to expect the audience to accept this claim and, if composing a persuasive argument, engage with the proposed action?

If the teacher or a peer group is the genuine audience targeted in the piece, what is possible to know or accurately imagine about them as readers?

What does this audience need and how does that affect the choice of modality and medium for composing?

Any of these audience analysis questions can lead writers to engage with their own texts. One exercise would be for peers to ask noninvasive questions of each other (making the list together helps to achieve question appropriateness), serving the dual purpose of getting to know one another and learning about their peer audience for writing.

Conducting an audience analysis helps students frame their claims and reasoning with both imagined and real human readers in mind. For example, if a student wants to write a piece that praises a famous individual whose private flaws recently have emerged publicly, would the audience be able to move past them? How could the writer express what is admirable about this person without offending readers who disagree? Making the decision to write about such a person could lead the writer to open with a counterargument rather than leave it to the end, possibly spawning greater success. Alternatively, an astute audience analysis might lead the writer to select another subject altogether.

Rhetorical Situation and Purpose

Lloyd Bitzer defines a rhetorical situation as that which "calls the discourse into existence" (2). Writers, he argues, need to know "the contexts in which speakers or writers create rhetorical discourse." Bitzer continues: "How should [these contexts] be described? What are their characteristics? Why and how do they result in the creation of rhetoric?" (1). Ultimately, a rhetorical situation involves not only the writer, subject, audience, and the composition, but also exigence, purpose, and genre.

Discerning a project's rhetorical situation may not be up to the student entirely. The rhetorical situation is both its *context* and *background*, words often used synonymously for *exigence*; it reflects why a topic is important and how it is situated historically and in people's opinions and lives. Sometimes, instructors require a prewriting proposal that discusses exigence along with the writing's purpose. Teachers should instruct students regarding the project's rhetorical needs: Why are they writing? Who are the audiences? What is the rhetorical situation? How will they influence the audiences?

The purpose for a composition also is part of its context, or rhetorical situation in history, culture, genre, and audience. Purpose has been related to genre (see ch. 3) in that one might select the genre to accommodate the purpose. The notion of rhetorical purpose has been explored since classical times with Aristotle stating three purposes of rhetoric: *deliberative*, or legislative, as related to a law-making audience; *forensic*, or judicial, as related to a jury or an audience in the law courts; and *epideictic*, or ceremonial, in state occasions, as related to an audience who expects to hear praise or blame of a public figure or issue (33–39; I.iii [1358a–59a]). Cicero expands Aristotle's taxonomy by indicating the orator's job is to instruct, delight, and move the audience (*Ideal Orator* I.3). Campbell, in enlightenment rhetorical theory, expands Cicero's tasks of rhetoric to "enlighten the understanding, to please the imagination, to move the passions, or to influence the will" (1). In his twentieth-century *A Theory of Discourse*, James Kinneavy locates rhetoric and discourse to the triangle of reader, reality, and writer, with written language as the signal inscribed within the triangle (31; see fig. 7.1). Walter Beale theorizes that purpose combines a referential or tropological factor (i.e., "the degree to which it aspires to describe reality or not") and contemplative

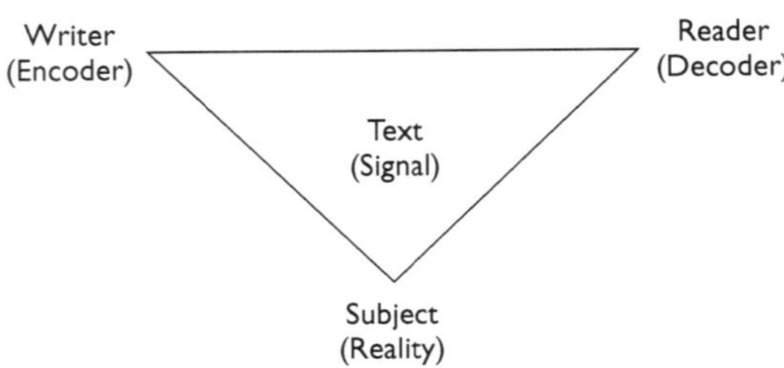

Figure 7.1. Kinneavy's discourse triangle. Kinneavy, p. 31.

or active factor (i.e., "the degree to which it aspires to effect action") (qtd. in Walzer 577). However these purposes are categorized or named, digitality itself does not affect their essential meaning for composing.

These theoretical approaches to rhetorical purpose have the common need to consider audience and determine what that audience wants or needs and how it relates to a goal or desired outcome. Few writing assignments—regardless of genre, technology used, or delivery method—make much sense to student writers without a purpose other than simply to do the assignment to improve their writing (or to get a grade). The often vague aim of writing improvement becomes more reachable when students have been given—or better, when they can choose—a goal with a specific, if imagined, audience for whom they can write. If students can select a genuine audience other than the teacher—perhaps their peers or readers of a website, journal, or blog—they can propose purposes specific to the audience and its context. In lieu of a genuine audience to provide feedback (see ch. 9), instructors like Professor Jackson can engage with the proposed audience and imagine themselves as that audience, providing feedback with them in mind. Of course, a composition instructor is always a teacher, so overtly expressing feedback from both perspectives can enliven evaluation and make potential revisions real for students (e.g., *When I imagine myself as a farmer you're addressing, I see X, Y, and Z in your argument. As your teacher, I also see A, B, and C.*).

Primary and Secondary Research

Good writing tends to be researched writing in that research happens whenever writers look outwardly to understand what others think and inwardly to reflect on their own thinking before writing. This statement is not an argument to resurrect the so-called research paper, with its problems of rigid expectations and student propensity toward plagiarism to fulfil those expectations. Instead, we agree with Rebecca Moore Howard and Sandra Jamieson in "Researched Writing" that research has inherent value of inquiry, and students should learn ways to accomplish it. From this perspective, whenever people write—even creative nonfiction, memoirs, and fiction—they must conduct research of some sort. Research offers writers facts, details, and earned opinions. Although everyone has opinions, often they begin as uninformed judgment—especially for younger students just individuating from their families. The opinions most worth reading—particularly in academic writing—are those informed through research, critical thinking, and dialogue.

Experiences, observations, and past learning all influence how people approach a topic. Writers have both biases and agendas—often unconsciously held and therefore unacknowledged—that guide them, which means they have particular viewpoints that may form their approach and specific goals for their compositions. Research can lead to more informed, thoughtful texts that acknowledge bias and agendas straightforwardly. Indeed, thoughtfully conducted research can be a form of self-reflection, leading people to greater self-awareness. Howard and Jamieson recommend the following approaches, adapted here, to avoid the hazards of the traditional research paper and to reengage students in the pleasures and benefits of research (236–42):

- Substitute other researched assignments for the traditional research paper.
- Emphasize connection to the writing topic over mechanics.
- Work with media specialists.
- Teach how to locate and assess sources to inform the writing.
- Teach focused, thoughtful reading.
- Teach skills like summary and paraphrase.
- Explore multimodal genres and approaches.

Many of these suggestions are addressed in chapter 5 as well as in this chapter. In this section, we address both primary and secondary research, not as a research methods course for advanced research projects but as ways to explore topics and deepen thinking.

Primary, or field, research develops new knowledge through such activities as observation, interviews, focus groups, and surveys or questionnaires. Students do not have to be in a research methods course to learn about field research (although, depending on the institution's rules, they may need approval from the human research protection office). Instructors can develop assignments that encourage students to step outside of reading about others' research and move into developing original data for analysis and explication. For example, they can be assigned to go to a local park to observe and record how people interact with monuments or memorials. To address access concerns, students with prohibiting contexts (e.g., overseas military students confined by wartime operations and sight-impaired or physically disabled students) can be offered other observation options that work better for them. Observation is a data-gathering practice that requires writers to use all their senses and then to describe both individual occurrences (e.g., *one man walked up to the memorial and sat down; fifteen people passed by it without apparent notice*) and the scene (e.g., *the day was gray, so the monument seemed to blend into the background*). This observation activity enables writers to disengage from text, the computer, and other traditional research strategies to engage with the subject.

Individual interviews and focus groups allow students to deconstruct their topics by developing questions to ask what participants think, believe, or have experienced. Such a process can break through preconceived notions, leading to more objective and better-informed viewpoints. Similarly, surveys and questionnaires require thoughtful, well-written questions to elicit meaningful responses. The mere process of constructing such tools (which, usefully, offers practical experience with technological tools), piloting them (possibly with peers, thereby enhancing peer interactions), and revising them before distribution can become a useful expository writing project. New data can inform any genre, whether written in alphabetic or multimodal texts. Any of these primary research processes can use digital tools—such as polling participants about their *Facebook* practices using *Facebook* posts as the survey means—but they also can encourage students to engage people face-to-face, in real time.

Most postsecondary composition projects require some level of *secondary research* that reviews what others have researched and analyzed.

Students may be confused by terminology because secondary research (an act) engages both primary and secondary sources (things). Primary sources include any original document or artifact like diaries or journals; manuscripts; letters and emails; recordings of talk, music, or movies; autobiographies and memoirs; and any sources that students may have developed through field research. Secondary sources typically have been written from studies about primary sources, including scholarly journal and magazine articles, textbooks, guidebooks, histories, and literary and other criticism. Many of these primary and secondary sources for secondary research can be retrieved through a library's physical holdings, database searches, and the Internet.

Secondary research will not be new to postsecondary students, who will have written research reports in high school. Regardless of how they consume such research, however, many students will stop reading before they have learned enough to know the topic well. This problem may result from an assignment with too short a deadline or too little latitude to enable writers to focus deeply. Secondary research cannot be accomplished well without reading skills in traditional print, digital text, and image-based sources (see ch. 6). Reading is a literacy that needs continued, overt attention and practice throughout one's life, particularly as more and different digital sources emerge. Often students fail to read deeply for research, claiming busyness, laziness, or boredom, which may be attributed to such personal qualities, although they also can result from reading challenges like dyslexia.

Finally, viewing and listening are research skills necessary for primary and secondary research, and they can enhance student writers' idea and thesis development. Viewing a presidential speech or news briefing regarding a natural disaster enables students to observe and record impressions of the central person's demeanor and body language. Because of his students' concerns outlined in chapter 1, Professor Jackson should teach his students to listen well, which enables them to hear and record the speaker's words, pace, tone, and apparent emphasis. Both skills, particularly when employed while observing the primary event and not filtered through a commentator's account of the event, can enhance research. Because viewing and listening most often are enabled digitally and not as a onetime live event, students can review and relisten to test their own understanding and find their own potential biases.

Organization

Organization, or arrangement, has been taught in various ways over the centuries. Organizing a composition, whether oral, written, or multimodal and whether brief or long, entails both a global approach to the whole text and a series of local approaches at the point (for oral), paragraph (for written), and node (for webtext) junctures. In an alphabetic essay, for example, each paragraph should be arranged to appeal to readers' sense of logic, build cohesion, or engage pathos or ethos at the right time. Within each paragraph, its points should comprise interesting and logically coherent statements. Each sentence should be clear, comprehensive, and engaging. Organization strategies come in different forms, including traditional outlining that guides students to compose according to the structure they create, reverse outlining, and storyboarding ideas into slides with text and drawings. Simple storyboarding can be accomplished visually and tactilely by drafting and reorganizing using note cards.

Although we like to see students have freedom for organic arrangement, they also benefit from time-tested strategies that are logically accessible to readers. Thus, lessons in organization might involve analyzing other texts for arrangement approaches. Classical educators often used the topoi for assisting orators with arrangement, who needed to present the best case extemporaneously and quickly. Organizational topoi include order of occurrence, historical chronology, general to specific, importance, function, and size. The topoi also are useful for arranging both globally (the whole text) and locally (within paragraphs and sentences) because they provide simple-to-follow patterns that guide content development and expression. Professor Jackson is teaching his students to organize with the topoi suggestions shown in example 7.2.

Example 7.2. Topoi as Arrangement Patterns

Cause and Effect Analysis

What it is: An examination of why something happened or what its consequences are or will be or both.

How to use it: The cause and effect pattern can help writers organize in terms of effects to cause(s), cause(s) to effects, and orders of occurrence, importance, complexity, and length of term.

Classification and Division

What it is: A pattern that enables analyzing a plural, multipart, or complex subject and breaking it into groups and subgroups.

How to use it: Classification and division, whether used individually or combined, provide outlining strategies.

- The outline will be balanced among the parts, leaving writers able to see whether they have addressed constituent parts equally.
- The final organization can use the divided or alternating organization cf comparison and/or contrast.

Comparison and/or Contrast

What it is: A means for finding likenesses and/or differences within and among topics.

How to use it: Choose one of two patterns, called *divided* (*block*) and *alternating* (*switch*).

- Divided: Enumerate all the qualities of one subject being compared and/or contrasted and then the qualities of the other subject. Requires a clear thesis and transitions to guide readers.
- Alternating: Address both subjects head-to-head, one quality at a time offering more control over how readers come to understand the subject(s)

Definition

What it is: A process of explaining what something is and is not, what it includes and excludes, and what its purposes are.

How to use it: Organizationally, a definition may be assisted by deduction, which begins top-down with the definition and works to a specific case study or exarrple; or it may be addressed inductively with a bottom-up arrangement that collects a series of examples and defines the subject based on them.

Description

What it is: An illustration of how something looks, feels, tastes, smells, sounds, cr simply is in its inherent state of being; static or dynamic (process).

How to use it: Arranging material by order of

- significance (e.g., more to less important)
- occurrence (e.g., when something happened or will happen)
- spatiality (e.g., from right to left or top to bottom)
- logic (e.g., hierarchical by ranking parts from least to most important cr through their connections one to the other, inductive by recreating a ciscovery process for the reader, and internal, or built-in, by describing as the item or event seems to call for)

Narration

What it is: A story related to an event—fictitious or true—such as anecdote, l fe episode, observation, memoir, autobiography, or biography, among other genres.

How to use it: Narration carries various organizational strategies:

- Organizational choices influence invention as writers may move among the narrative's parts, supplying plot details, character actions, and interpersonal dialogue as the narrative unfolds in the arrangement scheme.

- Narration can be organized chronologically in time from first to last (or, alternatively, from later to earlier events), by characters' perceptions, thematically, and in multiple other ways.

Process

What it is: A dynamic description of how to do something or a narrative of how a problem came to be, why it is a problem, and what steps might resolve it.

How to use it: Process can be organized by multiple patterns:

- straight line (e.g., how to make a pot roast) or cyclical (e.g., describing a tour bus route from beginning to its ending place)
- simple (e.g., how I built a cabin) or complex, with two or more things happening simultaneously (e.g., the back-end processes of a conference or demonstration)
- unique as a one-time event (e.g., building the Chesapeake Bay bridge tunnel) or repeated (e.g., building a series of skyscrapers)
- through logical, orderly steps (e.g., raising prize-winning roses) or continuously with no specific order (e.g., the historical destruction of an indigenous culture)

Testimony

What it is: An appeal to reliable authority, usually a public figure or an expert's research, including what others interested in the subject believe to be true.

How to use it: Testimony can be used to emphasize or highlight a person's experience:

- Move from the greater voices to the lesser ones.
- Consider past facts and apply them to likely future occurrences.
- Use narrative arrangement to set up a story about the authority being cited.

Drafting, Feedback, and Revising

Process theory emerged in counter to current-traditional theory (or "pre-process," per Chris M. Anson), which emphasizes the written product over how to teach students to get to that product (Anson, "Process" 216). In process theory, concomitant with focus on writing processes is an equal focus on improving the writer and not the text (North, *Making*), which means that imperfect text can be evaluated as strong text in the making. Other process-focused elements Anson highlights are the belief that writing is more than the sum of its parts; teaching should be "student centered"; writing can be part of the thinking process rather than the product of thinking; and—of enormous importance in shifting how writing is taught—writing is a "socially dynamic effort" as opposed to being an "individual effort" ("Process" 216). Hence, writing has become understood as a process of drafting, receiving feedback from an audience—often peers or tutors and sometimes teachers—and redrafting, or revising. How these phases cycle is something writers individualize.

One way to teach drafting is to describe it as actions involving making choices for either alphabetic or multimodal compositions. Even the acts of scripting and storyboarding for multimodal projects are drafting, as students compose narration to supplement a presentation, video, or podcast. Professor Jackson collects these drafts to give early feedback before projects are fully fleshed out. We suggest that instructors model drafting for students by writing and revising an original brief argument for them in whatever genre and using whatever technology best fits the course and purpose (see chs. 5 and 8).

In-process drafting has recursive parts, each of which can generate new ideas, directions, or steps. Drafting, which is unique to each writer, might have the following characteristics (adapted from Hewett, "From Topic"):

Drafting begins with choice of topic or, when a topic is required, choosing a perspective on that topic.

Invention narrows the topic and develops a thesis, reasons, examples, proofs, and details. Invention considers audience for guidance on how to accomplish its potential purpose. Brainstorming may occur with topic selection before narrowing can begin.

Writing begins with an initial draft, sometimes called a *zero draft* to indicate its low-stakes nature, that is likely unfit to show to others. It may have disconnected words, phrases, thoughts; incomplete sentences; scribbles; and drawing.[2] The writing is rough, unready for public viewing.

With time, more writing, and more thought, composing continues and leads to a preliminary draft, one that will be revised several times. A *preliminary*, or *early*, *draft* begins to have the shape and genre characteristics expected for the audience and purpose. It is ready for (ungraded, formative) feedback from teachers and peers. Students benefit from instruction on how to read and use feedback. Some writers may not understand how to take what is provided and use it in revision and may ignore it, feel embarrassed, or experience undue frustration.

Revising follows to create a second, third, or even fourth preliminary draft. The writer makes choices among the feedback received to improve and strengthen the message and its expression. If no other feedback sessions are provided by classmates or the teacher, then students may want writing center tutors or embedded writing fellows to offer thoughts.

Revision ends—despite knowledge that the piece is not finished—when drafting leads to a *presentation draft*, one that has been edited for style and correctness, formatting, and other polishing actions. Presentation drafts are as ready for class or instructor review as possible.

Revision begins again after additional formative feedback, leading to improvements that create a *publication draft* for the portfolio or other course requirement; this draft receives a summative response if it is graded. Ideally, people other than peers and instructors read published pieces.

As described in this example process, the writing has developed over time using a series of potential steps with numerous, recursive writerly choices. Any individual's writing process may be more recursive than this list allows, often cyclical with students revisiting these various stages. The writing process likely includes these steps at some point, however.

The drafting → feedback → revision process can be represented through the commonly adapted communications triangle we have used in various parts of this book. At its simplest, the triangle looks like figure 7.2, with the student writer interacting with the assignment text,

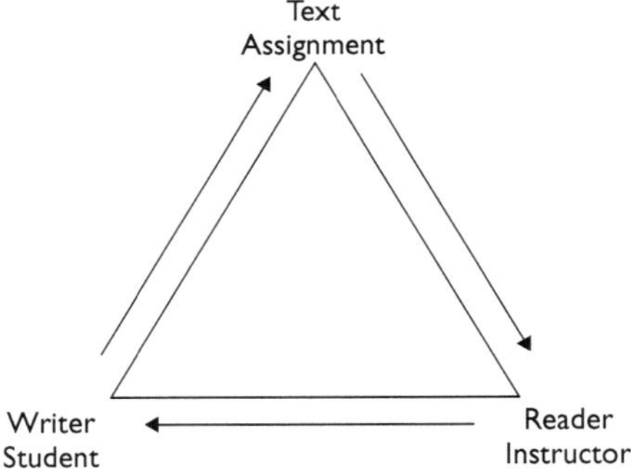

Figure 7.2. Adaptation of Kinneavy's communications triangle revised for instructors and students. Hewett, *Reading*, p. 61.

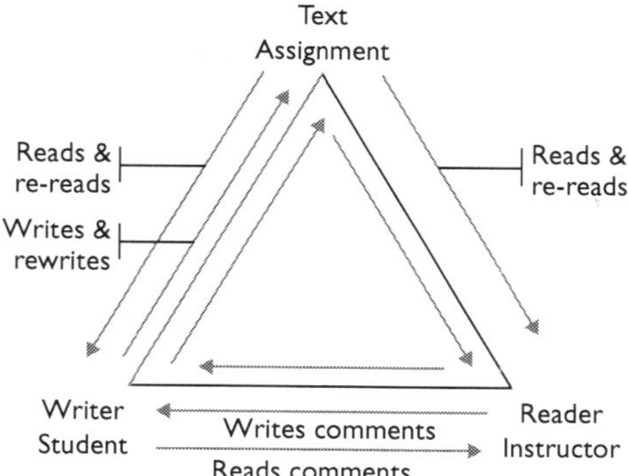

Figure 7.3. Communications triangle with linear interactions between instructor and student. Hewett, *Reading*, p. 62.

the instructor reader interacting with the student's assignment text, and the student writer receiving the instructor reader's feedback. Yet the interaction that composition instructors expect to occur is more complex than this simple one-time cycle. Figure 7.3 uses the same communications triangle configuration to suggest that complexity with a linear process wherein instructor and student interact (presumably through a learning management system [LMS]) in a back-and-forth manner. Given process pedagogy's theory that both drafting and reading occurs multiple times, this figure indicates that recursion happens and may affect writers through their write-rewrite and read-reread cycle.

This illustration is still insufficient, however, particularly given the ease with which instructors and students can and do respond to and share writing in progress using digitality (even in on-site courses). Linearity is fine in figures, but it cannot adequately model the instructor-student read-write-read cycle. Figure 7.4 is an attempt to illustrate the nonlinear, reciprocal, complex cycle of the drafting → feedback → revision process, wherein students have multiple options to revise from feedback, instructors have multiple options for both formative and summative feedback, and the movement between these options represents publishing text that students and instructors read and respond to.[3]

The etymology of *revise*, of course, is "resee," and teachers have various approaches, many digital, to help students resee their projects. Some of these approaches provide opportunities for students to see their words from different perspectives:

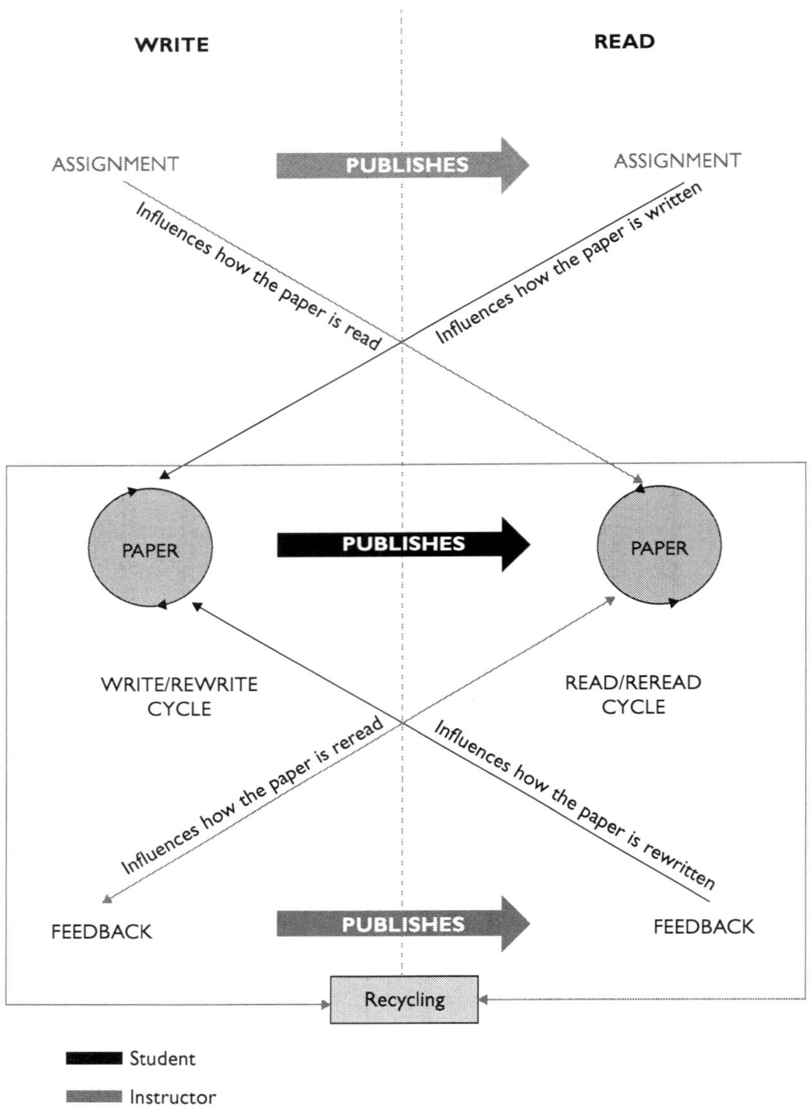

Figure 7.4. Nonlinear write-read process for drafting, feedback, and revision. Hewett, *Reading*, p. 63.

Reverse Outlining. Students create an outline after drafting, checking to see that sections and paragraphs each say something that logically follows the previous idea and leads to the next.

What I Said versus What I Mean. Students read the text aloud to hear what is written and consciously question whether it faithfully conveys what it was intended to say. This process benefits from a second reader to listen and read aloud.

Color-Coding. Using different highlighters on a hard copy or on the computer screen, students code connected points with the same colors or code only the thesis, topic sentences, and other main points. They check the conclusion points against the introductory and thesis points for intersections.

Multimodal Revising. Students orally record possible changes, using pictures or video to record what was composed versus what was intended, or test different mediums for the project.

Self-Reflection Exercises. Students write about writing choices, strategies, and other issues outlined in the assignment or assessment rubric.

Advantages from drafting and revising do not change in digital settings, but how these processes occur changes based on composing tools used, classroom setting, and alphabetic and multimodal technologies that spur different learning and writing practices. In other words, drafting and revising remain critical processes, but they may operate differently in digital settings. Thirty years ago, student writers might not have had the time to rewrite by hand or retype a paper multiple times to complete new drafts that generated different thinking, added deeper detail, or took the writing in a new direction. Simple lack of time might have accounted for poor or insufficient revision in these cases. The redundancies of rewriting by hand or retyping, however, are mitigated in a word processing world that enables file renaming for overlaying subsequent drafts on the original; as such, instructors should look to other reasons—also possibly time-related—for lack of redrafting. They should consider digital changes when assigning writing and teaching drafting. For example, drafting and redrafting can occur through text-to-voice for audio reconsideration, audio-video drafting for instructional review, or voice-to-text.

Likewise, instructing students about how to give, receive, and use feedback for improved compositions may change. Peer response groups (see chs. 4 and 9) still may meet face-to-face, but they also may meet online, typically using asynchronous groups in the course LMS, requiring a different approach to offering and receiving feedback. Feedback can occur through video, audio, text, and in person. Nonetheless, whether feedback is global, local, or both matters for how students understand their revision job (see ch. 9 for feedback processes and content).

Style

Style is more about expressing a message well than about correctness, although correctness makes texts more acceptable to academic readers particularly. Erika Lindemann addresses style as "word choice" (177). Also called *eloquence*, style is one of the five classical canons of rhetoric. According to Paul Butler in *The Writer's Style*:

> Style is a way of writing, the *manner* in which we use vocabulary, word choice, tone, voice, figures of speech (like parallelism or irony) and many other language features to achieve *effects* in writing or speaking. *How* something is said—its *style*—is intrinsically related to *what* is said—its content. The study of style asks, *how* are specific effects produced, either consciously or unconsciously, in our use of language? (9–10)

Writing courses, particularly first-year writing, have many outcomes more basic than eloquent expression, which may be why style rarely gets its due; course time restrictions potentially make advanced writing courses better suited for extensive stylistic work. Additionally, most students learn little of style because its constituent components of sentence correctness (i.e., grammar, usage, and mechanics), word choice, register or formality levels, and sentence-level clarity tend to be addressed individually and as error-focused rather than holistically and as meaning enhancing. Educators attuned to cultural competence regard these constituent parts as appropriate or rhetorically powerful rather than as correctness issues (Inoue, *Antiracist*; Matsuda; Miller-Cochran). Style is crucial to alphabetic text and also to how messages are composed multimodally. From a rhetorical perspective, style is an art of effective language use, "integral to meaning" (Butler 14).

It is not uncommon for educators to refer to teaching elements of style (Butler) and grammar (Kolln and Gray) rhetorically. This meaning-focused approach offers writers options for enlarging sentence-based choices instead of constraining them with rigid grammatical rules, making guidance more welcoming and friendly as well as potentially more helpful to those wishing to develop individual voices. In *Style: Lessons in Clarity and Grace*, Joseph Williams and Joseph Bizup, referring to H. L. Mencken's ideas, write that "no one learns to write well by rule, especially those who cannot see or feel or think. . . . I also know that the more clearly we write, the more clearly we see and feel and think. Rules help no one do that, but some principles can" (8; see also Strunk and White). We think style instruction should consider students' potential familiarity with written language. For example, what is cliché, trite, or stale language to instructors may be students' first attempts at elegant writing through imitation, and they may be proud to add such language to their repertoire. Gentle guidance toward eloquence rather than stark notations of "overused" or "banal" is preferable.

Editing and Polishing

Attending to editing and polishing any composition means being aware of register, usage, mechanics, and grammar, among other concerns. Addressing these issues can lead to better style. Certainly, style comprises more than error avoidance, but helping students begin to understand and notice their common error patterns works for some learners. Giving students a digital error correction log for their personal use may help visual learners acquire skill by notating where and when they make errors and how they corrected them (see ex. 7.3).

Example 7.3. Student Error Correction Log

Possible errors	Assignment	Number of occurrences	Corrections	Comments
Fragment				
Run-on				
Parallelism				
Shift in person				
Shift in tense				
Shift in number				
Comma needed				
Comma added				
Capitalization				
Contraction				
Other punctuation				
Quotation correctness				
Internal citation				
Bibliographic entry				
Other				

Digital composing means simple spelling and grammar errors can be corrected using word processing software checkers. Yet problems abound. First, the software might select a word or phrase that is correct in the piece's context and offer incorrect or inapt correction selections; inexperienced writers might make the incorrect choice to change their word(s). Second, the software might provide a series of corrections for a misspelling, for example, and writers who do not know better may choose the wrong spelling for an originally misspelled word. Perhaps more interesting are errors inserted into text through voice-to-text software, which might mistake *ketchup* for *catch up* or *voting* for *boating*, for example. Human eyes (and ears) are necessary to check for correctness; reading aloud from a hard copy or screen is still a good strategy.

Sentences and words tend to get helpful coverage in style guides and handbooks (e.g., Lindemann chs. 10 and 11). The Internet provides student writers with easy access to usage, grammar, and mechanics rules (or so-called standard American English). Therefore, many people never purchase or use a hard copy handbook—a concern Professor Jackson has with his students. Teaching students how to find what they need in a current handbook offers a lifelong reading and writing literacy skill. Such instruction minimally involves teaching why and how a handbook is useful;

building coursework around the handbook to assimilate learning into writing;

orienting students to the table of contents, index, and topic organization;

explaining the handbook's common vocabulary;

introducing students to special-interest sections: multilingual needs, style development, error consideration;

giving students miniassignments (accomplishable online, whether the handbook is hardbound or digital) to become acquainted with where to find assistance for common writing concerns corresponding to their own writing needs; and

using the handbook regularly in response to one or two writing concerns per draft, as an adjunct to—not substitute for—teaching using the students' own texts.

Thoughtful proofreading and use of handbooks lead to more polished pieces ready for publication.

Publishing

Publishing, or delivering, the finished composition, has not always received due attention partly because instructors have been the primary audience. Many teachers still expect students to publish their compositions as traditional essays strictly using alphabetic text with standard margins, titles, and pagination. Although students might give the instructor a hard copy in person, the ubiquity of LMSs (see ch. 4) makes digitally posting texts more likely; there, instructor-readers retrieve student work and either print or read it online. Contemporary students, however, have several delivery options that were not as accessible even ten years ago. Digital delivery offers a combination of modes—including sound, image, and video—for publishing in digital formats like websites, blogs, and social media platforms. Digital delivery allows authors to transform the message, and it lets the audience interact with the message and sometimes rewrite the text itself if the publication site (e.g., a wiki) allows for audience interaction and collaboration. A live audience's exigence means students need knowledge of the various distribution options at their fingertips; knowing how audiences will "access, engage, and interact" with the project leads students to critically consider design and presentation (Porter, "Recovering" 208).

Professor Jackson and other instructors should consider different publication options and broaden their understanding of acceptable composition delivery, which is linked to composing genre and therefore to how students' messages are shaped. For example, although students can deliver their ideas as traditional alphabetic projects, they can publish such essays with internal links from one section to another, giving readers different options for reading the text. Continuing this example, instructors can assign ePortfolios, which not only provide such internal links but also accommodate capstone projects that can be circulated for a wider audience (see ch. 8 in this volume and chs. 4 and 6 in Tiffany Bourelle, Beth L. Hewett, and Scott Warnock's *Administering Writing Programs in the Twenty-First Century*). Delivery also includes composing alphabetic text with multimodal features and publishing it to a class website for live reader commentary. Such public delivery makes the audience real, strengthening students' sense of purpose and rhetorical situation.

Oral presentations of the composition return students to ancient oratorical practices as seen in TED Talks, an example of online, free, talk forums for presenting worthwhile ideas. Podcasts return students to radio, where the aural supersedes the visual; to accommodate audience access needs, students should provide scripts or transcriptions. For students who speak better than they write or who have writing disabilities or other access needs, presenting some compositions orally may increase their learning while demonstrating their composing skills. Such oral composition can be captured on video for a *YouTube* recording using slideware or speaking from notes, which may benefit shy students who want to perfect a presentation through editing. To develop both a better understanding of access issues and to be inclusive, students can provide an accessible PDF of the talk on the publication site or they can enable closed captioning.

Briefer compositions—perhaps short topic proposals or assignments that turn a phrase—can be delivered using SMS or instant messaging, texting, or *Twitter*. Social media offer other delivery options, each with its own rhetorical conventions. Blogs also offer nontraditional, interesting delivery spaces. We recommend considering different delivery options, enabling students to learn the rhetoricity of their composing work as real, important, and part of a lifelong literacy education.

Reflection

Reflections, particularly self-reflections, are imperative, whether conducted orally, through alphabetic text, or multimodally expressed, and whether completed in on-site or online settings. Reflection's metacognitive nature requires both self-recognition and articulation of processes, choices, and thinking, enabling students to see how their cognitive learning, expressive skills, and personal growth have developed throughout the project. These skills are often understood at a deeper level through self-reflective practices. When students reflect on their learning and choices, they own their identities as twenty-first-century writers. Kathleen Blake Yancey notes in *A Rhetoric of Reflection* that reflection encourages a "growth of conscientiousness," allowing students to be 'agents of their own learning" ("Introduction" 5). In "A Multimodal Task-Based Framework for Composing," Jody Shipka expresses that goal setting, which can occur with pre- and postreflections of students' choices and goals, can encourage more robust revision. When multiple modalities are added, students experience "opportunities to develop and express their identities" (Vasudevan et al. 447), suggesting a richness of self-teaching and self-acceptance potential. Claire Lauer argues in "Examining the Effect of Reflective Assessment on the Quality of Visual Design Assignments in the Technical Writing Classroom" that students' multimodal projects become better, more rhetorically sound texts when students are asked to self-reflect. Student reflection is clearly a tool widely used in the teaching of composition, but it also can be used in evaluation (see ch. 9).

Reflection enables writers to explain their processes, why they approached the task as they did, what they liked or believed was strong, and what they disliked or believed was weaker. Such introspection cements learning; Yancey calls the different approaches to reflection *reflection-in-action* ("Introduction" 13), *constructive reflection*, and *reflection-in-presentation* (14). Reflection involves both "*looking forward*" to one's goals and "*casting backward*" to one's actions (Silver 168).

Digital settings can enhance reflection activities. In "Reflection in Digital Spaces," Naomi Silver offers suggestions for engaging digital tools as well as multimodal reflection techniques, any of which can combine text and multiple media: "Working with students as they discover the rhetorical affordances and constraints of various digital tools for their writing, as part of digital rhetoric pedagogy, supports as well the development of a digital reflective curriculum" (187). Her students' uses of reflection have led to her changing her own feedback processes to be more multimodal (188). Undoubtedly, when self-reflection is written, videoed, or audio-recorded, others can learn from them, too. Peer response to reflections teaches all parties; for example, instructors can learn how students approach the course and how the course might be adjusted. Reflection about one's composing processes and products is such a powerful learning tool that instructors may employ it for every major assignment and for some of the minor, scaffolded activities too.

Reflections are helpful throughout the composing process. For example, in journals, students write about their progress and approaches to composing; in an LMS space that is private to student and instructor, a confidential metacognitive dialogue can happen between student and teacher. Even if journals are not used, students should write prereflections in the style of Shipka's statements of goals and choices, where students pitch ideas for the project, including their individual project's goals (*Toward a Composition* 113–25). These statements minimally should include choices of audience, rhetorical situation and purpose, and medium so instructors (and potentially peers) can guide student writers in making better, more rhetorically effective choices. They should include students' goals for the project, which the instructor can use to guide evaluation.

Often, students do not recognize that self-reflections help them relearn course concepts, and they may think the instructor is their audience. Although this assumption is partly true, reflection is an interaction with oneself and should be retaught to help students use reflections for learning. Students often do a poor job writing reflections because instructors do not teach this genre, assuming students already know it. Therefore, instructors can incorporate reflection labs where students are presented with former student projects (or sample resources found on the Internet or shared among instructors) and are asked to consider the author's rhetorical choices that are evident or missing from the text. Students can freewrite or answer questions about audience, purpose, research, organization, or the general rhetorical effectiveness of the project. Learning to reflect upon others' work can be turned inward to one's own work, which is a way of researching one's own writing processes and content.

Conclusion

The twenty-first century's digitality requires that faculty members and students explore the potential of all processes and types of composing without losing the programmatic structures that facilitate the development of discrete writing skills. It is important to give students as complete a toolbox of composing strategies and technological options as possible. Multimodal composing should complement, not replace, traditional alphabetic composing. The emphasis should remain on rhetorical considerations instead of technology or the idiosyncrasies of a student's processes; instructors should acknowledge, however, that various processes, including those of medium choice and technology use, are key to composition. Starting small, giving students choices, and requiring reflection ensures they will learn the rhetorical concepts behind composition, regardless of challenges that arise during the process.

NOTES

1. A heuristic comprising particle, wave, and field for a uniquely multidimensional, nine-point grid to explore a topic's "contrastive or identificational features, its place within a dynamic flow or larger system, and its nature as a system itself with component parts" (Edwards 717; see R. Young et al.).

2. Such drawings further substantiate the conjoined nature of alphabetic and multimodal texts; see Reichert Powell, *Writing*, for additional perspective.

3. For a complete review of this drafting process contextualized by deep connections between reading and writing, see Hewett, *Reading* 61–65.

8

Designing and Scaffolding Assignments

Professor Jackson wants to do a better job of teaching by taking advantage of composition's inherent digitality. He plans to improve how he develops, tests, and presents content and assignments based on the program's outcomes—and to do so with digitality in mind. He particularly wants to encourage students to read, understand, and compose alphabetic and multimodal texts. Scaffolding strategies for different course purposes, including traditional essay development, multimodal composition, and various genres will help him accomplish these goals.

Regardless of modality and even in a well-designed course, students must teach themselves much more than instructors think. When the classroom is technologically enhanced for presenting, sharing, and posting assignments, students must read and comprehend—often without the teacher's verbal instructions. Indeed, when instructors do not write readable text and do not design instructional texts well, they inadvertently set students up for failure. When students fail to read well (i.e., when they fail to understand necessary instructional content or assignment goals), they also fail to write or learn to write and compose according to desired outcomes (Hewett, *Reading*). The intensively literacy-based nature of all technologically enhanced courses is a much neglected area, and we argue that students' success begins with well-designed, clearly articulated assignments that encourage students to understand both what they are being asked to learn or create and how to do so. We present strategies for developing and presenting such material and assignments to help students succeed; these strategies are effective practices for teaching all students, including multilingual writers.

A Process for Designing Effective Assignments

Setting students up for success involves careful design in every aspect of assignment creation and evaluation.

Choose Topics Wisely

The best assignments give students choices of topics, audience, rhetorical situation and purpose, and medium. Many teachers have told us they do not want their students to write about cliché, overdone, or contentious topics. Although students may themselves raise such topics for discussion, instructors should avoid assigning them unless they are critical to the course's purpose and students are taught to address them responsibly. Additionally, although instructors may not universally agree, we believe they should keep personal bias out of responses to students' topics whenever possible and openly acknowledge and work beyond their biases when necessary. The National Council of Teachers of English recognizes this challenging issue in its "NCTE Beliefs about the Students' Right to Write": "Teacher feedback should avoid indoctrination because of personal beliefs and should be respectful of both the writer and [the writer's] ideas." We think this advice is crucial to effective assignment design—particularly for first-year writing (FYW) students—because helping students choose potentially fruitful rather than inflammatory topics about which people simply will not agree is the best way to avoid unnecessarily and harmfully inserting one's bias in feedback. We suggest prompting students to write about timeless archetypal themes or the nature of reading and writing as acts. Alternatively, prompts about real, local community-based situations offer rhetorical situations that ask students to research what affects them and their neighborhoods, campus, and communities, offering potentially invigorating rhetorical situations that enable student writing to have an impact on their lived spaces.

Write Assignments Clearly

In the digital era, many students first see their assignments as files or pages in a learning management system (LMS). Reading text from a screen is different from reading from hard copy (Jukes et al.; see also ch. 6). Therefore, what is applicable to online writing instruction concerns nearly all composition students: "Providing readable OWI assignments is not as much about *what we ask students to write* as it is about *how we present those assignments to students.*" Writing an assignment is a reading consideration and an access issue: How well can students read the assignment? The best assignments use "clear expository writing and process analysis" (Hewett, *Reading* 208). Therefore, we provide this advice for writing readable assignments that clearly convey the tasks:

> Be straightforward.
>
> Try out your own assignments (addressed below).
>
> Offer ample examples.
>
> Build in redundancy to improve memory and comprehension.
>
> Use formatting and visual cues: make use of white space, format elements thoughtfully, use icons and formatting tools (208–25).
>
> Use clear language.
>
> "Give relevant information in the right order."
>
> "Help people find information quickly" (26Ten 5).

Perhaps the most important item of this advice is to be straightforward. Instructors like to express friendliness when giving guidance, yet it may render as informal, unclear discursiveness; other approaches, however, can develop a sense of teacher presence and connectedness with students (see chs. 10 and 11). Linguistically direct speech acts that clearly convey what students must do and when are crucial; Beth L. Hewett calls these *semantic integrity* (*Online Writing Conference* 116–29, 183–91 and *Reading* 179–89). Such speech includes thoughtfully developed declarative, interrogative, and imperative statements. Suggestions and hints are linguistically indirect and generally unhelpful because they are harder to interpret. Overt suggestions, for which students can make actual choices, should begin with phrases such as *I suggest you XYZ, I think ABC, or you may choose among X, Y, and Z.* Helpful formatting elements include bolding and highlighting due dates. Infographics and videos that aid reading are especially useful for accessibility (*Reading* 217–25). Example assignments in this chapter use such approaches.

Consider Outcomes

Rightly, WPA Garcia has told her faculty members that all assignments should address the program's global outcomes for student learning and the local outcomes for the specific course. Programmatic and course outcomes should be folded into assignments and scaffolded, supplemental exercises must match those outcomes. In fact, everything instructors do should align with programmatic and course outcomes, from the assignments to activities to portfolios, if required. To begin, instructors must structure assignments according to pedagogical goals:

What should students learn through this assignment?

What are the assignment goals?

How do they match with programmatic and course goals?

How does this assignment fit into the overall course structure and curriculum?

Question 1 indicates instructors should draft the assignment according to what students are expected to learn. For instance, if students need to learn a genre, then both the rhetorical situation and conventions for composing within that genre must be clear in the assignment. Questions 2 and 3 indicate instructors must determine the assignment's specific goals and align the assignment with the course outcomes. For example, if students need to learn online team writing, the assignment should teach elements of coauthoring a project using asynchronous and synchronous technologies. Question 4 suggests instructors should examine the assignment regarding its place in the term's sequential structure. If the assignment is major and requires learning new, complicated software or drafting multiple revisions, it may occur last in the term sequence with smaller-stakes projects leading up to it. Such sequencing is especially important when assigning multimodal projects. By first understanding outcomes that guide their practices, instructors can engage backward design, meaning they lay the groundwork with overarching outcomes to decide what students should be learning and then build lessons to help students achieve these goals.

Select Textbooks

Typically, WPA Garcia engages a textbook committee for examining and selecting required or recommended textbooks that align with outcomes. Before considering assignments, instructors should first review any prescribed models for teaching and mandatory or self-selected course texts.

For instance, many programs approach writing through genres. These might include restaurant, play, or park reviews in which students attempt to persuade the audience to frequent or avoid these spaces. Other genres might include writing to negotiate or persuade, teaching problem-solving proposals. Some textbooks offer a thematic or idea-based approach and include readings to provide possible content. Textbooks should be examined with regard to various factors, including accessibility of hard copy and digital resources, alignment to the program's outcomes and values, representation of local student culture and demographics, quality of case studies and examples, appropriate length for course or term, and cost to students (also an access issue). Where instructors can make their own choices, they should start with accessible texts and programmatic objectives, working down through this list.

Practice Scaffolding

Scaffolding is a process that, done well, leads to more active learning. Generally, instructors scaffold when they "break the task into smaller, more manageable parts"; "use 'think alouds', or verbalizing thinking processes, when completing a task"; "use cooperative learning, which promotes teamwork and dialogue among peers"; "use concrete prompts, questioning, coaching, cue cards, or modeling"; and use strategies like "activating background knowledge and offering tips, strategies, cues, and procedures" (Pinantoan). When a writing course's total outcomes are scaffolded through a series of assignments or parts of individual assignments, students receive doable tasks that teach particular skills, learn processes for task completion, experience collaborative learning, and follow prompts and models that suggest how activities can proceed.

Activity theory suggests that students learn by doing an activity and through the social nature of completing the task. Victor Kaptelinin, Karl Kuutti, and Liam Bannon indicate in "Activity Theory" that activity theory, rooted in Marxist philosophy, is based on the philosophical principle that the human mind as it develops "can only be understood within the context of meaningful, goal-oriented, and socially determined interaction between human beings and their material environment" (Kaptelinin et al. 190). Activity theory insists on active, student-centered learning, either collaborative or individual, if students are to grow as writers; although this learning can be individual, it is still situated in a social context, meaning that everything students construct is essentially created for various audiences within society (Bazerman, "Discursively Structured Activities"; Britton et al.; Sannino et al.).

In "Sound Engineering," Jody Shipka notes that, not only with multimodal composition but also with more traditional alphabetic essays, activity-based theory enables students to negotiate the meaning they make through various modes. With multimodal composition particularly, there are no set rules students must follow; instead, they are responsible for determining their objectives and outcomes for their productions—the "conditions and contexts of their work" (358). In a discussion of her classes, Shipka stresses the importance of leaving choices of modalities, construction, circulation, and delivery to her students:

> An activity-based multimodal theory of composing facilitates greater communicative flexibility by providing students with a series of open-ended tasks that ask them to consider how even a seemingly simple, straightforward, and relatively familiar communicative objective might be accomplished in any number of ways and with any number of semiotic resources depending on how they choose to frame or coordinate their response to that objective. (358)

Choices prompt students to take active roles in learning, setting goals for themselves and their projects. Thoughtfully developed activities that work toward course outcomes supplement strong assignments. This chapter's assignment examples use both scaffolding and activity theory, aligning with chapter 7's composing processes and approaches.

Determine and Teach Rhetorical Skills

Here we present an argument assignment for which the topic must require probable, or practical, reasoning (see chs. 1 and 3). No matter the specifics, students benefit from ongoing discussion and skills practice (e.g., analysis of ethos, pathos, and logos; developing a claim). Although Professor Jackson might avoid introducing hot-button topics in the classroom, he can ask students about their local concerns, such as what is happening in city or campus communities. Based on their responses, he can organize a debate, courtroom style. For instance, students might say they are concerned that their common student area is becoming "too healthy" by eliminating all fast foods and offering only whole food options. Alternatively, students can suggest topics and the class can vote about which to discuss or they can debate issues from textbooks and readings. To facilitate an argument or dialogue about an issue, instructors can

> Ask students to sit on one side of the room if they support a particular position (defense) and the other if they do not (prosecution). Undecided students can sit in the middle and be the jury. (Fully online courses can use breakout rooms, LMS small groups, or discussion boards for this work.)

> Assign all students to read and annotate at least four arguments: two in support and two against the position. The jury also must complete the readings to enable informed decisions.

> Allow students to volunteer for such roles as opening and closing lawyers, witnesses based on specific cases surrounding the issue, and so on.

> Conduct the debate as a trial, allowing it to come to a natural end.

With classes that have experienced this process once, consider shaking up certainty about the debated issue by redesignating students who support the given position to argue against it and those not in support to argue for it. Argumentative elements should be evident to students, and instructors can preteach such elements or approach them as students go along. Prior to class-based discussions, students can write reflections of what they learned regarding argumentation and the issue's pro-con positions. Not all students will enjoy participating in such a process, and instructors should clarify that the lesson is not about changing others' minds but about engaging argumentation, listening, dialoguing, and considering other legitimate viewpoints.

Establishing open dialogue through potentially low-stakes debates on local topics early in the term can create space for more productive dialogue when especially difficult topics arise. Any topic, however, has the potential to be contentious or triggering for those involved or affected by it. As such, instructors must set respectful ground rules, including that racist, sexist, or other inflammatory statements will not be tolerated.

When students show confusion about these rules or make earnest mistakes, these communicative errors become teaching opportunities. Although open dialogue should be embraced, all students should have a role in assignments like this example debate, which is especially important if their opinions change midway—a possibility in productive dialogue. The course syllabus should encourage students to talk with the instructor if they feel uncomfortable about course topics or situations that occur. As we address in chapter 10, instructors should seek to establish a functional community of practice (Lave and Wenger) assisted by reasonable ground rules. Teachers should moderate and facilitate debate and discussion, modeling civil and effective listening and speaking behaviors—a skill set Professor Jackson's students certainly need. Through reflection and discussion at the lesson's end, instructors and students can integrate what they learned about other points of view.

State Goals

A good assignment starts with clearly stated goals that reflect why students must complete the project and what they can expect to learn. Because programmatic or course outcomes typically are written for assessment and not for students' uses, assignment goals should be written to connect to the outcomes while clearly stating what students should learn. Heidi Harris and colleagues indicate that online students particularly need explicitly stated connections among the assignment and course goals and outcomes. This connection is especially critical when students create portfolios for which they reflect on their learning of course outcomes.

For example, the goals of a persuasive argument that offers a proposed solution (see ch. 3) may be to write a convincing persuasive argument with proposed solution, analyze an audience for a persuasive argument, recognize the genre conventions of arguments that move people to action, and use research to support such an argument. Course goal statements can be brief, and the course outcomes that align with the assignment goals should follow: *While completing this assignment, you also will be addressing the following course outcomes.*

Offer Choices

Although instructors make many decisions for students in assignments, allowing students to select such focal points as rhetorical situations may engage their desired purposes for composing. Instructors also can enable students to invent their own rhetorical situations, which is arguably harder than simply being given one. Conferencing helps when giving students such invention options. Of course, students need different assistance at lower course levels. When encouraging FYW students to invent a rhetorical situation, for example, it is helpful to offer them the writing's purpose (e.g., writing to analyze or to evaluate). In other words, do not expect students to self-determine both the context and purpose for writing when they are learning other core skills. Choices among assignment prompts also is critical, increasing access for students in various life situations. As Susan Miller-Cochran notes, such alternatives are imperative when working with multilingual students, who might not be familiar with local cultural contexts. Giving students assignment choices is one way of providing equal access culturally as well as technologically.

Instructors also can ask students to choose their project genre and medium after offering acceptable options and parameters. For example, given one of Professor Jackson's assignments (see ex. 8.1), his students need to know that a typical public service announcement (PSA) is one to two minutes, providing them a target length. Yet he can allow students to discover such parameters before providing them. Professor Jackson can scaffold an activity that introduces PSA examples and lead discussions that enable self-discovery of such conventions. By scaffolding such learning, he can connect learning through the assignment: *Remember our discussions of PSA conventions when creating your own.* This connective tissue teaches students that class discussions are important for achieving outcomes, encouraging their active participation. We suggest providing students with two or three choices of medium and then scaffolding the assignment by discussing the parameters of each, offering options for thinking beyond the choices provided.

To best address accessibility, instructors should offer no-cost, easy-use options while not requiring students to use certain software or create something within a specific medium that would require them to purchase or use particular software programs outside the LMS. Allowing students choices gives them opportunities to create alphabetic and multimodal texts using mobile technologies (e.g., creating a video or writing text using a file-sharing application). Although there may be pedagogical reasons for limiting students' choices, students should be given other options or workarounds, as example 8.1 illustrates.

Example 8.1. Sample Medium Choices

Your genre is a public service announcement (PSA). Remember our discussions about parameters of PSA conventions; keep your PSA to under two minutes. Although you must provide a written transcript, you may use any software to create either project listed below. See the course LMS for various tutorials. Choose radio or TV or discuss with me.

- **PSA for Radio (Sound Project).** If you choose radio, remember that the PSA should use another communicative mode along with voice (e.g., sound, music, or other aural elements).
- **PSA for TV (Video).** If you choose television, remember that the PSA should use more than one communicative mode (e.g., images, narration, sound, or others).
- **PSA for a Medium of Your Choice.** If the above choices do not work for your audience and purpose, talk to me about what you want to create.

Although instructors can give students free rein when choosing a medium, for example, we suggest conferencing with students early or requiring brief project proposals to pitch ideas before drafting. Because online students typically conference online, often asynchronously, they may benefit from several choices for which the instructor can offer specific guidance.

Sit in the Student Seat

After designing assignments, instructors should complete the projects themselves—start to finish—putting themselves in students' roles and using the course environment in which students will work (e.g., on-site, hybrid, fully online). By completing the drafted assignments themselves, instructors learn where the assignment succeeds and fails. Instructors should ask themselves the following:

What was most challenging about completing this assignment?

How can I revise my assignment to be clearer?

What do I need to teach students to do before they start drafting?

What additional resources should I provide to students?

How much time did I need for this assignment? To determine how much time students might need, double or triple your time depending on their skill levels. Give them this information for their planning purposes.

Through reflection on the composing process, instructors can revise the assignment and rescaffold accordingly. In addition to the instructor doing the assignment, peer teachers may participate since they can give more objective feedback. This process can be part of ongoing, paid professional development.

After reflecting on the composing process and revising accordingly, instructors may add a section on helpful hints to assignments (see Selfe, *Multimodal Composition* 21). These tips offer direct advice, such as starting the project early, planning sufficient time, remembering to save each draft, having a technology backup, creating a script before recording, or anything else instructors learned from completing the drafted assignment. Students might add to these tips, thus creating a community resource.

Construct Rubrics

We recommend in most cases that the final element of assignment development is constructing a feedback rubric comprising expected outcomes. Rubric specifics should match the assignment's focal points. Students must know how they will be evaluated when composing; discussing the benchmarks guides students in informed project composition. Instructors can cocreate rubrics with students, giving them voice in evaluation criteria and ensuring they clearly understand course outcomes. Such democratic teaching best follows teaching genre conventions and discussing what comprises a good project (see Shor). Rubrics help instructors cross-check course scaffolding and assignment clarity, and students may use them as composing guides and for peer review. We discuss and illustrate rhetorically focused rubrics in chapter 9.

What to Include in a Scaffolded Assignment

Chapter 7 addresses several processes that writers might use when composing, including genre conventions; rhetorical invention and brainstorming; audience analysis; rhetorical situation and purpose; organization; drafting, feedback, and revising; style; editing and polishing; and publishing. Here, we discuss how to teach these processes; some are exemplified through Professor Jackson's scaffolded miniassignments.

Genre Conventions

Students need to learn the conventions of the genres they will compose. One way to scaffold such learning is to provide a sample text and ask them to conduct a genre analysis. In a genre analysis, students

> categorize by rhetorical situation, apparent purpose, audience, and such, to find likely genre conventions;
>
> confirm observations by reading a corresponding textbook chapter or other instructional material and additional examples of the genre; and
>
> return to the genre analysis and revise it, noting whatever is missing.

This activity produces a genre master list or style sheet to which students can refer when brainstorming, drafting, and reflecting. Instructors also can teach genre conventions by asking students to find and analyze outside genres, presenting them to the class. To add a team element, students can do a think-pair-share activity in small groups to discuss their selected genres. Such activities help students prepare to brainstorm for composing.

Asking students to think about genre conventions and how they have changed over time (particularly regarding multimodality) can connect genre with rhetorical situation and purpose. For instance, the podcast is often considered an evolution or extension of radio programs that might have aired in the past (see ch. 3). When students are prompted to trace that evolution, noting when, how, and why the conventions have changed, they gain heightened awareness of their own composing.

Students also can consider genres within genres. For example, the podcast might be considered social media if the composer asks for dialogue with the audience in its posted space. Because often there are no clear definitions for certain genres, and some genres' purposes and audiences are changing based on human interaction and use, instructors should talk about changing genre conventions and rhetorical purpose. With social media like *Twitter*, for example, users often post hashtags where the audience can discuss ideas. Hashtags, therefore, are a genre within a genre and have rhetorical purpose when included in a post. Such discussions extend students' learning of genre and rhetorical purpose while sparking creative project ideas.

An assignment should outline the genre conventions and guide students to the textbook or other instructional material. This outlining, shown in example 8.2, should include specifics the instructor expects in the project.

Example 8.2. Genre Conventions Miniassignment

Because this is a persuasive argument that proposes a solution, in this miniassignment, you will do the preliminary work *before* you start writing. Specifically, you need to research the problem and find potential solutions for it, outlining one solution in detail. A good persuasive proposal typically

- outlines the problem with research, which shows that you have done your homework and know enough about the issue to offer a reasonable solution
- acknowledges the problem can have many solutions and suggests what a few might be—these are counterarguments—working toward showcasing the "best" one
- focuses on presenting one solution and arguing why it is best through research and evidence
- offers a call to action, which depends on who the audience for the proposal is

For more information on the proposal genre, see chapter X in your textbook [or instructional video or pages X–Y]. This information also offers various ways you can organize your project.[1]

Rhetorical Invention and Brainstorming

Invention and brainstorming can happen at any point in the composing process, as students continue to think, research, and write. Providing, modeling, and inviting students to try options from chapter 7 helps broaden their repertoire. Example 8.3 is a heuristic assignment that follows example 8.2's proposal assignment.

Example 8.3. Invention and Brainstorming Miniassignment

For this exercise, read or watch the local news to brainstorm your topic. While watching,

- take notes and follow up on anything interesting through deeper reading or viewing
- use an unstructured freewrite to explore a topic without stopping for ten minutes (or use a structured format with Burke's pentad or other questions)
- narrow the topic by writing an elevator pitch (i.e., a thirty-to-sixty-second persuasive speech) to tell me what you plan to write about

I will provide feedback to get you started and suggest research or a possible appropriate communication medium.

Invention certainly can occur multimodally. For example, if instructors provide students with an expository assignment for which they must observe, analyze, and evaluate favorite places, they can physically visit the place and take photos. Scaffolding this project toward the final assignment could require students to create a blog in a shared online space to outline how they plan to use the photos and discuss why and how each image is important to the overall message. Peers could be asked to read and respond to two or three blogs. A variation asks students to create brief videos in which they discuss their composing plans. Such scaffolded assignments not only assist in invention but also enable students to start thinking multimodally early in the project.

Audience Analysis

The twenty-first century has provided unique opportunities for teaching about audiences and how to appeal to them. Professor Jackson has learned, for example, that his students need to analyze social media to better understand the audience. Because the use of social media has changed who responds to societal happenings—broadening the circle—audience needs have changed. Where social media began as platforms to communicate events with friends and family, such platforms have morphed into argumentative spaces among those who know each other well and those with peripheral knowledge of other users. Students need not join social media or participate in the conversations to learn how these platforms engage audience, purpose, and medium. With platforms evolving, class discussion should consider how people are communicating on these platforms, perhaps pulling (anonymous) conversations into the classroom and asking students who the audience is and the users' communicative purposes. Some social media platforms enable people to block those who disagree with them. In such cases, who becomes the audience? People who think alike? What about the audience members who read but do not enter the conversation? What if they feel marginalized or silenced? Such audience analysis activities are not easy, but instructors can use social media as teaching tools without encouraging students to get involved, staying with the audience analysis (or other) goal at hand.

Many topics under discussion in society have real consequences and can be triggering for those who are affected by them. As hard as it may be to incorporate these lessons into the classroom, activities surrounding audience, purpose, and medium, combined with discussions of what it means to be open-minded, intellectually generous, and inclusive, can encourage students to recognize when and how to interact with others in an often polarized society. As we suggest in chapter 10, offering trigger warning language in the syllabus will help students recognize that discussions might be controversial and activate unexpected feelings.

Teaching audience analysis can be done creatively for any genre in any educational setting. Here are some methods for helping students learn to examine audiences:

Provide examples of audience analysis as guidance.

Ask students to analyze advertisements for audience, pointing out what brings them to their conclusions.

Ask students to hypothesize what might motivate such an audience: desires, fears, pleasures, knowledge, expectations.

Initiate additional active learning by asking students to bring, photograph, or video items they analyzed and discuss the intended audience with the class.

An assignment should explicate expectations regarding audience. We suggest leaving these decisions to students, guiding them to understand to whom they may want to argue based on their topics and interests. Example 8.4 illustrates one assignment requesting audience analysis.

Example 8.4. Audience Analysis Miniassignment

Choose your audience depending on your topic. For instance, if you are writing about the problem of your neighborhood not participating in a recycling program, your audience might be neighbors, the head of the homeowner's association, or the local mayor, depending on your choice of solutions. But it probably will not be the president of your college unless your neighborhood is, indeed, the campus. See the difference? The audience must be able to do something based on the selected problem, solution, and call to action.

Analyze this audience according to its characteristics:

- Who are they?
- What are their likely age ranges?
- What stake do they have in the problem?
- What types of emotions might this problem create in them?
- How might they be persuaded to act?

Remember that you must account for your choice of audience in the final reflection.

Rhetorical Situation and Purpose

The rhetorical situation, often called the *context for writing*, provides important background for the problem being addressed and why. To prompt thinking, instructors can provide two sample student projects—one that could be improved upon and another that is well crafted—anonymized with student permission. Students can identify the rhetorical situation for each piece, discuss the projects' strengths and weaknesses, and explain changes they would make to enhance them—a discussion that can occur face-to-face on-site, synchronously online, or asynchronously using discussion boards. Afterward, students might discuss ideas for their own projects, brainstorming with peers about any alphabetic and multimodal elements they might include to make clear the rhetorical situation. By first analyzing sample projects, students learn what they like and dislike about projects similar to their own and effective design elements for particular audiences. This process enables students to outline, draft, or storyboard their projects before full-on composing begins.

For a persuasive argument with a proposal, instructors might ask students to consider a local issue, as in example 8.5.

Example 8.5. Rhetorical Situation Miniassignment

Identify a current issue you find problematic in your community. You may consult local newspapers, news channels, social media sites, and so on. Look for something you have not written about before, and answer the following questions.

- What issue has emerged in your community that you feel passionate about?
- Why is it an issue?

- What is some of its history?
- Why do you care?
- Why should others care?
- What types of solutions could solve this problem?

Remember you will not be able to solve the major problems of the world or even of this local situation. Your job is to thoughtfully enter the conversation with reasons and actions that may possibly help.

This example rhetorical situation assignment is sufficiently vague to give students freedom to find an exigent issue that interests them while specifically local enough to steer them from more globally contentious issues. Some advanced course instructors may want to introduce a genre and help students find their own rhetorical situation to create more choices, but it is a good idea to start small with the first assignment and build skill requirements as the term progresses.

The purpose of a composition is different from but related to rhetorical situation. One's purpose regards not the situation but why one plans to write about it and what one hopes may come from the composition. The *why* is best answered by some individual interest in the issue and not just "because I have to do this assignment." Conversations about purpose often work well in conjunction with discussing audience. For instance, if students are writing about social media, they need to consider writers' purposes and their intended audiences, as shown in example 8.6.

Example 8.6. Purpose Miniassignment

Identify a social media platform you can explore for this assignment:

- What are the purposes of the social media platform you have selected to write about?
- What purposes might writers have when they post to social media? Are they trying to persuade the audience? Are they informing by posting links to articles?
- What does reposting of certain articles imply about the writer's purpose?
- How has the purpose of this social media platform changed over time?
- Who aligns with those changes and who does not?

Students may think they know the purpose of a social media platform, and often they can explain why someone may have developed a profile and for what purpose. But conversations are necessary regarding how they know the author's intentions or why they think they do.

Through what means, choices, or modes is the author communicating a purpose? Research will help them be better informed.

Primary and Secondary Research

Chapter 7 explains how *primary* and *secondary* research differ. Although most students engage in secondary research, they may do so insufficiently. Chapter 6 explains why some students read poorly about their topics. Research may become more relevant to students' lives and topics when they are prompted to write about something that affects their everyday lives. Beyond developing assignments around rhetorical contexts that prompt students to consider community-based issues, instructors can use examples of so-called fake news to help students learn about broader issues. Example 8.7 provides a research activity.

Example 8.7. Research Miniassignment

Find an example of "fake news" in both print and multimedia formats.

- Based on your examples, what is the definition of "fake news"?
- Analyze the purpose and audience for these examples.
- Research the issue to learn about other positions and narrative lines. Look at the back trail through various sources used in the post to evaluate source credibility.
- Rewrite or recreate the piece based on the newly found information.
- Write a reflection about research (and ethos) in the composing process.

Although, again, such an assignment might devolve into uncivil discourse about what is a fact, instructors can help steer discussions and compositions back to the research effort and away from opinions—even informed ones—that are off the assignment's point.

Organization

Using organization patterns in chapter 7, instructors should provide sample genres that are organized differently and ask students to discuss whether and why the arrangement works. Arrangement matters globally in how the content is paragraphed and locally within paragraphs and sentences. It is helpful to review organizational strategies for each assignment, since how one arranges material affects how audiences receive and understand it. When possible, students' organization of their projects should come organically: They should find an arrangement that fits the topic, genre, audience, rhetorical situation, and purpose. Yet they should not ignore the organizational patterns available to help them make such organic choices.

There is no one way to organize a specific genre, and often multiple organizational patterns might work. We resist the idea that a project must have a set introduction, body, and conclusion, especially if it is multimodal. Consider that, although movies and television programs often have an end, some conclude with a cliff hanger. Narratives begin in the middle or even the end. Sometimes readers need to know why they are reading something before they precisely understand what they are reading. Therefore, organization should be considered fluid in some cases, making reflection especially important since organization is a rhetorical choice for which students must account when breaking so-called rules for traditional organizational patterns.

Drafting, Feedback, and Revision

Teaching drafting in the twenty-first century can be done in many innovative ways, as chapter 7 describes. Students are no longer bound to handwriting or typing a draft drawn directly from their minds. Instead, they can storyboard the layout of an essay or multimodal project or draft a script that may help them record narration. Students can dictate their project and revise the resulting transcript. This drafting method may be especially helpful for multilingual students who use translation software and for students with writing disabilities, who may know what they want to say but are stymied by inscription. Depending on the project type, such as essays and comics or graphic narratives, students can create a rough sketch to receive formative feedback during the early drafting process (see ch. 9). Digital tools enable students to present preliminary drafts with voice-over at certain stages to explain to peer reviewers and instructors how they plan to progress.

Peers' and instructors' formative feedback assists students with rethinking and revising in-progress compositions. Students not only should receive formative feedback from peers, instructors (see ch. 9), and writing center consultants (see ch. 11) but also should learn how to read and interpret such feedback. When feedback is semantically clear—particularly to students in asynchronous online settings who must read and infer outside the instructor's presence—students have a better chance of interpreting it as intended. Nonetheless, they should be told whether and how they are expected to use the feedback provided and taught how to choose the best feedback for improving the project at hand. Moving from feedback to choice to revision often means showing students how a comment may be applied and what deep revision looks like: that revision requires more than changing a sentence or word and that revising one part of a piece often necessitates similar adjustments in other parts to match the argument's overall development.

Style

As chapter 7 notes, many good texts provide guidance about how to help students rhetorically with style. We recommend teaching one or two major style lessons during each assignment to scaffold and encourage more powerful stylistic choices throughout the term. For example, one assignment might teach conscious uses of active and passive voice with the goal of learning how to choose each. Students benefit from learning to use the strong, direct tone of the subject + verb + object to indicate powerful action. They equally benefit from learning to emphasize the passive voice of action over the actor, which business writing, advertisements, political statements, and news stories often engage. Such style instruction is a useful way to combine reading, analysis, and writing options in one miniassignment. Similarly, teaching cohesion strategies (such as from Williams and Bizup's *Style*) raises awareness both in reading and writing, allowing students to see how texts that are easiest to follow may be challenging (but worthwhile) to compose.

Editing and Polishing

Editing is another skill students must address, seeking improvement over time. Editing, which has many possible actions, can challenge students' skills in fun ways. For example, one exercise is to ask students to write a one-thousand-word essay. Then, in class, ask them to edit that essay down to five hundred words, using peer review and self-reflection activities after an initial attempt. Asking them to edit again to four hundred or three hundred words solidly teaches brevity and hard, but consciously made, word choices. Spell- and grammar-checks help with editing, but they are just one tool. Although everyone can benefit from an outside editor, students can become good self-editors. They should learn to read their work aloud and listen carefully to the words they speak. Reading aloud clarifies performance and competence errors because writers may read aloud what they wanted to say (i.e., their competence) rather than what they wrote (i.e., their performance). Reading aloud can be done alone, with a peer or tutor, or in student-teacher conferences. Even asynchronous students can live-conference with instructors through free videoconferencing software, the phone, or synchronous document-sharing software.

We teach that correctness is the final, local issue to address in any composition. Saving close editing for a second, third, or fourth draft helps students learn to focus on the global issues in an initial round of peer review, especially as the class progresses and they become familiar with what to expect for each assignment. Additionally, leaving close editing for last helps forestall the natural inclination to keep what "sounds good" but does not contribute to the content or argument. Polishing is a part of that level of editing, and it includes formatting in print text and checking links in multimodal digital texts.

Example 8.8 is a student prompt for teaching editing and polishing. Instead of having students simply point out errors, the assignment teaches grammar and punctuation in context.

Example 8.8. Style, Editing, and Polishing Miniassignment

Find examples of poorly written sentences in a document from another class or your workplace. You'll know them by any difficulties you have in reading the document. You'll also want to select examples of poorly written sentences from your own writing. When finding examples, select a problem sentence and the sentence before and after it for context.

- Email the sentences to me or bring them to class for compiling.
- In pairs, review and correct the sentences in context. Discuss the errors and how the revision corrected or eliminated the mistakes.
- Return to your own drafts and look for similar concerns or swap drafts with peers to suggest likely errors.

Publishing

Chapter 7 describes zero, preliminary, presentation, and publication drafts in the order of readiness for readers. The final draft of any essay or project is a publication draft, technically ready for circulation beyond the instructor. When projects are published to the Internet, they are available for anyone who finds them to read. Unfortunately, projects often are not seen beyond the instructor and classmates. Sometimes, if a portfolio is a capstone project, it might be seen by others as students work toward degree completion.

Having a genuine audience is an important part of composing with purpose. Instructors might collaborate with other instructors across the disciplines, asking them to coevaluate portfolios or leave feedback about how students' work touches on future coursework. This process eliminates the composition vacuum of disconnected publication, where the project never leaves the classroom.

Partnering with instructors of required courses, such as a first-year sequence or an upper-level writing class required for majors offers teachers opportunities to learn what other instructors are doing and to compare their own students' work. This collaboration can be work intensive, but it can be manageable when accomplished in a trade-off system wherein instructors ask their students to peer review students' work from other classes and write reflections about that experience. Technical communication instructors might integrate usability testing, a commonly required outcome for twenty-first-century technical communicators, for reviewing portfolios. The learning is reciprocal: technical communication students gain practical experience while students creating the portfolio gain feedback from outside readers. Of course, such collaboration works particularly well with ePortfolios (see below and ch. 9), which are more efficient for outside audiences than hard copies.

When instructors do not have access to such collaboration, students still benefit by publishing to websites and interacting with readers there. To encourage interaction with live audiences, instructors can ask students to create op-ed pieces for their local papers or to write brief letters to the editor that might receive response; a more traditional assignment might require students to email or mail such letters. Students can consider the outside audiences' feedback, revise accordingly, and reflect on why they made those changes.

When asking students to publish online, instructors should talk about online trolls and how to handle them. Because social media audiences are unpredictable—and often unkind—instructors should avoid them, instead asking students to send the completed project to the intended audience, who, with luck, will respond. Even if they do not respond, students can be prompted to discuss how another publication venue might generate more or different responses. These types of publication opportunities increase actual circulation and interaction with audiences outside academia.

Specific Requirements

After outlining the processes discussed above, instructors need to provide specific requirements that may or may not change across assignments. If the assignment is text-based, this section should include such parameters as types of research, length, and citation style. Example 8.9 illustrates how brief such requirements might be.

Example 8.9. Specific Requirements for Alphabetic Proposal

Your persuasive argument with the proposal should include at least five credible outside sources found through the college library. One must engage primary research and two others must be peer-reviewed research articles; the other two may be trustworthy news sources. For (primary) field research, I recommend conducting an interview with someone affected by the issue. We will develop sample interview questions in class. Ask me if you are unsure whether your sources are reliable.

Use MLA style for in-text citations and works cited. Your project should be at least two thousand words, about eight double-spaced pages, using twelve-point Times New Roman font. Post the paper through the LMS.

Reflection

Reflection is a key element to all assignments, no matter the other parameters. Composing a reflection not only helps solidify learning but also aids instructors in project evaluation (see ch. 9). Within reflection, instructors should ask students to consider their audience and talk through why and how their intended audience might approach or use the text. Students should consider their rhetorical situations and purposes as tied with audience. These choices should prompt them to write about why their selected composing medium is the best choice for communicating the message.

Reflections are about composing at all stages of the project. For example, after reading through an assignment, students can write about challenges they might encounter and brainstorm ideas; they also can write about their struggles with technology. When posted to a confidential space between student and instructor, students can receive guidance through the challenges and get suggestions for making different choices.

To guide students to understand and account for their rhetorical choices, instructors can prompt students to talk through examples of relevant alphabetic text and multimodal projects; they should comment on the author's choices of audience, rhetorical situation, and purpose. Students might review two projects composed in different mediums and evaluate them for these elements. For example, when a project calls for choosing between an online blog and an online op-ed piece, instructors can direct students to examples that have similarities and differences between them. It helps to prompt students to note differences between potential audiences for each project and how the authors' stylistic and design choices are geared toward these different audiences. Understanding differences among mediums encourages students to think about and reflect on their own choices of medium and content; this exercise of rhetorical understanding can be implemented at any time in the assignment's scaffolding. When possible, instructors can ask former students to share self-reflections and corresponding projects; self-reflections are personal, but some students are happy to share. Students may be asked to give feedback on the author's reflections: Where can the author improve the reflection? Where can the choices be made clearer? What can be expanded upon?

Within reflections, students can write about their interactions and challenges with composing, including challenges with technology if the project is multimodal. These types of reflections on technology allow students to think critically about the process that comes with learning new genres and software and how to apply these concepts to future learning practices; such a reflective practice promotes technological literacy. All reflection ideas can be tied to teaching various genres, with an emphasis on helping students understand and reflect on their learning during the composing process.

Prompting reflection might engage questions, per example 8.10.

Example 8.10. Self-Reflection Miniassignment

For this project, write a self-reflection accounting for your communicative choices. This reflection solidifies your learning and helps me evaluate your project, so carefully consider and answer all questions:

- What is the rhetorical situation for your project?
- What is its purpose? How well does the piece achieve its purpose?
- Who is the audience?
- How did this audience affect your choice of medium? In other words, why is the selected medium the best choice for your audience and your rhetorical situation and purpose?
- What other rhetorical decisions had an impact on your topic, medium, or use of outside sources?
- What were the challenges with this project? How did you overcome them?
- What did you do well in this presentation draft that I'm evaluating? What could you improve on if you had more time or access to other resources (e.g., technology or sources)?
- What else should I know about the project and your choices?

Reflection offers at least two critical benefits. First, it is a genuine writing-about-writing exercise that engages the vocabulary and spirit of composition. Second, it is a metacognitive exercise that individualizes learning, encouraging writers to ground insight and understanding of themselves as writers from their own work.

The Portfolio Assignment

Students need opportunities to revise based on instructor feedback, and portfolio development allows for such revision. Portfolios can demonstrate not only a single assignment's improvement through early drafts to a polished one but also students' abilities to apply learning from one project to another. Portfolios have many different faces and construction processes, and we do not recommend only one. We have had good experiences with the processes illustrated below, however. In this section, we offer an example portfolio assignment that instructors like Professor Jackson can use for one course or across sections. This portfolio assignment can be used for student self-assessment, instructor evaluation of the students' performance in the class, and programmatic assessment. We begin with guidance for creating the portfolio assignment.

As with the activities that lead to assignments, the assignments that lead to portfolios require careful scaffolding, ensuring checkpoints while helping instructors keep up with project feedback. Developing the portfolio can be an ongoing project that prompts continual reflection and learning transfer (see ex. 8.11), or it can be developed at the end of the course. We recommend asking students to use the writing center for feedback on presentation drafts when possible. As some institutions offer exam weeks, students might be allowed to complete or post the portfolio as their final project or exam, providing time to revise based on feedback and ongoing development throughout the term.

Simply calling a draft *preliminary* or *presentation* can help students understand that no draft is final. Even presentation drafts may receive instructional feedback they should consider before revising to publish it to the portfolio. Therefore, students could revise all projects or only a few for portfolio presentation. They might be asked to do one creative revision to a project of their choice, changing the audience, purpose, and medium, for example. In a class where only some projects are multimodal, this approach works well, but if all projects are multimodal, students might be required to revise only one project based on instructor feedback while providing one or two others they are proud of for the portfolio. Allowing students to revise creatively for the portfolio enables instructors to test multimodality skills. Another approach is to assign a piece the instructor will not evaluate formatively, requiring students to exercise their agency, newly gained skills, and resources. Finally, reflections for any newly developed pieces as well as learning letters reflecting on the entire portfolio are necessary to this major project. For an ePortfolio, as described below, the reflection might reside on the home page. Instructors and programs not set up for ePortfolios might use hard copy folders or digital files posted to the LMS.

Designing the ePortfolio Assignment

Just like any assignment, the ePortfolio assignment must start with clear goals, and the instructions should also explain what a portfolio comprises. We recommend using ePortfolios per the Conference on College Composition and Communication's "Principles and Practices in Electronic Portfolios." Therefore, providing students links to example ePortfolios and teaching required software are important steps. Example 8.11 provides a sample department-wide portfolio assignment with multimodal elements, written to a student audience.

Example 8.11. ePortfolio Assignment for Students

Goals

You will create an ePortfolio, an electronic document, using our ePortfolio software. It lets you demonstrate what you learned this term about

- writing, rhetoric, and multimodal communication
- how you have approached the course outcomes
- broader core skills and knowledge

Unlike a final exam, in which you respond to a few questions, the portfolio encourages you to write about and present a wide range of skills and knowledge learned throughout the term.

Rhetorical Situation

Create a portfolio that illustrates how well you have learned the course outcomes. The portfolio uses self-reflection and the projects you have created throughout the term. Consider the elements that best represent your work, including essay and project drafts, reflections, multimedia, and anything else that best represents your learning.

Audience

You have three primary audiences: your peers, instructor, and yourself. As this ePortfolio will be posted to the Internet, however, the secondary audience includes anyone who might find and read it, including other instructors at this school. Creating this ePortfolio teaches you about your composing processes; reading it teaches your classmates about their own composing processes by learning about yours. Your instructor is also the audience because you are showcasing what you have learned, enabling thoughtful evaluation. Although it may seem that your instructor is the most important audience because of grading, you also are an audience to your own work. You've come a long way, and it's time to recognize that work!

Purpose

Remember you are creating an argument about your learning, so each outcome reflection should make a clear case for what and how you have learned, convincing your audience that you learned these outcomes through both the self-reflections and the actual essays and projects pieces published in the portfolio.

Genre Conventions

A typical course portfolio has the following items:

- an overarching learning letter containing self-reflections about learning course outcomes and your writing and revising processes
- all revised projects created in the course in their polished form
- drafts of all projects to showcase process work
- multimedia components that complement your written work
- project reflections if assigned by your instructor

Specific Requirements

The portfolio assignment asks you to perform five major tasks:

- *Use course outcomes listed at the end of this document and in your syllabus as a guide.* The portfolio should assert through its content: "This is what I have learned in light of the learning outcomes for this course." Write how you have met each outcome. Watch the Portfolio Video that explains how you will make these assertions throughout the course. [Note to instructors: This video is especially important in online courses because it provides accessible initial instructions outside alphabetic text.]

- *For each skill or knowledge area you include, provide evidence of your learning* from the composing activities you conducted this term. Refer to examples from those texts and activities to show what you learned. Think of your own work as evidence, and cite peers from peer review or discussion boards, instructor feedback, and your own self-reflections. You may use anything from the course as evidence of your learning. In addition, you may include all drafts of your projects to showcase your composing process, as well as all project reflections you have created.

- *Revise all major writing assignments based on instructor and peer feedback.* The extent of the revisions necessary will depend upon how close the assignment was to being portfolio ready when you originally posted it for formative feedback. Make each project the best you can. Your outcome reflections in the learning letter should include discussion of your final revisions.

- *Craft a home page for your portfolio.*
  - o Tell your instructor about yourself and what you learned over the term.
  - o Use this space to reflect on your learning and how it can be useful in your future education or life after college.
  - o Writing at least five hundred words, reflect on your revisions of each major project, explaining why you made them and how they enhance the ePortfolio. Instead of writing textually, you may develop a short reflection video for this home page, showing the revisions you made to each project and highlighting areas in the text you improved.

- *Ensure your project represents multimodality.* Include videos, links to other web pages, images, graphics, and other media that help make your argument. You may use sources you have not personally created. Cite appropriately.

These specifics are guidelines that depend on department policies and outcomes. Minimally, however, they should guide students to review, restate, and address the outcomes. Students should argue for having learned those outcomes using evidence from the term's projects and explain the forms that evidence might take. After including the specifics and course outcomes, we suggest the portfolio assignment contain a rubric (see ch. 9).

Scaffolding the ePortfolio Assignment

The scaffolding of any portfolio assignment is complex and should be clear to instructors and students. Professor Jackson and other instructors should introduce the portfolio during the course's first week because students should start creating it immediately, continually adding to it throughout the term. Requiring a portfolio always assumes instructors will provide formative feedback at drafting checkpoints. Students should interact with each other and receive peer review on their portfolios, and they should write ongoing self-assessments based on their work and progress. As the culminating assignment, the portfolio can be a collection of artifacts that include students' best work, as well as self-reflections and peer assessments of their work.

Example 8.12 provides a rough outline of portfolio scaffolding in a sixteen-week term (changeable for any course length); we skip some weeks purposefully to be used for incorporating portfolio checkpoints or discussions at the instructor's discretion. This scaffolding is developed for three five-week units, leaving one week for revisions, also alterable. The final week can be used either for revisions or to conference with students for a collaborative evaluation (see ch. 9). Although we highlight ePortfolios, such scaffolding can be used with paper-based portfolios. This example is written with instructors as audience.

Example 8.12. Scaffolding the ePortfolio Assignment for Instructors

Week 1. Introduce students to the ePortfolio assignment sheet. Ask students to read the corresponding textbook chapter or provide outside readings about ePortfolios. When teaching online, create a video explaining the ePortfolio and your expectations. We recommend using videos for online students, but they also are helpful in on-site classes.

Week 2. Provide a template for creating the ePortfolio. The WPA or course administrator should create this template through easy-to-use, typically free software. Providing a template does not limit students' creativity, especially when requiring them to revise compositions and reflect on those choices. Students can be asked to complete a rhetorical analysis of the portfolio template, talking through what worked in the original template, what did not, and why and how they made changes to represent their personalities and overall learning. For online classes, videos should demonstrate how to find that template and make changes. Add tutorials for how to use the software for creating the ePortfolio.

Week 3. Assign students to post their templates with changes made and a short analysis of these changes. This checkpoint ensures instructors can open the ePortfolio. For online classes, students can share their ePortfolios in discussion boards and be prompted to offer feedback on the design elements.

Week 5. Assign students to post project 1, along with reflections written for each corresponding outcome in the assignment. Depending on the selected outcomes for the reflection, they should account for their rhetorical choices made while composing. Recall that regarding assignment design, we encourage instructors to highlight the course or program outcomes (in some cases these are the same); at this point, students should be writing self-reflections about meeting those outcomes in the portfolio. If a course has nine outcomes, for example, for this first unit, they could respond to three, those that align with the outcomes listed on the assignment sheet. Students have now created their project, written about at least three course outcome areas, and posted all this work at the end of the first unit. Students should be told to place the project in the portfolio and create their outcome reflections directly in that portfolio, giving instructors access to the link. Offer feedback on the project and the portfolio-in-development simultaneously. To save themselves time at the end of the term, advise students to revise the project and portfolio reflection before they post project 2 at the end of the next unit.

Week 6. Prompt students to start adding multimodal elements to the ePortfolio. This checkpoint can occur any week before the end of the second unit.

Week 8. Ask students to complete necessary revisions for project 1 and the outcome reflections based on instructor feedback.

Week 10. Assign students to post project 2 with project reflections written in the outcome areas. For instance, if students must work toward an understanding of three more course outcomes, they should write outcome reflections in each of these areas, again providing the link to the ePortfolio with their revised project 2 and outcome reflections written directly in the portfolio. After providing feedback on the project and the portfolio outcomes, instructors might check whether students have revised project 1 and its corresponding outcomes based on instructor feedback.

Week 11. Prompt students to continue adding multimodal elements to the ePortfolio. This checkpoint can occur any week before the end of the third unit.

Week 12. Ask students to have completed necessary revisions for project 2 and the outcome reflections based on instructor feedback.

Week 15. Assign students to post project 3 with project reflections written in the outcome areas for this project. As before, if students are required to work toward an understanding of three more course outcomes, they should write outcome reflections in each of these areas, again providing the link to the ePortfolio with their revised project 3 and outcome reflections written directly in the portfolio. After providing feedback on the project and the portfolio outcomes, instructors might check whether students have revised project 2 and its corresponding outcomes based on instructor feedback.

Week 16. Advise students to use this week to revise all projects and outcome reflections, even if they have already done so, enabling them to continue to improve their compositions based on the most recent lessons. Encourage them to add more to the outcome reflections, discussing how each project helped them learn the outcomes, not just the corresponding project. For instance, if project 1 asked them to respond to outcomes one through three, then students should return to their outcome reflections and talk through how projects 2 and 3 helped them learn those outcomes, too. Finally, prompt students to check that their multimodal elements are relevant and complement their written text.

Outcome Reflections in the Portfolio

As we mention in chapter 9 on portfolio evaluation, WPAs may require that students must respond to some outcomes. Whenever possible, students should respond to all course outcomes, however, not merely the ones being assessed for that year, and should write in-depth self-reflections (White, "Scoring" 591). Students should be expected to learn all course outcomes, such as those from the Council of Writing Program Administrators' "WPA Outcomes Statement." When a course or program has upwards of ten outcomes, however, we recommend implementing the scaffolding system outlined above for the outcomes that will be assessed and any other outcomes the instructor wants to focus on for self-assessment of the specific course. The same principle is true for compressed-term courses.

Although outcome reflections are the cornerstone of portfolios, students often have trouble writing them because outcomes typically are written for instructional assessment purposes and not for students. Therefore, in the first week, instructors might ask students to write about what the outcomes mean to them and to reword the outcomes in language they can better understand. After this exercise, students can peer review what others wrote and revise their own outcomes statements. For each unit, instructors can ask students to discuss corresponding outcomes for that project, giving students a chance to draft self-reflections before they post portfolios at the end of the unit. Using the LMS for this discussion enables students to see what others are writing and instructors to comment on their ideas. Alternatively, students can draft outcome reflections and use peer review to see other reflections and receive feedback on their own.

Toward the end of the term, instructors should facilitate a discussion regarding all the outcomes, prompting students to return to their first outcomes discussions and impressions. The goal is to learn how their understanding has evolved since that first-week discussion. We suggest asking them to consider how their outcomes learning may transfer to the broader society outside academia, either in their careers or when communicating generally, helping students better understand why they were asked to create course essays and projects.

Students often have trouble using their own coursework as evidence, so we suggest all instructors—not only those teaching online—should conduct digitally based discussions of topics and outcomes. Using the LMS, this online portion of the class becomes an archive from which students can pull evidence of their learning. Additionally, students may have trouble using direct quotations of their work as evidence. This challenge requires that students make assertions and arguments about their learning, using coursework for evidence instead of outside research. If the course has been scaffolded to teach argument and research (and we advocate it should be), students can be prompted to draw on their knowledge of these rhetorical aspects when making similar arguments in their portfolios.

Designing Effective Multimodal Assignments

Most essay and multimodal assignments can be developed using the guidance provided above. Because multimodal texts are relatively new to composition curricula, however, we offer additional assignment development details.

Before introducing multimodal assignments, instructors should identify why they would teach such projects within their curriculum. Educators should examine pedagogical goals before designing or redesigning assignments to help students acquire multimodal, technological, and digital literacies:

- What do I know about multimodal composition?
- Why am I teaching multimodal composition?
- How can I change my existing assignments or curriculum to add multimodal elements?
- What do I still need to learn about teaching multimodal composition?

Answers help instructors develop a well-informed pedagogy.

Both new and experienced multimodal project instructors may benefit from adapting existing alphabetic text assignments to multimodal projects before reinventing an entire curriculum. Existing assignments already have delineated outcomes, which may be transferable to multimodal projects, particularly if they are taken from the Council of Writing Program Administrators' "WPA Outcomes Statement." Instructors for FYW courses may be able to add multimodal outcomes to their syllabi, interweaving rhetorical elements to keep the focus on the critical considerations that guide multimodal composing. If adding multimodal outcomes to the entire course is not possible, instructors may add them to one assignment. Providing clear outcomes regarding multimodality, as in example 8.13, sets expectations that multimodal composition elements are crucial twenty-first-century skills.

Example 8.13. Repurposed Assignments

Outcome: To help students compose in multiple genres for a variety of audiences and purposes, choosing appropriate mediums (or media) for communication.

- Think about what mediums best suit different audiences. How do such mediums influence the affordances and constraints of certain modes?
- Using this knowledge, repurpose an existing essay for a new rhetorical situation, changing the medium to fit the new choice.
  - Regarding a persuasive argument with a proposal, if you choose a local problem like recycling, an appropriate alphabetic text medium might be a newsletter with multiple pages, columns, borders, and images.
  - Add video clips, images, or sound-bites.
  - Reflect on and explain the changes.

Text-based projects with multimodal elements still require in-text citations and references. Citing media or images requires new thinking about citation, which can be scaffolded within the assignment. Students also need to learn about copyright, especially if they are remixing (e.g., editing and splicing existing videos) compositions like *YouTube* videos. Instructors should teach the ethics of using digital work and attributing it to authors (DeVoss and Porter; Dubisar and Palmeri).

Teaching Technology and Design

Some students will need instruction for software. Instructors can create and provide tutorials for reference, which are especially useful in online classes; they can ask students to create their own brief tutorials for future students regarding their preferred software. Creating tutorials anchors students' understanding of the technology and teaches them through active learning to use only the most integral rhetorical approaches to the genre of instructions, audience needs, and rhetorical situation. Instructors should consider teamwork when incorporating multimodal composition; pairing students who are comfortable with technology with those who are not enables them to teach each other. Nonetheless, instructors should take active roles in teaching multimodal composition and not delegate all such teaching to students. After all, teachers must try new approaches, too, which we address in our companion volume, *Administering Writing Programs in the Twenty-First Century*, by Tiffany Bourelle, Hewett, and Scott Warnock.

Students may not know that learning technology for composing is a critical literacy. Therefore, design elements also matter: the use of font style, size, and color; format; images, tables, and graphs; sound bites, music, and voice. Links between rhetoric and design become clear when students choose these elements based on audience needs, the project's purpose, and specific context. In *Literacy in the New Media Age*, Gunther R. Kress claims it is irresponsible to ignore design as an essential literacy. Students should learn to connect alphabetic text with other modes into one theme, reviewing the intended effect of each mode choice and the combined effect they have toward the overarching message (see Kress, *Multimodality* 79–102). In "Impossibly Distinct," Anne Frances Wysocki argues for considering design concepts such as content and form because each influences the other while having different levels of visual (or aural) weight; authors can play with form and content in visual ways to influence the audience and their reactions, making design considerations important to all texts (138). Teaching design may be more important in technical communication courses where the concept is typically part of course or programmatic outcomes. In those cases, instructors should focus on teaching design in structured ways.

Using a preexisting template in common word processing and design software is an easy way to introduce multimodal composition and the importance of design. Another way to approach design and rhetorical considerations is to assign students to conduct a rhetorical analysis of a selected template, as example 8.14 does.

Example 8.14. Template Analysis

Consider the various templates you might use for the upcoming major assignment in this course and answer these questions before you begin drafting; there also are questions to answer after you complete a first draft:

- Why did I choose this template?
- What are the affordances and constraints of using this template?
- What design elements did I change and why (e.g., font, text boxes, background color, image shape)?
- After the text is drafted: Now that I've designed this text, would another template work better to convey my message? Why or why not?
- How did I manipulate the template to best serve my needs? The needs of my audience?

The template analysis helps students consider the use of templates and how they might be ineffective for conveying certain messages. This type of assignment can be paired with a short lesson on design and textbook readings.

Teaching and Scaffolding Technology

When is it appropriate to teach technology during a sequence and how much should instructors focus on it? When designing courses to promote critical thinking about technology, instructors should enable students to teach themselves through frequent media labs (T. Bourelle and Hewett).[2] A typical media lab might consist of students watching a *YouTube* or how-to video provided by software designers. Students would try the software and complete a low-stakes assignment to show they have done the lesson. A good media lab assignment also scaffolds the assignment; for example, after the composition of an alphabetic PSA text, an assignment might prompt students to create a video PSA for television or a sound PSA for the radio. During another media lab, students could be asked to download movie or screen-capture software to create a short video pitching their ideas. The media lab itself should be multimodal, with students using a combination of alphabetic text, image, narration, or sound. Instructors should comment on students' uses of various modes and give suggestions for drafting the proposal project based on the pitch. Another media lab in this same lesson might prompt students to create a sound project wherein they outline research that supports their arguments.

Simply playing with the technology while working in low-stakes assignments generates critical thinking. Media lab assignments not only ensure students play with new technology well before the final project is due but also allow students to play productively and fail safely. Low-stakes assignments provide freedom to experiment and test new technology without fear of being graded on how well they use the software. Media labs also offer students opportunities to consider the technology rhetorically and to critically construct an audience and message. These labs are not necessarily designed to teach students software functionality but rather to help them understand how to use technology effectively to convey a message. Testing new technology and creating small, low-stakes projects with these technologies may help students become more comfortable, courageous, and independent when approaching more complicated software.

Students should be given choices for both low-bridge technology (such as open-source software) and high-bridge technology (more sophisticated programs such as for graphic design) because either can produce rhetorically effective projects as well as lead to substantive, metacognitive reflections about the process of creating them (D. Anderson). Since all twenty-first-century composition engages digitality, media labs may assist any type of composing, whether with collaborative multimodal composing software or alphabetical word processing software. Starting small requires instructors to determine and work from students' current technological literacy; some may not have familiarity with or access to high-bridge software, and others may not know how to use the low-bridge software that appears ubiquitous. We suggest creating numerous media labs for students to start where they are—some students may want to play with and learn different word processing features, building up to higher-bridge software; others may want to challenge themselves with more creative software for manipulating modes.

Reflection also is important for students when considering technology choices. They can write prereflections, informing instructors about technologies they plan to use in their final projects, examining the affordances and constraints, and explaining why and how they plan to use the technologies. In "Toward a Rhetorically Sensitive Assessment Model for New Media Composition," Crystal Vankooten encourages students to write prereflections that consider the functional and rhetorical literacy goals they have for the project, and these can easily be added to the media lab assignment. When posting final projects, students should write postreflections, not only explaining choices of audience, context, purpose, and medium, but also whether they chose the software they tested in the media lab for the final project and why. Instructors should prompt students to consider how the software contributed to the overall communication message, making this postreflection an opportunity to inform instructors about their experienced learning curves: How long did I spend learning the software? How did that affect the composing process? Will I use the software again? Why or why not? How can the technology be used outside classrooms? Reflections that return to prereflections can guide students in understanding how technology shapes communications. Vankooten suggests linking the post- and prereflections, guiding students to a greater awareness of their composing and reflection processes, specifically how to offer evidence-based rationales for their rhetorical choices.

Teaching and Learning Technology

In the digital era, students need to learn necessary rhetorical literacies, which include using more than one mode to communicate. No matter the technology offered and its affordances, students benefit from understanding the rhetorical aspects of their text-based and multimodal choices. Whether instructors should teach the technologies themselves, however, is a challenging question. Principle 2 of the Conference on College Composition and Communication's online writing instruction position statement states: "An online writing course should focus on writing and not on technology orientation or teaching students how to use learning and other technologies" (CCCC, Committee 11). Hewett explains that

> a writing course should be primarily about writing—whether that writing is an alphabetic essay or a multimodal composition. When essay writing instruction is supported through technology, then only the selected technology is necessary for the course and students need to become functionally and rhetorically literate in it alone. When the writing instruction teaches a multimodal composition, again only the selected technology is necessary for the course and students need to become functionally and rhetorically literate in it alone. ("Grounding Principles" 47)

The goal of this principle was to make "clear that OWI teachers and students alike do not need to be technology experts, computer programmers, or Web designers" (45–46). The Global Society of Online Literacy Educators locates similar considerations regarding access in its online literacy instruction principle 1, tenet 2: "Use of technology should support stated course objectives, thereby not presenting an undue burden for instructors and students."

We provide this background to argue for balancing composing instruction with media requirements. Although we suggest teachers should approach technology instruction, particularly for multimodal curricula and in online environments, we also believe that expectations should be modest and appropriate to curricular outcomes and students' access needs. Media labs engage students to test new software on their own—with instructors providing reasonable assistance. In multimodal composition assignments, where media use and composition's rhetorical considerations are both part of the composing process, software selection and rhetorical goals should be balanced against "undue burden." When students practice in media labs and write metacognitive reflections of both the work and their technology choices, they learn to think critically about composing in the digital era. Approaching composition with all forms of digitality up front also helps students understand the limitations and potentials of various modes and technology for composing, allowing them to make independent choices regarding audiences, rhetorical situations, purposes, and communicative media. These choices encourage students to understand themselves as twenty-first-century composers who can succeed in life and the technology-driven workforce beyond academia.

Overcoming the Challenges of Technology-Based Composition Processes

Many students are challenged by alphabetic writing tasks; many more will be unaccustomed to composing with new mediums or modes beyond (and with) alphabetic text. Student buy-in is important from the beginning, but instructors also must engage. Many teachers do not know how to use newer technologies; many do not wish to learn. We suggest that in the short term they should ask other instructors who are knowledgeable to lead their class through media labs. In the long term, it will benefit them to increase their technology skills, taking Professor Jackson's lead.

Access is a common problem with contemporary composition. Many students do not own a computer or tablet and may find it difficult to access campus labs and create projects, particularly those that require them to record their voices or use sound. Campus labs may not provide sound recording or video recording software on their computers, or computer labs may no longer be available, as some are closed or downsized because of the false perception that all students have appropriate hardware (or because of mandatory remote learning from events such as the COVID-19 pandemic). These problems make integrating any composing technology more difficult. In these cases, we suggest instructors enlarge parameters for students, letting them choose their own medium for communication and software for production. Instructors should not encourage students to use video or sound production or other technology unless their institution provides access to it or students express comfort with it.

Finally, undoubtedly, the environment in which composition is taught makes learning different. Teaching composition in fully online or hybrid settings has advantages, including posting various tutorials for students to review when approaching software. Regardless of setting, instructors must account for various learning styles, using multimodal tools to teach concepts and model multimodality, with videos as supplemental resources. They need to connect individually with all students, as chapter 10 emphasizes. Instructors should provide ample time for discussion of sample projects, parameters, and conventions of genres, as well as opportunities for process work like drafting and revising, regardless of environment.

Conclusion

Designing assignments is a first step in creating a curriculum, and assignments are the roadmap for students to start the composing process. Instructors should create assignments that are clear and straightforward, allowing students to make choices, whether of audience, rhetorical situation, purpose, or medium. As we have illustrated, scaffolding assignments is the course backbone. Everything instructors use should work toward increasing students' understanding of course outcomes. Scaffolding also should encourage students to take risks; instructors should take these risks alongside their students. Teaching exposition and argument are critical for students, who also need to learn about genre, rhetorical choices, research, and more. Portfolios can illustrate students' conceptual learning (and, by extension, course outcomes) by treating them as a term-long project that works on a feedback-revision cycle. Simultaneously, students should be revising and crafting their work to improve as writers and critical thinkers for the twenty-first century.

NOTES

1. Here are two additional ideas for genre assignments that can be scaffolded as outlined in this chapter: (1) The writing-about-writing genre focuses on the study of writing itself, and using models helps students to do that. For instance, after students have read about the revision process from a rhetoric composition scholar, ask them to draft and revise a short writing piece—a blog post, a short report, or even an email—using at least three drafts. Have them package the drafts by pasting them into a *Word* document, using a different font color for each draft and providing a time-stamp and a length-stamp. Do this work yourself, too. Ask students to read peers' or your drafts to analyze the writing's progression, and comment on how the students' processes differ and are similar. (2) Creative nonfiction can be argumentative insofar as it has a goal of convincing or persuading readers. Asking for deep reading gives students fodder for creativity. For instance, supply several readings about the Holocaust

(or slavery in the United States) and take students to a local Holocaust (or African American history) museum or have them visit it virtually. Ask them to take on the persona of a family member of a person affected by the Holocaust (or by slavery). Have students write about a day in the life of the affected person from this point of view using all the knowledge they have gained from their reading and visit. This exercise is intended not to appropriate anyone's experience but to help students learn to see a person or situation from another perspective.

2. Adapted from the University of New Mexico graduate student Maya Alapin's technology labs.

9

Providing Response, Feedback, and Evaluation

Professor Jackson has been anxiously anticipating this day. Although he was eager to introduce more digitality to his courses, now he must respond to the assignments. Two classes are posting alphabetic text essay drafts, and one class is posting multimodal composition drafts—Professor Jackson's first try. He is uncertain whether his students have been successful—and whether he knows what success means—and he's worried about how he'll respond efficiently and effectively, given a fourth course with projects due next week. Fortunately, Professor Jackson is open to learning new response, feedback, and evaluation strategies.

In this chapter, we address asynchronous (e.g., alphabetic text, video and/ or audio, and screen capture) and synchronous (e.g., teleconference, video conference, and written chat) strategies for providing helpful response and feedback. We offer strategic principles drawn from studies of response-driven student revision. We also discuss the peer review and revision process relative to alphabetic, multimodal, and mixed mode documents. Specifically, we argue for using rhetorically focused rubrics and self-reflection to evaluate students' projects, both alphabetic and multimodal. We discuss how to develop various types of rubrics and then demonstrate evaluation in practice to illustrate formative and summative evaluation.

Response and Feedback Guide Students' Composing Processes

Scaffolding a course and providing consistent instructional feedback and support help students in any educational environment become active learners. As we discuss in chapter 8, activity theory can guide students to test new ways of composing; instructor feedback, however, is just as important and perhaps more so in fully online courses where feedback often constitutes the majority of the instructor-to-student interaction. Feedback can happen early, in the middle, and at the end of the writing process.

Formative Feedback (Early Process). Feedback preferably should start from idea inception through a conversation with instructors or peers or through a written proposal. A proposal pitch outlining what students want to write about, using what medium, and why helps everyone become clearer about project goals before the project has gone too far.

Formative Feedback (Mid-Process). Feedback provided throughout students' projects helps writers address challenges and shape their writing. Typically, students post drafts at specified points for instructional feedback, but they also may work with peers in response groups. Formative feedback is especially important in the creation of multimodal texts, as students benefit from different readers' impressions of their choices of audience, rhetorical situation, and purpose, and how these may influence medium choice before they begin composing (see Huot, *Rearticulating*). We address learning how to give, receive, and use feedback in this chapter.

Summative Feedback (End Process). Feedback on the final project is mostly summative, and it often includes a grade. Because our experience is that students may not read past the grade on final projects, portfolios change that dynamic, making no draft final (see ch. 8). With portfolio assessment, even summative feedback can have a formative nature, and mid-assignment drafts can be used to argue a case for a final course grade. In *Teaching and Assessing Writing*, Edward White suggests a final project grade left to itself does little to help students improve as writers (124).

When instructors offer feedback as a process and not as a one-shot compose-and-grade deal, students have opportunities to read, analyze, and synthesize what they have learned through the response and apply it to their compositions. A common view is that instructors should coach students, prompting them to see what does and does not work well in their drafts and guiding them to revision instead of directly telling them what to do (White, *Teaching*). Also common is the view that instructors should not appropriate students' texts, instead coaching through questions to lead students to a general understanding of how they themselves want to address the projects' challenges and weaknesses. Often, Lil Brannon and C. H. Knoblauch say, instructors have an idea of the "ideal text," or what they would recommend or want to see if they had written the piece (159; see also Sommers, "Responding" and "Revision Strategies"; North, "Idea"). Instead, instructors should listen to students, guiding them toward the students' own visions of their projects, helping them achieve their own purposes for communicating. Therefore, some mechanism is needed for instructors to consult with students throughout the writing process, asking them what they meant to say if the thesis is unclear or to clarify content points if the organization needs reshaping. These educators suggest questions can be direct: *The project seems to shift focus toward the end. What points do you want to leave with your audience? Where will you place the main takeaways?* Such linguistically direct, genuine questions using *who, what, when, where, why,* and *how* can help students see where they might have gone off track while leaving room for their decision making (Hewett, *Online Writing Conference* and *Reading*). Brannon and Knoblauch argue that coaching students to take authority over their writing and make revisions cannot happen if the instructional process allows only one draft for summative response.

Teaching and Structuring Revision

It is easier to tell students what changes to make than coach them through revision. It also is easier to focus on so-called standards of writing, quickly marking up what is incorrect by those standards. Yet feedback should encourage different thinking and lead to rewriting or even new composing actions, meaning instructors must engage the writing beyond copyediting. Hence, teachers may need to relearn how to respond to drafts (White, *Teaching* 124). They need to help students rethink, literally resee, the text from a reader's perspective. In "Multimodal Revision Techniques in Webtexts," Cheryl E. Ball explains that she encourages authors of *Kairos* webtexts to self-analyze the production strategy, getting them to think differently about their compositions. For students, we also recommend such reflection on all aspects of the composition; they should also be allowed to revise, perhaps for the portfolio, choosing a different textual or multimodal approach and comparing the differences in composing processes between the first draft and the creative revision.

Successful revision requires flexible instruction geared toward each student. It makes sense that students with disabilities and learning preferences may need more time to revise. They may need more help with finding ideas or attaining correctness, or they may need more time to revise because of limited technology access or a steeper learning curve associated with newer technology. Regardless of individual challenges, all students need extra time to revise multimodal projects because such revision requires a range of actions, from adding alphabetic and media content and editing to completely reconceiving and composing the project. Therefore, instructors should structure ample revision time. Students need up to a week to revise according to peer review, and possibly more time with instructional feedback. Again, portfolios provide a powerful way of offering extended revision time.

Like White, we suggest asking students to do freewriting or low-stakes writing like progress journals that do not require much instructor feedback while still prompting students to think through their ideas. Such writing should not be graded, encouraging speaking freely without fear of correction. Students also may be more comfortable revising if they have the freedom to make mistakes in early drafts of scaffolded assignments leading to final projects. Other successful instructional revision strategies include

> scaffolding the assignment with low-stakes exercises like brainstorming, freewriting, outlining, concept-mapping, and early drafting (see ch. 8);
>
> prompting students to test new ideas with freedom to fail;
>
> using media labs and low-stakes assignments to teach technology, test new software, brainstorm, and draft the assignment (see ch. 8);
>
> encouraging working with writing center tutors (see ch. 11); and
>
> engaging peer response for learning from writing in progress.

Engaging Peer Review

Peer review (see ch. 4) often benefits from having explicit guidance. Examples 9.1 and 9.2 illustrate what such guidance might look like in any given assignment. Note that peer reviews can occur completely through a separate peer response sheet, using the comments and track changes features on the students' own texts, or both. These choices tend to reflect instructors' preferences regarding authorial agency and collaborative connections.

Example 9.1. Peer Response Sheet for Student Completion

Summarize the writing (or multimodal project) in one or two sentences. *This writing is about* _________.

What was the purpose of this piece (the "so what")? *The reason the author wrote this text was* _________.

Who is the audience for this piece? *I think the writer was writing to* _________.

What do you like best about this piece? *Things I liked best about this piece are* _________.

What do you want to know more about that this piece should address? *Things I want to know more about are* _________.

Example 9.2. Rhetorically Focused Peer Response Sheet for Student Completion

Review the assignment directions carefully: Does the project *fulfill the assignment* ? Why or why not?

What is the author's *central or main point*?

Does the writer account for *audience* effectively?

How effectively does the author use *sources and evidence*? Are they too general? What specific advice can you offer (e.g., sources or reasoning)?

Is the project's *organization* clear? If not, why? Are the topic sentences helpful in guiding you through the project?

How *creative* is the project? Were you "wowed" by it? If not, why not?

Does the project look like a college-level assignment in terms of *format*?

Comment on the *grammar and mechanics*. Do recurring, glaring errors interfere with the project's message?

ON-SITE REVIEWING STRATEGIES

In-class peer review can be time well spent. Ways to set up an in-class review include the following:

Project Swaps. All students are assigned a classmate's paper to review, ideally using a clear set of criteria. Reviews can be set up randomly or in some structured way.

Pairs or Groups. Students can be set up in pairs or small groups to discuss and write about each other's papers.

Partner Reviews. Students are paired. Each pair receives two projects from two other students. The students spend the class time working together to create a collaboratively written review of each project.

ONLINE REVIEWING STRATEGIES

Peer review works just as well in hybrid and fully online courses. Scott Warnock and Adrienne Cassel recommend beginning from simplicity with document exchange occurring through email or learning management system (LMS) protocols. Guidelines and peer review questions for on-site peer reviews work online. Students again can work individually, in pairs or small groups, or as partners. The LMS typically allows small groups in which students might exchange and read several projects. Although reviews can remain private to the group's discussion, they can also be posted to a class-wide discussion using an attached document. One helpful online process is to make "comments . . . *accretive*, taking into account previous reviewers' comments so review comments aren't redundant" (Warnock and Cassel 109).

Elements of Response

Reviewing student drafts and evaluating final projects are part of the high literacy load instructors experience in the digital era (Griffin and Minter 153). Although reading essays has long been a challenging part of composition instructors' work, the amounts of reading and writing have increased through digitality, which encourages more writing. Therefore, we offer a response and evaluation process that may assist instructors in keeping their time and efforts tightly focused on what is most important.

Response to student writing should follow well-organized, repeatable patterns they can learn to expect, enabling them to make sense of what instructors believe are successful compositions. These patterns include what is to be evaluated, how the evaluation will look, and the selected response media.

What Is to Be Evaluated

Response should align with the goals provided in the assignment, which follow the course and programmatic outcomes (see ch. 3). For evaluation purposes, feedback should be provided in order of importance. We recommend a strategic blend between what Stephen North calls minimalistic-expressive and instructional-educational marking in "Training Tutors to Talk about Writing" regarding higher- to lower-order concerns, also known as global-to-local issues; such a blend illustrates the need for attending to major-to-minor issues respectively. These include idea fluency (i.e., content), form (i.e., organization and style), and correctness (i.e., mechanics, grammar, and citation use), as well as self-reflection.

In other words, if there is no content—if the thesis is missing or text is thin, undetailed, or does not address the stated thesis—then organization and correctness have no importance. Idea fluency must exist before worrying about sentences that would change if content is developed differently; similarly, correcting sentences anchors students in their current writing plan, often keeping them from seeking needed fluency. It is important to read through what students have written, however. Many writers—even experienced ones—do not express a true thesis in terms of what they really want to say until near the end of early drafts. That is because they may write their way into the draft, using the writing as a thinking activity (often unconsciously) and figuring out what they mean along the way. Yet inexperienced writers may not realize that, having finally found the crucial point, readers need them to state their new thesis idea at the beginning of the project and rework the text to address that new, often clearer idea. Instructors who recognize a late thesis can help students move it to the beginning for revising with that focused idea in mind.

Attending to fluency, form, and correctness in that order provides instructors a focused process for giving feedback and avoids overwhelming students. Thus, Richard Haswell's "Minimal Marking" describes how minimal marking for error has some benefit, although instructors should keep such surface-driven comments in their place. Below are some possible outcomes addressing these issues:

Fluency

- to write a persuasive argument with proposed solution
    - o provide a reasonable claim
    - o offer justifiable reasons for the claim
    - o use sufficient details and examples
- to analyze an audience for a persuasive argument
- to recognize and use the genre conventions of arguments that move people to action
- to use research to support reasoning and meaning
- to include multiple media in rhetorically effective ways

Form

- to arrange the argument using one of the organizational methods taught
- to organize according to the audience needs and rhetorical situation
- to write in a style that recognizes the intended audience's needs

Correctness

- to use grammar and mechanics appropriately
- to write readable prose
- to proofread well
- to use MLA (or other) citation and referencing correctly
- to meet style, format, and length requirements

Self-Reflection

- to provide critical self-reflection of composing choices and processes

Such outcomes should be made clear not only in the syllabus as course goals but also in each assignment, evaluative rubrics, and provided feedback.

How the Evaluation Will Look

Evaluation can be provided globally, locally, or through rubrics that include both; any of these will help Professor Jackson and assist his students in understanding their instructor's feedback. Here, we address the information each should offer.

Global Response

Global comments often are text-based paragraphs or brief letters to students, and they can be provided through audio or video media. Even when video and audio are recorded, the global and local provisions apply in that fluency and form are more important than correctness, and instructional response should attend to them first and with the most emphasis.

Offered mostly through prose or sentence-based talk, global response requires careful construction. In a process model based on formative feedback and revision opportunities, students must make a cognitive leap between the feedback they receive and how to revise and develop their writing using that feedback. Instructors might not realize that their intention for feedback may not match students' interpretations, which means teachers must learn to write and speak instructional text with simplicity and clarity in mind. Hewett theorizes from research that a linguistically direct approach to written and spoken response—*semantic integrity*—is particularly helpful in online settings where feedback often provides much of the teaching (*Online Writing Conference* 19; *Reading* 179). Semantic integrity grounds instructional language that provides sufficient information to students, offers clear guidance about potential next steps (which includes teaching students how to make choices and encouraging them to do so), and works to prompt new or different thinking. Such an approach is also important for any student whose composition is evaluated through digital means and whose teacher may not have face-to-face time or ability to discuss the feedback.

Feedback can be either straightforward (linguistically direct) or suggestive (linguistically indirect, per Hewett, *Reading* 179; see also Straub). It is best to use declarative, interrogative, and imperative statements that do not suggest or hint at what students might do and that are not linguistically indirect. Such clarity of instructional intention can help students—particularly online—interpret the feedback for use in a next draft. Brief mini-lessons can help teach students through their own writing, providing personalized feedback through a four-step intervention process (illustrated in exs. 9.3 and 9.4) that identifies problems. This process can also be used to identify what students are doing well and how strengths in their projects can be repeated. It is important to use models for repeatable strengths as well as for problems.

Four-Step Intervention Process

What is the problem? Identify *what* is the most important problem in projects, typically a higher-order concern regarding content or form, but possibly a style or lower-order correctness concern if projects are otherwise well developed.

Why is it a problem? Explain specifically *why* students' drafts are not working in their current state to help them make cognitive connections between feedback and revision.

How can this problem be revised and avoided? The notion of demonstrating *how* may worry instructors who are concerned about not appropriating students' texts, but appropriation is not possible when instructors teach two or more possibilities for moving forward, allowing students choice. Deliberate modeling of revision gives students strategies to imitate.

Do these steps to address the problem? Giving students something to *do*—a way to change the writing and an instruction to try a revision action—encourages needed revision. It may seem odd, but students often do not address problem areas that instructors merely have pointed out (Hewett, "Asynchronous Online Instructional Commentary" 42), indicating instructors can help by explicitly telling them to act.

Example 9.3. Approach to the Four-Step Intervention Process: What, Why, How, Do

College professors want students to contribute thoughtful and correct discussion posts that demonstrate you are thinking critically about the course material. That's why discussion makes up forty percent of the course grade. Although the situation you described does a good job of showing how you used your moral judgment in the eighth grade, there are so many grammatical and punctuation problems in this post that it's hard to understand, which is a problem. **[WHAT]** When readers cannot understand what you have written, they probably will not read all of it. **[WHY]**

You can avoid this problem by proofreading carefully. Try reading your post out loud, listening for what you say orally versus what you wrote. **[HOW]** Do this for every discussion post. **[DO]**

Example 9.4. Approach to the Four-Step Intervention Process: What, Why, How, Do

A report typically has an abstract that is written after the report itself is complete. It summarizes the main issues and findings of the report in about two hundred to five hundred words. You do not have an abstract. **[WHAT]** This is a problem because your assignment specifically calls for it. **[WHY]** To write an abstract, review the main parts of your report, find the key issues and results, and use them to write a summary. Then, place it at the beginning of the report as shown in your MLA guidance. **[HOW]** Do this essential work before you post the report to me in the portfolio. **[DO]**

Example 9.5 shows a lengthier, text-based global comment that praises the student where praise is due, offers two brief mini-lessons based on the student's own writing and uses the four-step intervention process, responsively addresses a class-wide problem, provides a series of action steps, and closes with encouragement.

Example 9.5. Global Comments

Dylan, your summary starts out strong. You summarize the article contents well. For the most part, your writing is clear, audience-focused, and interesting. Well done! You do have a problem with lack of detail throughout. This is a problem because your article was about eight pages long, and your summary was about one-third of a page. The length guidelines I gave you suggest how detailed you should be. To address this problem, reread the article and find additional pertinent details. You could include a description of how the mall imitates Main Street (using a description from the figure, for example), more summary from the final paragraphs of the article, or more information about the author's bias and your critique of it. Look for facts, figures, examples, or quotations that would make the summary stronger. Do these actions to improve your piece.

You have several sentences that are comma splices (you use commas to separate complete sentences without a coordinating conjunction). Look at those sentences again and use other punctuation (e.g., a semicolon) or a conjunction—or just rewrite them entirely.

Finally, your citation is wrong. Almost everyone in the class got these wrong, so I'll teach a short lesson in the LMS conference space. Basically, your book is an edited collection. You didn't get the citation from the original piece, so you cannot cite the original piece. Make sense? Here are your next steps:

- Work with your content first, then sentences and citation formats.
- Read the entire piece out loud to check for clear phrasing and punctuation.
- Carefully consider your peers' advice (and see what peers are saying about other people's summaries). How does it apply to your writing?
- Write and post your self-reflection with the essay.
- Remember to use internal citation for new material.
- Post as an attached document (not pasted into the box) by Sunday, 11:00 p.m. (ET).

Nice start, Dylan!

Although this global approach to feedback may seem lengthy, it does not take long to formulate, primarily because it does not attempt to address every problem or even problem sentences that likely would change if the student undertakes an in-depth revision. Below are five tips for providing faster, more effective global response on drafts. These same tips can be used to plan oral feedback through audio and video platforms.

Think formative, not summative. The goal is to provide problem-centered instruction. For formative commentary on drafts, help students take drafts to the next level of competence by addressing only key ideas or issues. For final paper commentary, address only the most important concerns that may assist with the next assignment or portfolio development (Hewett, *Online Writing Conference* 201–03).

Focus tightly. Select only two to three major concerns that, if addressed, would influence the meaning of the writing or take it to the next level of competence (higher-order concerns). Teach primarily about those concerns, avoiding the urge to sneak in lessons about the small, correctness-level stuff (lower-order concerns; 206–08).

Be straightforward. Use linguistically direct language. (1) *This paragraph needs to be revised.* This declarative sentence uses direct language to provide information about the writing. (2) *How will you revise this paragraph?* This interrogative sentence uses direct language to ask a genuine question about the writing. Interrogatives that begin with *wh-* and *how* are helpful question forms. (3) *Revise this paragraph.* This imperative sentence uses direct language to request or command the writer about the writing. (4) AVOID: *Shouldn't you revise this paragraph? Or Does this paragraph need revising?* Rhetorical and yes-no questions are particularly unhelpful because their intention is to gently push students toward an action; research suggests that students interpret them literally and address them as a choice. Suggestions are not helpful sentence forms UNLESS they are preceded with the phrase *I suggest you XYZ or I think you should XYZ* (203–06).

Teach; don't talk. Teaching with feedback involves asking genuine *wh-* and *how* questions, demonstrating, illustrating, explaining, modeling, and providing doable tasks with instructions to give them a try. Modeling is especially useful when personalized through examples of the student's own writing and directed to the student by name (197–200).

Format thoughtfully. Instructional text should engage one readable font (usually twelve point) and judicious uses of font styles (e.g., **bold**, <u>underline</u>, or *italics*; avoid **using** <u>all three</u> *in one response*), highlighting, bullets, and numbers. It also includes using the word processor's indentation, tabs, line spacing, page breaks, formatting icons, and other auto features (212–15).

LOCAL COMMENTS

Local comments may be helpful with or without global commentary. Typically, with global commentary, local comments are best used to engage lower-order concerns. When they substitute for global commentary, they might address higher-order concerns primarily. It is important to avoid correcting students' writing unless the goal is to demonstrate what editing at the sentence level looks like. Once their work is corrected, students are unlikely to risk unfixing perfectly good sentences by rewriting. Local comments might be embedded between brackets [ ] and bolded or in another color font (preferably not red, given its potential negative connection to past evaluation for many students). Or, they may be provided in comment balloons, as shown in example 9.6. Keep local comments friendly, brief, to the point, and straightforward.

Example 9.6. Local Comments in Comment Balloons

The following image provides examples of an instructor's local comments in the margins of a student's paper.

In the beginning, a family with a telephone in the home was considered fortunate. That early phone hung on a wall and connected the caller to an operator, who then connected to the desired party. The phone became more popular and its popularity meant that in some locations, a party line meant that any one person's conversation was open to hearing by neighbors sitting on the phone. The game of "operator" came about when people would listen to their neighbors' calls and tell others of the business. As with the game, news became muddled and morphed into something beyond reality and truth.

That early phone was replaced by the rotary dial phone used to dial most parties directly; the operator became most useful for long distance calls and for calls where the number was unknown. Only those who have used the rotary dial know the sound of the dial going around with the finger in the number and the whirring of the dial returning to its original place. No one wanted to call a wrong number when the dialing took so long, but then no one knew any different, so time was not of the essence.

In the 1970s, for more affluent families, the single phone in the house was replaced by multiple jacks that enabled extension lines. Still one phone account, but now one was not as limited as to where to talk. With the advent of the modern touchtone phone, traditional black Bakelite was replaced by white, blue, and pink colors—and the stylish "Princess Phone," designed to attract teenage girls.

When cordless phones were introduced, the communicator suddenly was unleashed: no more requirements to remain in the kitchen, bedroom, or living room. Television shows like *Magnum PI* advertised the luxury of the mobile phone—tied only to the house that connected the invisible line. What could be better than that?

The 1990s popularized the next technology because there is always something better than "that." Truly mobile phones could be connected in a car; in short time, these phones had cell towers as their links, and the cell phone was born. From the cell phone—which in the 21st century began to replace the home phone for many people—technological innovations included a camera and texting an alphanumeric message to another person's phone and the computing power of the Blackberry and the Droid. No longer leashed to a house or to a car, the phone unleashed itself from the limitations of human speech and launched itself into the Internet. Internet browsers now are a common part of such phones and people use their cell phones as watches, movie theatres, email receptors, restaurant finders, mapping systems (GPS), text message receivers and senders, twittering messages, and even as phones for voice connections.

Professor Jackson: I like how you have opened the paragraph, Tamara. It draws me into your topic.

Read this sentence aloud and listen for repetition. How can you revise it for greater clarity? Then, read all your sentences aloud—do they communicate your message?

Professor Jackson: Try dropping "of the business." What other changes would strengthen the sentence?

Professor Jackson: I can see and almost hear this action, Tamara!

Professor Jackson: This really is a rough-draft sentence. Revise it with your subject and verb in mind.

Professor Jackson: Flesh out this paragraph and the next ones to really connect with your readers through more detail. To meet the assignment requirements, use source citations that anchor what you're saying in what your readers can read independently.

Professor Jackson: While I really like the image of the phone unleashing itself, because it's kind of fun, you've given the phone human actions. The phone didn't launch itself into the Internet either. Think about whether to give people the action, which is what we expect as readers, or to give phones the action throughout, which would fully personify them. Right now, the personification is a bit odd to read.

Rubrics

Rubrics may be used to guide students' composing and instructors' evaluation processes. Students can refer to them when creating projects to ensure they have fulfilled necessary criteria, and peers can use them to give feedback to classmates. Based in assignment outcomes, rubrics should address enough criteria to guide but not overwhelm students. Construct between eight and fifteen items, which can be interchangeable with each genre taught. Example 9.7 offers an example of an analytic, impressionistic rubric that follows the fluency, form, and correctness order we recommend.

Example 9.7. Analytic (Impressionistic) Rubric

√ = draft

* = presentation (next) draft

Competency	Fails to meet competency	Meets competency	Exceeds competency
Content fluency			
Presents a clear thesis.	√	*	
Introduction offers background, or reasons, for the thesis.		√	*
Introduction outlines why this issue is a problem, why people disagree about it, and the essay's main points.		√	*
Essay body summarizes one source article about the issue.			√ *
Source author's position is presented in an unbiased manner.	√		*
Relevant support includes facts, figures, examples, and quotations.	√	*	
Conclusion summarizes the source author's position and critiques it for objectivity, weaknesses, or strengths without inserting student's own bias.		√ *	
Organization (form)			
Essay is unified by summarizing and discussing only one article or essay.		√	*
Paragraphs address the assignment's requirements.	√	*	
Style and expression			
Writing is clear and precise.		√ *	
Sentence meaning is clear.		√	*
Grammar and mechanics (correctness)			
Essay is substantially free of major errors in grammar, spelling, punctuation, and mechanics and completely free of distracting errors.	√	*	
Introduces and explains paraphrases and quotations correctly and completely.			√ *
Uses MLA [APA] guidelines for in-text citations and works cited [references].		√	*

Different types of rubrics include analytic and holistic rubrics.

Analytic rubrics separate each criterion, allowing instructors to evaluate them individually, as with example 9.7. Analytic rubrics work well for formative evaluations prior to or as part of portfolios. Created without scores, they break down each criterion according to three categories: students fail to meet, meet, or exceed the criterion. Using marks rather than numerical scores, holistic rubrics offer an impression from right to left and top to bottom of how well students have fulfilled the assignment's requirements. For example, students can see quickly that they did well if most of their checks—particularly those in the top third—are on the right side of the page.

Holistic rubrics use specific criteria, but offer an overall judgment, or score, regarding the quality of the project. Analytic rubrics are good for formative while holistic rubrics are good for summative evaluation, or the final project that needs grading. Holistic rubrics also save time, as they generate one final score for the project, and they are often used in portfolio evaluations.

Example 9.8 highlights criteria that can be used in a rhetorically focused evaluation of a student project and offers questions to guide rubric creation, whether analytic or holistic.

Example 9.8. Rhetorically Focused Grade-Based Rubric Criteria

A, Above Average. Writer has thoughtfully considered and carefully crafted the content within the project and included relevant details. Project is organized and presented to the intended audience in a logical manner, including the multimodal element. No conventional errors evident.

B, Effective. Writer tries to consider and craft the content in an effective way, but the text may include some irrelevant details. Project is organized logically for the intended audience, including the use of multimodality. Some errors evident but do not detract from the overall message.

C, Satisfactory. Writer should do more to consider and craft the content to make an effective argument. Project may include irrelevant details or follow tangential lines of reasoning, indicating a clear need for restructuring. Significant errors throughout.

D, Needs Improvement. Writer must do more to identify the audience and central purpose of the piece, revising to make a clearer argument. The project's information is disorganized and does not work to forward a thesis. Errors are distracting.

F, Fails to Meet Criteria. The writer has made no attempt to identify the audience and purpose, causing the argument to fail. The project's information lacks organization or is incomplete. The writer has failed to revise considering feedback, mechanical errors, or both.

Example 9.9 highlights rubric material with a criterion for a multimodal project; this rubric could also guide an alphabetic text-heavy project, as well as an ePortfolio, however, as we discuss further in the sections below.

Example 9.9. Rhetorically Focused Multimodal Project Rubric Criteria

Argument, Evidence, Support, or Research. Does the student use solid argument, evidence, and supporting details, or some variation? Does research support the topic? Is the research used in an unbiased and fair manner? *[This criterion is relevant depending on the course and genre.]*

Audience. Has the student chosen the appropriate audience for the project? Does the project meet the needs of the intended audience?

Purpose. Has the student developed a project that indicates the purpose of the project?

Genre Conventions. Does the student understand what the genre entails? Does the project demonstrate those standard genre conventions? *[This criterion should be drafted according to the unique features of the genre. What are the features of the genre? Word accordingly.]*

Organization. Is the thesis evident? Does the piece have an overall theme? Does the text-image arrangement lead to understanding the argument?

Multimodal Component. Do selected modes work together to form a cohesive argument and drive the thesis? Are all modes relevant? Has the student chosen the appropriate medium for the intended audience and purpose? *[If the project is multimodal, this criterion is necessary.]*

Style, Grammar, and Mechanics. Is the document error free? Has the student used the proper citation manual? *[This criterion also can include citation standards.]*

Reflection. Has the student thoughtfully and critically accounted for the rhetorical choices made? Are these choices reflected in the project; do the choices match what is conveyed in the self-reflection?

Selected Response Media

The third element of response involves selecting appropriate technologies for giving feedback to the student. Typically, formative and summative feedback are provided using alphabetic text, in conferences (see ch. 10), and in video and audio formats. In all feedback, we recommend following the fluency → form → correctness order, focusing most on higher-order and less on lower-order concerns. Instructor response may be the most overt and concrete way instructors teach students one-to-one; feedback thereby constitutes genuine teaching opportunities particularly in the digitally enhanced, hybrid, and fully online settings (Hewett, *Online Writing Conference* 50). Therefore, we consider providing feedback of all kinds a form of conferencing (whether in alphabetic text, images, or audio and/or video) particularly in online settings (see also Hawisher, "Electronic Meetings").

Regardless of the learning environment, either online or on-site, it has long been argued that live one-on-one conferences help students improve their writing. Muriel Harris states in *Teaching One-to-One* that conferences teach students the writing process, "coaching the student through the '-ings' of writing—thinking, planning, drafting, revising, and editing—even when these occur almost simultaneously" (9). She stresses that the conference enables individualizing the instruction to the students and their compositions: "Generalities from the classroom or textbook can be brought down to the reality of a specific piece of writing" (9). For instance, in summative written feedback, instructors may indicate the conclusion is weak and teach about how to fix it, but without the chance to change a grade through revision, students likely will not pay attention to this instruction. However, in synchronous or asynchronous, formative conferences, instructors can become writing coaches and guide students through various approaches to rewriting the conclusion. Ideally, formative feedback would address the drafted conclusion, enabling students to revise it. When such an issue arises in summative evaluation, however, instructors should explicitly teach students how to transfer the lesson to the next project. Conferencing for such specifics may help students make the cognitive leap between the conclusion in this essay and how to address future conclusions—which would represent learning transfer.

Although many students prefer and need alphabetically written feedback, which we have discussed, recent scholarship suggests other students may learn through multimodal instruction (Brick and Holmes; Mayer and Moreno; Stannard, "Screen Capture Software"), especially screen capture (Gilboy et al.). Giving strictly alphabetic feedback undoubtedly is helpful and students are accustomed to it, yet it can be time intensive despite the targeted feedback tips provided above; therefore, instructors may want to test screen-capture programs that limit feedback to a few minutes, forcing them to stay focused and not overwhelm the student (Stannard, "Using"; Warnock, "Responding"). Screen-capture software often is free and may operate within an LMS. Simply put, screen capture shows the instructor's screen with the student project on display, allowing instructors to record voiceover with their feedback, walking students step-by-step through a project. In "*Camtasia* in the Classroom," Mary Lourdes Silva reports that "[s]tudents who preferred the visual/audio modality of the teacher commentary videos cited their conversational quality, clarification of expectations, and reference to more global issues in writing" (1). Instructors should inquire regarding their institution's FERPA rules, as some will require instructors to use the screen-capture software housed in the LMS to avoid student privacy issues, especially if grades are assigned through this feedback.

Not all students, of course, prefer screen-capture feedback. In "Responding to Student Writing with Audio-Visual Feedback," Warnock finds that the gold standard is still the one-to-one, face-to-face conference. For the best access for all students, particularly concerning visual versus aural learners and those who learn better from images than text, we recommend mixing response media during the term, potentially reaching each student with the preferred media at some point. Another approach is to poll students at the beginning of the term to target the most commonly desired media the most often or to provide feedback according to individual preferences; such accommodation is especially helpful for certain learning challenges like reading and auditory processing disabilities. As many free screen-capture programs do not offer transcription services, it is important to ask students whether they can access the video as well as what format they prefer. Combination feedback works well, such as *Microsoft Word* comments and teacher commentary videos. In all cases, instructors should familiarize students with how feedback will occur and teach them how to use it to their best advantage—and explain whether they are required to use it to improve grades.

In multimodal courses, screen-capture feedback can model multimodality for students, helping them create multimodal projects for which written feedback may not be as effective. Students can use screen-capture software to create videos with voice-over; then instructors can screen-capture over these videos, recording their own feedback and pausing students' videos to discuss their features (much like a director's commentary). Screen-capture allows instructors to point to specific parts of a project and discuss them in a conversational manner organic to the project's strengths and weaknesses.

Multimodal options beyond screen-capture videos include making audio files, which can ease both teacher and students into increased technology use. Audio feedback has its limitations, including challenging students to follow along by viewing projects while listening to the feedback; in a video, cursor movement provides that navigational help. If instructors are uncomfortable using screen-capture or audio feedback, conferencing software (often included in LMSs) enables screen sharing with students. Instructors can highlight and point to places in the students' projects, leading them through each section by bits. Similarly, instructors can engage synchronous composing software while in a video conference or even on the phone to offer response and teach revision. Possibilities abound!

Peer Review as Evaluation

Peer review offers an outside perspective from classmates. In "Composing Multimodality," Joddy Murray states, "Trial and error or improvisation may work intuitively to get the text invented and made material in the medium in which the student is working, but the final product must be carefully considered and assessed against audience expectations" (346). Although classmates may not be the project's intended audience, they can provide a fresh perspective regarding what they see and how the piece works for its intended purpose; when encouraged to imagine themselves as such, they also can review from the intended audience's perspective. Peer review is good for both students under review and reviewers themselves because composing insights transfer among them. For instance, peers may see that the project being reviewed takes more risks or tests out new mediums, giving them confidence to try new things, too. Reviewing others helps students see their own projects more critically, especially when peer review strategies are guided by instructors and course outcomes.

Students may focus on correctness over fluency and form, so instructors can provide guided peer review that involves questions to answer about the project; these might be derived from rubric criteria or areas where instructors know students struggle. The guiding questions should have rhetorical focus to prompt reviewers to consider the audience, rhetorical situation, and choice alignment with medium. If instructors have taught the assignment before or completed it themselves, as we recommend, they can steer students through potential stumbling blocks, guiding peers to help writers in these areas. Students might be required to develop their own questions for peer readers. Instructors can prompt students to think about where they struggled and ask peers to help them think through concepts. Instructors should model peer review for students, which can be done through feedback to an example student project or through previous course peer feedback (after receiving permission).

For multimodal projects, instructors can prompt students to give each other screen-capture feedback, enabling them to play with technology, think about multimodality, and consider how and when such media are useful for communicating. Prompting students to create self-reflections about their peer review experiences—both as authors and readers—can address text-based and multimodal feedback. Using screen-capture peer feedback also might help fully online students become more comfortable with one another. Some students may not immediately be comfortable giving screen-capture feedback, so instructors should be flexible about students' needs.

General advice for peer review includes the following:

Provide students word count and video length guidance for the review.

Make the peer review worth a grade.

Require students to self-reflect on whether, how, and why they used peer advice in revision, potentially worth points.

Ask students to review more than one peer's project to view different composing styles and to provide at least one peer review in case a reviewer does not follow through.

Prompt students to review each other's work throughout the composing process, from brainstorming, outlining, and drafting through final portfolios.

If certain students fail to provide feedback, pair them with each other.

Reflection as Evaluation

Reflection is perhaps the most important evaluation tool. Writers are well poised to talk about what works and what does not in their own pieces. Students' self-reflections can guide instructors in their evaluations of projects because they should include students' rhetorical choices. Jody Shipka reminds educators in *Toward a Composition Made Whole* that reflection can illustrate students' decision-making process in the alphabetic essay, multimodal, and mixed mode composing processes while encouraging metacognition. Shipka expresses that self-reflection "allow[s] instructors to frame their response to students' work in increasingly efficient, purposeful, and constructive ways by focusing on the specific goals and choices students have selected and shared with the instructor" (290).

For example, if a student reviews a restaurant in a text-based essay with the purpose of persuading local citizens to patronize it, that choice might limit circulation outside the classroom setting. If the student's choices are illustrated in a prewriting reflection, the instructor can guide the student toward a medium choice with wider circulation, such as a text-based blog that could include images or other media. Students' postreflections can then guide instructors in evaluation, as instructors consider the following:

- Are students' choices having the intended effect?
- Have students articulated the appropriate audience?
- Are the choices students say they have made evident in the created text?

Such articulation of choices makes self-reflection crucial. Students can express why they made certain choices, which can guide the instructor in reading or evaluating the text, but if their choices do not ultimately make sense, the reflection provides clues as to how and why they should return to the drawing board. Students should be prompted to write project reflections, especially for multimodal projects. These self-reflections can be separate from the ePortfolio reflections discussed in chapter 8. If the course outcomes also ask students to consider audience, purpose, and medium choices, students can simply write self-reflections regarding course outcomes specific to the project (as long as they account for rhetorical choices made throughout the composing process).

If students have media labs, they can write statements of goals and choices about their software choices (see ch. 7). When students post final project drafts, they can reflect on their choices of software and their struggles; self-determined challenges can help instructors focus on the rhetorical choices behind the project instead of its design—the bells and whistles—which can be critical for students without access to certain technology or those with less familiarity regarding certain software. In "Multimodal Composing, Appropriation, Remediation, and Reflection," Donna Reiss and Art Young express that focusing on students' self-reflections helps instructors guide evaluation toward rhetorical choices: "We don't require expertise in video production or painting from our students; we do require commitment, critical thinking, engagement with content, and thoughtful composing where multiple communicative elements interrelate" (179–80). Requiring students to examine their own processes is perhaps the best way to teach them to make thoughtful, rhetorical composing decisions.

Instructional Evaluation in Practice

To illustrate evaluation in practice, in this section, we present two of Professor Jackson's student-created projects, obtained with institutional review board permission and anonymized.

Evaluating a Text-Heavy Project

In example 9.10, Professor Jackson's students created a review for which the scaffolded assignment broke down genre conventions, including how to write a critical discussion that persuades the audience (chosen by the students) to visit a place in the students' city. As part of the review genre, students needed to discuss the common audience expectations of a review, including what outside research, such as interviews from patrons, might be convincing. The assignment asked students to choose their medium according to their intended audience; choices included a newsletter one might find in a travel agency or a blog the local online news. Regardless of medium, students were required to use alphabetic text and at least one other mode to communicate. Therefore, while the medium was multimodal, there was still a strong written word component.

We focus here on an alphabetic text-heavy project from Tamara, a student who used low-bridge technology for her review. Although the project is considered multimodal, the written word is the predominant communicative mode. Instructors could assign this project as simply an alphabetic essay or as an initial foray into multimodality by asking students to manipulate *Microsoft Word* templates, which is low-bridge software.

Example 9.10. Tamara's Review of The Standard Diner

Tamara visited The Standard Diner, a favorite among her city's locals. She created a newsletter, and she chose to manipulate a *Word* template, using a two-column format that would allow her to include photos or other images. A two-column format enabled an aesthetically pleasing organization (see fig. 9.1). She began her review with research about diners, walking readers through how the classic diner became an American cultural mainstay, as well as how The Standard Diner itself was started. With this research, she met the criterion of *evidence, support, argument, or research* and set up her argument that this particular restaurant is unlike other "standard" diners readers might encounter.

Tamara's review describes the traditional look and feel of diners, juxtaposing words with images of the exterior and interior, giving the

Tamara Jones

THE STANDARD DINER

Not the Standard Dining Experience

The United States of America is home to people from all around the world and with that comes an eclectic variety of cuisine to choose from. Growing up as a military brat, I had the opportunity to expose my palate to some unique and tasty dishes, so I like to fancy myself as an amateur food connoisseur. However, I've found that even the finest gourmet foods just cannot compare to the simplest diner classics. Diners have been a long established part of our culture long before the time of drive-thru ordering was even a thought. But what exactly makes a standard diner?

The first diner was founded in 1872, by a man named Walter Scott who abandoned his job in order to pursue a career in the culinary world. He quit all other work to become a street vendor and, using a horse drawn delivery van with large wagon wheels he modified himself, he filled orders for the people walking by him on the streets of Providence, Rhode Island. Lunch wagons and food carts may not seem like the typical diner to some, but it was the beginning of a food revolution. His street side success drew notice and soon others were buying wagons to sell food—some were

and french-fries or club sandwiches that people associate with their ideal diner staples.

The Diner Experience, 2012 Road Trip

Figure 9.1. Tamara's review of The Standard Diner.

audience a sense of what she portrays. Tamara adheres to the genre conventions at this point, offering opinions about the diner's service and food, which a restaurant review's audience would expect. But, whereas she does well at describing the restaurant itself, she does not describe the food as thoroughly. Tamara states, "[E]ven their grilled cheese sandwiches [were] served unlike anything else I had ever seen—with several different types of cheeses, a jam made from heirloom tomatoes, a balsamic vinegar syrup, and brioche with green chili." When writing about the fries, Tamara describes their look and taste, adding an enhanced photo illustrating the seasoning on each fry. Her choices of images augmenting the written text indicates a strong understanding of design and format, adhering to the criterion of *multimodality*. All her images are relevant. The *Word* template appears to mimic the style of a restaurant menu, further indicating an understanding of the medium and review genre.

Tamara accounts for her rhetorical decisions in her self-reflection. She explains why she included some of the images with the text, stating, "I also tried to give my audience a good *feel* of the establishment by emphasizing on the visual aspects of the diner—the décor, the atmosphere, the look of the food—and on the smells. . . . The senses truly played a role in aiding my description of the diner." She explains her choice of medium, saying:

> I chose to write my review as a newsletter. I tried to compose it as something that might be found on the front desk of a hotel. [The textbook authors] wrote about incorporating credibility to writing through the use of *ethos* and I have lived in hotels and worked in hotels, so I know from both sides of the counter how helpful those newsletters can be. I have found newsletters to be more detailed and a tad more reliable than an online review found on yelp.com or such.

Tamara's own experience living and working in hotels helped her understand the audience's needs, prompting her to choose a newsletter format over an online review that might not reach the same audience. Her reflection enabled us to determine that Tamara understood the rhetorical concepts of audience and purpose, choosing the best medium for delivery of content. She even commented on the document's ethos as print-based rather than designed for a popular review website, which indicates further understanding of rhetorical concepts.

In formatively evaluating Tamara's project (ex. 9.11), we use the example 9.9 rubric, with its rhetorical focus, attention to genre conventions, and multimodal criteria. In the following evaluations, we use the example rubric with modified criteria, focusing on each criterion to discuss the effectiveness (or lack thereof) of each project. We have put the criteria found in example 9.9's rubric in bold to illustrate Tamara's issues and to model how instructors can guide students using rubric elements, as well as focus on fluency, form, correctness, and the four-step intervention process (shown as ***italicized boldface*** in brackets [ ] for the reader's benefit). We note here that Tamara's project earned solid praise, and we tried to balance that praise with revision guidance.

Example 9.11. Tamara's Text-Heavy Restaurant Review Project Formative Evaluation

Hi Tamara,

Reading your project makes me hungry! I love your use of quality images like the fries. The seasoning really stands out, and they give the audience a sense of what type of food they will be getting at The Standard Diner. As a frequent visitor of The Standard Diner, I enjoyed reading your thoughts about the food, service, and atmosphere. These are the **genre conventions** one might expect to find in a restaurant review. I can tell you did your **research** by interviewing patrons, and what they said supports your opinion. You also include research about how the diner was founded—a lot of it I didn't know! The piece is well organized and flows nicely from one paragraph to the next, walking your reader through your argument for visiting. In your **self-reflection**, you mention that your **audience** might be patrons of a hotel, and this newsletter format works because they might look for it in the hotel lobby. What other format could you have used if this review would be found in a hotel? [***Genuine, not rhetorical question.***]

Although the genre conventions are evident and you definitely make an argument for visiting this restaurant (your persuasive **purpose** is clear), you also should describe the food using words to complement the images. [***What***] I do like how you use a picture of the fries when describing them (you're making excellent use of **multimodality** here!), but I found myself wanting more textual description of the rest of the food because I wanted to see and maybe taste it with you. [***Why***] To address this problem, add more food description of foods other than the fries. [***How***] Also, I'd like to see a variation of pictures to keep me interested. [***What, Why***] Instead of two pictures of the outside of the building, what other pictures might be more relevant? For instance, you talk excitedly about blackberry soda, which I think you should show. [***How***] I also recommend that you either wrap the text around the images, keeping a nice flow of **multimodality**, or use the same size pictures everywhere, so they all use the same column width. [***How***]

For a more polished piece, I'd like to see you work on interweaving your quotations from research with lead-ins to the sentences and explaining them more for your audience. In terms of **correctness**, you have issues with commas that come before coordinating conjunctions. For instance, you say, "The presentation was simple yet neat and it smelled amazing." **[What]** This is a simple, yet important problem in connection with the sentence work we did this term. **[Why]** Remember that if what comes after the coordinating conjunction is an independent clause (in other words, a full sentence: noun plus verb), then you need a comma before the coordinating conjunction (like before the "and" in the sentence I pulled from your project). **[How]**

Overall, I think you composed a fantastic draft! Let me know if you have any questions as you revise this piece for the next due date. **[Do]** Contact me for help if you want to choose a different medium beyond the newsletter if you decide that hotel patrons are truly your **audience**. **[Do]**

Evaluating a Multimodal Project

A multimodal project without extensive written text does not necessarily need a different rubric as example 9.11 suggests. Instructors may want to ask students to create a text-based response to the assignment as well as a supplemental multimodal component, but both mediums can be evaluated using a similar rhetorically focused rubric. In this section, we highlight a multimodal project for which students had to create a persuasive argument with a proposed solution illustrating a local problem. Professor Jackson required them to research and suggest possible solutions, giving the audience a final call to action. We review Tim's project (shown as ex. 9.12), for which he created a multimodal persuasive proposal in the genre of a PSA, which could be distributed on television (video), radio (sound project), or some other medium that clearly met the intended audience's needs and the composing purpose. We include this example to illustrate the importance of the written reflection, not the use of technology. The reflection indicates Tim struggled with understanding the rhetorical concepts behind composing: It was limited in that he wrote little, suggesting he had trouble expressing the rhetorical choices behind his multimodal composing process.

Example 9.12. Tim's Multimodal PSA Project

Tim created a video PSA using high-bridge technology, as it evidences his ability to integrate sound, image, and text within *iMovie*. In the video, Tim clearly identifies the problem he is addressing: that his state board of education could evaluate teachers of any discipline based on students' performance across all disciplines at any given primary or secondary school. For example, an art teacher could receive low evaluations if the students at a particular institution received low scores in math and science. The student's video attempts to address this issue, provide doable solutions, and suggest a call for action.

In figure 9.2, the first slide, Tim asks his audience, "Did you know, teachers will be graded on students who aren't even in their classes?" He then transitions to the question "How is this fair?" using the same background and font with no sound in the background.

On the next slide, Tim inserts the sound of children screaming coupled with an image of a red letter *F* flashing briefly. The letter is followed by the image of an unhappy toddler. After these brief images, the student reverts to the original style of text slides, using the gray background with white font, but he uses different fade-in animation between slides. He includes a slide stating, "I didn't think so," before telling his audience, "But that's how the new evaluation system works." The final slide calls the audience to action: "Contact the Public Education Department Now and Tell Them What You Think."

The length of the video was within the genre parameters, as students were encouraged to make their PSAs three minutes or less. Thus, the short length is not necessarily indicative of poor quality; instead, Tim's choices of images, sound, and text make the project problematic. At first glance, however, viewers might consider this video to be an example of sound design. The student used a gray background with white text to create contrast and make the text stand out, and the screaming children appeared at the appropriate time in the video, paired with the flashing *F* and the unhappy toddler. The transitions between slides are seamless,

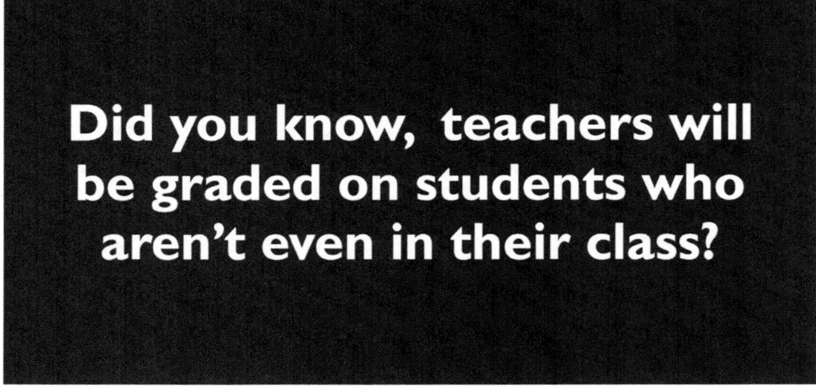

Figure 9.2. Argument question in Tim's multimodal PSA project.

and the text was on the screen for an appropriate amount of time. With an initial viewing, instructors might be inclined to give high scores for the production. With more attention to genre conventions, research, audience, and purpose, however, it becomes clear that there are problems beyond the student not understanding the PSA genre conventions

First, although the issue of how teachers are evaluated has loomed large in the public sphere, this student's video does little to explain the problem beyond suggesting that there is one and that the new evaluation system is unfair. Under the criteria of *genre conventions* and *research*, the student did little to outline the problem and give the audience context for it, including evidence or research to support the perceived unfairness. Despite the call to action in the final slide, there is no mention of possible problem solutions, indicating the student perhaps did not understand the genre conventions of a persuasive argument with a proposal.

Second, Tim's audience is unclear. Based on the video's text that constitutes the call to action, we can surmise that the audience for this PSA was local citizens who care about their educational system. There is little mention of the evaluation system already in place for teachers or how to reach their public education department (PED), however; this leaves the audience at a loss when trying to understand exactly what they should be addressing when writing to their PED or even how to get in touch with the organization if they wanted to voice their concerns. There was little mention of the audience in Tim's self-reflection to support any assertions. He stated, "My purpose was to let the PED (Public Education Department) know that the public has concerns and that the law must be changed" (his parentheses). From this reflection, it seems the audience is the PED, which would make the call to action inappropriate. Perhaps it can be inferred that the video was for an audience who would act and let the PED know how they feel. Tim's word choice in his reflection is slightly confusing, however, suggesting the PED itself was the audience. Tim needed more guidance for justifying his choices and explaining how the video was structured for his audience, further clarifying for the instructor (and himself) the rhetorical choice of audience. With this clarification, the instructor could help Tim either create a new PSA for his actual intended audience of the PED or guide Tim to better understand that local citizens are the audience, who require more information regarding the problem, solutions, and what they should do about the issue.

Third, the project lacks in organization, since there are modes overlapping and interacting, but not for any notable purpose. The way that sound (i.e., children crying), images, and text slides were edited together suggests that Tim is a proficient technology user; however, the crying toddler image during phase two of the video and the soundtrack of children screaming do not speak to the problem of teacher accountability and evaluations or enhance the author's message. The use of images, sound, and text is confusing and confounds the PSA's purpose, which also is a criterion in example 9.9's rhetorically focused rubric.

Our formative evaluation of Tim's project appears in example 9.13. As with Tamara, we have set up the feedback with each criterion in bold to guide readers and the student to the rubric. We again use the four-step intervention process (shown in the first three paragraphs as ***italicized boldface*** in brackets [ ] for readers' benefit; readers may identify the steps used in the rest of the evaluation).

Example 9.13. Tim's Multimodal PSA Project Formative Evaluation

Hi Tim,

Thanks so much for sharing your project with me. I think that your use of a grey background contrasts with the white text, making it really stand out, and the video itself has a nice flow without breaks. I can tell that this is an idea you are passionate about. As I really want to know more, please share why you are so passionate about this topic when you write your final project reflection. **[*Do*]**

There are some problems you should address in revision, so let's turn your passion toward figuring out how to get the main point you are trying to convey to the right audience. First, in your **self-reflection**, you say that your **audience** was the Public Education Department (PED) and your **purpose** was to let them know that the public has concerns and that the law in question must be changed. In the last slide, you state, "Contact the Public Education Department Now and Tell them what you think"; this call to action suggests something that the general public can do. Somehow, this statement leads me to believe that the audience is the general public, not a specific group like the PED. **[*What*]** If the PED is truly your choice of audience, then the call to action is not speaking to the right people. **[*Why*]** How can the call to action be changed to better suit this audience? **[*Genuine, not rhetorical question*]** If the PED is your audience, notice that your self-reflection does not accurately convey your audience, which is a problem you need to fix in revision. **[*What*]**

Either way, your call to action makes me question whether an audience of the general public might have a stake in this problem. **[*What*]** The **audience** you choose needs to have a stake in how the teachers are being evaluated, or they should be affected by the problem. Does this problem affect parents or students or administrators or the general public in that different schools get lower ratings? I'm not sure, but I am confused, which is a composing problem for you. As your primary reader, I should be able to understand who is affected and why. **[Why]** To address this problem, conduct some research and figure out just who this law has an impact on and why it is a problem. **[How]** That said, set up the rhetorical problem a little better in the beginning. **[Do]** What is the fundamental issue and why is it a problem? What are possible, doable solutions? Who is this problem affecting the most? Only when your project can answer these questions can you figure out who your audience truly is and what the call to action really would be. This groundwork also will help you meet the criteria of **research** as well as **genre conventions**, especially if you set up a solution to the problem more clearly and in detail.

After you figure out who your audience is and the general call to action, then you can look at the images you use in terms of **multimodality**. For instance, the toddler crying and the screams behind this image really get the audience's attention, but why do you use the toddler's image and the screams? Once you do more research and determine the audience who is most affected, try to gain the same impact using images that are more powerfully geared to them. Again, your composing decision depends on who your true **audience** is. Your use of images will probably change according to the decisions you make about audience based on what group you determine is the most impacted by the problem; these choices will certainly determine how you organize the piece. Will you highlight the problem in the first slide? The solution in the second? I like how the call to action is at the end, so that organization might stay the same, but the actual call to action will need to change with your revisions of audience and purpose. Go back to our textbook to see sample organizational tactics for the proposal genre. Come see me in conference for a discussion of potential next steps.

After you revise, we can talk through **genre conventions** because you will want to post your reference sheet with appropriate citations for your research. At that point, we also can look more at **mechanics**.

Let me know if you have any questions! As a teacher, I'm quite interested in this topic, so I genuinely want to know more about the problem and its possible solutions. When will you meet with me?

Implications for Evaluation in Practice

Readers may assume Tamara was able to produce a more rhetorically sound project because of her use of low-bridge technology like *Microsoft Word*, leading to a better-produced project that allowed her to focus on the rubric criteria, not the technology. Although this assumption may be accurate, Tim stated his prior knowledge of *iMovie*, leading us to believe he chose the technology based on experience with the software and not because video was the best choice of medium. Either way, Tamara's project was rhetorically effective, and she accurately reflected on her choices. She clearly understood the need to use different media and why. Tim, however, was unable to justify his choices of audience and purpose in his reflection, and his lack of understanding of the rhetorical considerations was evident in his video. Professor Jackson might assume Tim was using technology for technology's sake without understanding what images, sound, or text would be the most effective for the audience.

In addition, both students were prompted in their self-reflections to talk through their uses of software and the struggles they encountered. In a reflection for another project, Tamara states that "using the technology felt more creative and a bit more involved, and I enjoyed learning how to use the video editing program I used to make [the project]." Tamara's comment clearly illustrates the goals of the media labs—to help students feel more comfortable with playing and experimenting with new software they think might be the best choice in conjunction with the chosen medium. In contrast, Tim noted he was already proficient with *iMovie* for making videos, which is not necessarily a valid reason for choosing a medium. Instructors should encourage students to choose the appropriate medium regardless of their comfort level, focusing on the reflection to guide the evaluation, not the overall design. Such focus can allow a project with technical flaws to pass the evaluation.

To be clear, Tim is not solely at fault for his project's shortcomings. This project seems like a first, preliminary draft where Professor Jackson should provide formative, not summative, feedback. He could have assigned a media lab to scaffold the final project, asking students to use video or sound (the two choices of mode) and to clarify the audience choice, structured as a pitch where students walk the instructor through the audience, purpose, medium, and modes they planned to use. At this point, Professor Jackson could have commented that the choices of images and sound did not match Tim's stated choice of audience, guiding him to rethink his approach. Professor Jackson also could have scaffolded the assignment to better ensure that students would outline and research their chosen problem by assigning a supplemental annotated bibliography, complete with research that not only helped to establish the problem but also attempted to provide potential solutions. Tim's project flaws clearly reveal the need for scaffolding a project and providing a formative evaluation. See Sonya Borton and Brian Huot's "Responding and Assessing" for additional support in multimodal project evaluation.

Evaluating an ePortfolio

ePortfolios allow students to collect their work online, including drafts of projects in varying stages, to showcase their best work and to reflect on what they have learned throughout the semester.

The Process of ePortfolio Review

As chapter 8 indicates, a portfolio is a collection of students' best work; it includes a range of drafts from zero to presentation, new projects not yet viewed by the instructor, student self-reflection, and other possible compositions. An ePortfolio simply is a portfolio presented online which is necessary for multimodal projects and, more important, invites a range of outside readers other than instructors (CCCC, "Principles and Practices"). Evaluating an ePortfolio is challenging, as the document typically is robustly large when completed. Instructors should be commenting on portfolio contents throughout the term, and students should be revising all along from instructor feedback. This formative approach spreads out the evaluative work, which helps Professor Jackson—especially given his four-course load.

Similarly, in ePortfolios peer review is more manageable when accomplished in conjunction with specific projects. Students can peer review outcome reflections paired with individual projects when they review the corresponding project, allowing them to see the author's argument for learning course outcomes in both self-reflections and the project itself. ePortfolio peer review can also occur toward the end of the course if instructors limit what they must read (e.g., the multimodal aspect). Sheer volume makes evaluation unwieldy if evaluation is left until the end.

In chapter 8, we also mention students can review each other's work and write self-reflections about their peer review process throughout the term. This suggestion for labor-based contract grading offers another way to evaluate students' performance. Asao B. Inoue defines labor-based contract grading as a system "that calculates final course grades purely by the labor students complete, not by any judgments of the quality of their writing" (*Labor-Based Grading Contracts* 3). He challenges instructors to work with their students to make collaborative judgments, assigning evaluative scores of students' work together; this approach could include several steps:

- Engage a cycle of rubric-building with students.
  - o Create rubrics collaboratively.
  - o Ask students to use the rubric to guide them in project creation.
  - o Engage written or oral peer review based on that rubric.
  - o Prompt students to reflect on their work, including process and revision.
- Meanwhile, throughout the course, students collect artifacts, including peers' evaluations, their own self-reflections, and their projects.
- Meet with students to negotiate the final portfolio's evaluation (54).

Inoue's process relies on mutual agreements with students based on their individual goals for assignments and the rubric they had collaboratively created. Although also work-heavy, he argues this process allows marginalized students, including multilingual students who may not have the same access to standardized English, to have agency in how they are evaluated and to express themselves by showcasing and talking through their work and individual goals. For other ideas regarding ePortfolio practice, see Regina Collins, Norbert Elliot, Andrew Klobucar, and Fadi Deek's "Web-Based Portfolio Assessment."

ePortfolio Evaluation in Practice

Evaluating an ePortfolio is like evaluating a multimodal project, especially when instructors use a rhetorically based rubric like that in example 9.9. Instructors can use the same rubric by rewriting the criteria to include the broader scope of a capstone project and its overarching outcomes.

To illustrate what an ePortfolio evaluation looks like in practice, we again use Professor Jackson's student Tamara's portfolio and reflections. Tamara chose to redesign the template, using a different background than the one offered in the LMS. She selected white with black text boxes on her home page (see fig. 9.3).

First, Professor Jackson might comment on the text's readability; white on black is hard for many readers to see. The criterion of *multimodality* could guide this feedback. Tamara offers her audience guidelines for navigating the ePortfolio on this home page, writing that she made

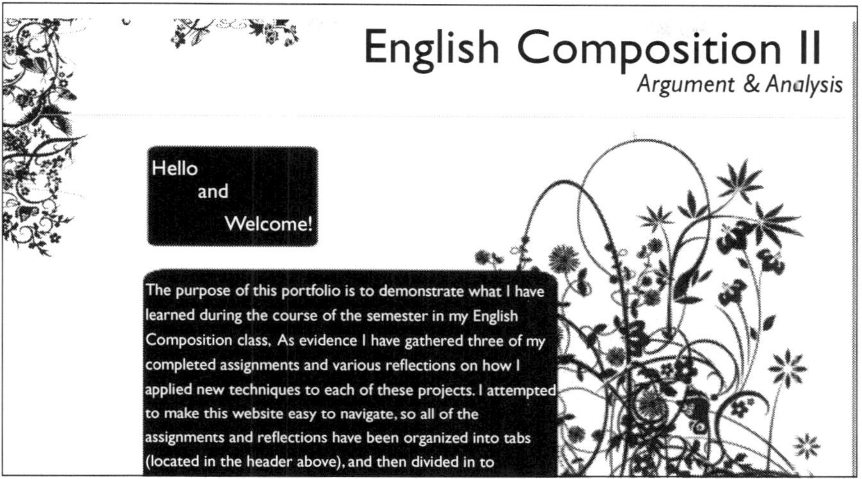

Figure 9.3. Home page of Tamara's ePortfolio.

the pages easy to navigate with all assignments and reflections organized into tabs and divided into subpages. She added guidance to readers who might become lost, explaining how to return to the home page. These additions mitigate some of the white-on-black visual concerns. To showcase her learning of *purpose*, Tamara included revisions of three projects, including the multiple drafts she created for each; Professor Jackson could review these under *genre conventions* to ensure the student has made revisions and accounted for those changes in the project or outcome reflections. Tamara commented on the purpose of the ePortfolio in the home page (see fig. 9.3), stating that its goal was: "to demonstrate what I have learned during the course of the term in my English Composition class. I have gathered three of my assignments and various reflections on how I applied new techniques to each of these projects."

Regarding *multimodality*, the remaining ePortfolio pages do not have black text boxes with white text, making them visually stronger. The pages remained within the black and white theme, however, providing readers with a uniform pattern and allowing Tamara to express her unique personality. The images used throughout were like those showcased in her earlier assignment, addressable with *multimodality*. She provided videos, including a PSA to support her persuasive project's research, and she linked to *Yelp* for other reviews of The Standard Diner.

On other pages in Tamara's ePortfolio, some of the text box text is not spaced properly. Professor Jackson might offer a final comment on how she could integrate the text box quotations seamlessly with her own text, given that direct intervention with that skill might be wasted energy at this point.

Because Tamara also used text boxes to support how she learned from her self-reflections, Professor Jackson might comment on how to integrate quotations into her writing, perhaps under the criterion of *evidence, argument, support, or research*. This critique is especially important if the course goals are to use outside research and integrate others' views with her own. Although Tamara demonstrated ability to quote from the textbook, when she used instructor or peer quotations, she set them off from the text using text boxes. Although this aspect could be a design choice, it signals possible discomfort with integrating evidence into the text's body. We noted that problem in Tamara's review project, indicating a pattern of quotation struggle.

Finally, Tamara discussed how all three projects helped her learn the course outcomes. She talked through her rhetorical decisions for medium and mode choices and discussed her own project goals, which she believed she would take into future compositions. Overall, Tamara's ePortfolio is a good example of what students can produce throughout the term, insofar as the instructor guides them in choosing appropriate artifacts, revising their projects and self-reflections, and reconsidering their medium and mode choices.

Example 9.14 illustrates our final, formative evaluation of Tamara's ePortfolio with bolded criteria from example 9.9's rubric and keeping the four-step intervention process in mind.

Example 9.14. Tamara's ePortfolio Formative Evaluation

Hi Tamara,

I can tell you really worked hard on this ePortfolio. The portfolio is thoughtfully **organized**, with drafts of each project included for quick reference, and each page houses multimodal images that lend to the overall thesis: an argument for what you have learned this term.

All three projects represent **multimodality**, including your newsletter review, newspaper op-ed commentary, and video proposal. I think your revision of the theme and background expresses your personality, which makes me believe the audience is one who might want to get to know who Tamara is. Right now, you say that your **purpose** is to showcase your work, so I assume the **audience** is the class. If so, what do you want them to take away from reading this portfolio? How can you be clearer in your home page?

To return to **multimodality**, I'd also like you to think about how some of your text boxes are placed in the pages. Some of the text needs proper spacing, and the words should wrap around the text boxes seamlessly. But also consider what goes into the text boxes and whether they are necessary. Text boxes are often used as quick, soundbite references for an audience, but in your portfolio, you always use them as evidence of your learning. This is a potential problem if you don't know how to integrate quotations with your text. I encourage you to keep on working to integrate quotations, as doing so is a key part of the **conventions** of writing arguments.

Each project has been carefully revised (adhering to the criterion of **genre conventions**), as is evident in your inclusion of the drafts of projects and your **evidence** in your **reflections**; you've demonstrated taking your peers' and my comments for final drafts into consideration. You do use the textbook a lot as evidence. What other support from the class could count as **evidence**? Return to discussion boards and journals to talk through what your peers said that helped you brainstorm or revise. What about what you wrote in your brainstorming journals? How did your freewriting spark you to compose your final projects?

As a final project in this course, this portfolio represents all you have learned in the class, from multimodality to revision to using evidence. Since you have one more week, use my feedback to revise before posting the portfolio for a final grade. I'm happy to clarify anything or to meet if you need help.

Conclusion

Although there are many elements and moving parts to providing feedback, instructors should collaborate with students, working as coaches to help them shape their writing. We have illustrated that formative evaluation combined with ongoing revision are critical to students' meeting of composition outcomes. Evaluation must be combined with revision if instructors expect students to develop as writers. Ongoing evaluation and revision help ensure students understand the rhetorical concepts of composition and can identify these concepts within both the projects and accompanying self-reflections. Such strategies as peer review should aid students in receiving formative feedback, and instructors can guide the process by creating rubrics that coach students toward more rhetorically effective projects. Whether the project is multimodal, a small-stakes media lab, or capstone portfolio, the principles remain the same: students need feedback frequently. Instructors should guide them in fluency, form, and correctness and use students' self-reflections to understand their rhetorical choices and evaluate projects.

10

Promoting Effective Communication

Professor Jackson always used to have success with his class conversations; this term, however, he's having a miserable experience with two of his classes. He can't figure it out: the classes are lifeless, apathetic, even a little hostile. He has tried various strategies, but nothing seems to work. He wants to make changes, but he doesn't know how. How can he turn these classes around and have fruitful discussions where students are learning from and respecting each other? How can he start future classes on the right track from day one?

As we address throughout this book, there is no single way to conceive of or teach composition; as with all literacy-based courses, however, teaching writing is dependent on communication. In this chapter we outline some communication strategies to help instructors promote successful communication with and among students and in different environments. We include establishing a community of inquiry (CoI) and offer online collaborative theories and concrete strategies for collaborative discussion and writing groups in various on-site and online settings. Although these strategies are intended to establish communication and productive, respectful dialogue, instructors must acknowledge that every course, section, and student is different—not every strategy will work in every situation, which is part of what makes teaching in the twenty-first century so challenging. These strategies can guide instructors in creating classroom environments that promote critical thinking, student-to-student learning, and productive dialogue among classroom participants.

Establishing the Classroom Environment

As the learning facilitator and class leader, the instructor—like Professor Jackson—is primarily responsible for creating a classroom environment conducive to engaged learning. To do that effectively, the classroom structure must allow students to learn from each other and the instructor. One way to create what may be called a *student-centered classroom* is through the CoI framework, which seeks connection among fellow inquirers. Students should be charged to learn together, with the instructor as a guide to acquiring knowledge and a facilitator of an atmosphere conducive to learning. A CoI aids in constructing deep, meaningful knowledge among all who participate when its three presences interact: teaching, social, and cognitive (Swan et al.). The framework relies on instructors establishing their own teaching presence while encouraging students to be more socially present, whether through on-site discussions or in digital spaces; the combination of these two presences can facilitate cognitive presence for deeper engagement with and learning of course outcomes.

In "The First Decade of the Community of Inquiry Framework," D. Randy Garrison, Terry Anderson, and Walter Archer indicate the CoI model was introduced to "define, describe, and measure the elements of a collaborative and worthwhile" educational experience (6). The CoI framework has been adopted broadly in education and, notably, in courses that use technology to facilitate instruction, including fully online classes. Instructors using the CoI framework should create a figurative and literal space where students can integrate new knowledge with their existing knowledge, leading them to design a course based on social interaction and the instructor's input (Hilliard and Stewart). It is no surprise that the CoI framework finds a natural home in technologically enhanced courses when instructors focus on blending the three presences in a student-centered classroom.

Teaching Presence

Instructors should set up communication between themselves and their students, but they also need to create safe spaces for students to learn from each other and metacognitively reflect on their learning. It may be easier for teachers to establish their presence in on-site classrooms because of the physical closeness and face-to-face interaction, but it certainly is possible online. One simple way to establish teaching presence in on-site settings is to smile and greet each student by name. Being available before class begins enables a positive atmosphere of friendly connection. Another way is to be available to students using different technologies, regardless of the teaching environment. For example, office hours can be conducted in person or by phone, text-based chat, or videoconferencing software. Other ways to establish this presence include creating short, weekly video announcements for students to enable them to see the instructor "in person" while learning what is expected that week. Instructors can establish presence through screen-capture feedback (Stannard, "Using"), synchronous video (Cho and Tobias), and multimodal instructional tools (T. Bourelle et al., "Designing"; B. Rubin et al.).

In an online writing course, teaching presence is critically important; not only is it imperative that instructors introduce and manifest themselves as active and genuine but also that they create venues for students to explore ideas with instructor feedback guiding them. To establish greater presence, instructors can use audio or screen-capture technology to communicate the overall course structure, walking students through how to navigate the course, retrieve assignments, post documents, and other processes. Thoughtfully posted sound bites and live chat (text) messages can communicate that instructors are temporally present through the course shell, welcoming live comments and questions regardless of modality. *Instructor sharing journals* are resources in which instructors can reflect on positive happenings in the course for students to see and respond to. Similarly, *student sharing journals* allow students to reflect on readings, question assumptions or beliefs, and grapple with difficult concepts in the safe space of semiprivate, nonjudgmental sharing with instructors, who only comment briefly to question, praise, and guide critical thinking. Such insight into what students might be struggling with allows instructors to craft activities and readings based on expressed needs.

In "Why Do Student Development and Course Climate Matter for Student Learning?," Susan A. Ambrose and colleagues suggest instructors must create presence from the onset, looking first at their syllabus language, as this document often establishes the instructor's personality (176). Online, the syllabus is one of the first documents students read, perhaps even before watching any video that introduces the instructor and class. The syllabus' tone can provide students insight into the instructor (also see ch. 5). Is the tone punitive or encouraging? Does the instructor appear approachable? Are there opportunities to meet with the instructor, and are they clearly outlined? Because the syllabus often is considered a contract between instructor and students, instructors must consider how the language and tone of the syllabus encourage students to be active in the course and in their learning. Inclusive language also is important, so instructors should ask students their personal pronouns and use them. Helping students understand what kinds of language are acceptable is another way to establish a firm, guiding presence that provides safety. Instructors can define qualities of racially motivated or other hate speech or intolerance, for example, or they can engage students to develop their own definitions by which they agree to abide.

Student Presence

Developing a strong student presence requires engaging students in meaningful social interactions where they can get to know each other and connect in respectful dialogue. In on-site settings, teachers often ask students to discuss what they have read or what they are writing; such discussions may fall short of instructor expectations, and technologically enhanced (often asynchronous) discussions may also flounder. Chapter 5 addresses specific strategies for developing effective online discussions. One method for improving challenged discussions includes reversing the responsibility by asking students to engage in online discussions prior to the synchronous meeting or assignment due date. Instructors can assign student-led (or moderated) discussions where the students choose a reading and one or two students lead that day's discussion; if everyone is promised such an opportunity, students have incentive to be good communicators for their peers. Students need explicit parameters for these discussions, which might include providing a summary of the text and creating an activity that helps them understand and apply the concepts to their own projects. The student leaders—assisted by the instructor as a mentor or coach—can be prompted to develop a multimodal presentation or discussion component in their format of choice; in online courses, they could screen-capture or video record a slideware presentation for this element. Regardless of format, the instructor should model how to lead a discussion, illustrating how to deconstruct a text and lead successful activities and discussions. Then, the instructor should aid student leaders in moderating and keeping the class on task. Conferencing with students before their student-led discussions enables instructors to guide them and ensure activities are appropriate and respectful of other learners, which can create more confident student interactions.

Cognitive Presence

Cognitive presence is the crux of the course community as it focuses on helping students develop critical thinking skills and learn content specific to course outcomes. A course should be designed with attention to cognitive presence, wherein teaching, student, and cognitive presences work in conjunction to help facilitate critical thinking skills development (Garrison et al., "First Decade" 6). Instructors can implement the CoI framework by starting with course outcomes. Then, they can determine objectives or goals beyond required course outcomes. For example, a writing course in which argumentation is an important outcome might have an objective of creating a safe space wherein students grapple critically, yet civilly, with difficult current events. Alternatively, a goal might be that students experience and interact with texts from a diverse pool of authors and perspectives. As we mention throughout the book, another course objective might be that students develop technological literacy. The possibilities of objectives are endless, but they should support—not supplant—course and departmental outcomes.

Based on the outcomes and objectives, instructors should design courses that allow students to grapple with ideas and then actually do something with those ideas, such as create a project that illustrates the concepts being learned or argue for a position or change. One way to encourage cognition through technology is to have students record themselves brainstorming, keeping a journal of short sound bites to do think-aloud processing. As we mention in chapter 8, students can be prompted to engage in media labs in which they brainstorm or freewrite about their projects in different modes, enabling them to play with technology and progress toward project completion. Finally, they should be encouraged to reflect on the ideas that occur during the initial brainstorming, drafting, or project completion; these reflections can be developed in alphabetic text or other modes. Students can be encouraged to screen-capture their projects, walking the instructor through draft changes and how the changes improved the project. Alternatively, they can create vlogs that update the instructor on their drafting progress and reflect on changes they are making throughout. Any activity using reflection engages metacognition and potentially improves cognitive presence.

Instructors must consider course content carefully, including readings and projects. We have talked extensively about creating multimodal assignments that allow students to choose their own medium and technology for composing and the negative implications stemming from assuming all students have equal technology access. Similarly, instructors must consider the reading diversity they bring to the course, noting which authors dominate the syllabus; whenever possible, they should incorporate texts from various authorial ethnicities, cultures, and genders, bringing in potentially marginalized perspectives. Deeply incorporating—not merely adding one or two texts to meet a minimum requirement—such diversity may encourage students to share their own perspectives more freely (Ambrose et al. 179). Including diverse perspectives can encourage students to question and critically examine their ideas, assumptions, and biases (Garrison et al., "Critical Inquiry" 96). Because students may not enter the course with the ability to question potentially deeply held personal beliefs, however, the instructor's thoughtful presence can help facilitate this cognitive growth.

In their webinar Employing Equity-Minded and Culturally Affirming Teaching Practices and Virtual Learning Communities, Frank Harris, III, and J. Luke Wood argue for equity as a fourth presence, which we enfold here to encourage a mindful approach to cognitive presence. They argue that underserved students, including students of color, experience invisibility in online classes, specifically that what they say does not matter, which would indicate the instructor has not done enough to include all students in the discussion or perhaps has allowed hostile or inappropriate comments to occur unaddressed. Jon P. Humiston, Sarah Marshall, Nicole Hacker, and Luis Cantu, in "Intentionally Creating an Inclusive and Welcoming Climate in the Online Learning Classroom," suggest that marginalized students may gravitate toward online classes where there is a certain amount of anonymity. At the same time, research warns of the potential erasing of identity and diversity that comes with the online course (de Montes et al.). Therefore, instructors need to be mindful of all students and establish a pedagogy that aims "to connect course content, teaching practices, and assessment to each individual" (Humiston et al. 181). In their companion webinar, Addressing Racial Bias and Microaggressions in the Online Environment, Harris and Wood suggest a course needs to be designed as a "mirror" for marginalized students by using media with authors or actors from different backgrounds, cultures, and ethnicities. Instructors should encourage (not force) students to share their stories, integrate a variety of diverse texts and learning strategies, and encourage an understanding of student backgrounds (Humiston et al. 181), facilitating discussions in a way that addresses hostility or microaggressions against marginalized authors of texts or students who do choose to share (see discussion of microaggressions below). In "Rhetorical Listening Pedagogy," Wenqi Cui asserts that using media from a variety of authors encourages students to listen to the voices of marginalized groups and promote "cross-cultural communication"; but before "reaching an understanding or [a willingness] to negotiate, listeners may need time and a place to think, digest, and reflect on what they hear from speakers who are from different groups" (5). Carefully selected course materials from authors with diverse backgrounds and cultures, followed up with reflections and mediated discussions that allow space for all students to enter the conversation, can aid in forming a course that encourages them to thrive and learn from each other in a true CoI (see also Khadka, *Multiliteracies*).

Effective Communication in Collaborative Groups

Group work is an established way to create student presence. Collaboration in written and spoken group projects is highly touted as a twenty-first-century outcome (e.g., CWPA), yet it is difficult for students to achieve. By *collaboration*, we mean more than putting students into peer response groups or asking them to discuss a reading or issue. We particularly mean groups that are asked to work together to create a joint writing or other literacy project. There may be separate deliverables, one for each student, or there may be one deliverable per group. In technologically enhanced settings especially—but also on-site—developing and supporting functional collaborative writing groups can be challenging. Students need to learn how to engage in genuinely collaborative, effective, efficient action. They need skills to develop and abide by time management decisions and strategies for interacting on-site, online, or both, particularly with student peers they do not know well or who do not participate fully. They also need specific instruction about how groups develop and function. Here, we provide concrete strategies for collaborative discussion and writing groups in both on-site and online settings.

In "Developmental Sequence in Small Groups," research psychologist Bruce W. Tuckman observed collaborative groups and discerned a four-stage model of working group activity, adapted here, necessary to develop functionality: *forming, storming, norming,* and *performing.*

> **Forming**. A group is coming together, becoming familiar with the task, creating ground rules (even if the instructor provided ground rules already, the group forms its own naturally), and developing relationships with each other.
>
> **Storming**. Participants may find themselves resisting the task, how it is to be accomplished, or how group members are behaving toward the task or each other. In this stage, group members dissent, test their values, and may be hostile or polarized. Some groups refuse to work together; instructors should set the stage by letting groups know they may experience this phase and must work through it.
>
> **Norming**. Group members are beginning to work past their differences, find commonalities, and seek harmonious ways of working together. They try to avoid dissension in favor of getting the work done, and they can accept each other better while feeling more comfortable expressing their own thoughts.
>
> **Performing**. The group has developed "functional role relatedness," which means it focuses on problem solving and adapts more flexibly to the roles (which may change fluidly among students at this point) necessary to complete the project successfully (387).

Adjourning is an additional stage Tuckman and Mary Ann Jensen named in 1977 in "Stages of Small-Group Development Revisited." Its importance here is in understanding that once a group has moved through all four phases, they need the space or means to conclude the group's interactions. The ending of group work changes how students interact with each other, and a celebratory discussion or other positive act may help with separation. Tuckman's group work stages may help instructors and students better understand that group collaboration is hard for everyone, not just them, and that given the tools and the will to proceed with civility, tasks can be accomplished cohesively.

In "Collaborating Virtually to Develop This Book," Charlotte Robidoux and Beth L. Hewett highlight strategies that can encourage successful group collaboration. They studied collaborative writers in action where participants were heavily invested with group writing but did not function well collaboratively, allowing Robidoux and Hewett to extrapolate principles that might help instructors teach student collaborators:

> *Develop a culture of collaboration* (408). Determine whether writers should change each other's texts or whether people individually own the text. Consider the group as individuals and encourage them to talk about their writing history regarding collaboration. Be clear about what they must, should, or could do in the project. Remember that academic rules against plagiarism, often defined as using other's words in one's own writing without proper attribution, may frighten some students away from touching what could be a collaborative text, instead making it singly authored. Address the differences between plagiarism and collaboration clearly.

> *Find and promote leadership* (412). Not everyone needs or wants to lead; for each project, one leader typically suffices. If the same group is used for other projects, roles should rotate, but students should feel comfortable enough with their instructors' care of them to express when being a leader will not work for them (e.g., at midterm). Instructors should step in as needed, not betraying confidences and helping the group compromise. They should respect students who trust them "with their hard work" (415), but they should take as active a facilitator role as needed.

> *Establish trust* (415). Trust comes first from knowing one another, accomplishable through several brief, low-stakes team-building activities, ranging from ice breakers to teaching each other

a low-bridge technology. Trust is about having a functional group size for the project, understanding the goals, listening to group members thinking through those goals, learning something about everyone's values regarding the composition course, and promptly addressing emerging issues with confidence and kindness.

Use tools and collaborative modes effectively (420). Students should learn about tools and ways to communicate and work collaboratively through whole class settings before conducting group work. Then, the group needs to "frontload sufficient time to choose and test the tools selected" for the project (423). Group work should not be hurried; participants need time to form, storm, norm, and perform. Group members should be immersed in the tools they will be using, so instructors should teach about those tools by modeling their use and asking students to use them.

Create structure (424). Instructors should initially create workable group structures, outlined by Joanna Wolfe (see discussion below and in ch. 5). Although not all group members will function comfortably in a structured work pattern, the outlined boundaries of what is to be done, how, and when offers a reasonable point from which the group might vary with the instructor's permission. Once groups have functioned well more than once, they may be more fluid and flexible in structurally outlined projects.

Measure and track performance (428). Instructors should not be the only arbiters of group performance. Students should reflect about their own and others' work to build an after-action report of the team's interactions and products. What are the expectations? How can they be measured? How can the group track its own performance, the project's meeting deadlines, and overall expectations? When groups work out these measurements with instructors or present them to instructors as collaboratively developed, they likely will strive to meet them.

Wolfe's *Team Writing* is helpful for developing student presence through group work. To begin, Wolfe recommends establishing clear guidelines for the group project, whether it is a high-stakes assignment or a low-stakes activity. Questions for instructors, adapted here, include the following:

- What are the ground rules for groups working together?
- What is the required result in terms of individual and group deliverables?
- How should students post or present the project?

The ground rules are perhaps the most important part of starting groups out right. They can be established from the beginning by giving students the following tasks, also adapted from Wolfe (13–14, 42–43):

- Keep a progress report during the project, establishing who did what and when.
- Establish and clarify roles during the project, determining who will do what with the assignment and the final deliverable project. (Instructors can switch roles for different group projects throughout the term, ensuring everyone learns the different tasks connected to roles.) Roles include the following:
  - *a project leader* who calls and runs meetings, assigns parts to group members, and takes primary responsibility for communicating the group's progress and needs with the instructor
  - *a scribe-secretary* who takes notes, sends out meeting date and time reminders, and gathers the project parts from everyone (if joint submissions are required)
  - *writers* who draft the project; per chapter 5's description of collaboration, determine whether the group will write together simultaneously, either face-to-face or through collaborative software; divide the task into parts for individual composition that will be combined later; or layer the task by taking turns with the project
  - *writers* who create the multimodal portion of the project; again establish whether it is done individually or as a group and, if as a group, when and how
  - *editors* who revise the project in its final stages
- Evaluate one another anonymously, each student reflecting on their own work and that of all group partners. (Such anonymous evaluations can guide instructors in feedback while encouraging students

to do their share of the work; if they know they will be evaluated by their peers, they are more likely to follow through with their tasks.)

Even with articulated ground rules, groups will not always function well—per storming—and the student-to-student learning process may break down. Just as collaborative group work is important to establish student presence, it can promote teaching presence; instructors should check in periodically with groups and change group members if needed. Ultimately, instructors must facilitate group work, guiding students to a final project. Even when group dynamics are poor, students learn valuable communicative and strategic lessons for working in teams that can transfer to the home and workplace.

In the digital, globally connected era, instructors should design courses so students interact with one another through technology as well as face-to-face because both types of interaction are crucial to future work. In technologically mediated classrooms, students can talk asynchronously through discussion boards, leaving screen-capture feedback for their peers to add a personal touch and establish communication. They can meet through videoconferencing software and set up collaborative workspaces, enabling them to work in the document simultaneously or leave each other comments after an asynchronous composing session.

Collaborative group work establishes student presence, yet given the many communicative channels available, students in any environment may struggle with having a productive dialogue, may allow the worst interactive strategies from social media to leach into school interactions, and may not know the guidelines or communicative rules of any medium. Therefore, they need strategies for engaging in effective dialogue that both are respectful of various ideas and promote critical thinking.

Creating Space for Productive Dialogue

As theories about the social construction of knowledge have become ingrained in teaching practices, instructors have learned to use conversation as ways of building knowledge. Although scholars in all disciplines have discussed the ubiquity of social construction approaches, these approaches have taken hold particularly in composition courses (e.g.,

Bruffee, *Collaborative Learning*). The endless talk of a writing course helps students learn and think, creating the foundations of better writers.

There is no magic to facilitating good conversation among students, as Professor Jackson is learning. Moderating course conversations is a major facet of the teaching art. Of course, good moderating practices can be learned, but there is no easy template, as a dizzying array of variables can affect conversations, including time of day, a strong student who acts as catalyst (and is missed when absent), a student who talks too much, and so on. Instructors must act as moderators. For online teaching, instructors must make sure students stay on task, and instructors also need to know when to navigate the conversation back on topic if students stray too far. Instructors with strong communication skills guide conversation and prompt students to consider questions or topics they may not have considered, reserving their own opinions. Finally, instructors need to stop conversations when they become problematic or off task (and often must return to them for further exploration), which can be challenging.

In courses that are mainly online, including some hybrids, the pressure to create good communication environments is high, since the dialogue—often written asynchronously and disconnected by threading—that students establish may be their primary way of representing themselves in the course. As Scott Warnock says to teachers, "[O]ne of the biggest pressures in teaching writing online is rethinking your communication with students" (*Teaching* 14). Written discussions are infinitely complex, but these simple strategies, some connected to effective practices in on-site courses, can help encourage and sustain genuinely dialogic conversation:

> In prompts and follow-up posts on threads, ask open-ended questions that require higher-order thinking.
>
> Work more inherently with students' written talk by asking them to refer to or quote each other, potentially fueling conversation by engaging classmates as thinking beings.
>
> Use multiple deadline tiers, so posts are not bunched up at the end of the week or deadline, encouraging more give-and-take dialogue.
>
> Use student moderators to place responsibility for dialogue on students. As Donald E. Hanna, Michelle Glowacki-Dudki, and Simone Conceicao-Runlee write in *147 Practical Tips for Teaching*

Online Groups about such practices, "Most people learn best by doing or by teaching others what they're learning" (147).

Try to achieve a just-right level of posting in response to students.

Instructors should model participation, responding in ways that generate critical thinking and asking questions of students' posts to encourage response beyond one-word answers. Students need to see instructors reading and responding to the discussion posts with thoughtfulness before they can fully understand what makes a good post. If a discussion goes off topic, the instructor must steer the conversation back to the main point.

Establishing a Respectful Learning Environment

Teachers can never predict how a discussion will go; unanticipated social and emotional factors arise, changing the dynamic and complicating the learning experience (Ambrose et al. 155). Especially when students have personal experiences with the topic, what begins as a fruitful discussion can quickly turn, becoming emotionally charged and potentially disrespectful. Instructors must realize that postsecondary students (particularly younger ones) are still developing cognitively, emotionally, and socially, and instructors can help but will not be the only guides through that process (155). Thus, instructors can show students the multiplicity of ideas surrounding an issue, teaching that argumentation is not about being right but about listening to all opinions, informing one's own opinions through research, and sifting through what might be presented as fact but is actually opinion. Students need to learn to challenge each other respectfully and acknowledge that other students in the class also are working and thinking through these issues critically. No one including the instructor, will have all the answers—particularly regarding human problems for which there are no certain answers—but dialoguing can illuminate an issue's many sides.

It is also important to recognize, however, that students have real, lived experiences; their opinions likely have been formed based on these experiences, and instructors must honor them and recognize that some students may not want to talk about them or may not be open to questioning some beliefs in a public forum. In this case, instructors can focus on helping students by posing questions in feedback on student projects and encourage students to conference with them; these actions help to build trust and illustrate the benefits of collaboration, which can then be translated to the open forum of peer discussion. Ambrose and her colleagues note that when students do take risks in the classroom, speaking their own opinions in productive ways that do not marginalize other students, instructors should validate those risks and ask students to further discuss the alternative opinions (178). With this validation, students may be prompted to share or discuss topics productively.

As John Duffy indicates in "Ethical Rhetoric in Unethical Times," instructors should proceed with caution and humility; what has worked in the past—the tried and true lesson plans and syllabi—may not work for every class or student, especially when students are linked into social media and learning to question what they see and hear. Instructors need to embrace challenged moments; respond calmly and tactfully if heated discussions arise; model acceptable, respectful behavior; and take responsibility for shutting down hateful, intolerant speech. Duffy explains that educators cannot insist on students thinking one way. They should embrace dissensus because it involves ongoing conversation and negotiation—not closure—allowing for evolving viewpoints, yet they should provide respectful guidance. Like Jacqueline Jones Royster and Gesa E. Kirsch in *Feminist Rhetorical Practices*, we believe instructors have a responsibility to "engage dialectically and dialogically, to actually use tension, conflicts, balances, and counter balances more overtly as critical opportunities for inquiry in order to enable a conversation" in the twenty-first-century classroom (71).

Students can be invited to self-reflect on heated discussions, asking themselves what they learned that they did not already know or how they felt when talking through the issue. They can ask themselves what they actively could do better in the next discussion. Even the simple act of asking how dissensus can be productive (or not) can help students learn to think through opinions before speaking while allowing themselves to speak out when they disagree or believe injustice has occurred. Likewise, instructors should challenge themselves to self-reflect on what they could do differently the next time a heated discussion arises. Written instructor reflections also provide notes about any negative incident as a record for their personal files should a need for accurate recollection arise.

Instructors can and should have real, honest conversations with students after a heated discussion. Having previously identified the elements of hateful or intolerant speech, they can engage this conversation at the beginning of the next class meeting or the next day if such a problem emerged asynchronously online, giving everyone time to process the event. They should gauge the students and the climate to understand what the right moment is to deconstruct what happened, make any necessary amends (and allow students to do so too), and discuss what might be done differently. If heated discussions arise in online spaces, instructors should step in and moderate quickly or even stop the discussion altogether, making the judgment call to remove inflammatory posts. Indeed, some students may feel emboldened by the relative anonymity of online classrooms and make comments they would not in face-to-face conversations. Contentious discussions can occur even when readings or posts seem benign or unlikely to start controversy. Instructors should politely reach out to students privately as needed—and publicly when possible—to explain why some posts were removed and reiterate the class rules (which should be clearly outlined on the syllabus) of respectful engagement and netiquette. As in on-site environments where the discussion occurs through oral talk, students need opportunities to reflect in private spaces like journals or together in a moderated discussion board. Above all, instructors should check discussion boards frequently to ensure that the process is running smoothly and that productive dialogue is occurring.

Recognizing Ineffective Dialogue and Behaviors

To promote effective dialogue, teachers must model the behaviors they wish to see. As we explain in chapter 1, societal issues arise, and students grapple with what they hear, see, and read in the media. Although instructors may have their own opinions, they need to reserve them and give students space and full attention. If problematic assumptions or stereotypes come to light, the instructor should provide space for everyone to question why those assumptions or stereotypes are, indeed, problematic. As the National Council of Teachers of English Committee against Racism and Bias in the Teaching of English suggests in *Qualities of Anti-Racist ELA Curricula*, instructors can use such instances to open discussions of racism and issues of marginalization. In "Racism in Schools and Classrooms," authors George J. Sefa Dei and Rowena Linton offer theory and practice for facilitating these conversations in the classroom, starting with instructors acknowledging and working through their own implicit biases; creating a safe space for classroom discussion; helping students develop racial literacy by learning to critically read, hear, and appreciate diverse and potentially unfamiliar experiences; and guiding students to reflect on ideas of bias and assumptions. As we previously discussed creating a safe space in the classroom for productive dialogue (and in other places encouraged the inclusion of diverse texts), much of our discussion below seeks to help instructors understand implicit bias.

Implicit bias in instructors and students can manifest in microaggressions, which may indicate not having challenged one's ways of thinking. In "Making Commitments to Racial Justice Actionable," Rasha Diab, Thomas Ferrel, and Beth Godbee assert that "racism is enacted in small, regular, and everyday micro-inequities and micro-aggressions" (26); based on their work, our discussion intends to bring microaggressions to light and encourage instructors to understand their origin and problematize them. Implicit biases that may manifest in microaggressions can affect how instructors approach students, as well as their writing, thereby impacting student success. We encourage readers to peruse our companion book, *Administering Writing Programs in the Twenty-First Century*, by Tiffany Bourelle, Beth L. Hewett, and Scott Warnock, in which we offer concrete strategies for helping instructors realize and address their implicit biases, strategies that can be reframed for students.

Ambrose and her colleagues describe a continuum of course climates and note that both ends can be marginalizing. On one end, the climate may be explicitly marginalizing, and, on the other end, it may be implicitly marginalizing. Explicitly marginalizing climates can be overtly hostile and discriminating, and implicitly marginalizing climates can be inadvertently hurtful through seemingly harmless comments, sometimes made by the instructor. Although either climate can hurt students and be detrimental to the course dynamic, implicit assumptions can be especially harmful because they may not be challenged by those who are targeted, leaving them feeling diminished. Stereotypes and microaggressions, often implicitly expressed, also can affect students' learning (Ambrose et al. 170–71). To model effective dialogue and behaviors, instructors must learn to recognize microaggressions—which tend to embrace stereotypes—avoid them, and teach students to avoid them too. Professor Jackson should reflect on his current classes to consider whether some of the communicative dissension stems from microaggressions.

In "Racial Microaggressions in Everyday Life," the psychologists Derald Wing Sue and colleagues define *microaggressions* as "brief and commonplace daily verbal, behavioral, and environmental indignities, whether intentional or unintentional, that communicate hostile, derogatory, or negative racial slights and insults to the target person or group" (273). In their research, they consider three types of primarily race-based microaggressions. *Microassaults* are "an explicit racial derogation characterized primarily by a verbal or nonverbal attack meant to hurt the intended victim through name-calling, avoidant behavior, or purposeful discriminatory actions" and may be purposeful acts (274). *Microinsults* are "characterized by communications that convey rudeness and insensitivity and demean a person's racial heritage or identity" and may be comprised of "subtle snubs, frequently unknown to the perpetrator" that are clearly insulting to the recipient (274). Finally, *microinvalidations* are "characterized by communications that exclude, negate, or nullify the psychological thoughts, feelings, or experiential reality of a person of color" (274). The authors also identify nine microaggression classifications with distinct themes (282–83), as applicable to those in helping professions.

Sue and colleagues focus on racial microaggressions, and we expand them because educators encounter differences beyond race, ethnicity, and culture; students (and instructors) also diverge in language skills, learning preferences, physical and learning challenges, and sexual orientation (280). As a helping profession, education has an inherent power structure that can be abused easily. Educators make mistakes, but they can change their talk with focused, conscious efforts. To illustrate, we adapt Sue and colleagues' nine microaggressions to example educational scenarios and suggest one of many possible problematic and disturbing messages they could convey. We include these examples to help instructors think through how harmful microaggressions are.

Alien in One's Own Land. Assuming students to be foreign born
   because of race, ethnicity, or name.
Example: An instructor assumes an Asian American student is an
international student and automatically states she should be in an
ESOL course. Possible message: You are not American.

Ascription of Intelligence. Assigning a degree of intelligence based
   on race, ethnicity, name, learning challenges, and so on.
Example: A WPA asks a student who discloses dyslexia, *Are you sure
you're ready for college?* Possible message: People with learning disabilities will not succeed.

Color Blindness. Indicating that race does not need to be
   acknowledged.
Example: An instructor tells the class, *I don't see color* or *We should emphasize similarities and not differences.* Possible message: Your racial
experiences are not valid.

Criminality or Assumption of Criminal Status. Suggesting that
   race, ethnicity, or cultural background marks one as dangerous
   or deviant.
Example: A WPA tells a visibly tattooed student who is frustrated about
her writing course grades to see a school counselor about her "anger issues." Possible message: You have low grades because you are trouble.

Denial of Individual Racism. Locating oneself outside any prejudice or biases.
Example: When asked by the class how racial differences affect his
teaching, an instructor says, *Race has no effect on my teaching.* Possible message: Your racial or ethnic experiences are not important
enough to explore (see also Soto Vega and Chávez for more on acknowledging the particularity of racialized groups, as well as of individual students within those groups).

Myth of Meritocracy. Asserting that racial, ethnic, cultural, and
   physical or learning differences do not play a part in educational success.
Example: An instructor tells a student who uses a wheelchair, *I made
it through college, and I had many life challenges. You can, too, if you put
your mind to it.* Possible message: The playing ground is even, and if
you fail, it is your fault.

Pathologizing Cultural Values and Communication Styles. Giving value only to standardized forms of American English.
Example: An instructor tells a Black student who speaks using African American Vernacular English in written discussion posts, *We don't use that kind of language in this class, and your participation grade will be marked down because of it*. Possible message: Always assimilate to the dominant language.

Second-Class Status. Focusing positive attention only on White students or those who have no noticeable differences.
Example: The instructor refuses to use students' pronouns for personal address, saying, *You look like a woman, so I'm going to call you "she" or "her."* Possible message: Students must conform to conventional gender norms.

Environmental Invalidation. Revealing a systemic bias toward only one race, ethnicity, or culture.
Example: An instructor who requires students to read a textbook with primarily White, male authors. Possible messages: You are an outsider. You do not exist.

Seemingly minor aggressions have current impact but also a cumulative effect, which lead to a "psychological toll . . . on recipients' well-being" (Sue et al. 279). It is important to observe student needs and behaviors, think before speaking, and create inclusive courses. Even the best-intentioned educators make mistakes, though, and students also may use microaggressions when speaking during discussion. When someone raises the likelihood that a teacher used a microaggression, we advise immediately stopping, thinking before responding, and approaching the issues straightforwardly with humility. Likewise, it is imperative that teachers respond to student-used microaggressions, tactfully pointing out why that language is problematic and the potential harm of using it. We have adapted the mindfulness facilitator Lee Mun Wah's process for responding when educators or students have misspoken and should make amends. Immediately after realizing there has been a hurtful incident,

be patient, listen, and don't rush to an apology or solution;

stay with the relationship and process; and

remember that empathy and sincerity are the gateways to understanding and compassion.

When someone is offended by your comments, say the following:

What I heard you say was that ________.

Tell me more what you meant by ________.

What angered you about ________?

What hurt you about ________?

What's familiar about ________?

What do you need or want from ________?

Process the incident with the class:

Tell the class one thing you heard. Use the exact words.

What did you appreciate about what happened?

What did you notice was the turning point?

What came up for you in watching this? What's familiar?

What's hard about what happened?

What good came from processing or discussing the incident?

What did you learn today about listening and responding?

The reality of microaggressions or any other speech or physical acts that might be offensive is that they may happen despite instructors' best efforts: It is impossible to know what will happen and how students may react on any given day. Although we acknowledge that a democratic classroom is desirable, democracy ends when the instructor must take the lead. Democracy can be enabled by civil, respectful conversation modeled by instructors, guided by student needs, and facilitated by turn-taking. Allowing a multitude of voices is possible by passing a talking stick or microphone in the traditional or technology-enhanced setting and using a lineup or hand-raising feature in a learning management system or videoconference, where enabled; the instructor should ensure that all students are heard, however. Yet instructors are in charge not by election but by necessity, which means they are responsible for creating a safe learning environment. Sometimes, safety means stopping the activity, disallowing further discussion, and engaging methods like Wah's or others in this chapter. At some point, volatile moments must end.

Finally, as mentioned, instructors should try to help students recognize implicit bias that may manifest in microaggressions, taking time to help them recognize microaggressions and why they are problematic, which can open the door to more productive conversations. We encourage readers to continue educating themselves, starting with theories we provide in this chapter (see also *How to Be an Antiracist* by Ibram X. Kendi), as well as those found in chapter 4 of *Administering Writing Programs in the Twenty-First Century*.

Building Trust

Recognizing and respecting cultural differences are key aspects in building trust and developing cultural competence, which can provide greater opportunities for students to succeed.

Cultural Competence

Culturally competent digital-era educators remember that using technology can help some students who wish to remain more anonymous and potentially harm those whose very anonymity enables other students to express unkind or unhelpful opinions and biases. Students' affiliations can be hidden in computer-based environments and communications. Therefore, it is important to "address communication needs immediately, for poor communication delays and inhibits relationship-building, leads to errors in understanding, and creates a stressful [and unsafe] environment for [students] who are already distressed" (Rothman 39). Potential areas of engagement, trust, and relationship building to discuss with colleagues and, possibly, with students include understanding how contact is initiated and with whom, who to include in a conference, formality and form of address, eye contact, physical distance, and physical contact (42). Each of these is discussed in what follows.

For example, consider family background and possible hierarchy when determining who to contact and how to initiate contact. Is the student from a patriarchal family where the father may phone on the student's behalf? Regarding FERPA, the law requires instructors to protect student privacy, which should be accomplished in such a way as to respect cultural positioning. What happens if a parent calls to curse about a student's failing grade? To whom would the problem be reported while keeping the student's needs and privacy in mind? Educators are challenged to comprehend the gist of the communication and contextualize it without allowing it to interfere with teacher-student relationships.

Given FERPA, the answer to the question of who to include in a conference is clear: the student. If the student's cultural or (dis)ability background demands a parent, sibling, or other mediator, however, how can instructors determine what to say, where, and when? In a writing conference with a student peer group, similar concerns might arise when peers are from different cultural backgrounds or when the peer group contains only students from a single minority. Learning to communicate well within such settings increases teachers' ethos and enables more trusting relationships with all students because they do talk among themselves to complain about perceptions of unkindness or unfairness and, sometimes, to praise a teacher's communication skills.

Respect is key when choosing to formally address students as *Mr.* and *Ms.* or by first names, preferred names, or pronouns. Similarly, respect underlies choosing one's teacherly form of address (e.g., *Mr., Ms., Dr., Professor,* or first name). Some might think these choices concern leveling the interaction, but the transactional educational relationship is always in play. There never is a fully leveled interaction when grades and credits are involved; some students may argue that they paid for credits and, therefore, hold the power. Even in naming and address, culture is a factor. In August 2018, a ten-year-old student was disciplined by his teacher for addressing her as "Ma'am" (Hafner). Yet he had been raised to use that form of address as a politeness requirement with adults, and teachers particularly.

Learning to make appropriate eye contact is both a function of maturity and cultural customs. There can be a power-based motivation to who holds and who breaks eye contact; typically, the person of lesser status breaks contact first. Males and females likely have been acculturated differently to how and when to hold eye contact, and age also may factor. Students' ethnic groups may have acculturated them to look to the side rather than into instructors' eyes; indeed, instructors from such cultures may have to learn new ways of making and holding eye contact with colleagues and supervisors so they experience the interaction as respectful while holding their own power.

It may be hard to know how much physical distance to keep when conferencing with students or even when talking with students in a classroom. Educators should take cues from students, watching for such closed body language as leaning back or crossing of arms when instructors crouch next to their desks or sit nearby. Students might be more comfortable overall (as it is difficult to adjust for every scenario) if instructors place an empty chair next to or across from theirs for such conversations. Desks provide a hard space for writing while they increase personal distance, leading to questions about whether students should sit next to or across from instructors. Online instruction provides its own challenges because physical distance is built in, but a sense of connection still must be created. Educators can choose to make that connection through asynchronous email or messaging, which adds time and distance (and comfort for some) or through synchronous chat, which requests immediate response and requires spontaneity.

With physical contact, teachers have multiple challenges to consider. We write this book in the Me Too era, when people in power have been called out publicly and vociferously not only for blatant sexual offenses but also for being too close physically, for unwanted or nonconsensual touching, and for holding someone's hand in a sexualized or misinterpreted manner. Beyond inappropriate touching that both individuals instinctively know is wrong but has been allowed or excused in the past, one must consider whether a student in tears or *any* student should be touched. Never touch a student without asking for permission and paying careful attention to the response. People from some cultures do not touch or hug others, particularly teachers; instead, they bow or nod the head slightly. That gesture of respect can be used by people of all cultural backgrounds to designate attentive caring while showing respect for the dignity of others' personal space. Educators should attend to institutional rules about keeping office doors open when meeting with students. These actions are self-protective, legally smart, and sensitively caring.

Cultural Humility

Trust building requires everyone to behave well. From instructors, it particularly requires a high sense of cultural awareness, which is crucial to working with every student on a case-by-case basis. Because people certainly differ among and within groups, we suggest educators exercise cultural humility whenever they do not know what to do. Sometimes, this stance requires asking students what makes them comfortable yet acknowledging and respecting that students may not feel secure enough to share. Other times this stance can be fulfilled through *preparation, respect, environment,* and *presentation* (PREP). We have adapted these skills from the health care professionals Daniel E. Epner and Walter F. Baile to represent approaches to writing studies education, which by nature may involve more emotional closeness with students than other academic disciplines. These skills are particularly valuable for individual conferences, and they may be applied in person, on the phone, in videoconferences, in synchronous chat conferences, and in asynchronous conferences through a learning management system or email. As table 10.1 outlines, these foundational skills are relevant to working with all students, which can help greatly toward treating them uniquely yet uniformly with respect, dignity, and cultural competence.

Table 10.1. PREP Principles for Cultural Humility

PREP

Preparation Establish the right frame of mind and plan before meeting students.
Respect Show respect since students are vulnerable and need our assistance as teachers.
Environment Create a comfortable and safe setting for students.
Presentation Represent the profession and the work we do in a dignified manner.

Principles	Relevant skills, phrases, and examples
Principle 1 Everyone has a profound need to be heard and to be understood. Inviting students to tell their stories is itself therapeutic. Exploring students' concerns gets you tuned in to their agendas. Encouraging the telling of one's personal history allows students to feel as if you are interested in them as people, not only as students.	Listen attentively when students talk. Explore: *Tell me [Write] more about ______ if you feel comfortable doing so.* Allow space (silence) in the conversation. Use open-ended questions to invite students' narratives: • *Please tell me what you understand about yourself as a writer (or as a student).* • *What would you like to discuss today?* • *Tell me about your family's experiences with ______ (e.g., education).*
Principle 2 All people really care about is being cared about. Telling students you will treat them respectfully—and then doing so—builds trust and rapport. Responding to emotion with empathy allows students to feel you are tuned in to them.	Create the right atmosphere. Be friendly, greet everyone in the room, and sit at eye level when not walking around. Respond to emotion with empathy. • *I wish things were different.* • *This must be very difficult for you.* • *I can see you were hoping for better news.*

Principles	Relevant skills, phrases, and examples
Principle 3 Family is an extension of students. Almost all people have a profound love for and loyalty to family, especially immediate family. Asking students about their families when appropriate opens an emotional window.	Acknowledge the work of the family: • *I am impressed by the love between you and your family.* • *You have done a great job supporting your ________ through [this crisis or experience].* • *What do your children understand about your goals in college?*
Principle 4 Words can harm, and words can heal. As the saying goes, "It is not what you say but how you say it." Giving information in a way that students understand strengthens your connection to them.	Be clear, avoid jargon, and keep explanations geared to students' range of understanding. People need the truth, especially hard truths, to be delivered sensitively. Step back to allow students to take in and share such truths.
Principle 5 Physical touch is a powerful force that can be destructive or healing. Be respectful and ask before reaching out to touch students.	Watch for cues about comfort levels when deciding whether to offer a handshake. If you do not know how to greet someone, simply smile and nod respectfully.
Principle 6 Nonverbal cues are powerful. People transmit as much or more information by nonverbal cues as they do by words.	Be perceptive and adaptive. Strong emotions, such as fear, sadness, pain, and anxiety, are usually obvious. Allow students opportunities to put these emotions into words if they want. Establish eye contact with students that is commensurate with their eye contact with you. If they avert their gaze, adjust your eye contact commensurately
Principle 7 Faith (morality or values) is important to many people. Faith (morality or values) often becomes increasingly important during times of duress and vulnerability and when invited to discuss it. Show respect and support by validating students' rights to their own approaches to faith, morality, or values. Do not ask students to write about their spiritual, ethical, or moral lives if you are not prepared to honor each student's experience. At the same time, do not assume everyone has the same experience with faith or lack thereof.	If a student mentions faith in the context of composition, explore: • *What role does faith (morality or values) play in your life?* • *How has your faith (morality or values) helped you during challenging times?* Show respect: • *I respect your faith in ________.* • *I see that you have learned ________ as a moral code that you trust.*
Principle 8 Allow students as much control as possible. Focus immediately on the issue students are most concerned about. When possible, give them the power to make decisions relative to their learning and time commitments. Negotiate the content and flow of the conversation to give students some control over the meeting. Respect students' needs and priorities as long as they are reasonable and, sometimes, even if they are unreasonable.	Explore • *What is your understanding of your work in this course?* • *What would you like to discuss (or what are your goals) today?* When students need guidance, confidently help them make well-informed decisions.

Although these principles can help instructors when communicating with students, they also can help model interaction behaviors. Instructors and students alike need to be active listeners, and this is often a learned behavior that comes with time and practice. Opening discussion with *This is what I hear you saying* enables discussion participants, including the instructor, to dialogue by paraphrasing what other participants have said, which can help students feel heard while allowing them to clarify aspects that may have been misunderstood.

Additionally, using thoughtfully chosen words for self-expression can help. For example, opening a statement with *I think* or *I believe* encourages speaking from one's intellect or values system, whereas opening with *I feel* encourages speaking from emotion, an approach that often gets school-based conversations into trouble. Similarly, modeling first person pronoun use and encouraging students to do the same reinforces ownership of thoughts, beliefs, and feelings. The contemporary trend to put one's statements into second person creates a linguistic gap between the statement and its owner that may make it easier to speak thoughtlessly. When educators model behaviors and interactions for students in the classroom and in conferences, students can learn how to build trust with one another and challenge each other's ideas, not the actual person speaking them.

Turning to Administration for Help

Teaching in the twenty-first century is challenging. As we suggest in earlier chapters, however, composition as a field has changed because of cultural, social, economic, and political influence; these same changes have consequences and effects on students. They also have real consequences for instructors, and instructors may find themselves victims of racial microaggressions (see DeCuir-Gunby et al. for more guidance). As such, it can be hard to manage classroom discussions let alone teach students to write. We hope instructors like Professor Jackson are comfortable turning to their WPAs or department heads for guidance. In our *Administering Writing Programs in the Twenty-First Century*, we offer strategies for training instructors to teach in the twenty-first century, including how to help instructors develop an anti-racist pedagogy; therefore, instructors may want to read this companion book when such training is lacking at their institutions. Instructors also can observe one another and talk through influential teaching practices and their unique challenges and experiences, which is a strategy that may help Professor Jackson with his current classroom challenges.

Conclusion

Students not only are educators' primary audiences; they are the primary reason educators exist. Instructors can do everything in this chapter to humanize composition (see ch. 2), yet as humans themselves, mistakes are inevitable. Good communication is hard work! If students approach instructors with concerns, upset feelings, perceived microaggressions, or senses of having been misunderstood, we recommend generously listening to learn their experience of what has happened. Sometimes a listening ear is all that is needed: *Please teach me about what you are experiencing.* Usually, a humble, proactive stance is possible: *What can I learn from this incident? Is there anything I can change for the better?* As with the other issues of human communication outlined in chapters 1 and 2, there is not always a clear-cut correct and incorrect stance; practical reasoning leads to a broader, kinder understanding of human problems—as applicable to the classroom as to composition subject matter. Instructors must learn effective communication strategies to teach them to and interact with students.

11

Supporting Students

Midway through the term, Professor Jackson's classes are doing well overall. Professor Jackson has run into a range of issues, however, and not all of them are directly connected to work in the course. One student has written about and then elaborated on his issues with anxiety, which have worsened this term. Several students have expressed problems with the course learning management system, which have prevented them from submitting work on time—they don't seem to know where to turn for help. Two other students have asked about study and meeting spaces on campus. Several students seem to have inadequate time management habits. Professor Jackson has emailed WPA Garcia requesting guidance.

This chapter addresses various support aspects and avenues for students like those Professor Jackson has this term. We discuss how to encourage students to seek support and how instructors themselves can receive the help they might need from these support systems, especially considering the communication concerns discussed in chapter 10. These support structures range from technological, or IT, assistance to services such as mental health counseling. Among the many helpful support systems are reading, writing, and multiliteracy centers, which are distinctly literacy based and crucial to composition instruction; therefore, we end the chapter with a detailed discussion of such centers, including how they might be reconceived as integrated literacy centers that together address composition in the digital era.

Essential Support in a Contentious Age

We must reiterate, as we discuss throughout this book, that twenty-first-century composition classrooms can be contentious learning spaces. Students therefore need support in various areas, such as determining how to communicate appropriately and civilly. It can be especially challenging to provide such support in the myriad teaching and learning environments, but there are basic approaches that can guide educators.

Reducing Contention

The confluence of digital composing platforms, easy (and sometimes uncontrolled) dissemination of texts, and potentially acute polarization of viewpoints about issues can lead to difficult moments in writing courses, whether in reading student writing or during conversations. Therefore, being especially thoughtful in determining course themes and assignment topics is one of the most essential support practices instructors can introduce. As chapters 1 and 7 recommend, teachers should make use of rhetorical approaches to composing, which means helping students recognize that issues about which people argue typically do not have one correct or workable answer. Probable reasoning methods can help student writers come to grips with the various sides of issues and then use research to argue the positions and proposals they think make the most sense. Engaging contentious topics to practice rhetorical approaches, however, is not always necessary to students learning useful composing skills. In other words, it may serve students better to explore and argue more potentially satisfying issues, such as local community problems, campus-based concerns, and universal themes (e.g., the nature of learning, the hero archetype). Students need respectful agency from instructors linked to their developing skill levels. Hot-button issues and current events themes that particularly interest instructors might best be introduced at upper-level and seminar courses in which students presumably have stronger composing skills and better senses of themselves as critical thinkers and writers. To this end, in addition to teaching rhetorical composing strategies, we recommend using topics about writing or reading or those with specific purposes (e.g., service-learning) to engage students.

A Respectful Course Environment

Writing instructors should make clear that their class spaces are respectful and safe. Many institutions provide easy-to-access language about respectful course environments for both students and their instructors. Appropriate material can be included in the course syllabus. There should be language about support for students in areas such as gender and sexual harassment, and instructors should understand their role when students approach them, whether these conversations are based on occurrences inside or outside the course. Writing program administrators should include these considerations in preservice and professional development training.

A respectful course environment is often built around instructor efforts, including things like content or trigger warnings on course materials. These materials have been the source of some professional conversation and even controversy, but instructors should consider how such warnings might assist or otherwise affect their students, a thought process that is, of course, rhetorical. The University of Michigan's "Introduction to Content Warnings and Trigger Warnings" provides a good primer on these types of warnings. Content warnings signal that potentially sensitive material will be in the course. Their intent is to prepare students by letting them know what is coming up, enabling students to engage with the material or to disengage as needed for their well-being. Trigger warnings are a specific type of content warning that signals content that may be especially psychologically or physiologically challenging to some individuals, particularly those with post-traumatic stress. Such warnings often let students know that readings, writing assignments, media presentations, and the like might include such material as sexual assault, violence, child abuse, abduction, death or dying, mental illness, racism, or homophobia ("Introduction"). We encourage instructors to carefully consider why they are including such readings and for what purposes; if they are deemed necessary for furthering discussion and learning, instructors should prepare students for what they are about to read.

Content and trigger warnings can be provided not only on the syllabus but also on the course website in or outside the LMS, which is something WPA Garcia has suggested to Professor Jackson and other faculty members. The University of Michigan's document expresses that such warnings can occur as *a blanket warning* for the course description if challenging content is a necessary and common part of the course that students will encounter weekly;

an in-syllabus warning regarding specific material that can be flagged using keywords for the units and weeks in which students will encounter it;

the course website or separate document warning, for when instructors prefer not to use keywords on the syllabus;

personalized warnings that indicate instructors' attempts to flag content with keywords and invite students to let them know if there are any individualized warnings that may be needed; and

just-in-time email and in-class warnings for potentially challenging content that was not planned for at the time of the initial course syllabus or website construction.

Finally, these warnings are not provided to let students out of work but to enable them to determine whether the course will work for them, converse with instructors about their needs, and prepare themselves emotionally with support structures. As stated above, we recommend avoiding many of these potentially challenging content issues in most writing courses, yet we realize that triggering issues are a normal part of human life and may arise naturally. As such, supporting students is a critical concern.

Communicating Support Information

Undoubtedly, given the humanistic nature of composition instruction and the emotional connections many writers experience with their projects, students may see writing instructors as potentially safe allies and listeners to their concerns both in and outside the course. Composition instructors are therefore poised to advocate for students who seek their assistance. Thus, instructors should know what is available at the school and be able to connect students to various support entities when necessary. Even if composition instructors are well-versed in student support services, that knowledge will not be useful unless they communicate the information to students in easily available, user-friendly, redundant ways, including—but not solely—an accessible, downloadable syllabus.

Embedding everything in the LMS is great unless the students experience technology issues that preclude web access. If students have the printed syllabus, they can call or find an alternative means of contacting support services. Many institutions and writing programs have boilerplate language that lists campus support services, including web links, phone numbers, and available hours. Instructors should provide this information not only on the syllabus but also through links on the LMS, and they should review it in a first-week conversation regardless of teaching environment. Contact and hours information should include campus security and safety, academic advising, office of disability, information and computing technology support, mental health counseling center, health-and-wellness center, literacy centers (e.g., reading and writing centers), bookstore, library or media center, registrar's office, and multilingual student support.

The sections below suggest additional information that a syllabus or other document or LMS space should address.

Engaging Respectful On-Site and Online Discussions

For the same reasons that they can work so well in courses, discussion board conversations offered in any course environment can introduce a range of communication issues since they are asynchronous, writing-based, and—although usually not anonymous—allow for indirect commenting that, although it may be minimized as just the writer's opinion, still has human repercussions. Instructors relying on these conversations should develop rules and guidelines specifically for these interactions, as we describe in chapter 5. Regardless of the classroom environment in which the discussion occurs, these rules should be included on the course syllabus as well as discussed in class. Online environments can be wonderful for creating, sharing, and reading student writing, but they also can encourage behaviors—often migrated from unmoderated social media talk habits—that instructors would not tolerate in on-site conversations.

General Support to Expect from the Instructor

It can be interesting to talk to instructors in other disciplines, in courses that deal primarily with knowledge dissemination or content delivery. Sometimes, these instructors are surprised to hear about the depth of personal connection that occurs among students and between instructors and students in composition courses, but such is the nature of the profession. Composition instructors draw fundamentally on assignments like literacy narratives and journals that students often use to explore deep ideas and areas of their lives, or they may ask students to debate and write about classic topics that have challenged rhetoricians for centuries. Instructors should be mindful of these dynamics and, through language in the syllabus, express overtly where students can turn to vent or decompress after an especially thoughtful or even heated conversation, which might help Professor Jackson's student who is experiencing heightened anxiety this term. As the information about content and trigger warnings clearly indicates, instructors will not always be able to solve student problems that stem from course material or course interactions; nonetheless, they should be aware of how they or someone else might be an ally or listener after class or during a project's development.

Office of Disability or Special Services

Because accessibility underlies this book's pedagogical approach, the topics of disability and student connection to the offices that support such students are covered in depth in chapter 2. Offices of equality, equity, diversity, or accessibility obviously must be accessible to students who need them, both on-site and online. Students, for instance, should be able to acquire access or disability verification forms in ways that are easily transmittable to instructors in electronic formats. Instructors should become well acquainted with the disability services' supportive goals, strategies, and means for connecting with students.

Accessibility Support

All support services for students should be provided with primary consideration for access; therefore, specific attention must be given to the *support environment* (i.e., on-site, fully online, hybrid), *support modality* (i.e., synchronous or asynchronous), and *support medium* (i.e., face-to-face, phone, video, email) per principle 13 of the position statement on online writing instruction (OWI) by the Conference on College Composition and Communication (CCCC; CCCC, Committee 26). If institutions offer learning both on-site and online in geographically distributed, distance-based environments, then support services ranging from the registrar to IT support to counseling must account for students who are not physically on campus and whose time zones may not align with that of the institution.

This universal obligation for accessibility does not mean it is always easy to provide. Accessibility costs money, time, and effort, especially when it has not been addressed proactively. Instructors will confront issues regarding accommodating student needs. How do instructors help students by providing necessary accommodations without singling out or publicly identifying students? Typically, one-on-one discussions can occur through in-office conferencing, phone, or email. As important, how can instructors personally connect students to needed services? Whatever guidelines are in place for an on-site setting, how will they be handled in an online setting in which instructors and students meet only virtually? These are examples of access issues connected to student support that should be the subject of robust conversations in postsecondary programs, departments, and institutions.

Health, Wellness, and Similar Supports

In many cases, an educational institution is a mini-city, and the residents and citizens will need basic services, such as health care. Instructors should learn how these services operate. Does the school, for instance, have an open clinic for ill or injured students? What is the first point of access for such a clinic: phone, text, email, website appointment, or walk-in? Higher education administrators like WPA Garcia also need to pay attention to students' need for mental health support (Kitzrow). Support facilities often are available on-site on a walk-in basis, which may leave out distance-based students. Particularly during times when most students are learning remotely, such as during the pandemic, institutional administrators must be creative in addressing mental health, connecting students with support professionals through videoconferencing and phone, for example. We advocate that these efforts go beyond simple interfaces and provide support experiences similar to those for traditional, on-site students. Beyond the issue of accessing the actual place for receiving care, composition instructors may experience students who express desire for help with mental health concerns. WPAs should proactively inform instructors about how to listen and act. Is it appropriate in the institution's view to offer to phone the counseling center to make an appointment in the student's presence? To phone the counseling center and then hand the phone to the student? To walk the student to the building that houses the counseling center? Mental health is a delicate, critical issue about which it is crucial to act appropriately and in an institutionally approved manner.

STUDENT CRISIS

Instructors may not realize it, but on many campuses, they are considered *mandatory reporters*, especially in situations of sexual violence but also in cases of discrimination, bullying, and threat of violence. Mandatory reporters are required to report these cases when they learn about them. This reporting obligation creates pressures on writing instructors like Professor Jackson as acutely as it does on other types of faculty. After all, writing teachers spend their lives cultivating the thoughts of students and reading about them. Highly emotional compositions often result. Students may be experiencing emotional distress due to housing and food insecurities caused by the pandemic, or they may be victims of hate crimes or are deeply affected by discrimination in various ways. As with other aspects of student health and wellness, instructors and their students should understand campus rules and regulations, and specific information and resources should be made available to students.

STUDENT LIFE

Institutions of higher education have put enormous amounts of money and resources into enhancing student experiences on their campuses. We believe, in the spirit of the CCCC OWI principle 2, which emphasizes that teachers should teach writing and not be required to teach technology, that writing teachers should stay focused on the pedagogical aspects of their instructional lives (CCCC, Committee 11). Although largely beyond the focus on this book, student life matters hold some importance for writing instructors, who may ask students to connect with their campuses as part of their writing experiences or even as direct subjects of their writing projects.

ON-CAMPUS STUDENTS

On-campus students have a wide variety of resources available: recreation and fitness facilities, intramural sports, Greek societies, clubs, theater activities, musical events, and the like. These resources constitute student support structures that contribute to student life experiences. Although it is not composition instructors' responsibility to make sure students engage in these resources, they can be one of the many sources of information about them. Students may be heartened to know their instructors attend and use some of these resources themselves, making them more familiar and real. It is important to remember, as chapter 2 states, that between thirty-three and ninety-one percent of students were over age twenty-five in 2017–18 ("Most"), and these returning adult learners—or so-called nontraditional students—tend to have families and full-time jobs. Therefore, it is helpful to acknowledge their potential limitations in using campus resources and also to know about campus-based childcare; here again, having the number handy or offering that number to students who may not have thought about it can be all they need to experience themselves as part of campus life.

DISTANCE-BASED STUDENTS

Institutions of higher education can be faced with hurdles in making their distance-based students feel connected to the school. When students attend courses online and are locally based, they often can make use of campus resources. When the online students are geographically distributed—as with rural, military, and some prison-based students, for example—their ability to participate in anything extramural (and even in some required coursework, as explained below for commuting students) is severely limited. In this case, although students may not be able to join the campus and local populations in using campus student life resources, they may be included by, for example, requesting that the campus theater film its productions and provide the recording to distance students at the same fee students would pay on campus. Whenever copyright or other proprietary rights would not be infringed upon, instructors can videoconference online students to on-campus resources necessary to the course. In constructing a list of student support services, writing instructors should plan such work-arounds to help create learning-centered communities inclusive of all students.

COMMUTING STUDENTS

Students who commute may have restrictions and obstacles unlike their on-campus—or even fully online—colleagues. Many institutions have dedicated spaces for such students to work between classes and meet, and some have special services and programming established to assist commuting students in having a richer and more successful academic and overall experience. Instructors must consider such students from the perspective of access, whether the issue is campus life or educational requirements. For example, if an instructor requires that a collaborative team meet face-to-face five times, how will that work for nontraditional students with limited on-campus availability? How can the entire team surmount this challenge without the commuting students becoming the nonparticipating, problematic members?

LIBRARY AND MEDIA CENTER

Libraries remain key sites to help composition students with their work, but from our teaching experiences it appears that, particularly for first-year students, libraries are woefully underutilized and underappreciated. Students often do not realize the incredible intellectual support network that is a library, and many do not know about the vast electronic resources that schools make available—and that students, in higher education institutions at least, pay for. Composition instructors should always provide clear, up-to-date library links in multiple places in their course materials, and they should look into specific resources for their courses; this practice is particularly useful in first-year writing (FYW) programs, which often partner with libraries to provide focused workshops and LMS-friendly electronic materials, ranging from general topics like research to help for particular assignments. Media specialists can assist students not only through the class—both with on-site visits to the library and online visits linking course participants with the library's resources—but also individually in person. Students need to know where the physical library is, that there are stacks with print-based materials in it, how to use the Dewey decimal system and the Book Industry Standards and Communications system, and how to access and use the library's electronic databases. Media center specialists provide this help one-on-one, and students need to learn not to be afraid to ask for their assistance.

BOOKSTORE

The cost of and access to books and other course materials are hot topics. Instructors should have some understanding of how students access course materials and interact with the bookstore. Many rent textbooks and some buy them, hoping to return them for cash after the term. In those cases, students will be reluctant to write in the books or otherwise mark them up as study and writing resources. If writing instructors order books that students should keep as resources, they also should engage with those texts regularly in and out of class and teach students how to use them well. In many cases, regulations now require that teachers provide students with course textbook costs before the term starts. Instructors in large FYW programs may have texts chosen for them, but they still should understand what students must do to acquire them. These guidelines are equally important for online and on-site students. Instructors should consider whether in truncated terms of, for example, six or eight weeks, online students will be able to acquire their books in a timely enough manner to be able to make full use of them. If not, it is likely students simply will not purchase them and may be unprepared for their work. Thus, information about bookstore services is important for all students.

Registrar and Institutional Infrastructure

Many postsecondary instructors who read this book will be teaching first-year students, who are the most unfamiliar with the institutional structure. Again, institutions must accommodate students who are spatially and temporally at a distance. Instructors need not be experts about how the central billing office works, but they might at least be mindful of these services. Perhaps time can be a bigger obstacle than distance, as students may be enrolled in an institution that is open when they are not available due to work, travel, and other realities. These students still may have billing questions, add-drop issues, and all the problems students encounter when interfacing on campus with the school. Hence, FYW instructors particularly are likely to work with students who have bureaucracy issues: they cannot complete the requirements for adding the course, register for the next term, or use a library resource because their account is on hold, for example. One straightforward strategy we have emphasized in this chapter is that instructors should post materials on their syllabus to help students in this area. Although, again, the expectation is not that a composition teacher transforms into a financial counselor, directing students to the proper resources can help them more quickly resolve these problems and focus on their coursework.

Technology Support

Principle 10 of the CCCC's OWI position statement is clear: "Students should be prepared by the institution and their teachers for the unique technological and pedagogical components of OWI" (CCCC, Committee 21). Although instructors and even administrators may not always have much control over technology support, we emphasize that the approach and philosophy of institutions should be that they supply necessary supports, so students can learn composition in technological environments. Students need strong IT support, but the instructor and even the writing program should not be the first line in supplying that support. Thinking particularly about access, Sushil K. Oswal writes, "Educational institutions spend millions of dollars to purchase computer equipment that cannot be used by all students" (253). Instructors are likely not on the front end of such purchases, but they can consider more closely how such equipment, apps, and interfaces will function in their classes, as we discuss in chapter 2. If instructors have technological know-how and want to be helpful, it is fine to occasionally assist, but LMS issues and other digital interface issues should not necessarily fall to instructors or even their programs. Institutions have first-level responsibility for these problems. To this end, Professor Jackson should know where to point his students with LMS problems, so they can get the most efficient and reliable assistance.

Pedagogical Course Support

Overall technology help is simply the first level of such support for students. Students also need to be prepared for the challenges of an online writing-literacy course. As CCCC OWI principle 10, effective practice 10.1 states, "Students need to be introduced to the writing-course specific uses of the LMS" (CCCC, Committee 22). As has long been the case, considerable literature exists regarding how to teach online and distance content courses, whereas less literature exists regarding how to teach online writing-literacy courses, which is a major impetus for this book's focus on teaching composition in the digital era. Of course, such writing-literacy courses are fundamentally different, and focused support is necessary, such as how to develop writing and responding environments, respond to student writing with teaching in mind, and facilitate the dialogic experience so crucial to such courses. This book has been developed to help instructors support students in these and multiple other pedagogical areas where technology is involved.

SUPPORT FOR MULTILINGUAL STUDENTS

Multilingual education is not just a robust subdiscipline within writing studies but also its own separate disciplinary area within education. Educators' work with multilingual students overlaps with many of the access conversations throughout this book. Here, we simply want to emphasize that instructors should be aware of the resources on campus for multilingual students. We discuss writing and other literacy centers in detail below, but many campuses have a unit or service of an English learning or language center that is designed to help students who do not speak and write primarily in English. Often, such centers will have specialists in languages and perhaps even the learning styles and research approaches particular to certain cultures. Instructors should have information on the syllabus about these support services, but they also should learn as much as they can about supporting multilingual students enrolled in their courses. WPAs should offer such training or guide them to it when requested; professional development, which we discuss at length in chapter 4 of *Administering Writing in the Twenty-First Century*, by Tiffany Bourelle, Beth L. Hewett, and Scott Warnock, should be financially supported by the writing program or institution whenever possible.

Literacy Center Support

These centers, whether reading, writing, multiliteracy, or integrated, offer key support services to students in writing courses. Instructors should locate these resources, discover the services they provide, potentially establish a relationship with them, and encourage students to use their services.

Reading Centers

Many, though not all, postsecondary institutions have reading centers designed to supplement students' reading abilities. It is fair to say that in many cases such reading centers have a developmental or remedial function intended to bring students up to speed with reading postsecondary-level texts. Skills with which they assist include annotating texts, visual memory, remembering material, pronunciation, study strategies, research skills, vocabulary development, and spelling. In some cases, reading center work involves testing reading abilities prior to matriculation; if students do not achieve certain scores, they may need to pass a basic, non-credit-bearing reading course and attain a particular score on a final assessment prior to taking credit-bearing courses. In other cases, students use reading centers for the tutoring offered in making sense of reading that may be more complex or sophisticated than they are used to. Multilingual students and those with reading disabilities may receive such help, particularly with pronunciation and vocabulary.

Sometimes reading centers (or other student support centers) educate students about fundamental skill sets for efficient time and project management. Workshops, webinars, and one-to-one coaching with time and project management can make the difference between success and failure, particularly for asynchronous online settings that students may interpret as being easier, since classes do not meet in physical spaces on regular days. Students in FYW classes, who are still acculturating to college-level work with professors' less intense monitoring of homework and learning, may need to pay special attention to time and project management strategies to build new habits, especially for working in digital settings.

Given the extreme (and exciting) digital-era changes in reading materials and the skills necessary to surmount those changes, which we describe in chapter 6, reading centers may need to consider the research about building neural pathways and biliterate brains and how reading in print—both long and shorter texts—differs from reading on digital screens. Reading is complicated by the multiple genres and forms texts take and the technologies through which they are distributed, as well as the varied messages and rhetorical purposes students must deconstruct from texts. Even strong readers who would never be considered developmental or remedial may benefit from assistance with contemporary postsecondary reading. If reading is a lifelong literacy skill and has changed as much as we argue it has, then reading center work should include ongoing skill development as much as or even more than remediation.

Writing Centers

Both WPAs and writing instructors must be aware of and collaborate with those in writing center studies. One-on-one writing center instruction between consultant and writer—particularly in online settings but also on-site—complements and supplements the one-on-one feedback that occurs between teacher and writer and, to an extent, among peers. Knowing how and why writing centers tend to operate as they do, the theories that ground them, and how these professional writing spaces are changing to meet twenty-first-century students is crucial to building the professionally respectful and collaborative partnerships that are so valuable to student writers.

On-Site Writing Centers

Writing centers have long been recognized as spaces where students can receive personal assistance with their writing, assistance that may not have been available to them or is at least different from what they receive in a teacher-centered classroom. As far back as 1974, Doris Sutton and Daniel Arnold studied the effectiveness of the tutorial assistance in remedial writing in comparison to classroom lectures and discussions, concluding that the individualized instructional method found in tutorial sessions had a significantly "beneficial effect upon the later English grades of the students" they studied (in M. Harris 16). A decade later, Kenneth A. Bruffee argued that students really needed a peer-driven writing center, as students avoided expertise-driven writing tutoring "in droves," as it "seemed to them merely an extension of the work, the expectations, and above all the social structure of traditional classroom learning" ("Collaborative Learning" 87).

Since the 1930s, when writing centers first appeared in colleges, three paradigms have predominated as models of how writing should be taught, and these align with paradigm shifts in composition:

Current-Traditional Rhetoric. Within the current-traditional method, the tutor often focused on isolating errors and formal weaknesses in the text (i.e., grammatical correctness).

Expressivism. Through the expressivist approach, tutors helped students develop so-called authentic writing, asking questions, having discussions to generate ideas, and prompting students to discover and think about ideas at greater length.

Social Constructionism. In social constructionism, tutor and student negotiate meaning and make knowledge together, coming to an agreement regarding what or how the writing might develop. Unlike expressivism, social constructionism maintains that instead of students learning through self-discovery, knowledge is created together between the student and tutor.

In practice, even with these paradigm shifts, many writing centers see traces of all three in their tutorial sessions. Andrea A. Lunsford, in "Collaboration, Control, and the Idea of a Writing Center," argues for a fourth model of a collaborative center that unites all three paradigms and focuses on collaboration, wherein consultants (also variously called *tutors, coaches, readers,* and *mentors*) view "knowledge and reality as mediated by or constructed through language in social use, as socially constructed, contextualized, as, in short the product of *collaboration*" (37). Within this type of collaborative center, "power and control are constantly negotiated and shared" (41), and students can have power they may not have access to in traditional classroom settings. Through sharing not only ideas but also power, students ultimately learn how to improve their writing processes. Regardless of what approach consultants take in responding to students, one goal is to change the way writers look at their own writing.

For Stephen North, as he articulates in "The Idea of a Writing Center," the main objective of a writing center is to change the writers rather than the writing (27). Consultants may be trained to help students change their processes and approaches to writing, not just the projects they bring into a session. By asking students questions about their writing, consultants attempt to help students ask self-reflective questions when composing and revising future essays, stimulating inner dialogue and broadening writers' views of themselves as composers. Consultants become participant-observers, charged to change the ritual of composing, interfering and getting in the way of the process but leaving the writing process itself changed (29). Although they may comment on higher-order concerns, including genre, thesis, argument, or expression of thought, consultants' main goals typically are to ask questions to get students to recognize potential issues or problems in the text, enabling them to ask themselves these questions in the future. Writing center praxis and theories stress that tutors will not fix students' papers (in part because the writing is not broken but merely in progress), but they will coach students to improve their overall composing processes. Unfortunately, many instructors mistakenly want writing center consultants to correct papers or inoculate students against error, as has been well documented in writing center literature.

Instructors who want to work closely with their writing centers can talk with the director and provide assignment instructions and context as to what will be assessed in students' projects within each assignment. It is good practice to have ongoing conversations with the director, at both the program and course levels, especially if many students are asked to access services at certain points during the term. Instructors can introduce students to writing center services by

> providing writing center services information on the syllabus;
>
> inviting a writing center consultant to visit the class (on-site, online, or both) and discuss its services;
>
> requiring students to use writing center services at least once during a project's development cycle;[1] and
>
> explaining the value of a writing center consultation and asking students to give it a try, encouraging them to develop specific questions that help focus the session.

Online Writing Centers

Recently, more writing centers have become equipped to help students at a distance. In fact, according to CCCC OWI principle 13, effective practice 13.2, writing centers must offer help not only at a distance for online students but also through the same learning environment and modality as the instruction being offered in those courses (CCCC, Committee 27). Such practices became overtly critical during the 2020 COVID-19 en masse movement to remote education. Sometimes called online writing labs (OWLs), these online centers offer one-on-one tutoring through digital technology.

Asynchronous tutoring occurs through paper-submission portals, typically requiring assignment instructions for context; consultants then respond with questions, comments, and mini-lessons based on the student's own writing to help in revision. Responses may occur using text-based formats as well as video and audio. Hewett, in "Asynchronous Online Instructional Commentary," argues that linguistic clarity, in terms of semantic integrity, direct (not directive) speech acts, using students' own writing in focused examples and mini-lessons, action steps, and rhetorically considered formatting, are all necessary parts of effective online conferences (see also *Online Writing Conference*). Asynchronous conferences probably occur more frequently than synchronous ones, given that technology access must be available both to consultant and students.

Synchronous tutoring occurs through real-time conferencing platforms that can include audiovisual and text-based chat features with screen and document sharing options. Document sharing options particularly encourage collaborative exchange of composing ideas and knowledge between participants. Students and consultants who prefer real-time interactions may gravitate to synchronous tutoring because questions can be addressed right away and without the lag time of asynchronous interactions. The real-time setting and the limitations such a setting presents for consultants to read texts, however, may better suit it to broad, global issues like brainstorming ideas, thesis development, and targeted grammar and mechanics lessons over the particulars of what is occurring in any one project (Hewett, "Synchronous"). The environment, modality, and medium should be selected as much for student educational setting and preferences as for those to which writing center leadership may be partial. Finally, synchronous tutoring benefits from the same effective conferencing strategies outlined above for asynchronous tutoring.

The more that online writing centers offer online support, the more the discipline is engaged in researching its efficacy, as Rebecca Babcock and Terese Thonus have demonstrated in *Researching the Writing Center*. Hewett has long offered a view of online writing centers as being an essential part of writing programs—both on-site and online ("Theoretical Underpinnings"). Research supports this idea. After conducting a small-scale study of how medium affects conferencing, in "Comparing Technologies for Online Writing Conferences," Joanna Wolfe and Jo Ann Griffin reported finding that "although some lore suggests face time is the ideal form of communication . . . OWI may offer pedagogical benefits rivaling—or even exceeding—those of face-to-face conferencing" (86). Similarly, in "Moving Online," Gene Thompson found that in a small center in Japan, opening up digital resources and capabilities met students' needs more effectively. For their work in "Interactional Dynamics in On-line and Face-to-Face Peer-Tutoring Sessions for Second Language Writers," Rodney H. Jones, Angel Garralda, Davis Li, and Graham Lock coded and compared online and face-to-face interactions, finding "that different modes of communication facilitate the construction of different kinds of relationships between peer-tutors and clients"; the researchers found that face-to-face interactions appeared "to lend themselves to more hierarchical relationships in which tutors take control of the discourse," whereas online interactions "seem to lead to more egalitarian relationships, with clients controlling the discourse more" (16; see also ch. 4).

Embedded Tutors

We include embedded tutors within this writing center section, although WPAs can provide their own consultants, often called *writing fellows*. Embedded tutors work in a structured way to offer feedback and form a classroom community of writers helping other writers. Embedded tutoring can help instructors with daunting writing response workloads, as the tutors offer in-process feedback during composing. This extra feedback is especially helpful during multimodal composing processes, as we discuss in chapter 8, and tutors can aid students by reading texts from the perspective of the students' intended audiences. When provided in addition to in-class peer review, this feedback offers students opportunities to learn from knowledgeable peers who not only are trained in the writing center to offer feedback but also—because they are embedded into the course and experience the course content with the students—are familiar with the specific content and culture of that course. Writing center educators and instructors can work with embedded tutors to ensure they have a strong understanding of course goals and projects, including how to offer formative feedback during the writing process. If embedded tutors are working in fully online and hybrid courses, administrators should train them on the unique features of online courses and how students may be challenged, including access-wise, by strictly online assignments. Instructors can work with embedded tutors to norm assignment feedback, enabling tutors to provide feedback during the writing process much like the instructor would but without the accompanying evaluative positionality. To ensure that tutors and instructors agree regarding feedback strategies, instructors can provide tutors with sample projects created by former students and create norms for feedback on the project by asking tutors to practice giving feedback on these sample projects. Experienced instructors can help tutors anticipate challenging parts of assignments although, as we argue in chapter 8, instructors always should create assignments from the student seat to best anticipate and understand possible challenges.

Embedded tutors can be coached to leave formative feedback with student portfolios. Since portfolios often represent a substantial portion of grades, embedded tutors should be prompted to look at early drafts or the checkpoints detailed in chapter 8. Both instructors and embedded tutors can give feedback on early portfolio drafts. Embedded tutors should be provided with course learning outcomes and successful portfolio examples from previous students. Instructors need to coach embedded tutors to review portfolios for revisions and outcome reflections. If multimodality is a goal, embedded tutors should work with the students to choose rhetorically appropriate images, videos, graphics, and links. They also should be coached to help students learn to write substantial reflections and provide evidence of their learning, places where students often fall short.

Working with embedded tutors may seem like a lot of effort for the instructor, and it does take time; these tutors can make instructors' teaching and response lives more efficient and, ideally, more effective, however. Additionally, the unique nature of embedded tutors as postsecondary students themselves can help form a course community of caring about each other's success, which is proven to aid in student retention. By facilitating discussions and reaching out to struggling students, embedded tutors can form peer-to-peer relationships with students. Embedded tutors can be mentors and writing coaches to students, keeping them involved and active, which can be particularly valuable in online writing courses (T. Bourelle et al., "Teaching").

Multimodal or Multiliteracy Centers

The work of the writing center support has shifted, as has all of education, because of digital technologies. According to Babcock and Thonus, "The question is not *why* or *whether* writing centers should be multiliteracy centers or *whether* they should work with tutees in multiple modes. The question is *how* writing centers can rebrand themselves and create new spaces for their work within an expanded mission" (285). Although the paradigms of good writing center work, much like good composition and literacy work overall, remain stable, approaches must change because of the affordances (and requirements of) of digital technology. In *Multiliteracy Centers*, David M. Sheridan and James A. Inman suggest that multiliteracy centers, although not yet prominent on many campuses, strive to be "spaces equal to the diversity of semiotic options composers have in the 21st century" (6). Diversity within the writing center includes having rhetorically savvy consultants who can support semiotic options as well as help students be reflective in multimodal practice. In other words, center administrators should decide what types of support they can provide (e.g., they may help students with ePortfolios but not podcasts). Similarly, if assigning these types of assignments, instructors should contact center directors to learn what support options consultants provide (e.g., can they tutor multimodal projects?) as well as what types of technology the center makes readily available to students to work with on their own or in collaboration with tutors (e.g., voice recorders, video cameras, and video-editing software).

Some institutions have come onboard with multiliteracy centers and others have implemented makerspaces, which mainly exist to help guide the creativity and creation of projects, from the digital to the physical. For instance, some students may need help creating and editing a video, whereas others may need assistance with an architectural project, building a smaller-scale model of a building they wish to design. In keeping with the importance of expanding instructional skills in the digital era, makerspaces offer a place wherein students can acquire the technological skills—if not always the rhetorical knowledge—they may need to produce multimodal projects. Students also need assistance with creation, brainstorming, outlining, and any other rhetorical conception ideas, all the way through production. Although makerspaces and multiliteracy centers require funding, students need them, particularly when creating digital compositions, and funding issues should not prevent this help. Even if the center does not have the technology to support the tutoring of some multimodal projects, consultants should be prompted to brainstorm with students and talk through their rhetorical choices and composing process, guiding them to further think through their decisions.

Integrated Literacy Centers

Reading centers. Writing centers. Multiliteracy centers. Broken apart, siloed, and separated from one another, they singularize three critical, foundational, digital-era literacy skills as if each skill could be taught well apart from the others. We believe these literacies are not best handled as singular meaning-making activities. Each is intricately connected to the other—particularly with the fluidity of twenty-first-century composition. Therefore, we recommend rethinking this type of student support and moving to build integrated literacy centers that address the biliterate brainwork of contemporary print-based and screen-based reading; the varied genres, processes, and technical tools necessary to writing; and the increasingly digital multimodal projects that nearly always engage text, among other media. Rhetorical principles and their intricate reliance on one another hold these literacies together. One cannot read if nothing is written. One cannot write if one cannot read. Reading begins in childhood with images and symbol systems. Images and symbol systems make up much of the material postsecondary students read (consume) and therefore should write (produce). Rhetorical processes for critically thinking about, researching, and constructing expositions and arguments link them, regardless of medium.

In her review of Sheridan and Inman's edited collection *Multiliteracy Centers*, Catherine Gabor writes: "Readers might fret, 'Not only do I have to transform the Writing Center into an MLC [multiliteracy center], but now I also have to'" _______ (3). Readers should complete the sentence for what worries them. Given the scope of this book, we are aware readers might fret about our argument for yet another interdependent task for twenty-first-century literacy educators. We also realize how hard these literacy educators have worked to carve out their singular professional spaces in a postsecondary system that often devalues them as merely remedial teachers and tutors. Yet, just as composition course instructors cannot ignore the need to understand and teach reading, alphabetic text-based writing, and multimodal composition as their core digital-era job, neither can reading-writing-multiliteracy center directors and consultants. We believe literacy support center educators do need to expand and intersect the scope of their work, embracing their identities as Generalists 3.0. Encouraging students to engage the assistance that integrated literacy centers can offer as a common place for learning new literacy skills removes the stigma of remediation, and it gives them a space—much as architecture, computer science, or engineering students have spaces—for learning and practicing these skills.

Conclusion

Supporting students means providing them with essential information and teaching them when and how they might use services designed to help them. Books have been written about many of the individual components of student support we describe in this chapter. Sometimes students are not able to use these resources, and sometimes they simply do not use them. Supporting students also means rethinking the current ways things are done, as with separately housed and funded literacy centers. We believe it is the job of educators, from the instructors through the layers of administration, to make sure writing students are in courses in which their support needs are met. That way, students can focus on the primary goal: learning the skills and content of the composition instruction they receive.

NOTE

1. Writing center community conversations about required visits reflect disagreements. At one time, the thinking was that required visits were not good practice, as they forced reluctant writers to the center, using scarce appointment resources, and making such visits unpleasant. Recent conversations on professional email lists (e.g., *WCenter*) have shifted, as directors suggest required appointments may have fortunate effects for writers, even when initiated with a course requirement.

12

Imagining the Future of Composition

Professor Jackson feels like, finally, he has a good grasp on teaching in the twenty-first century's digital era. Nonetheless, understanding the changes that have occurred over the past decade and more recently during the COVID-19 pandemic response has made him more aware of the inevitable changes to come. He is more cognizant, as well, of societal fissures that may affect the writing course. Professor Jackson wants to roll with the changes, make the best decisions, and ensure he is prepared for the future. Teaching writing is his passion, and he wants to remain employable. Although WPA Garcia is facilitating Professor Jackson's growth as a strong Generalist 3.0, he wonders what his job will look like in the upcoming 4.0 era.

No one can expect instructors to learn or even keep up with all new technology, and they should be protected from the assumption that they will do so, per the Conference on College Composition and Communication's online writing instruction (OWI) principle 2 (CCCC, Committee 11) and online literacy instruction (OLI) principle 1 of the the Global Society of Online Literacy Educators (GSOLE). Therefore, we encourage educators to approach technology without trepidation, viewing composition in a new light—one that insists on rethinking communication strategies and matching them with insightful teaching. Yet we also encourage those in the writing studies field to help create these changes. As Joyce Locke Carter indicates in her 2016 CCCC chair's address, composition educators need to be at the forefront, guiding the technology development that most supports civil conversation and thoughtful uses of rhetoric. The now globally connected world is at a crossroads. Everywhere, people are communicating through digital means; it is nothing at all to work through video meetings from North America to Asia on a home computer or mobile phone.

This book was written under the premise that many instructors want support in preparing themselves and others for teaching twenty-first-century composition, whether that instruction occurs fully online, as a hybrid, or in more traditional on-site, albeit technologically enhanced, spaces. As we have argued, all writing instruction is inflected by digitality, one step further from Beth L. Hewett and Scott Warnock's 2015 statement in "The Future of OWI" that "OWI is composition writ large because OWI enables teaching students to write with, through, and about the next wave of writing technologies" (547). Furthermore, as we argue, all writing instruction must, by its very nature, encompass reading and multimodal composition, as indicated in numerous position statements such as GSOLE's "Online Literacy Instruction Principles and Tenets": "online literacy instruction (OLI) in reading, alphabetic writing, and multimodal composition is taught in traditional and digital settings, engaging teachers and scholars of reading and composing across a range of disciplines." In that vein, as we continue to be astounded (and thrilled) by the changes in literacy education, we recognize that the writing studies field must have some tough discussions and make some challenging changes to address even a few of the possible futures facing composition instruction in this third decade of the twenty-first century.

The Future: Language and Literacy Education

With the growth of multimodal and digitally enhanced daily communication, writing instructors now can see that they are, indeed, literacy educators and that writing involves much more than producing a readable academic essay written in alphabetic text. Thus, as educators, writing studies professionals as literacy experts are challenged to define practices broadly. No one could have predicted the revolutionary effect the Internet would have on college instruction, and the twenty-first century's shift in teaching and learning environments from on-site to technologically enhanced to hybrid and fully online is but one of those changes. Similarly, no one could have predicted the mass emergency move to remote education in early 2020 that brought virtual education to everyone's reality, a reality that is taking on a life of its own moving forward. Change begets change, of course, so below we cautiously refer to a few of the current conversations happening both in the field and more broadly, encouraging readers to think about these discussions. How can educators help shape current and future composition practices, including the practices surrounding language use and how it is taught in postsecondary institutions, the continuing changes occurring in composition, students' needs for usable course structures and civil discourse, and fair and equitable treatment of faculty members—particularly those who are part-time—including professional development opportunities?

From Writing to Literacy

If writing instruction is more than teaching alphabetic writing, then the idea of writing qua writing is too limiting. Composition educators need to conceptualize their collective instructional work more broadly as *literacy*, a future that opens the door to seriously engaging reading and multimodality in digital settings, including the changes and instability that technology has wrought regarding students' needs for developing rhetorical maturity and for their future workplace potential. Furthermore, multimodal composition cannot be taught to students if the instructors themselves do not have adequate preparation and support for their work, an issue of access. Thus, it is incumbent on writing program administrators (WPAs) to provide effective teacher training for multimodal composition even if they first need to learn multimodal tools to become the trainers themselves. For online education, this reconception minimally would shift language from OWI to OLI, but the implications have resonance in composition more generally.

First, no longer can the digital rhetoric of multimodal composition be placed in a silo outside composition instruction with the misbegotten idea that alphabetic and multimodal texts should be taught separately. A thoughtful union of these composing processes and products should be addressed—albeit at different levels for students of differing abilities and needs—at some point in the postsecondary composition education. Second, some scholars (e.g., Carillo, *MLA Guide* and *Securing*; Horning, "Writing" and *Reading*) rightfully have criticized how overlooked reading is in the writing classroom. As we describe throughout, there is no sound reason for this division; in fact, a primary excuse may be that writing educators simply are not trained to consider literacy more broadly. We believe instructors must be trained to better prepare students to read text consciously using biliterate brains and to oscillate among texts, as well as prepare students for reading videos and listening to sound bites, critically considering what they see and hear. This future is not only achievable but necessary.

A reconceptualization also would call for literacy centers that unite support for reading, alphabetic writing, and multimodal composition, whether in a commonly shared literacy center space or as a single integrated unit. We know from professional experience just how hard each of these support centers have worked to establish their own niches within an academy that often does not see their importance and considers their work to be remedial at best. But we believe strongly in an interdependent relation among these literacies, made not only more necessary but also more possible in the digital era. For integrated literacy centers to work, the educators staffing each support center must be assured they can join ranks with their fellow literacy professionals without, bluntly speaking, potential harm to their employment. Therefore, administrators at every level must foster the literacy center educators' satisfaction with their intricate, complex, and rhetorically interrelated tasks. Above all, WPAs—particularly those who are tenured or have other assurances of job security—should be mindful of the considerable list of items above that are connected to student literacy support. They should engage with the separate literacy centers to devise an integration plan that works for the unique institutional setting and student population. Then, they should work with literacy center administrators to connect with and teach the institution's administration how and why such an integrated literacy center program is necessary. The literacy educators—both administrative and their consultants—must be well supported fiscally through sufficient staffing, pay, professional development, job retention, and promotion, as well as temporally so they can provide the time students actually need with the twenty-first century's complex rhetorical and technological literacy tasks. We are aware that this future is not easily achieved, but the need for student support in these areas is so vital that every effort must be made to implement such foundational support structures.

Continuing Hybridization of Composition Instruction

Writing instruction's inherent connection to digitality is here to stay and will only continue to evolve. Composition instructors are using digital tools in one way or another in almost all classes, even if only to receive drafts or discuss web research articles. Hewett and Warnock write in "The Future of OWI," "We believe one major change in OWI will be the gradual—but not necessarily slow—diminishment of distinctive features between a hybrid online writing course and one that traditionally has been considered onsite and face-to-face" (548). They mean that the line, a blurry one revealed by the uncertainty in nomenclature such as *hybrid*, *blended*, and the like, will become even less distinct; even newer terms like *spatio-hybrid* and *chrono-hybrid* will require additional rethinking (see ch. 4 for more information regarding these terms). Instructors do not need to venture into fully online writing courses to think about, take advantage of, and—yes—be challenged by digital composition environments. They already inhabit this future!

Although we acknowledge the pitfalls of technological determinism, the concept that technology will dictate behaviors and even social structures, we also see that experiments with digital tools and applications can help instructors productively rethink their teaching, much as we have stressed throughout the book with our emphasis on reading and multimodality. Digitality invites the field to rethink every aspect of its theory and praxis. For example, every learning management system has a suite of tools and applications that, when explored, can offer new perspectives on how instructors conduct peer review, respond to student writing, organize students into groups, and even help students take notes. Teachers who are open to such opportunities can reinvigorate their teaching styles and approaches. As indicated by the yin and yang of OWI principles 3 and 4 (CCCC, Committee 12, 14) and GSOLE OLI principle 3, tenets 4 and 5, instructors can migrate and adapt current teaching approaches and develop appropriate new ones—all without sacrificing their fundamental teaching selves.

Paying Attention to the Student and to Studenting

A recent trend in academe is the conversation surrounding user-centered experience in composition classrooms, and a major theme of this book is access. Many instructors are challenged in all environments to work with students, helping them to better understand their experiences with course curriculum, including such course documents as assignment sheets and syllabi. Administrators work with their institutions to perform usability tests of online courses to serve students taking the courses and, in training practices, to guide instructors to design their courses for actual students, not just hypothetical ones that might take their courses (see T. Bourelle et al., *Administering Writing Programs*; Bartolotta et al.). In "User-Centered Design as a Foundation for Effective Online Writing Instruction," Michael Greer and Heidi Harris state, "Online writing instruction as a discipline stands to benefit from a deeper engagement with the practices and mindset of user experience design because of the changing dynamics of our students" (15); they refer to OWI, but we believe their words relate to teaching literacy in the digital era overall. Even when usability testing of course design and curriculum cannot occur, instructors should be talking with their students to learn what works, what does not work, and what is unclear. These access issues are crucial to teaching and learning.

Writing studies should conduct more field and empirical research regarding the needs of the diverse student population entering the twenty-first-century classroom. How can educators best offer anti-racist and diversity-aware instruction? How can they honor students' language uses (for only one example) and prepare them well for life beyond school? Some of the conversations we hear in conference meeting rooms and hallways and read on email lists include asking how instructors do and should approach teaching standardized English in the classroom while honoring the various ways that students use language and engage dialogue in spaces outside the classroom walls. As we suggest in our introduction, there are no easy ways to approach these facets of education because they are human issues with no certain answers; thus, they require conversations open to the probable reasoning we have argued throughout this book. Certainly, discussions must be had at conferences, in scholarship, in departments, and even inside classrooms with students. Educators will create this future by active talk and listening, by cooperative dialogue, and certainly through skillful rhetorical interactions.

To underscore the importance of this work as it relates to student success, writing studies scholars have been involved in vigorous research about code switching, code meshing, and translanguaging, often discussing which of these terms should be applied regarding language use as well as how to address them in postsecondary classrooms. Beyond discussion of the terms, teachers and scholars alike have argued for valuing the variety of languages, dialects, and registers used by students in the twenty-first century (Perryman-Clark; Williams-Farrier; V. Young et al.; V. Young). These areas of inquiry are not new—recalling the National Council of Teachers of English's *Students' Right to Their Own Language*—but their widespread emergence in writing classes will be. One only need look at popular first-year writing course textbooks to see that mainstream writing instruction is not sure how to proceed. Although it is increasingly recognized that teachers cannot simply and uncritically advocate standardized written English as a way to "protect" students down the line, there are good, interesting challenges about how to teach such approaches, including teachers' uncertainty about their own knowledge and beliefs about language use.

Moreover, all writing instructors must become more aware of their part in developing courses that encourage equality and inclusion. In *Culturally Sustaining Pedagogies*, Django Paris and H. Samy Alim argue that this goal must not be seen as getting students "of color to speak/write/ be more like the middle-class White ones" (3). It is crucial, they indicate, that instructors must recognize, value, and honor cultural, linguistic, and racial diversity, which are core values that we advocate for in this volume and in our companion volume, *Administering Writing Programs in the Twenty-First Century*. Faculty members like Professor Jackson should strive to integrate a diversity of materials into a course. Chapters 2 and 10 of this book challenge faculty members to understand and work toward approaching their implicit biases as a barrier to student success and using communication strategies that will help when barriers become clear. Specifically, instructors should read about anti-racist pedagogies (see Condon and Young; Inoue, *Antiracist Writing Assessment Ecologies*). Everyone in writing studies should participate in this important work, not only reading about anti-racist pedagogies, but also implementing research into them and, minimally, investigating their own practices.

Finally, as society and the media people use to communicate continue to change, it is critical to examine how rhetoric, especially dialogue, is taught. Dialogue will occur in future spaces people have not yet imagined. In chapter 8, we note that such media will evolve, changing their audience and purpose; new platforms will be invented, and students undoubtedly will use these for communicating. Even if instructors do not use these communicative channels as much as students, they still have a duty to teach responsible, ethical ways of interacting with others in these platforms. We argue that educators should teach students not only to think critically, but also to listen and read critically, responding to one another with sensitivity and compassion. This duty does not mean instructors should guide students to think (or believe) a certain way, but rather that they should guide students to think about all the issues surrounding a topic, who might be affected, how different lived experiences shape opinions, and how to honor those differences when inevitable disagreements arise. Ultimately, just as educators need to consider the human element when teaching, they must help students understand the human element and need for probable reasoning in all ways of communicating.

Contingency in Writing Studies Instruction

We have talked a great deal in this book about studenting and what students need from their composition experiences in the digital era. That is as it should be in a rhetoric for writing instructors. There is another human element that needs more attention, however: composition instructors themselves, which includes all those who teach reading, alphabetic writing, multimodal composition, and the rhetorical and technological literacies incumbent on them. As we argue in *Administering Writing Programs in the Twenty-First Century*, contemporary instructors like Professor Jackson benefit from training to teach composition in the digital era, but they need support. We describe teaching writing and literacy, composition and rhetoric as open-ended and exciting—the latter is the exact word we use at times in this book—but we recognize that for many, teaching writing often becomes a cross-the-finish-line slog because of pay, work conditions, and contingency issues. This is a book about teaching primarily, but we hope readers will step into WPA Garcia's shoes for a few minutes. She must be concerned with the macro teaching conditions of literacy instruction because those conditions relate to teaching perhaps more directly than in other disciplines.

Far too many faculty members at any given institution are contingently employed, and in some regions, this largely unseen army often teaches most composition classes across multiple institutions. This condition does not recognize the reality that both extensive knowledge and tremendous creativity go into rhetorically and technologically strong literacy instruction, and that creativity particularly needs time and mental space to flourish. Those freeway flyers who teach six, seven, or eight sections of writing at four, five, or six schools—those who are teaching fully loaded sections that add up to well over one hundred students per term—will find scant time for the professional development that builds great Generalist 3.0 teaching or that permits of future Generalists 4.0. There are playbooks for writing instructor activism, and this book cannot take on that role, but we acknowledge the challenge of building professional conversations among people who do not have the time: This is a long-standing problem of writing program administration that the field needs to address through systematic changes, treating all instructors like valued faculty members. The current employment structure, as well as its nomenclature of contingency and adjunction, must be reexamined, as part-time educators are the faculty members so often pulling the heaviest burden of the important literacy work described in this book. (Because it may seem undignified to call teaching composition a burden, perhaps we should be clearer and say that teaching composition to upwards of one hundred students in sixteen weeks or less is, indeed, a burden.) Because of their high teaching load—necessitated by embarrassingly insufficient wages—they will be overwhelmed trying to keep up with composition's evolution in both what they are required to teach and what they know they should teach in the digital era, potentially harming their ongoing employability.

Not only does the current faculty structure in postsecondary composition hurt the very people it relies on but also the entire writing studies field by giving the unfortunate and entirely incorrect impression that "anybody can teach English" and that these anybodies can be treated with disdain within the academy. No. This belief must be quelled by the very people who have allowed it to continue in far too many institutions. As we have shown in every chapter of this book, the multiliteracies of reading, alphabetic writing, and multimodal composition require thoughtful, intellectually deep, pedagogically (and andragogically) skilled, and communicatively wise educators. When the silos of individual literacy territories are removed, the need for educators' intelligent, interdependent work is revealed, and it becomes clear that this critical literacy work of writing instruction and all it entails requires educators who are compensated fairly, given ample professional development, and provided a genuine faculty voice.

Ongoing Professionalization and Certification

Deeply connected to contingency issues is that of professional development. Despite the extraordinary amount of intellectual and, yes, physical labor that goes into teaching reading, alphabetic writing, and multimodal composition, the writing studies field has too few agreed-on professional standards, pillars, or guidelines of excellence beyond the Council of Writing Program Administrators' contested "WPA Outcomes Statement." Higher education more broadly suffers from this problem, including how to use these practices effectively in the classroom, but it is accentuated in writing studies, if for no other reasons than there are so many people who teach in these areas and contingency and professional equality are such significant problems.

The primary writing studies organizations have not served as certifying bodies, with some exceptions, such as the tutoring and tutor training certifications offered by the College Reading and Learning Association. We attempt to cover a lot of ground in describing and advising what teaching writing in the twenty-first century is about. One book—or even a library of them—cannot do the entire job, however. Educators are needed to prepare other educators. For that reason, we call for a future in which writing-studies-driven certifying bodies provide necessary human-based—albeit digitally enhanced—education for twenty-first-century writing instructors. Certification processes and the professionalization that accompanies them would be good for writing studies educators—if such processes were created by actual instructors to address the specificities of contemporary literacy instruction in the digital era. For instance, many who teach in online writing programs have discussed with us the challenges of undergoing certification by Quality Matters, which has excellent tools to evaluate online learning offerings, but is limited, as is the case with many aspects of the conversation around online learning, in that its focus is on content courses. As an alternative, GSOLE has developed a broad certification process for literacy-focused tutors and teachers. This realizable future can benefit faculty of all disciplines, given that literacy education is the task of the entire academy.

Why should researchers, WPAs, and all composition instructors be aggressive here? They might view the need to prepare themselves and others for Generalist 3.0 (and 4.0) work as analogous to how composition treated the machine grading of student writing: The field did not act, and now these types of applications have spread like kudzu (Haswell, "Automatons"), yet they do little to help teaching and learning. If educators do not design professional development standards and processes that make sense based on writing class and program outcomes—as well as on the characteristics inherent in genuine student writing—without question such standards and processes will be defined for them by outside entities and implemented upon the field. Going forward, composition instructors need to join in professional organizations to construct and pilot ways of teaching one another the best, most effective practices of literacy instruction available for digital-era education. Teaching literacy in the digital era introduces human elements to instruction, on-site and online, that are difficult to see in more content-based courses. To this end, writing studies educators should consider how digitality provides entrée into empirically developed professional development that should inform student-centered teacher training going forward.

Conclusion

The field of writing studies remains intricately connected with what happens in classrooms. Joseph Harris indicated as much in naming *A Teaching Subject* as the title of his historical perspective on the field. From the stores of composition and rhetoric knowledge, we have aimed to build an approach to teaching that reflects long-standing practices while also considering the technologies and contexts of the twenty-first century. Writing studies has been experiencing a general push toward reproducible, empirical work. In considering our pedagogically driven book, we offer a straightforward instructional model—certainly not novel—that may be usable to develop more standardized research studies of writing and writing instruction across multiple institutions. Perhaps with such studies, effective (if not best) practices can emerge, leading to recognizable and shareable new knowledge about accessible teaching practices, student composing, and writing and literacy improvement.

This book provides context and application for instructors like Professor Jackson to teach in contemporary composition classroom settings. Nonetheless, instructors should remain flexible with their teaching styles and approaches, rhetorically considering why and how they engage with digitality in their classes. These skills will help them no matter what technological and pedagogical changes they may encounter throughout their teaching careers.

No one could have predicted the communication changes that have occurred and have had an impact on society after the Industrial Revolution. As we argue in chapter 1, composition and its rhetorical connections continue to evolve, and the future remains (delightfully) uncertain, such that educators can build a future that meets students' composing needs for academe and their world-at-large communications. The writing studies field also continues to evolve, opening the future to thoughtful research and engaged collaboration among educators while encouraging them to approach digital technology with excitement and to review composition in a new light. In this chapter, we have reimagined the critical literacies of reading, alphabetic writing, and multimodal composition as the new digital-era composition, urging instructors to be prepared for change while encouraging them that such change will come through them with exciting advancements in how writing and literacy are taught—and studented.

We hope the insights and advice in this book will guide composition instructors into and through the next, Generalist 4.0 phase of rhetorical, cultural, and digital change.

Notes on the Authors

Beth L. Hewett is a well-known expert in online literacy instruction, the founding president of the Global Society of Online Literacy Educators, and the founding owner and executive coach of Defend and Publish, an online academic writing-coaching business. She is the author or coauthor of numerous books, articles, and book chapters regarding writing in the digital era. Her books include *Administering Writing Programs in the Twenty-First Century*, *The Online Writing Conference: A Guide for Teachers and Tutors*, *Reading to Learn and Writing to Teach: Literacy Strategies for Online Writing Instruction*, *Foundational Practices of Online Writing Instruction*, and *A Scholarly Edition of Samuel P. Newman's* A Practical System of Rhetoric. Currently, in response to the losses surrounding the COVID-19 virus, she is working on her fourth book about grief and bereavement support.

Tiffany Bourelle is an associate professor in the Department of English Language and Literature at the University of New Mexico, where she teaches multimodal composition and professional writing. Her research focuses on enhancing pedagogy in composition and technical communication classes, in both face-to-face and online formats. She is lead author of *Administering Writing Programs in the Twenty-First Century* and coeditor of *Women's Professional Lives in Rhetoric and Composition: Choice, Chance, and Serendipity*. Her work has been published in such journals as *Technical Communication Quarterly*, *WPA: Writing Program Administration*, *Computers and Composition*, and *Kairos: A Journal of Rhetoric, Technology, and Pedagogy*.

Scott Warnock is professor of English and associate dean of undergraduate education in the College of Arts and Sciences at Drexel University. He is the author of *Teaching Writing Online: How and Why* and coauthor of *Administering Writing Programs in the Twenty-First Century* and, with

Diana Gasiewski, *Writing Together: Ten Weeks Teaching and Studenting in an Online Writing Course*. His work includes numerous chapters and journal articles about online writing instruction, computers and composition, and educational technology. Warnock served as president of the Global Society of Online Literacy Educators from 2018 to 2020 and cochair of the Conference on College Composition and Communication Committee for Effective Practices in Online Writing Instruction from 2011 to 2016. He has maintained the blog *Online Writing Teacher* since 2005.

Works Cited

Adams, Dale, and Robert Kline. "The Use of Films in Teaching Composition." *College Composition and Communication*, vol. 26, no. 3, 1975, pp. 258–62.

Adler-Kassner, Linda, and Elizabeth Wardle. *Naming What We Know: Threshold Concepts of Writing Studies*. Utah State UP, 2015.

Alexander, Jonathan, and Jacqueline Rhodes. *On Multimodality: New Media in Composition Studies*. Conference on College Composition and Communication / National Council of Teachers of English, 2014.

Ambrose, Susan. A., et al. "Why Do Student Development and Course Climate Matter for Student Learning?" *How Learning Works: Seven Research-Based Principles for Smart Teaching*, John Wiley and Sons, 2010, pp. 153–87.

Americans with Disabilities Act of 1990, as Amended. *ADA National Network*, www.ada .gov/pubs/adastatute08.htm.

Anderson, Daniel. "The Low Bridge to High Benefits: Entry-Level Multimedia, Literacies, and Motivation." *Computers and Composition*, vol. 25, no. 1, 2008, pp. 40–60.

Anderson, Floyd D., and Matthew T. Althouse. "Five Fingers or Six? Pentad or Hexad?" *K. B. Journal*, vol. 6, no. 2, Spring 2010, p. 1.

Anderson, Paul V. "Professional and Technical Writing/Ethics/Cultures." 2019. *Wikibooks: Open Books for an Open World*, 17 May 2020, en.wikibooks.org/wiki/ Professional_and_Technical_Writing/Ethics/Cultures.

Andriotis, Nikos. "What Is Just-in Time Training (and the Best Practices to Adopt It for Your Business)." *eFront*, www.efrontlearning.com/blog/2017/10/just-time-training -best-practices-adopt-business.html.

Anson, Chris M. "Process Pedagogy and Its Legacy." Tate et al., pp. 212–30.

Apps, Jerold W. *Mastering the Teaching of Adults*. Krieger Publishing, 1991.

Arbaugh, J. B. "How Classroom Environment and Student Engagement Affect Learning in Internet-Based MBA Courses." *Business Communication Quarterly*, vol. 63, no. 4, 2000, pp. 9–26.

Aristotle. *The "Art" of Rhetoric*. Translated by John Henry Freese, Harvard UP, 1982. Loeb Classical Library 193.

Augustine. *De doctrina Christiana*. Oxford UP, 1995.

Babcock, Rebecca Day, and Terese Thonus. *Researching the Writing Center: Towards an Evidence-Based Practice*, rev. ed., Peter Lang, 2018.

Bacon, Francis. *The Advancement of Learning*. 1605. Paul Dry Books, 2001.

Bakhtin, Mikhail. *The Dialogic Imagination: Four Essays*. Edited by Michael Holquist, translated by Caryl Emerson and Holquist, U of Texas P, 1981.

Ball, Cheryl E. "Multimodal Revision Techniques in Webtexts." *Classroom Discourse*, vol. 5, no. 1, 2014, pp. 91–105.

———. "Show, Not Tell: The Value of New Media Scholarship." *Computers and Composition*, vol. 21, no. 4, 2004, pp. 403–25.

Ball, Cheryl E., and Colin Charlton. "All Writing is Multimodal." Adler-Kassner and Wardle, pp. 42–43.

Baron, Dennis. "From Pencils to Pixels: The Stages of Literacy Technologies." *Literacy: A Critical Sourcebook*, edited by Ellen Cushman et al., Bedford, 2001, pp. 70–84.

Bartholomae, David, and Anthony Petrosky. *Ways of Reading: An Anthology for Writers*. 6th ed., Boston: Bedford / St. Martin's, 2002.

Bartolotta, Joseph, et al. "Revising the Online Classroom: Usability Testing for Training Online Technical Communication Instructors." *Technical Communication Quarterly*, vol. 26, no. 3, 2017, pp. 287–99.

Bawarshi, Anis S., and Mary Jo Reiff. *Genre: An Introduction to History, Theory, Research, and Pedagogy*. Parlor Press, 2010.

Bazerman, Charles. "Discursively Structured Activities." *Mind, Culture, and Activity*, vol. 4, no. 4, 1997, pp. 296–308.

———. "Writing Expresses and Shares Meaning to Be Reconstructed by the Reader." Adler-Kassner and Wardle, pp. 21–23.

Bean, John C. "Computerized Word-Processing as an Aid to Revision." *College Composition and Communication*, vol. 34, no. 2, 1983, pp. 146–48.

Bennett, Milton. J. "Becoming Interculturally Competent." *Toward Multiculturalism: A Reader in Multicultural Education*, edited by Jaime S. Wurzel, Intercultural Resource Corporation, 2004, pp. 62–77.

Berlin, James. "Contemporary Composition: The Major Pedagogical Theories." *College English*, vol. 44, no. 8, Dec. 1982, pp. 765–77.

———. *Writing Instruction in Nineteenth-Century American Colleges*. Southern Illinois UP, 1984.

———. "Writing Instruction in School and College English, 1890–1985." *Short History of Writing Instruction: From Ancient Greece to Twentieth-Century America*, edited by James L. Murphy, Routledge, 2012, pp. 183–222.

Berthoff, Anne E. *The Making of Meaning: Metaphors, Models, and Maxims for Writing Teachers*. Heinemann, 1981.

Bessette, Jean. "Queer Rhetoric in Situ." *Rhetoric Review*, vol. 35, no. 2, 2016, pp. 148–64.

Bitzer, Lloyd. "The Rhetorical Situation." *Philosophy and Rhetoric*, vol. 1, no. 1, Jan. 1968, pp. 1–14.

Bizzell, Patricia, and Bruce Herzberg. *The Rhetorical Tradition: Readings from Classical Times to the Present*. Bedford, 2001.

Blair, Hugh. *Lectures on Rhetoric and Belles Lettres*. Edited by Harold F. Harding, Harvard UP, 1982. 2 vols.

Blair, Kristine. "Teaching Multimodal Assignments in OWI Contexts." Hewett and DePew, pp. 477–98.

Blair, Leslie. "Teaching Composition Online: No Longer the Second Best Choice." *Kairos*, vol. 8, no. 2, 2003, kairos.technorhetoric.net/8.2/binder.html?praxis/blair/index .html.

Bolter, Jay David, and Richard Grusin. *Remediation: Understanding New Media*. MIT Press, 2000.

Borton, Sonya, and Brian Huot. "Responding and Assessing." Selfe, *Multimodal Composition*, pp. 99–112.

Bourelle, Andrew, et al. "Multimodality in the Technical Communication Classroom: Viewing Classical Rhetoric through a Twenty-First-Century Lens." *Technical Communication Quarterly*, vol. 24, no. 4, Aug. 2015, doi:10.1080/10572252.2015.1078 847.

Bourelle, Andrew, et al. "Sites of Multimodal Literacy: Comparing Student Learning in Online and Face-to-Face Environments." *Computers and Composition*, vol. 39, no. 1, 2016, pp. 55–70.

Bourelle, Tiffany, and Beth L. Hewett. "Training Instructors to Teach Multimodal Composition in Online Courses." *Handbook of Research on Writing and Composing in the Age of MOOCs*, edited by Elizabeth Monske and Kristine Blair, IGI Global, 2017, pp. 348–69.

Bourelle, Tiffany, et al. *Administering Writing Programs in the Twenty-First Century*. Modern Language Association of America, 2021.

Bourelle, Tiffany, et al. "Designing Online Writing Classes to Promote Multimodal Literacies: Five Practices for Course Design." *Communication Design Quarterly Review*, vol. 5, no. 1, 2017, pp. 80–88.

Bourelle, Tiffany, et al. "Teaching with Instructional Assistants: Enhancing Student Learning in Online Classes." *Computers and Composition*, vol. 37, no. 2, 2015, pp. 90–103.

Bowen, Tracey, and Carl Whithaus, editors. *Multimodal Literacies and Emerging Genres*. U of Pittsburgh P, 2013.

Bowie, Jennifer L. "Beyond the Universal: The Universe of Users Approach to User-Centered Design." *Rhetorically Rethinking Usability: Theories, Practices, and Methodologies*, edited by Susan K. Miller-Cochran and Rochelle L. Rodrigo, Hampton Press, 2009, pp. 15–31.

Brandt, Deborah. "Accumulating Literacy: Writing and Learning to Write in the Twentieth Century." *College English*, vol. 57, no. 6, 1995, 649–68.

Brannon, Lil, and C. H. Knoblauch. "On Students' Rights to Their Own Texts: A Model of Teacher Response." *College Composition and Communication*, vol. 33, no. 2, 1982, pp. 157–66.

Breuch, Lee-Ann Kastman. "Faculty Preparation for OWI." Hewett and DePew, pp. 349–87.

———. "Post-Process 'Pedagogy': A Philosophical Exercise." *JAC*, vol. 22, no. 1, 2002, pp. 119–50.

Brick, Billy, and Jasper Holmes. "Using Screen Capture Software for Student Feedback: Towards a Methodology." IADIS International Conference on Cognition and Exploratory Learning in the Digital Age, Jan. 2008. *IADIS*, 2021, www.iadisportal.org/digital-library/using-screen-capture-software-for-student-feedback-towards-a-methodology.

Britton, James, et al. *The Development of Writing Abilities (11–18)*. Macmillan Education, 1975.

Bruffee, Kenneth A. "Collaborative Learning and the 'Conversation of Mankind.'" *College English*, vol. 46, no. 7, Nov. 1984, pp. 635–53.

———. *Collaborative Learning: Higher Education, Interdependence, and the Authority of Knowledge*. Johns Hopkins UP, 1993.

Buber, Martin. *I and Thou*. Translated by Ronald Gregor Smith, 2nd ed., Macmillan, 1958.

Buckingham, David. "Digital Media Literacies: Rethinking Media Education in the Age of the Internet." *Research in Comparative and International Education*, vol. 2, no. 1, 2007, pp. 43–55.

Burke, Kenneth. *A Grammar of Motives*. 1945. U of California P, 1969.

———. *A Rhetoric of Motives*. U of California P, 1969.

Burroughs, Siew C. "Rhetorician." Enos, pp. 630–31.

Burton, Gideon O. "Content/Form (Res/Verba, Logos/Lexis)." *Silva Rhetoricae*, rhetoric.byu.edu/Encompassing%20Terms/Content%20and%20Form.htm.

Butler, Paul. *The Writer's Style: A Rhetorical Field Guide*. Utah State UP, 2018.

Campbell, George. *The Philosophy of Rhetoric*. Edited by Lloyd F. Bitzer, Southern Illinois UP, 1988.

Carillo, Ellen C. *MLA Guide to Digital Literacy*. Modern Language Association of America, 2019.

———. *Securing a Place for Reading in Composition: The Importance of Teaching for Transfer*. Utah State UP, 2015.

Carroll, Lewis. *Jabberwocky*. Illustrated by John Boyden, Farthing Press, 1976.

Carter, Joyce Locke. "2016 CCCC Chair's Address: Making, Disrupting, Innovating." *College Composition and Communication*, vol. 68, no. 2, Dec. 2016, library.ncte.org/ journals/CCC/issues/v68-2/28886.

Cassorla, Leah Frieda. *The Shifting Sands of Authority in the Age of Digital Convergence.* 2015. The Florida State U, PhD dissertation.

Chaiklin, Seth. "The Zone of Proximal Development in Vygotsky's Analysis of Learning and Instruction." *Vygotsky's Educational Theory and Practice in Cultural Context*, edited by Alex Kozulin et al., Cambridge UP, 2003, pp. 39–64.

Chemin, Anne. "Handwriting vs Typing: Is the Pen Still Mightier Than the Keyboard?" *The Guardian*, vol. 16, December 2014, theguardian.com/science/2014/dec/16/ cognitive-benefits-handwriting-decline-typing.

Cho, Moon-Heum, and Scott Tobias. "Should Instructors Require Discussion in Online Courses? Effects of Online Discussion on Community of Inquiry, Learner Time, Satisfaction, and Achievement." *The International Review of Research in Open and Distributed Learning*, vol. 17, no. 2, 2016, doi.org/10.19173/irrodl.v17i2.2342.

Cicero. *Cicero II:* De inventione, De optimo genere oratorum, Topica. Translated by E. W. Sutton and H. Rackham, Harvard UP, 1988. Loeb Classical Library 386.

———. *De inventione.* Cicero, *Cicero*, pp. 1–346.

———. *De oratore: Books 1–2.* Translated by E. W. Sutton and H. Rackham, Harvard UP, 1988. Loeb Classical Library 348.

———. *The Ideal Orator (De optimo genere oratorum).* Cicero, *Cicero*, pp. 347–73.

———. *Rhetorica ad Herennium.* Harvard UP, 1989. Loeb Classical Library 403.

Collins, Regina, et al. "Web-Based Portfolio Assessment: Validation of an Open Source Platform." *Journal of Interactive Learning Research*, vol. 24, no. 1, 2013, pp. 5–32.

Collison, George, et al. *Facilitating Online Learning: Effective Strategies for Moderators.* Atwood Publishing, 2000.

Condon, Frankie, and Vershawn Ashanti Young. *Performing Antiracist Pedagogy in Rhetoric, Writing, and Communication.* WAC Clearinghouse / UP of Colorado, 2017.

Conference on College Composition and Communication (CCCC). "CCCC Promotion and Tenure Guidelines for Work with Technology." *Conference on College Composition and Communication*, National Council of Teachers of English, Nov. 1998, rev. Nov. 2015, cccc.ncte.org/cccc/resources/positions/promotionandtenure.

———. "CCCC Statement on Globalization in Writing Studies Pedagogy and Research." *Conference on College Composition and Communication*, National Council of Teachers of English, Nov. 2017, cccc.ncte.org/cccc/resources/positions/globalization.

———. "CCCC Statement on Second Language Writing and Multilingual Writers." *Conference on College Composition and Communication*, National Council of Teachers of English, 2014, rev. May 2020, cccc.ncte.org/cccc/resources/positions/ secondlangwriting.

———. "Disability Studies in Composition: Position Statement on Policy and Best Practices." *Conference on College Composition and Communication*, National Council of Teachers of English, Mar. 2020, cccc.ncte.org/cccc/resources/positions/disabilitypolicy.

———. "Principles and Practices in Electronic Portfolios." *Conference on College Composition and Communication*, National Council of Teachers of English, Mar. 2015, cccc.ncte.org/cccc/resources/positions/electronicportfolios.

———. "Principles for the Postsecondary Teaching of Writing." *Conference on College Composition and Communication*, National Council of Teachers of English, 2013, rev. Mar. 2015, cccc.ncte.org/cccc/resources/positions/postsecondarywriting.

———. "Students' Right to Their Own Language." *College Composition and Communication*, vol. 25, no. 3, 1974, 1–32.

Conference on College Composition and Communication (CCCC), Committee for Effective Practices in Online Writing Instruction. *A Position Statement of Principles and Example Effective Practices for Online Writing Instruction (OWI)*. National Council of Teachers of English, Mar. 2013, www.ncte.org/library/NCTEFiles/Groups/CCCC/OWIPrinciples.pdf.

Cope, Bill, and Mary Kalantzis, editors. *Multiliteracies: Literacy Learning and the Design of Social Futures*. Psychology Press, 2000.

Corbett, Edward P. J. *Classical Rhetoric for the Modern Student*. Oxford UP, 1965.

Council of Writing Program Administrators (CWPA). "WPA Outcomes Statement for First-Year Composition (3.0): Approved July 17, 2014." *Council of Writing Program Administrators*, 2014, wpacouncil.org/aws/CWPA/pt/sd/news_article/243055/_PARENT/layout_details/false.

Crowe, Adam S. *A Futurist's Guide to Emergency Management*. CRC Press, 2015.

Crusius, Timothy W., and Carolyn E. Channell. *The Aims of Argument: A Rhetoric and Reader*. Mayfield, 1995.

Cui, Wenqi. "Rhetorical Listening Pedagogy: Promoting Communication across Cultural and Societal Groups with Video Narrative." *Computers and Composition*, vol. 54, Dec. 2019, pp. 1–14.

Daiute, Colette A. "The Computer as Stylus and Audience." *College Composition and Communication*, vol. 34, no. 2, 1983, pp. 134–45.

DeCuir-Gunby, Jessica, et al. "African American Professionals in Higher Education: Experiencing and Coping with Racial Microaggressions." *Race Ethnicity and Education*, vol. 23, no. 4, 2020, pp. 492–508.

Dei, George J. Sefa, and Rowena Linton. "Racism in Schools and Classrooms: Towards an Anti-Racist Pedagogy of Power and Systemic Privilege." *The Compassionate Educator: Understanding Social Issues and the Ethics of Care in Canadian Schools*, edited by Allyson Jule, CSP Books, 2019, pp. 271–92.

De Montes, L. E. Sujo, et al. "Power, Language, and Identity: Voices from an Online Course." *Computers and Composition*, vol. 19, no. 3, Oct. 2002, pp. 251–71.

DePalma, Michael-John. "Tracing Transfer Across Media: Investigating Writers' Perceptions of Cross-Contextual and Rhetorical Reshaping in Processes of Remediation." *College Composition and Communication*, vol. 66, no. 4, 2015, pp. 615–42.

DePew, Kevin Eric. "Moving toward Generalist 2.0 as a Strategy for Addressing Diversity." *CCCC Blog*. 6 Jan. 2011, cccc-blog.blogspot.com/2011/01/moving-toward -generalist-20-as-strategy.html.

———. "Preparing for the Rhetoricity of OWI." Hewett and DePew, pp. 439–67.

DePew, Kevin, and Heather Lettner-Rust. "Mediating Power: Distance Learning Interfaces, Classroom Epistemology, and the Gaze." *Computers and Composition*, vol. 26, no. 3, 2009, pp. 174–89.

Descartes, René. *Discourse on Method*. 1637. Discourse on Method *and* Meditations on First Philosophy, translated by Donald A. Cress, 4th ed., Hackett Publishing, 1998, pp. 1–45.

Devitt, Amy J. "Genre." Tate et al., pp. 146–62.

DeVoss, Dànielle Nicole, and James E. Porter. "Why Napster Matters to Writing: Filesharing as a New Ethic of Digital Delivery." *Computers and Composition*, vol. 23, no. 2, 2006, pp. 178–210.

Dewey, John. *Democracy and Education: An Introduction to the Philosophy of Education*. Macmillan, 1916.

Diab, Rasha, et al. "Making Commitments to Racial Justice Actionable." Condon and Young, pp. 19–40.

Downs, Doug, and Elizabeth Wardle. "Teaching about Writing, Righting Misconceptions: Re-envisioning 'First-Year Composition' as 'Introduction to Writing Studies.'" *College Composition and Communication*, vol. 58, no. 4, 2007, pp. 552–84.

Dryer, Dylan B., et al. "Revising FYC Outcomes for a Multimodal, Digitally Composed World: The 'WPA Outcomes Statement for First-Year Composition (Version 3.0).'" *WPA: Writing Program Administration*, vol. 38. no. 1, 2014, pp. 129–43.

Dubisar, Abby M., and Jason Palmeri. "Palin/Pathos/Peter Griffin: Political Video Remix and Composition Pedagogy." *Computers and Composition*, vol. 27, no. 2, 2010, pp. 77–93.

Duffy, John. "Ethical Rhetoric in Unethical Times: Five Strategies for the Writing Classroom." *Teacher-Scholar-Activist*, 30 Apr. 2019, teacher-scholar-activist.org/ 2019/04/30/ethical-rhetoric-in-unethical-times-five-strategies-for-the-writing -classroom/.

———. "The Good Writer: Virtue Ethics and the Teaching of Writing." *College English*, vol. 79, no. 3, 2017, pp. 229–50.

Edwards, Bruce. "Tagmemics." Enos, pp. 715–19.

Elbow, Peter. *Writing without Teachers*. Oxford UP, 1998.

Emig, Janet. *The Composing Processes of Twelfth Graders*. National Council of Teachers of English, 1971.

Enos, Teresa, editor. *Encyclopedia of Rhetoric and Composition: Communication from Ancient Times to the Information Age*. Garland Publishing, 1996.

Epner, Daniel E., and Walter F. Baile. "Wooden's Pyramid: Building a Hierarchy of Skills for Successful Communication." *Medical Teacher*, vol. 33, no. 1, 2011, pp. 39–43.

Estrem, Heidi. "Writing Is a Knowledge-Making Activity." Adler-Kassner and Wardle, pp. 19–20.

Fahle, Kimberly. *Collaboration and Community in Undergraduate Writing Synchronous Video Courses (SVCs)*. 2019. Old Dominion U, PhD dissertation.

"Family Educational Rights and Privacy Act (FERPA)." *U.S. Department of Education*, 15 Dec. 2020, www2.ed.gov/policy/gen/guid/fpco/ferpa/index.html.

"Fast Facts: Distance Learning." *National Center for Education Statistics*, US Department of Education, 2019, nces.ed.gov/fastfacts/display.asp?id=80.

"FERPA." *Protecting Student Privacy. U.S. Department of Education*, studentprivacy.ed .gov/node/548/.

Fleckenstein, Kristie S. *Embodied Literacies: Imageword and a Poetics of Teaching*. Southern Illinois UP, 2003.

Fleming, David. "Rhetoric and Argumentation." Tate et al., pp. 248–65.

Flower, Linda, and John R. Hayes. "A Cognitive Process Theory of Writing." *College Composition and Communication*, vol. 32, no. 4, 1981, pp. 365–87.

Fogarty, Daniel. *Roots for a New Rhetoric*. Bureau of Publications, Teacher's College, Columbia U, 1959.

Freese, John Henry. Introduction. Aristotle, pp. xi–xxxi.

Freire, Paolo. *Pedagogy of the Oppressed*. Translated by Myra Bergman Ramos, Herder and Herder, 1971.

Gabor, Catherine. Review of *Multiliteracy Centers: Writing Center Work, New Media, and Multimodal Rhetoric*, edited by David M. Sheridan and James A. Inman. *Praxis: A Writing Center Journal*, vol. 1, no. 9, 2012, pp. 1–3.

Garrison, D. Randy, and Zehra Akyol. "The Community of Inquiry Theoretical Framework." *Handbook of Distance Education*. Edited by Michael Grahame Moore, Routledge, 2013, pp. 122–38.

Garrison, D. Randy, et al. "Critical Inquiry in a Text-Based Environment: Computer Conferencing in Higher Education." *The Internet and Higher Education*, vol. 2, nos. 2–3, 1999, pp. 87–105.

———. "The First Decade of the Community of Inquiry Framework: A Retrospective." *The Internet and Higher Education*, vol. 13, nos. 1–2, 2010, pp. 5–9.

Gee, James Paul. *Teaching, Learning, Literacy in Our High-Risk High-Tech World: A Framework for Becoming Human*. Teachers College Press, 2017.

Gee, James Paul, and Elisabeth R. Hayes. *Language and Learning in the Digital Age*. Routledge, 2011.

Gere, Anne Ruggles. "Talking in Writing Groups." *Perspectives on Talk and Learning*, edited by Susan Hynds and Donald L. Rubin, National Council of Teachers of English, 1990, pp. 115–28.

Gilboy, Mary Beth, et al. "Enhancing Student Engagement Using the Flipped Classroom." *Journal of Nutrition Education and Behavior*, vol. 47, no. 1, 2015, pp. 109–14.

Glazier, Rebecca A. "Building Rapport to Improve Retention and Success in Online Classes." *Journal of Political Science Education*, vol. 12, no. 4, 2016, pp. 437–56.

Glenn, Cheryl, and Krista Ratcliffe, editors. *Silence and Listening as Rhetorical Arts*. Southern Illinois UP, 2011.

Global Society of Online Literacy Educators (GSOLE). "Online Literacy Instruction Principles and Tenets." *Global Society of Online Literacy Educators*, 2020, www.glcsole .org/oli-principles.html.

Gos, Michael. "Nontraditional Student Access to OWI." Hewett and DePew, pp. 309–46.

Graff, Gerald, and Cathy Birkenstein. *They Say, I Say: The Moves that Matter in Academic Writing*. W. W. Norton, 2018.

Grant, M., and H. Thornton. "Best Practices in Undergraduate Adult-Centered Online Learning: Mechanisms for Course Design and Delivery." *Journal of Online Learning and Teaching*, vol. 4, no. 3, 2007, pp. 346–56.

Greer, Michael, and Heidi Harris. "User-Centered Design as a Foundation for Effective Online Writing Instruction." *Computers and Composition*, vol. 49, no. 3, 2018, pp. 18–24.

Griffin, June, and Deborah Minter. "The Rise of the Online Writing Classroom: Reflecting on the Material Conditions of College Composition Teaching." *College Composition and Communication*, vol. 65, no. 1, 2013, pp. 140–61.

Hafner, Joshua. "North Carolina Boy Punished for Calling Teacher 'Ma'am' at School, Report Says." *USAToday*, 27 Aug. 2018, usatoday.com/story/news/nation-now/ 2018/08/27/boy-punished-calling-teacher-maam-north-carolina-report-says/ 1108472002/.

Hairston, Maxine. "The Winds of Change: Thomas Kuhn and the Revolution in the Teaching of Writing." *College Composition and Communication*, vol. 33, no. 1, 1982, pp. 76–88.

Handayani, Nani Sri. "Emerging Roles in Scripted Online Collaborative Writing in Higher Education Context." *Procedia: Social and Behavioral Sciences*, vol. 67, 2012, pp. 370–79.

Hanna, Donald E., et al. *147 Practical Tips for Teaching Online Groups*. Atwood Publishing, 2000.

Harrington, Susanmarie, et al., editors. *The Outcomes Book: Debate and Consensus after the "WPA Outcomes Statement."* Utah State UP, 2005.

Harris, Frank, III, and J. Luke Wood. Addressing Racial Bias and Microaggressions in the Online Environment. *Cora Learning*, coralearning.org/webinars/.

———. Employing Equity-Minded and Culturally Affirming Teaching Practices and Virtual Learning Communities. *Cora Learning*, coralearning.org/webinars/.

Harris, Heidi, et al. "A Call for Purposeful Pedagogy-Driven Course Design in OWI." *Research in Online Literacy Education (ROLE)*, vol. 2, no. 1, 2019, www.roleolor.org/a-call-for-purposeful-pedagogy-driven-course-design-in-owi.html.

Harris, Joseph. "The Essay as Form in a Digital Age." Reichert Powell, *Writing*, pp. 123–37.

———. "The Idea of Community in the Study of Writing." *College Composition and Communication*, vol. 40, no. 1, Feb. 1989, pp. 11–22.

———. *A Teaching Subject: Composition Teaching Since 1966*. Prentice Hall, 1996.

Harris, Muriel. *Teaching One-to-One: The Writing Conference*. National Council of Teachers of English, 1986.

Haswell, Richard H. "Automatons and Automated Scoring: Drudges, Black Boxes, and Dei ex Machina." *Machine Scoring of Student Essays: Truth and Consequences*, edited by Patricia Freitag Ericsson and Haswell, Utah State UP, 2006, pp. 57–78.

———. "Minimal Marking." *College English*, vol. 45, no. 6, 1983, pp. 600–04.

Hawisher, Gail E. "Electronic Meetings of the Minds: Research, Electronic Conferences, and Composition Studies." *Re-imagining Computers and Composition: Teaching and Research in the Virtual Age*, edited by Hawisher and Paul LeBlanc, Boynton, 1992, pp. 81–101.

———. "Research Update: Writing and Word Processing." *Computers and Composition*, vol. 5, no. 2, 1988, pp. 7–27.

Hawisher, Gail E., and Cynthia Selfe. "The Rhetoric of Technology and the Electronic Writing Class." *College Composition and Communication*, vol. 42, no. 1, Feb. 1991, pp. 55–65.

———. "Studying Literacy in Digital Contexts: Computers and Composition Studies." *Exploring Composition Studies: Sites, Issues, Perspectives*, edited by Kelly Ritter and Paul Kei Matsuda, Utah State UP, 2012, pp. 188–98.

Hawisher, Gail E., et al. *Computers and the Teaching of Writing in American Higher Education, 1979–1994: A History*. Ablex Publishing, 1996.

Herzberg, Bruce. "Ramus, Peter (1515–1572)." Enos, pp. 587–88.

Hewett, Beth L. "Asynchronous Online Instructional Commentary: A Study of Student Revision." *Readerly/Writerly Texts: Essays in Literary, Composition, and Pedagogical Theory*, vols. 11–12, nos. 1–2, 2004–05, pp. 47–67.

———. "Characteristics of Interactive Oral and Computer-Mediated Peer Group Talk and Its Influence on Revision." *Computers and Composition*, vol. 17, no. 3, 2000, pp. 265–88.

———. "From Topic to Presentation: Making Choices to Develop Your Writing." *Writing Spaces: Readings on Writing*. Edited by Charles Lowe and Pavel Zemliansky, vol. 1, Parlor Press, 2010, pp. 59–81.

———. "Fully Online and Hybrid." Tate et al., pp. 194–211.

———. "Grounding Principles of OWI." Hewett and DePew, pp. 33–92.

———. *The Online Writing Conference: A Guide for Teachers and Tutors*. Bedford / St. Martin's, 2015.

———. *Reading to Learn and Writing to Teach: Literacy Strategies for Online Writing Instruction*. Bedford / St. Martin's, 2015.

———. *A Scholarly Edition of Samuel P. Newman's* A Practical System of Rhetoric. Brill, 2020.

———. "Synchronous Online Conference-Based Instruction: A Study of Whiteboard Interactions and Student Writing." *Computers and Composition*, vol. 23, no. 1, 2006, 4–31.

———. "Theoretical Underpinnings of Online Writing Labs (OWLs)." *The OWL Construction and Maintenance Guide*, Edited by James A. Inman and Clinton Gardner, International Writing Center Association Press, 2002, www.defendandpublish.com/v2/wp-content/uploads/2011/05/OWL_Theory.pdf.

Hewett, Beth L., and Kevin Eric DePew, editors. *Foundational Practices of Online Writing Instruction*. Parlor Press, 2015.

Hewett, Beth L., and Christa Ehmann. *Preparing Educators for Online Writing Instruction: Principles and Processes*. National Council of Teachers of English, 2004.

Hewett, Beth L., and Scott Warnock. "The Future of OWI." Hewett and DePew, pp 547–63.

———. "Writing MOOEEs? Reconsidering MOOCs in Light of the OWI Principles." Monske and Blair, pp. 17–38.

"Higher Ed Course Design Rubric Standards." *Quality Matters (QM)*, 2021, www.qualitymatters.org/qa-resources/rubric-standards/higher-ed-rubric.

Hilliard, Lyra P., and Mary K. Stewart. "Time Well Spent: Creating a Community of Inquiry in Blended First-Year Writing Courses." *The Internet and Higher Education*, vol. 41, 2019, pp. 11–24.

Hodges, Charles, et al. "The Difference Between Emergency Remote Teaching and Online Learning." *Educause Review*, 27 Mar. 2020, er.educause.edu/articles/2020/3/the-difference-between-emergency-remote-teaching-and-online-learning.

Holpuch, Amanda. "US's Digital Divide 'Is Going to Kill People' as Covid-19 Exposes Inequalities." *The Guardian*, 13 Apr. 2020, www.theguardian.com/world/2020/apr/13/coronavirus-covid-19-exposes-cracks-us-digital-divide.

hooks, bell. *Teaching to Transgress: Education as the Practice of Freedom*. Routledge, 1994.

Horner, Bruce. "Modality as Social Practice in Written Language." Reichert Powell, *Writing*, pp. 21–40.

Horning, Alice. "Reading across the Curriculum as the Key to Student Success." *Across the Disciplines*, vol. 4, 2007, pp. 1–18, wac.colostate.edu/ATD/articles/horning2007.cfm.

———. *Reading, Writing, and Digitizing: Understanding Literacy in the Electronic Age*. Cambridge Scholars Publishing, 2013.

———. "Writing and Reading across the Curriculum: Best Practices and Practical Guidelines." *Reconnecting Reading and Writing*, edited by Alice S. Horning and Elizabeth W. Kraemer, Parlor Press / WAC Clearinghouse, 2013, pp. 71–88.

Howard, Rebecca Moore. *Standing in the Shadow of Giants: Plagiarists, Authors, Collaborators*. Ablex Publishing, 1999.

Howard, Rebecca Moore, and Sandra Jamieson. "Researched Writing." Tate et al., pp. 231–47.

Howard, Rebecca Moore, et al. "Writing from Sources, Writing from Sentences." *Writing and Pedagogy*, vol. 2, no. 2, 2010, pp. 177–92. *Equinox Publishing*, doi.org/10.1558/wap.v2i2.177.

Howell, A. C. "*Res et Verba*: Words and Things." *ELH*, vol. 13, no. 2, June 1946, pp. 131–42.

Hull, Glynda A., and Mark Evan Nelson. "Locating the Semiotic Power of Multimodality." *Written Communication*, vol. 22, no. 2, 2005, pp. 224–61.

Humiston, Jon P., et al. "Intentionally Creating an Inclusive and Welcoming Climate in the Online Learning Classroom." *Handbook of Research on Creating Meaningful Experiences in Online Courses*, IGI Global, 2020, pp. 173–86.

Hunzer, Kathleen M., editor. *Collaborative Learning and Writing: Essays on Using Small Groups in Teaching English and Composition*. McFarland, 2012.

Huot, Brian. *Rearticulating Writing Assessment for Teaching and Learning*. UP of Colorado, 2003.

Inoue, Asao B. *Antiracist Writing Assessment Ecologies: Teaching and Assessing Writing for a Socially Just Future*. Parlor Press, 2015.

———. "Friday Plenary Address: Racism in Writing Programs and the CWPA." *Writing Program Administration*, vol. 40, no. 1, 2016, pp. 134–55.

———. *Labor-Based Grading Contracts: Building Equity and Inclusion in the Compassionate Writing Classroom*. WAC Clearinghouse / UP of Colorado, 2019.

———. "2019 CCCC Chair's Address: How Do We Language So That People Stop Killing Each Other; or, What Do We Do about White Language Supremacy?" *College Composition and Communication*, vol. 71, no. 2, 2019, pp. 352–69.

"An Introduction to Content Warnings and Trigger Warnings." *Inclusive Teaching*, University of Michigan, 2021, sites.lsa.umich.edu/inclusive-teaching/an-introduction-to-content-warnings-and-trigger-warnings/.

Jenkins, Henry, et al. *Spreadable Media: Creating Value and Meaning in a Networked Culture*. New York UP, 2013.

Jewitt, Carey. "Multimodality and Literacy in School Classrooms." *Review of Research in Education*, vol. 32, no. 1, 2008, pp. 241–67.

Jones, Natasha N., and Miriam F. Williams. "The Just Use of Imagination: A Call to Action." *ATTW Blog*, Association of Teachers of Technical Writing, 10 June 2020, attw.org/blog/the-just-use-of-imagination-a-call-to-action/.

Jones, Rodney H., et al. "Interactional Dynamics in On-line and Face-to-Face Peer-Tutoring Sessions for Second Language Writers." *Journal of Second Language Writing*, vol. 15, no. 1, 2006, pp. 1–23.

Jukes, Ian, et al. *Understanding the Digital Generation: Teaching and Learning in the New Digital Landscape*. Corwin Press, 2010.

Kanuka, Heather. "Understanding E-Learning Technologies-in-Practice through Philosophies-in-Practice." *The Theory and Practice of Online Learning*, edited by Terry Anderson, 2nd ed., Athabasca UP, 2008, pp. 91–120.

Kaptelinin, Victor, et al. "Activity Theory: Basic Concepts and Applications." *International Conference on Human-Computer Interaction*, Springer, 1995.

Keller, Daniel. *Chasing Literacy: Reading and Writing in an Age of Acceleration*. Utah State UP, 2014.

Kendi, Ibram X. *How to Be an Antiracist*. One World / Ballantine, 2019.

Kent, Thomas, editor. *Post-Process Theory: Beyond the Writing-Process Paradigm*. Southern Illinois UP, 1999.

Khadka, Santosh. *Multiliteracies, Emerging Media, and College Writing Instruction*. Routledge, 2019.

Khadka, Santosh, and J. C. Lee, editors. *Bridging the Multimodal Gap: From Theory to Practice*. UP of Colorado, 2019.

Killoran, John B. "Reel-to-Reel Tapes, Cassettes, and Digital Audio Media: Reverberations from a Half-Century of Recorded-Audio Response to Student Writing." *Computers and Composition*, vol. 30, no. 1, 2013, pp. 37–49.

Kinneavy, James. *A Theory of Discourse*. W. W. Norton, 1971.

Kishimoto, Kyoko. "Anti-Racist Pedagogy: From Faculty's Self-Reflection to Organizing within and beyond the Classroom." *Race Ethnicity and Education*, vol. 21, no. 4, 2018, pp. 540–54.

Kitzrow, Martha A. "The Mental Health Needs of Today's College Students: Challenges and Recommendations." *NASPA Journal*, vol. 46, no. 4, 2009, pp. 646–60.

Knowles, Malcolm S., et al. *The Adult Learner: The Definitive Classic in Adult Education and Human Resource Development*. 5th ed., Gulf Publishing, 1998.

Kolln, Martha, and Loretta Gray. *Rhetorical Grammar: Grammatical Choices, Rhetorical Effects*. 6th ed., Longman, 2010.

Konstant, Shoshana Beth. "Multi-sensory Tutoring for Multi-sensory Learners." Murphy and Sherwood, pp. 108–11.

Kress, Gunther R. *Literacy in the New Media Age*. Routledge, 2003.

———. *Multimodality: A Social Semiotic Approach to Contemporary Communication*. Taylor and Francis, 2010.

Kress, Gunther R., and Theo Van Leeuwen. *Multimodal Discourse: The Modes and Media of Contemporary Communication*. Hodder Arnold, 2001.

Lauer, Claire. "Contending with Terms: 'Multimodal' and 'Multimedia' in the Academic and Public Spheres." *Computers and Composition*, vol. 26, no. 4, 2009, pp. 225–39.

———. "Examining the Effect of Reflective Assessment on the Quality of Visual Design Assignments in the Technical Writing Classroom." *Technical Communication Quarterly* vol. 22, no. 2, 2013, pp. 172–90.

Lauer, Janice M. "Topics." Enos, pp. 724–26.

Lave, Jean, and Etienne Wenger. *Situated Learning: Legitimate Peripheral Participation*. Cambridge UP, 1991.

Levine, Arthur, and Diane R. Dean. *Generation on a Tightrope: A Portrait of Today's College Student*. Jossey-Bass, 2012.

Lindemann, Erika. *A Rhetoric for Writing Teachers*. 4th ed., Oxford UP, 2001.

Lloyd-Jones, Richard. "Who We Were, Who We Should Become." *College Composition and Communication*, vol. 43, no. 4, 1992, pp. 486–96.

Lu, Min-Zhan, and Bruce Horner. "Translingual Work." *College English*, vol. 78, no. 3, Jan. 2016. *ThinkIR: The U of Louisville's Institutional Repository*, Faculty Scholarship no. 70, 2016, ir.library.louisville.edu/cgi/viewcontent.cgi?article=1062&context=faculty.

Luke, Carmen. "Cyber-Schooling and Technological Change: Multiliteracies for New Times." *Multiliteracies: Literacy Learning and the Design of Social Futures*, edited by Bill Cope and Mary Kalantzis, Psychology Press, 2000, pp. 67–88.

Lunsford, Andrea A. "Collaboration, Control, and the Idea of a Writing Center." Murphy and Sherwood, pp. 36–42.

Lunsford, Andrea A., et al. *Everything's an Argument*. Bedford / St. Martin's, 2004.

Lutkewitte, Claire. "An Introduction to Multimodal Composition Theory and Practice." Lutkewitte, *Multimodal Composition*, pp. 1–8.

———, editor. *Multimodal Composition: A Critical Sourcebook*. Bedford / St. Martin's, 2013.

Maclellan, Effie. "Reading to Learn." *Studies in Higher Education*, vol. 22, no. 3, 1997, pp. 277–88.

Magda, Andrew J., and Carol B. Aslanian. *Online College Students 2018: Comprehensive Data on Demands and Preferences*. The Learning House, 2018.

Marshak, Robert. "What's Between Pedagogy and Andragogy?" *Training and Development Journal*, vol. 37, no. 10, Oct. 1983, pp. 80–81.

Martinez, Diane, et al. "A Report on a U.S.-Based National Survey of Students in Online Writing Courses." *Research in Online Literacy Education*, vol. 2, no. 1, 2019, roleolor .org/a-report-on-a-us-based-national-survey-of-students-in-online-writing-courses .html.

Matsuda, Paul Kei. "The Myth of Linguistic Homogeneity in U.S. College Composition." *College English*, vol. 68. no. 6, 2006, pp. 637–51.

Matsuda, Paul Kei, and M. Cox. "Reading an ESL Writer's Text." *Studies in Self-Access Learning Journal*, vol. 2, no. 1, 2011, pp. 4–14.

Mayer, Richard, and Roxana Moreno. "Nine Ways to Reduce Cognitive Load in Multimedia Learning." *Educational Psychologist*, vol. 38, no. 1, 2003, pp. 43–52.

McCloud, Scott. *Understanding Comics: The Invisible Art*. Tundra, 1993.

McCluhan, Marshall. *Understanding Media: The Extensions of Man*. MIT Press, 1964.

McLeod, Susan H. *Writing Program Administration*. Parlor Press, 2007.

Miller, Carolyn R., and Ashley R. Kelly, editors. *Emerging Genres in New Media Environments*. Springer International Publishing, 2017.

Miller-Cochran, Susan. "Multilingual Writers and OWI." Hewett and DePew, pp. 291–308.

Mills, Kathy. *Literacy Theories for the Digital Age: Social, Critical, Multimodal, Spatial, Material and Sensory Lenses*. Multilingual Matters, 2015.

Moffett, James. "Coming on Center." *English Journal*, vol. 59, no. 4, Apr. 1970, pp. 528–33.

———. *Teaching the Universe of Discourse*. Boynton-Cook, 1983.

Monske, Elizabeth A., and Kristine L. Blair, editors. *Writing and Composing in the Age of MOOCs*. IGI Global, 2017.

Moss, Jean Dietz. "Dialectic(s)." Enos, pp. 183–90.

"Most Students Age Twenty-Five and Older." *U.S. News and World Report: Education*, www.usnews.com/best-colleges/rankings/most-over-25. Accessed 5 Aug. 2019.

Mrkich, Shannon, and Jeff Sommers. "Audio Response to Student Writing: WPA-CompPile Research Bibliographies, No. 26." July 2016, comppile.org/wpa/ bibliographies/Bib26/Audio_Response.pdf.

Mukavetz, Andrea Riley. "Females, the Strong Ones: Listening to the Lived Experiences of American Indian Women." *Studies in American Indian Literatures*, vol., 30, no. 1, 2018, pp. 1–23.

Murphy, Christina, and Steve Sherwood, editors. *The St. Martin's Sourcebook for Writing Tutors*. St. Martin's Press, 1995.

Murray, Donald. "The Listening Eye: Reflections on the Writing Conference." *College English*, vol. 41, no. 1, 1979, pp. 13–18.

———. "Teaching the Other Self: The Writer's First Reader." *College Composition and Communication*, vol. 33, no. 2, May 1982, pp. 140–47.

———. "Teach Writing as a Process Not a Product." *The Leaflet*, Nov. 1972, pp. 11–14.

———. *A Writer Teaches Writing*. 1968. Houghton Mifflin Harcourt, 1985.

Murray, Joddy. "Composing Multimodality." Lutkewitte, *Multimodal Composition*, pp. 325–50.

National Council of Teachers of English (NCTE). "NCTE Beliefs about the Students' Right to Write." *National Council of Teachers of English*, 31 July 2014, ncte.org/statement/students-right-to-write/.

———. *NCTE Framework for Twenty-First-Century Curriculum and Assessment*. 2013, https://cdn.ncte.org/nctefiles/resources/positions/framework_21stcent_curr__assessment.pdf.

National Council of Teachers of English (NCTE), Committee against Racism and Bias in the Teaching of English. *Qualities of Anti-Racist ELA Curricula*. *National Council of Teachers of English*, 2020, ncte.org/get-involved/volunteer/groups/committee-against-racism-and-bias-in-the-teaching-of-english/. PDF download.

———. *What Anti-Racist Language Teachers Do*. *National Council of Teachers of English*, 2020, ncte.org/get-involved/volunteer/groups/committee-against-racism-and-bias-in-the-teaching-of-english/. PDF download.

Nelms, Gerald. "Imitation Copying for Students." Handout, 2016.

Neuhauser, Charlotte. "Learning Style and Effectiveness of Online and Face-to-Face Instruction." *The American Journal of Distance Education*, vol. 16, no. 2, 2002, pp. 99–113.

Newkirk, Thomas. "The Writing Process—Visions and Revisions." *To Compose: Teaching Writing in High School and College*, edited by Newkirk, 2nd ed., Heinemann, 1990, pp. xiii–xxiv.

New London Group (NLG). "A Pedagogy of Multiliteracies: Designing Social Futures." *Harvard Educational Review*, vol. 66, no. 1, 1996, pp. 60–93.

North, Stephen. "The Idea of a Writing Center." *College English*, vol. 46, no. 5, 1984, pp. 433–46.

———. *The Making of Knowledge in Composition: Portrait of an Emerging Field*. Boynton/Cook Heinemann, 1987

———. "Training Tutors to Talk about Writing." *College Composition and Communication*, vol. 33, no. 4, 1982, pp. 434–41.

Nunes, Matthew J. "The Five-Paragraph Essay: Its Evolution and Roots in Theme-Writing." *Rhetoric Review*, vol. 32, no. 3, 2013, pp. 295–313.

Office for Civil Rights. "Protecting Students with Disabilities." United States, Department of Education, 2018, www2.ed.gov/about/offices/list/ocr/504faq.html.

Ong, Walter J., SJ. *Orality and Literacy: The Technologizing of the Word*. Methuen, 1982.

Oswal, Sushil K. "Physical and Learning Disabilities in OWI." Hewett and DePew, pp. 253–89.

Oswal, Sushil K., and Beth L. Hewett. "Accessibility Challenges for Visually Impaired Students and Their Online Writing Instructors." *Rhetorical Accessibility: At the Intersection of Technical Education and Disability Studies*, edited by Lisa Melonçon, Baywood, 2013, pp. 135–55.

Oswal, Sushil K., and Lisa Melonçon. "Saying No to the Checklist: Shifting from an Ideology of Normalcy to an Ideology of Inclusion in Online Writing Instruction." *WPA: Writing Program Administration*, vol. 40, no. 3, 2017, pp. 61–77.

Owens, Derek, and Tara Roeder. "Reclaiming Composition: A Twenty-first-Century Interdisciplinary Imperative." Reichert Powell, *Writing*, pp. 290–303.

Paine, Charles. *The Resistant Writer: Rhetoric as Immunity, 1850 to the Present*. State U of New York P, 1999.

Paris, Django, and H. Samy Alim, editors. *Culturally Sustaining Pedagogies: Teaching and Learning for Justice in a Changing World*. Teachers College Press, 2017.

Paull, Joanna N., and Jason Snart. *Making Hybrids Work: An Institutional Framework for Blending Online and Face-to-Face Instruction for Higher Education*. National Council of Teachers of English, 2016.

Perelman, Chaim. *The Realm of Rhetoric*. Translated by William Kluback, U of Notre Dame P, 1982.

Perelman, Chaim, and Lucie Olbrechts-Tyteca. *The New Rhetoric: A Treatise on Argumentation*. Translated by John Wilkinson and Purcell Weaver, U of Notre Dame P, 1969.

Perryman-Clark, Staci M. "African American Language, Rhetoric, and Students' Writing: New Directions for SRTOL." *College Composition and Communication*, vol. 64, no. 3, 2013, pp. 469–95.

Piaget, Jean. *The Language and Thought of the Child*. Routledge and Kegan Paul, 1959.

Pimentel, Octavio, et al. "The Myth of the Colorblind Writing Classroom: White Instructors Confront White Privilege in Their Classrooms." Condon and Young, pp. 109–22.

Pinantoan, Andrianes. "Instructional Scaffolding: A Definitive Guide." *informED*, 20 Mar. 2013, www.opencolleges.edu.au/informed/teacher-resources/scaffolding-in-education-a-definitive-guide/.

Plato. *Apology*. Plato, *Works*, pp. 89–134.

———. *Gorgias*. Penguin Books, 1960.

———. *Phaedrus*. Plato, *Works*, pp. 359–449.

———. *The Works of Plato*. Translated by B. Jowett, vol. 3, Dial Press, 1936.

Porter, James E. "Audience." Enos, pp. 42–49.

———. "Recovering Delivery for Digital Rhetoric." *Computers and Composition*, vol. 26, no. 4, 2009, pp. 207–24.

Pratt, Mary Louise. "Arts of the Contact Zone." *Profession*, 1991, pp. 33–40.

Prensky, Marc. "Digital Natives, Digital Immigrants." *On the Horizon*, vol. 9, no. 5, 2001, www.marcprensky.com/writing/Prensky%20-%20Digital%20Natives,%20Digital %20Immigrants%20-%20Part1.pdf

Quintilian. *Institutio oratoria: Books I–III*. Translated by H. E. Butler, vol. 1, Harvard UP, 1989.

Raimes, Ann. "Errors: Windows into the Mind." *College ESL*, vol. 1, no. 2. 1991, pp. 55–64.

Ramus, Peter. *Dialectica*. 1556. *A Compendium of the Art of Logick and Rhetorick in the English Tongue*, edited by R. F., Thomas Maxey, 1651. *Early English Books Online*, quod.lib.umich.edu/cgi/t/text/text-idx?c=eebo;idno=A49581.0001.001.

Rankins-Robertson, Sherry, et al. "Multimodal Instruction: Pedagogy and Practice for Enhancing Multimodal Composition." *Kairos*, vol. 19, no. 2, 2014, kairos .technorhetoric.net/19.1/praxis/robertson-et-al/index.html.

Reichert Powell, Pegeen, editor. *Writing Changes: Alphabetic Text and Multimodal Composition*. Modern Language Association of America, 2020.

———. "Writing Changes: Beyond the Binary of Writing versus Multimodality." Reichert Powell, *Writing*, pp. 1–18.

Reid, Ronald F. "The Boylston Professorship of Rhetoric and Oratory, 1806–1904: A Case Study in Changing Concepts of Rhetoric and Pedagogy." *Essays on the Rhetoric of the Western World*, edited by Edward P. J. Corbett et al., Kendell Hunt, 1990, pp. 261–82.

Reiss, Donna, and Art Young. "Multimodal Composing, Appropriation, Remediation, and Reflection: Writing, Literature, Media." Bowen and Whithaus, 2013, pp. 164–82.

Rice, Rich. "Faculty Professionalization for OWI." Hewett and DePew, pp. 389–410.

Richards, I. A. *The Meaning of Meaning: A Study of the Influence of Language upon Thought and of the Science of Symbolism*. Harcourt Brace, 1925.

Rilling, Sarah. "The Development of an ESL OWL, or Learning How to Tutor Writing Online." *Computers and Composition*, vol. 22, no. 3, 2005, pp. 357–74.

Robidoux, Charlotte, and Beth L. Hewett. "Collaborating Virtually to Develop This Book." *Collaborative Writing in Virtual Workplaces: Computer-Mediated Communication Technologies and Tools*, edited by Hewett and Robidoux, IGI Global, 2010, pp. 400–32.

Rodrigo, Rochelle. "OWI on the Go." Hewett and DePew, pp. 493–516.

Rothman, Juliet C. *Cultural Competence in Process and Practice: Building Bridges*. Pearson, 2008.

Rottenberg, Annette T., and Donna Haisty Winchell. *Elements of Argument: A Text and Reader*. Macmillan, 2011.

Royster, Jacqueline Jones, and Gesa E. Kirsch. *Feminist Rhetorical Practices: New Horizons for Rhetoric, Composition, and Literacy Studies*. Southern Illinois UP, 2012.

Rubin, Beth, et al. "The Effects of Technology on the Community of Inquiry and Satisfaction with Online Courses." *The Internet and Higher Education*, vol. 17, 2013, pp. 48–57.

Rubin, Claire. B., editor. *Emergency Management: The American Experience, 1900–2005*. Public Entity Risk Institute, 2007.

Rule, Hannah J. "Beyond Page Design: Writing as Multimodal Embodied Meaning." *Writing Changes: Alphabetic Text and Multimodal Composition*, edited by Pegeen Reichert Powell, Modern Language Association of America, 2020, pp. 62–63.

Russell, Thomas L. *The No Significant Difference Phenomenon: As Reported in 355 Research Reports, Summaries, and Papers*. North Carolina State U, 1999.

S., Jessie. "Note-Taking: Writing vs. Typing Notes." *StudySkills.com*, 16 Sept. 2018, studyskills.com/students/note-taking/.

Salisbury, Lauren E. "Just a Tool: Instructors' Attitudes and Use of Course Management Systems for Online Writing Instruction." *Computers and Composition*, vol. 48, 2018, pp. 1–17.

Sannino, Annalisa, et al., editors. *Learning and Expanding with Activity Theory*. Cambridge UP, 2009.

Sapir, Edward. *Language*. Ruppert Hart Davis, 1971.

Sapp, David A., and James L. Simon. "Comparing Grades in Online and Face-to-Face Writing Courses: Interpersonal Accountability and Institutional Commitment." *Computers and Composition*, vol. 22, no. 4, 2005, pp. 471–89.

Schreyer, Jessica. "Composing and Researching on the Move." *Mobile Technologies and Writing Classroom: Resources for Teachers*, edited by Claire Lutkewitte, National Council of Teachers of English, 2016, pp. 99–117.

Section 504 of the Rehabilitation Act of 1973. *Office of the Assistant Secretary for Administration and Management. US Department of Labor*, www.dol.gov/agencies/oasam/ centers-offices/civil-rights-center/statutes/section-504-rehabilitation-act-of-1973.

Selber, Stuart A. *Multiliteracies for a Digital Age*. Southern Illinois UP, 2004.

——. "Reimagining the Functional Side of Computer Literacy." *College Composition and Communication*, vol. 55, no. 3, 2004, pp. 470–503.

Selfe, Cynthia L. "The Movement of Air, the Breath of Meaning: Aurality and Multimodal Composing." *College Composition and Communication*, vol. 60, no. 4, 2009, pp. 616–63.

——, editor. *Multimodal Composition: Resources for Teachers*. Hampton Press, 2007.

———. "Students Who Teach Us: A Case Study of New Media Text Designer." *Writing New Media: Theory and Applications for Expanding the Teaching of Composition*, edited by Anne Frances Wysocki et al., Utah State UP, 2004, pp. 43–66.

———. "Technology and Literacy: A Story about the Perils of Not Paying Attention." *College Composition and Communication*, vol. 50, no. 3, 1999, pp. 411–36.

———. *Technology and Literacy in the Twenty-First Century: The Importance of Paying Attention*. Southern Illinois UP, 1999.

Selfe, Cynthia, and Patricia Ericsson. "Expanding Our Understanding of Composing Outcomes." Harrington et al., pp. 32–38.

Seward, Daniel. "Conversation Starters: Orchestrating Asynchronous Discussion to Build Academic Community among First-Year Writers." *Global Society of Online Literacy Educators*, 2020, www.glosole.org/conversation-starters-orchestrating -asynchronous-discussion-to-build-academic-community-among-first-year-writers .html.

Sheridan, David M., and Inman, James A., editors. *Multiliteracy Centers: Writing Center Work, New Media, and Multimodal Rhetoric*. Hampton Press, 2010.

Sheridan, David M., et al. *The Available Means of Persuasion: Mapping a Theory and Pedagogy of Multimodal Public Rhetoric*. Parlor Press, 2012.

Shipka, Jody. "A Multimodal Task-Based Framework for Composing." *College Composition and Communication*, vol. 57, no. 2, 2006, pp. 277–306.

———. "Sound Engineering: Toward a Theory of Multimodal Soundness." *Computers and Composition*, vol. 23, no. 3, 2006, pp. 355–73.

———. *Toward a Composition Made Whole*. U of Pittsburgh P, 2011.

Shor, Ira. *Empowering Education: Critical Teaching for Social Change*. U of Chicago P, 2012.

Silva, Mary Lourdes. "*Camtasia* in the Classroom: Student Attitudes and Preferences for Video Commentary or Microsoft Word Comments during the Revision Process." *Computers and Composition*, vol. 29, no. 1, 2012, pp. 1–22.

Silver, Naomi. "Reflection in Digital Spaces: Publication, Conversation, Collaboration." *A Rhetoric of Reflection*, edited by Kathleen Yancey, UP of Colorado, 2016, pp. 166–200.

Sirc, Geoffrey. *English Composition as a Happening*. Utah State UP, 2002.

Smith, Robin M. *Conquering the Content: A Step-by-Step Guide to Online Course Design*. Jossey-Bass, 2008.

Smith, Tania. "Elizabeth Montagu's Study of Cicero's Life: The Formation of an Eighteenth-Century Woman's Rhetorical Identity." *Rhetorica: A Journal of the History of Rhetoric*, vol. 26, no. 2, 2008, pp. 165–87.

Snart, Jason. "Hybrid and Fully Online OWI." Hewett and DePew, pp. 93–127.

———. *Hybrid Learning: The Perils and Promise of Blending Online and Face-to-Face Instruction in Higher Education*. Praeger, 2010.

Sommers, Nancy. "Responding to Student Writing." *College Composition and Communication*, vol. 33, no. 2, May 1982, pp. 148–56.

———. "Revision Strategies of Student Writers and Experienced Adult Writers." *The Writing Teacher's Sourcebook*, edited by Gary Tate and Edward P. J. Corbett. 2nd ed., Oxford UP, 1988, pp. 119–27.

Soto Vega, Karrieann, and Karma R. Chávez. "Latinx Rhetoric and Intersectionality in Racial Rhetorical Criticism." *Communication and Critical/Cultural Studies*, vol. 15, no. 4, 2018, pp. 319–25.

Spear, Karen. *Sharing Writing: Peer Response Groups in English Classes*. Heinemann, 1988.

Standards for the English Language Arts. International Reading Association and National Council of Teachers of English, 1996, cdn.ncte.org/nctefiles/resources/books/sample/standardsdoc.pdf.

Stannard, Russell. "Screen Capture Software for Feedback in Language Education." Second International Wireless Ready Symposium, NUCB Graduate School, Japan, 2008, wirelessready.nucba.ac.jp/Stannard.pdf.

———. "Using Screen Capture Software in Student Feedback." *English Subject Centre Archive*, Oct. 2007, english.heacademy.ac.uk/2016/01/16/using-screen-capture-software-in-student-feedback/.

Stefanakos, Victoria Scanlan. "Types of College Accommodations and Services." *Understood for All*, 2014–2021, www.understood.org/en/school-learning/choosing-starting-school/leaving-high-school/types-of-college-accommodations-and-services.

Straub, Richard. "Response Rethought." *College Composition and Communication*, vol. 48, no. 2, 1997, 277–83.

Strauss, Valerie. "1.5 Billion Children around Globe Affected by School Closure. What Countries Are Doing to Keep Kids Learning during Pandemic." *The Washington Post*, 27 Mar. 2020, www.washingtonpost.com/education/2020/03/26/nearly-14-billion-children-around-globe-are-out-school-heres-what-countries-are-doing-keep-kids-learning-during-pandemic/.

Strunk, William, Jr., and E. B. White. *The Elements of Style*. 50th anniversary ed., Pearson, 2009.

Sue, Derald Wing, et al. "Racial Microaggressions in Everyday Life." *American Psychologist*, vol. 62, no. 4, 2007, pp. 271–86.

Swan, Karen, et al. "A Constructivist Approach to Online Learning: The Community of Inquiry Framework." *Information Technology and Constructivism in Higher Education: Progressive Learning Frameworks*, edited by Carla Payne, IGI Global, 2009, pp. 43–57.

Takayoshi, Pamela, and Cynthia Selfe. "Thinking about Multimodality." Selfe, *Multimodal Composition*, pp. 1–12.

Tate, Gary, et al., editors. *A Guide to Composition Pedagogies.* 2nd ed., Oxford UP, 2014.

Thompson, Gene. "Moving Online: Changing the Focus of a Writing Center." *SiSAL (Studies in Self-Access Learning) Journal*, vol. 5, no. 2, 2014, pp. 127–42.

Thonus, Terese. "Tutoring Multilingual Students: Shattering the Myths." *Journal of College Reading and Learning*, vol. 44, no. 2, 2014, pp. 200–13, doi.org/10.1080/10790195.2014.906233.

Tobin, Lad. "Process Pedagogy." Tate et al., pp. 1–18.

Toulmin, Stephen. *The Uses of Argument.* Cambridge UP, 1958.

Tuckman, Bruce W. "Developmental Sequence in Small Groups." *Psychological Bulletin*, vol. 65, no. 6, 1965, pp. 384–99.

Tuckman, Bruce W., and Mary Ann Jensen. "Stages of Small-Group Development Revisited." *Group and Organization Studies*, vol. 2, no. 4, 1977, pp. 419–27.

26Ten. *Communicate Clearly: A Guide to Plain English.* Tasmanian Adult Literacy Action Plan, 2010–2015, Dec. 2015. 26ten.tas.gov.au/PublishingImages/Tools/26TEN-Communicate-Clearly-A-Guide-to-Plain-English-Current-September-2014.PDF.

"The UDL Guidelines." *CAST*, 2018, udlguidelines.cast.org.

Understood Team. "Seven Things to Know about College Disability Services." *Understood for All*, 2014–2020, www.understood.org/en/school-learning/choosing-starting-school/leaving-high-school/7-things-to-know-about-college-disability-services.

Vankooten, Crystal. "Toward a Rhetorically Sensitive Assessment Model for New Media Composition." *Digital Writing Assessment and Evaluation*, edited by Heidi McKee and Danielle Nicole Devoss, Computers and Composition Digital Press / Utah State UP, 2013, ccdigitalpress.org/dwae/09_vankooten.html.

Vasudevan, Lalitha, et al. "Rethinking Composing in a Digital Age: Authoring Literate Identities through Multimodal Storytelling." *Written Communication*, vol. 27, no. 4, 2010, pp. 442–68.

Vie, Stephanie. "What's Going On? Challenges and Opportunities for Social Media Use in the Writing Classroom." *The Journal of Faculty Development*, vol. 29, no. 2, 2015, pp. 33–44.

Vygotsky, Lev S. *Thought and Language.* Edited and translated by Alex Kozulin, MIT Press, 1997.

Wah, Lee Mun. *The Art of Mindful Facilitation.* StirFry Seminars and Consulting, 2005.

Walzer, Arthur E. "Purpose." Enos, pp. 576–77.

Warnock, Scott. "New Teaching Modality Terms: Chrono-hybrids and Spatio-hybrids?" *Online Writing Teacher*, 30 July 2020, onlinewritingteacher.blogspot.com/2020/07/new-teaching-modality-terms-chrono.html.

———. "Responding to Student Writing with Audio-visual Feedback." *Writing and the iGeneration: Composition in the Computer-Mediated Classroom*, edited by Terry Carter and Maria A. Clayton, Fountainhead, 2008, pp. 201–27.

———. "'Spatio-hybrid,' 'Chrono-hybrid,' 'Classroom,' 'Homework,' and Other Puzzling OLI Terms." Visions and Sites of Online Literacy Education: The Global Society of Online Literacy Educators Annual Conference, Jan. 2021. gsole.org/resources/Documents/WarnockOLITerms-GSOLEPlenary21.pdf. Presentation slides.

———. "Studies Comparing Outcomes Among Onsite, Hybrid, and Fully-Online Writing Courses." Apr. 2013, docs.google.com/file/d/0BygwPfTKm-RqSUtqcllyX3RQeEE/edit.

———. "Teaching the OWI Course." Hewett and DePew, pp. 151–82.

———. Teaching Writing Online: How and Why. National Council of Teachers of English, 2009.

Warnock, Scott, and Adrienne Cassel. "Teaching Writing Online." A Guide to Teaching the Norton Field Guides to Writing, edited by Richard Bullock et al., 5th ed., W. W. Norton, 2019, pp. 104–12.

Warnock, Scott, and Diana Gasiewski. Writing Together: Ten Weeks Teaching and Studenting in an Online Writing Course. National Council of Teachers of English, 2018.

Weaver, Richard. "Language Is Sermonic." The Rhetorical Tradition: Readings from the Classical Times to the Present, edited by Patricia Bizzell and Bruce Herzenber, 2nd ed., Bedford / St. Martin's, 2001, pp. 1351–71.

"Web Content Accessibility Guidelines (WCAG) Overview." W3C Web Accessibility Initiative, 17 Oct. 2020, www.w3.org/WAI/standards-guidelines/wcag/.

"What Are a Public or Private College-University's Responsibilities to Students with Disabilities?" ADA National Network: Information, Guidance, and Training on the Americans with Disabilities Act, Mar. 2021, adata.org/faq/what-are-public-or-private-college-universitys-responsibilities-students-disabilities.

Whately, Richard. Elements of Rhetoric: Comprising an Analysis of the Laws of Moral Evidence and of Persuasion, with Rules for Argumentative Composition and Elocution. 1828. Edited by Douglas Ehninger, Southern Illinois UP, 1963.

"What Is the Americans with Disabilities Act (ADA)?" ADA National Network: Information, Guidance, and Training on the Americans with Disabilities Act, Mar. 2021, adata.org/learn-about-ada.

White, Edward M. "The Origins of the 'Outcomes Statement.'" Harrington et al., pp. 3–7.

———. "The Scoring of Writing Portfolios: Phase 2." College Composition and Communication, vol. 56, no. 4, June 2005, pp. 581–600.

———. Teaching and Assessing Writing: Recent Advances in Understanding, Evaluating, and Improving Student Performance. Rev. and expanded ed., Jossey-Bass Publishers, 1994.

Williams, Joseph M., and Joseph Bizup. Style: Lessons in Clarity and Grace. 13th ed., Pearson, 2019.

Williams-Farrier, Bonnie J. "'Talkin' bout Good and Bad' Pedagogies: Code-Switching vs. Comparative Rhetorical Approaches." *College Composition and Communication*, vol. 69, no. 2, 2017, pp. 230–59.

Wolf, Maryanne. *Proust and the Squid: The Story and Science of the Reading Brain*. HarperCollins, 2007.

——. *Tales of Literacy for the Twenty-First Century*. Oxford UP, 2016.

Wolfe, Joanna. *Team Writing: A Guide to Working in Groups*. Bedford / St. Martin's, 2010.

Wolfe, Joanna, and Jo Ann Griffin. "Comparing Technologies for Online Writing Conferences: Effects of Medium on Conversation." *The Writing Center Journal*, vol. 32, no. 2, 2012, pp. 60–92.

Word, David L., et al. *Demographic Aspects of Surnames from Census 2000. United States Census Bureau*, www.census.gov/topics/population/genealogy/data/2000 _surnames.html. PDF download.

Wysocki, Anne Frances. "Impossibly Distinct: On Form/Content and Word/Image in Two Pieces of Computer-Based Interactive Multimedia." *Computers and Composition*, vol. 18, no. 2, 2001, pp. 137–62.

——. "Opening New Media to Writing: Openings and Justifications." Wysocki et al., pp. 1–42.

Wysocki, Anne Frances, et al. *Writing New Media: Theory and Applications for Expanding the Teaching of Composition*. UP of Colorado, 2007.

Yancey, Kathleen Blake. "Introduction: Contextualizing Reflection." *A Rhetoric of Reflection*, edited by Blake, UP of Colorado, 2016, pp. 3–21.

——. "Standards, Outcomes, and All that Jazz." Harrington et al., pp. 18–23.

——. *Writing in the Twenty-First Century*. National Council of Teachers of English, Feb. 2009, cdn.ncte.org/nctefiles/press/yancey_final.pdf.

Young, Richard E. "Invention." Enos, pp. 349–55.

Young, Richard E., et al. *Rhetoric: Discovery and Change*. Harcourt Brace Jovanovich, 1970.

Young, Vershawn Ashanti. "Should Writers Use They Own English?" *Iowa Journal of Cultural Studies*, vol. 12, no. 1, 2010, pp. 110–17.

Young, Vershawn Ashanti, et al. *Other People's English: Code-Meshing, Code-Switching, and African American Literacy*. Teachers College Press, 2014.

Zoellner, Robert. "Talk-Write: A Behavioral Pedagogy for Composition." *College English*, vol. 30, no. 4, Jan. 1969, pp. 267–320.